CONGRESSIONAL POLICIES, PRACTICES AND PROCEDURES

ELDER JUSTICE

ABUSE, LEGISLATION AND FINANCIAL EXPLOITATION

Congressional Policies, Practices and Procedures

Additional books and e-books in this series can be found on Nova's website under the Series tab.

CONGRESSIONAL POLICIES, PRACTICES AND PROCEDURES

ELDER JUSTICE

ABUSE, LEGISLATION AND FINANCIAL EXPLOITATION

VINCE D. ANDERSON
EDITOR

New York

Library of Congress Cataloging-in-Publication Data

ISBN: 978-1-53619-447-0

Published by Nova Science Publishers, Inc. † New York

CONTENTS

PREFACE

Seniors in nursing homes are among the people most vulnerable to life-threatening consequences of abuse and neglect. Across the country, that vulnerability is being exploited in unimaginably cruel ways in nursing homes that are unsafe, understaffed, and uninterested in providing even the most basic humane level of care. Chapter 1 looks at elder abuse and especially nursing home abuse.

Elder abuse is a complex issue. As such, it often leads to calls for a multifaceted policy response that combines public health interventions, social services programs, and law enforcement. Chapter.2 provides a brief legislative history of the Elder Justice Act, summarizes elder justice provisions enacted as part of ACA, and describes administrative efforts related to implementation and funding, along with several issues for Congress regarding the act's reauthorization

Elder financial exploitation—the fraudulent or illegal use of an older adult's funds or property—has far-reaching effects on victims and society. Chapter 3 examines the status of HHS's efforts to compile nationwide data through NAMRS on the extent of financial exploitation and the challenges involved, and (2) what is known about the costs of financial exploitation to victims and others.

Chapter 1 - This is an edited, reformatted and augmented version of Hearing before the Committee on Finance, United States Senate, One Hundred Sixteenth Congress, First Session, Publication No. S. HRG. 116–282., dated March 6, 2019.

Chapter 2 - Elder abuse is a complex issue. As such, it often leads to calls for a multifaceted policy response that combines public health interventions, social services programs, and law enforcement. To address this complexity, the Elder Justice Act was enacted on March 23, 2010, as part of the Patient Protection and Affordable Care Act (ACA, P.L. 111-148, as amended). The Elder Justice Act is intended to provide a coordinated federal response to elder abuse by emphasizing various public health and social service approaches to prevent, detect, and treat abuse. The Elder Justice Act is Congress's first attempt at comprehensive legislation to address abuse, neglect, and exploitation of the elderly at the federal level. *Elder Justice Provisions.* Enactment of the Elder Justice Act under the ACA contained certain public health and social services approaches to the prevention, detection, and treatment of elder abuse, primarily under the Department of Health and Human Services (HHS) authorities and administration. The elder justice provisions enacted under the ACA did not fully incorporate the comprehensive multidisciplinary policy approach (public health, social services, and criminal justice) envisioned in earlier versions of introduced legislation. Unlike earlier versions of the Elder Justice Act, which included a multidisciplinary approach that incorporated criminal justice provisions, the Elder Justice Act enacted under ACA did not include a criminal justice response for addressing the prevention, detection, and prosecution of elder abuse crimes under the Department of Justice (DOJ). With enactment of the Elder Justice Act under the ACA, criminal justice provisions were introduced as separate stand-alone legislation in subsequent Congresses. On October 18, 2017, the Elder Abuse Prevention and Prosecution Act of 2017 (EAPPA; P.L. 115-70) was signed into law establishing certain DOJ requirements with respect to investigating and prosecuting elder abuse crimes and enforcing elder abuse laws. In addition, Section 501 of P.L. 115-70 amended the Elder Justice Act to authorize certain court-appointed guardianship oversight activities under Adult Protective Services (APS) demonstration grants. *Federal Funding for Elder Justice Activities.* The authorizations of appropriations for most Elder Justice Act activities expired on September 30, 2014. However, Congress continues to appropriate some funding for authorized activities. To date, most programs and activities authorized under the Elder Justice Act have either not received funding since enactment or have not received funding at their previously authorized levels. For FY2020, the Further Consolidated Appropriations Act, 2020 (P.L. 116-94), provided $14.0 million in discretionary appropriations under the Elder Rights Support Activities line item appropriation within the Administration for Community Living's (ACL's) Aging and Disability Services Programs budget authority, of which $12.0 million is for the Elder Justice and Adult Protective Services program. ACL funding under the Elder Justice and Adult Protective Services program is also used for activities authorized under Older Americans Act (OAA) Sections 411 and 751. FY2020 funding of $12.0 million for the Elder Justice and Adult Protective Services program was the same as the FY2019 funding level. *Topics Covered in This Chapter.* This chapter provides a brief legislative history of the Elder Justice Act, summarizes elder justice provisions enacted as part of ACA, and describes administrative efforts related to implementation and funding, along with several issues for Congress regarding the act's reauthorization.

Chapter 3 - Elder financial exploitation—the fraudulent or illegal use of an older adult's funds or property—has far- reaching effects on victims and society. Understanding the scope of the problem has thus far been hindered by a lack of nationwide data. In 2013, HHS worked with states to create NAMRS, a voluntary system for collecting APS data on elder abuse, including financial exploitation. GAO was asked to study the extent to which NAMRS provides information on elder financial exploitation. This chapter examines (1) the status of HHS's efforts to compile nationwide data through NAMRS on the extent of financial exploitation and the challenges involved, and (2) what is known about the costs of financial exploitation to victims and others. GAO analyzed NAMRS data from fiscal year 2016 through 2019 (the most recent available); reviewed relevant federal laws; and interviewed officials from HHS, other federal agencies, elder abuse prevention organizations, and researchers. GAO also reviewed APS documents and spoke with officials in eight states, selected based on their efforts to study, collect, and report cost data; and reviewed studies on financial exploitation.

In: Elder Justice
Editor: Vince D. Anderson

ISBN: 978-1-53619-447-0

Chapter 1

NOT FORGOTTEN: PROTECTING AMERICANS FROM ABUSE AND NEGLECT IN NURSING HOMES*

Committee on Finance

Wednesday, March 6, 2019
U.S. Senate, Committee on Finance,
Washington, DC.

The hearing was convened, pursuant to notice, at 10:15 a.m., in room SD–215, Dirksen Senate Office Building, Hon. Chuck Grassley (chairman of the committee) presiding.

Present: Senators Crapo, Thune, Portman, Toomey, Scott, Cassidy, Lankford, Daines, Wyden, Stabenow, Cantwell, Menendez, Carper, Cardin, Casey, Warner, Whitehouse, Hassan, and Cortez Masto.

Also present: Republican staff: Evelyn Fortier, General Counsel for Health and Chief of Special Projects; and Kirsten Lunde, Professional Staff Member. Democratic staff: Anne Dwyer, Senior Health Counsel; and Matt Kazan, Senior Health Advisor.

* This is an edited, reformatted and augmented version of Hearing before the Committee on Finance, United States Senate, One Hundred Sixteenth Congress, First Session, Publication No. S. HRG. 116–282., dated March 6, 2019.

Opening Statement of Hon. Chuck Grassley, a U.S. Senator from Iowa, Chairman, Committee on Finance

The CHAIRMAN. I want to welcome everyone to our hearing today. The hearing is on a very extremely important topic: elder abuse. And I thank our witnesses for joining us today.

Elder abuse, and nursing home abuse in particular, has been a topic of ongoing concern of mine and other members of this committee for a long time. My involvement has gone on over a period of the last 2 decades. As former chairman of the Senate Aging Committee, as an example, I conducted oversight of the nursing home inspection process and convened hearings focused on enhancing standards and compliance across the nursing home industry.

More recently, I sponsored the Elder Abuse Prevention and Prosecution Act, a new Federal law that calls for the training of elder abuse investigators, collection of data on elder abuse, and collaboration among Federal officials tasked with combating seniors' exploitation. Its enactment was a top priority of mine in the 115th Congress, but Congress's work in this area seems never to be done.

Hardly a week goes by without seeing something about nursing home abuse or neglect in the national news. Every family has a loved one—a mother, a father, or a grandparent—who may someday need nursing home care. That makes this a topic of enormous concern, then, to every American. And today, two such Americans are here with us to share their heartbreaking experiences. They are both the daughters of former nursing home residents who were victims of abuse or neglect.

First we will hear from a friend of mine, Pat Blank, whose mother Virginia died at an Iowa nursing home due to horrific neglect. This facility was fined for the mistreatment of Virginia as well as another Iowan, Darlene Weaver. Second, I want to welcome Maya Fischer, whose 87-year-old mother, an Alzheimer's patient, was brutally raped by a nursing aide. In each of these cases, the victim's trust was betrayed by the very individuals who were entrusted to care for and protect them. Sadly, these are not isolated cases. They could have happened to anyone.

According to the Inspector General, a whopping one-third of nursing home residents experienced harm while under the care of their federally funded facilities. And in more than half of these cases, the harm was preventable. I remember that figure; one-third is pretty close to the one-third figure that cropped up in my hearings 20 years ago. Two years ago, the Inspector General also issued an alert warning the public about deficiencies cited at nursing homes in 33 States. A significant percentage of these cases involved sexual abuse, substandard care, and neglect.

It is our job to protect America's most vulnerable citizens and to prevent them from being victimized. Many, like the elderly mothers of Ms. Fischer and Ms. Blank, cannot speak for themselves. Some rely on wheelchairs and walkers to get up from their beds. Others have mental and cognitive disabilities that prevent them from communicating wrongdoing.

We depend on nursing homes to render the skilled nursing care that many of our loved ones cannot provide on their own. As chairman of the Senate Finance Committee, I will continue to make it a top priority to ensure our most vulnerable citizens have access to quality long-term care in an environment free from abuse and neglect, and I know that members of this committee share that goal, and particularly my partner, Senator Wyden.

I intend for today's hearing to shed light on the systemic issues that allow substandard care and abuse in America's nursing home industry and help lead the way to reforms. I hope to hear from our expert witnesses, for example, about why some nursing home abuse and neglect cases never even get reported to law enforcement. And that is required by law. I hope to hear that we fixed the weaknesses in the five-star rating system, and that we have cracked down on social media abuse. Every American listening today can be sure that I will continue shining the public spotlight on this issue as long as it takes to fix these problems.

It is my hope that the oversight work of this committee will prevent elder abuse from claiming more victims so that we will not need to call more witnesses to testify about the horrible abuse that we are going to hear about today, and so that other moms and dads do not experience that in a nursing home.

Thank you all for joining us. I look forward to your testimony, and I will call on Senator Wyden.

[The prepared statement of Chairman Grassley appears in the appendix.]

OPENING STATEMENT OF HON. RON WYDEN, A U.S. SENATOR FROM OREGON

Senator WYDEN. Thank you very much, Mr. Chairman. As you indicated, this will be another issue where there is an opportunity for you and I and committee members to find considerable common ground. And I look forward to working with you.

Colleagues, generations ago with Social Security, America closed the door to the whole idea of impoverished seniors living out their last years on poor farms. Decades later with Medicare and Medicaid, there was a guarantee that seniors would be able to get health care. To continue that hard work, one of the challenges our country faces now is ensuring that seniors in nursing homes are safe and well cared for. I want to be clear this morning: our best nursing homes meet a high standard of care, but tragically not all do in America.

Seniors in nursing homes are among the people most vulnerable to life-threatening consequences of abuse and neglect. Across the country, that vulnerability is being exploited in unimaginably cruel ways in nursing homes that are unsafe, understaffed, and uninterested in providing even the most basic humane level of care.

This morning the committee is going to hear stories of seniors being sexually and physically abused, starved, dehydrated, and left for dead. These stories, unfortunately, are not just isolated cases. Last November I released a report—a report that was produced by Finance minority staff called "Sheltering in Danger"—that examined the tragic deaths of 12 residents at a Florida nursing home where nursing home managers and staff failed to evacuate them after Hurricane Irma.

Just this week, a news report from Ashland, OR told the story of an elderly nursing home resident who was found with mold, ulcers, and infections after she went a week without bathing. In the news report, a nurse was allegedly stealing her pain medication, and, even after a trip to the hospital to treat her infections, the person who is charged with her care—according to the news report—continued to steal her medicine until she died 17 days later.

So as the committee examines these issues, there are a few specific matters that need investigation. First, the Trump budget comes out next week, and my sense is—I wish it was not the case— we will see proposed another draconian cutback on Medicaid. Medicaid helps cover costs for two out of three seniors in nursing homes. I am going to fight this proposal with everything I have got, because it would turn back the clock on efforts to improve care, and it would inevitably lead to more nursing homes closing their doors, which would especially work a hardship in rural America. We cannot see rural America turning into a sacrifice zone, but if we do not have rural health care and rural nursing homes, that is where you are headed.

Second, at a time when the Federal Government ought to be raising standards and rooting out harmful substandard care and those who provide it, regrettably the Trump administration and the Centers for Medicare and Medicaid Services are going in the wrong direction. The basic regulations on nursing homes go back several decades. Since then, a 2003 study found 20,000 complaints of exploitation, abuse, and neglect. Reports from the National Center on Elder Abuse found that only a small fraction of cases even get reported.

A 2014 report from the Department of Health and Human Services Inspector General found that a third of Medicare beneficiaries were harmed within a matter of weeks, just several weeks, after they entered the home. So in 2016, there was an effort to update basic safety rules. The update required nursing homes to develop plans to prevent infections. There were specific policies and procedures in that proposal to prevent abuse, neglect, mistreatment, and theft.

The proposal said that nursing homes should not pump residents full of psychotropic drugs. That seems about as basic as you can get. And it banned the practice of forcing seniors to sign away their legal rights with pre-arbitration contracts as a precondition of admission to a nursing home. Also, it proposed tougher financial penalties for homes that harm residents or fail to meet safety standards. Come 2017, under the banner of deregulation, the Trump administration said, "We are going to roll those changes back." Other examples related to the recommendations are in the "Sheltering in Danger" report. I am concerned that the Trump rollbacks will mean nursing homes are unprepared for natural disasters in the future. There still is no Federal rule mandating that nursing homes have emergency power generators.

Folks, this is not rocket science. It gets hot in the summers in the west and the south and all over the country. If you have a rule that does not require that nursing homes have emergency power generators, that is a prescription for trouble. So when I hear the Trump administration throw around the phrase "patients over paperwork," I think that somehow criminals and substandard caregivers are getting off the hook, because there is a likelihood that more vulnerable seniors get hurt.

I also share the chairman's view with respect to the Federal Government's rating system for nursing homes. At a hearing in the Aging Committee years ago—and I think I mentioned this once to the chairman—I pointed out that it was easier to get an accurate review of a washing machine than a nursing home. After that hearing, the Centers for Medicare and Medicaid Services created a new rating system that should have been a powerful tool for seniors and their families to sort out the good homes from the bad. As the chairman indicated—a view we share—it has not turned out that way.

Too much of the information that goes into the rating system is self-reported. It is not a reliable indicator of quality. For instance, one of the witnesses coming before the committee today will tell us about her mother passing away after suffering extreme neglect at a facility in Iowa. That home got top marks for quality: a five-star rating. So as the chairman indicated, this hearing needs to be part of the effort to accelerate fixes to the flawed rating system.

I am going to close with one last point. I know in my home State there are nursing homes and labor unions working together on common ground to try to set higher standards and raise the quality of care. As a young man, I was the co-director of the Oregon Gray Panthers, and I was named by our Governor to serve on the State Board of Examiners of Nursing Home Administrators, even though the industry got State legislators to vote to keep me off.

I finally managed to get on, and I spent a lot of time visiting seniors who lived in sordid conditions who needed a lot of help just to get through the day and who were victims of scams and abuses. So those memories are still very much on my mind.

I am pleased that the chairman has chosen to hold this very important oversight hearing, and I think we can all agree that what this is about is, seniors have a right to a dignified retirement. And this battle is not complete until that right to a dignified retirement is secure.

Thank you very much, Mr. Chairman.

[The prepared statement of Senator Wyden appears in the appendix.]

The CHAIRMAN. I hope you know that what I have pointed out, and what Senator Wyden has pointed out, that these issues come up whether you have Republican or Democratic Presidents. When I first got involved in it, it was a President of another political party. This is a systemic problem that does not seem to respond to whoever is in control of any bureaucracy here.

Before I introduce these first four witnesses, I want to say a friend of mine, Donna Harvey, is in the audience. When she was head of the Governor's Administration on Aging in Iowa, she and I collaborated on elder abuse policy for many years, and she now heads up the Northeast Iowa Area Agency on Aging. I want to recognize her past contribution to this effort as well.

Now to introduce our witnesses. The first one—I have already spoken about Patricia Blank, a constituent of mine and the daughter of a nursing home neglect victim from Iowa.

Then we have Maya Fischer from Seminole, FL, who is the daughter of a Minnesota nursing home abuse victim. We welcome both of you here.

Then we are going to have Dr. David Grabowski, health-care policy professor, Harvard Medical School, and a member of the Medicare Payment Advisory Commission, which is a commission that a lot of us on this committee pay a lot of attention to. Dr. Grabowski has conducted extensive research on aging and nursing home care.

We will then hear from Dr. David Gifford. He serves as senior vice president of quality and regulatory affairs for the American Health Care Association, which represents many of the nation's nursing homes.

We welcome all of you, and we are going to start then with Patricia, and then go to Maya, and then go to Dr. Grabowski, and then to Dr. Gifford.

Would you start? Make sure the red button is on.

STATEMENT OF PATRICIA BLANK, DAUGHTER OF NURSING HOME NEGLECT VICTIM, SHELL ROCK, IA

Ms. BLANK. Ladies and gentlemen, my name is Patricia Olthoff-Blank. I am from Shell Rock, IA. I want to thank you all for allowing me to present testimony this morning on this very important issue. It is important to me because my mother, Virginia Olthoff, died as a result of neglect at a nursing home where she had lived for nearly 15 years. As a matter of fact, today marks the 1-year and 1-day anniversary of her funeral.

One of the most frustrating parts about how she died is that during her 15 years at Timely Mission Nursing Home in Buffalo Center, IA, my family believed she was getting good care. Each time we visited, she seemed comfortable. She was dressed in regular clothes, not pajamas. She seemed to be clean and well-groomed. We were familiar with many of the staff, including the director of nursing, who went to high school with me and my brothers. There had always been good communication from the staff between my father—who lived just three blocks away from the facility until his death in 2012—and me, the eldest and only daughter.

After my father's death, I became the family member responsible for decisions, and the administrators called me often—and I appreciated hearing from them. "Your mom needs new glasses. She needs a haircut. Her toenails need to be trimmed. She could use some new underwear." They also contacted me and discussed each time her medication was altered. She had dementia and she communicated with the staff and with us, but not always knowing who we were. She just always thanked us because we were the nice people who came to visit. I was always invited to attend her yearly evaluation, which I did not attend in person because I live nearly 2½ hours away. But it was conducted during the week, and the staff always reported to me what had happened during that evaluation over the phone.

Fast forward to February 28, 2018, at 3 a.m. I received a phone call from the overnight registered nurse, who told me simply, "Your mother is moaning. What do you want me to do?"

I said, "Give her something for pain." And the nurse said, "Well, all we can give her is Tylenol." She asked me again, "What do you want me to do?" And I said, "Well, I think she needs to go to the hospital." So she said, "Okay," and hung up.

The next call I got was from an emergency room nurse at Mason City, which is about an hour and a half away from the facility, who said I had better come quickly because she was not sure that my mother would be alive in the hour or so that it would take me to get there. My husband, brother, and I were greeted by the emergency room doctor, who said my mother was extremely dehydrated and had sodium levels that were so elevated she likely had suffered a stroke.

He also said, "This did not just happen. I believe she has been without water or any type of fluid for 4 or 5 days, maybe for as long as 2 weeks." He also told us he was a mandatory abuse reporter, and he was going to report this.

I heard him say that, but I was so surprised that my mom was so sick at this point that it really did not register at the time. We held her funeral, as I said, March 5th of last year. After her funeral, I went on with my life, grieving her especially in April, because we shared a birthday. She would have been 88.

In July, I got a phone call from Clark Kauffman, a reporter from *The Des Moines Register,* who said he was sorry for my mother's death, and he wanted to know if I had any comments about a Department of Inspections and Appeals report. I had no idea what he was talking about, but then remembered the emergency room doctor had said he was going to make a report. He did report that to the Department of Human Services.

The report, 31 pages long, read like a horror story. According to numerous staff members, my mother had been eating very little and drinking almost nothing for almost 2 weeks. Where was my phone call then? The report also said she had been crying out in pain often. Where was my phone call then?

She did have a Do Not Resuscitate order, but was not having breathing or cardiac issues. The DNR states she is to be made comfortable with an IV for fluids, oxygen, and morphine or something for pain. None of that happened. The DIA report also mentioned that she had lost a considerable amount of weight. Again, where was my phone call?

I do want to thank the CNAs, the nurses, and others who do work in care facilities who do their jobs right. The facilities are often understaffed, and these people work for much less money than they should be paid. Please thank these people if you have a loved one in one of these nursing homes in nursing care.

I also want to thank the emergency room doctor who reported the neglect, and I want to thank Clark Kauffman from *The Des Moines Register* and other journalists who make time to read these lengthy reports and write stories about inspections so perhaps something can be done about the current situation, and family members will be notified when this happens.

I do have more ideas that I will just leave to the comment section to talk to you about later. So, thank you very much.

[The prepared statement of Ms. Blank appears in the appendix.] The CHAIRMAN. Ms. Fischer?

STATEMENT OF MAYA FISCHER, DAUGHTER OF NURSING HOME ABUSE VICTIM, SEMINOLE, FL

Ms. FISCHER. Chairman Grassley, Ranking Member Wyden, and members of the committee, thank you for the opportunity to be here today on behalf of my mother Sonja Fischer. My mother, suffering from advanced Alzheimer's, was a Medicare patient at Walker Methodist Health Center in Minneapolis. On December 18, 2014, at 4 a.m., a nurse walked into her room and witnessed a male caregiver, George Kpingbah, raping my mother.

My mother had suffered from Alzheimer's for 12 years. She was totally immobile, unable to speak, and fully dependent on others for her care. When I saw the nursing home's number on caller ID, I prepared myself for the worst, that my mother had passed away after so many years struggling with Alzheimer's. I was not prepared for what I heard. A nurse informed me that my mother had been sexually assaulted and was being transported to the hospital. And just like that, my mother became another statistic in the shocking reality of nursing home abuse. My mother, however, was so much more than a statistic. So, please allow me to tell you about her.

My mother was born in Jakarta, Indonesia in 1931. In 1942, the Japanese army invaded the Indonesian Islands. In the horror of war, soldiers were raping and killing women and young girls. My grandparents were left with no other option but to flee their homeland with their 12-year-old daughter.

My mother ended up in the United States, becoming a U.S. citizen and building a life for herself here in this country. She was a testament to the American dream. In this country, she was safe and she was happy, a world removed from the horrors of her youth.

It is impossible to imagine that at the end of her life when she had no ability to fend for herself, that she would suffer the very same horror her parents had fled their homeland to protect her from. At 83 years old, unable to speak, unable to fight back, she was more vulnerable than an infant when she was raped. The dignity which she always displayed during her life, which had already been assaulted by her disease, was dealt a further devastating blow by her caregiver.

I received a phone call that this unthinkable act had been committed against my mother during the week of Christmas 2014. This news was devastating not only for its immediate shock, but how it affected the memories we had of my mother and Christmases past. Now and for the rest of my life, when I think of my mother at Christmas, I will think of that horrifying call.

The sense of helplessness I felt trying to comfort her while she had a rape kit performed on her will always remain with me, as will the 9 hours I spent in the emergency room with her and the fear she must have felt with the bright lights and scary noises of monitors going off. I will remember the pain she went through having an IV drip so that, at 83, she did not contract a sexually transmitted disease.

My final memories of my mother's life now include watching her bang uncontrollably on her private parts for days after the rape with tears rolling down her eyes, apparently trying to tell me what had been done to her but unable to speak due to her disease. I still feel the guilt of not being able to take care of her myself and having to entrust her care to others only to have her subjected to this unthinkable assault.

I remember the difficult decision we had to make when we realized we could no longer care for her at home. We understood that we had to pick a nursing home for her, and we did everything we could to find the best place. We assured my mother that she would be safe and that she would not suffer. I can never overcome the guilt of realizing that these promises were not kept. She was not safe. She was raped. Could this rape have been prevented?

It is my understanding that other residents had previously complained of sexual misconduct while Mr. Kpingbah worked at the nursing home. I have learned that the Department of Health investigated these prior complaints, did nothing, and kept them hidden. I cannot help but wonder how my mom's, my family's, and my life would be different if the Department had not kept these allegations hidden.

Families struggle to care for their loved ones, do everything they can to find the best possible care and to make the best decision possible. We rely on information provided by the Department of Health, and we must have access to all of this information.

Please consider what I have shared with you today, how this crime has changed our lives forever, how it stole away the last shred of dignity that my mother had, and how it tarnished the memory of a decent and loving woman who had already suffered enough. Thank you.

[The prepared statement of Ms. Fischer appears in the appendix.]

The CHAIRMAN. Dr. Grabowski?

STATEMENT OF DAVID GRABOWSKI, PH.D., PROFESSOR, HARVARD MEDICAL SCHOOL, BOSTON, MA

Dr. GRABOWSKI. Thank you, Chairman Grassley, Ranking Member Wyden, and distinguished members of the committee. My name is David Grabowski, and I am a professor of health-care policy at Harvard Medical School.

I want to thank you for inviting me to testify today on this important issue of protecting older Americans from abuse and neglect in nursing homes. On a given day, roughly 1.5 million individuals receive care from approximately 16,000 nursing homes nationwide. These individuals have high levels of physical and cognitive impairment and often lack family oversight and financial resources. As such, these are among the frailest and most vulnerable individuals in our health-care system.

We spend roughly $170 billion annually on nursing home care. This sector is heavily regulated. Yet, quality issues persist in many U.S. nursing homes. I want to quote from a U.S. Senate Special Committee on Aging report. In this chapter, the committee identified the following nursing home abuses: a lack of human dignity, lack of activities, untrained and inadequate numbers of staff, ineffective inspections and enforcement, profiteering, lack of control on drugs, poor care, and the list goes on and on.

If this chapter does not sound familiar to the Senators and their staff, it is because it was published in 1974. I would acknowledge that the nursing home sector has made important improvements over the past 45 years. Nevertheless, many of the issues identified in the Senate report in 1974 persist today.

Often the number of nurses per resident is low and the staff turnover rate is high. Residents may develop new health problems after admission due to physical restraints and missed medications. Avoidable transfers of residents to the emergency room and hospital are frequent. Many residents suffer from abuse and neglect. And finally, the quality of life in many U.S. nursing homes is inadequate. And a large number of residents report feeling isolated and lonely.

So why is nursing home quality such a persistent problem going on multiple decades? I want to review four reasons that have been identified by researchers.

Reason number one for persistent low quality: we get what we pay for. Medicaid is the main payer of nursing home services, accounting for about half of all revenues and 70 percent of bed days. In many States, Medicaid reimburses at a rate that does not cover the cost of caring for these high-need residents. It is hard to run a high-quality nursing home when you are losing money on the majority of your residents. Low Medicaid payment rates also result in unnecessary emergency department and hospital transfers, which increase Federal Medicare spending on these services.

A second reason for persistent low quality: we have regulations that simply are not being enforced. Over the last several decades, we have seen quality improvements due to our regulatory system. However, cracks are clearly evident in the current quality assurance framework. Recent investigative reports have documented substantial lapses in oversight processes across multiple States. Importantly, it is the States that are largely responsible for implementation of oversight responsibilities, and many of the identified gaps have been specific to particular States.

A third reason for low quality: certificate of need or CON regulations which have stifled quality competition in many markets. Thirty-four States currently have CON laws in place to hold down nursing home spending. A CON law requires nursing homes to get permission from the State to build additional beds. Research has been fairly clear: nursing home CON laws serve as a barrier to competition and lower the quality of care. These laws also discourage capital innovation in a sector badly in need of modernization.

And a final reason is really a lack of quality transparency. CMS produces the Nursing Home Compare tool on the *Medicare.gov* website to facilitate better consumer choice by providing summary quality rankings. Evidence suggests that it is coming up short.

Unfortunately, Nursing Home Compare lacks information on many of the provider features that may be of the greatest importance to residents and their families. Beyond shortcomings in the website itself, relatively few nursing home consumers report being aware of—much less using—the Nursing Home Compare tool.

In summary, we have made important progress towards improving nursing home quality over the past few decades since the 1974 U.S. Senate report. I would assert, however, that the nursing home sector is better, but still not well. We have a lot of work left to do.

Significant quality-of-care problems persist at many U.S. nursing homes. These problems are related to how we pay for care, how we regulate providers, how we enforce existing regulations that are on the books, and the inability of residents and their advocates to monitor and oversee care. Unless we address these underlying issues, we will be discussing nursing home quality for another 50 years.

Thank you, Mr. Chairman.

[The prepared statement of Dr. Grabowski appears in the appendix.]

The CHAIRMAN. Dr. Gifford?

STATEMENT OF DAVID GIFFORD, M.D., MPH, SENIOR VICE PRESIDENT, QUALITY AND REGULATORY AFFAIRS, AMERICAN HEALTH CARE ASSOCIATION, WASHINGTON, DC

Dr. GIFFORD. Chairman Grassley, Ranking Member Wyden, and distinguished members of the committee, I would like to thank you for holding this hearing to address abuse and neglect. My name is David Gifford. I am a geriatrician, and I serve as the senior vice president for quality at the American Health Care Association. Previously, I was the Director of Health in the State of Rhode Island.

As we just heard, nursing homes miserably failed to keep the mothers of Ms. Blank and Ms. Fischer safe and healthy. You entrusted their care to the staff in those nursing homes only to see that trust violated. Their failure changed your lives forever.

I want to thank you for coming forward today to describe their abuse and neglect so that we can discuss ways to prevent this from happening again. Families and residents like you and your mothers, who are often at the most vulnerable and in the most need of care and support, should never have to worry about their physical safety, let alone experience what they have done.

Cases of neglect and abuse are inexcusable and should not happen ever. We are appalled and disgusted by these incidents. Chairman Grassley and committee members, thank you for making sure that these women are not forgotten. Our focus is to prevent horrific incidents like these from occurring. At the same time, I would like to recognize the thousands of dedicated and caring nursing home staff who care for the elderly, often in challenging circumstances.

AHCA represents nearly 10,000 of the 15,000 nursing homes in the country, including half the not-for-profit and half the government facilities. One of the privileges of my job is to travel around the country to meet the hard-working committed nurses, nursing assistants, and other staff. I have heard thousands of heartwarming accounts of how nursing home staff look after residents as if they are their own family members, helping them get back on their feet and return home or enjoy the remaining years with their families.

Listening to media stories, one might think the quality of care in nursing homes is getting worse. This is not true. I am proud to report that, in the last 7 years, the quality of care in nursing homes has improved dramatically. In early 2012, AHCA voluntarily launched a quality initiative, a member-wide effort to measurably improve care, and our members stepped up to that challenge. Since then our members have demonstrated improvements in 18 of 24 quality outcome measures by CMS, many of which relate to neglect.

For example, our members have decreased the number of elderly who develop pressure ulcers, prevented more residents from developing urinary tract infections, and prescribed fewer antipsychotic medications. For the first time among all health-care providers in the country, a nursing home in Idaho received the U.S. Department of Commerce's prestigious Malcolm Baldrige Award.

More needs to be done. Sometimes we fall short. Sometimes we fall very short, as we have heard today. So what can we do to help prevent future neglect and abuse cases? We have spoken widely with our members and reviewed many of the abuse and neglect citations. What we learned leads us to make the following three recommendations.

First, to further reduce incidents of neglect, a program is needed to attract and retain more nurses, aides, and health professionals such as social workers and activity coordinators. Staffing is the number one challenge I hear from our members over and over again. Unfortunately, there is a national workforce shortage. When nursing homes identify or train staff, they often leave and take jobs in a hospital. To recruit and retain high-quality staff, we suggest expanding to nursing homes the already successful Federal programs to use loan forgiveness to attract health-care workers.

Second, to prevent abuse we need to ensure that people we hire have never engaged in improper, neglectful, or abusive behaviors anywhere. We cannot do that nationwide and are deeply concerned. To complete our background searches, we recommend that nursing homes get easier access to the National Practitioner Data Bank maintained by HRSA.

Third, CMS needs to collect and post customer satisfaction ratings. Nursing homes are the only health-care setting without such information. Giving residents and family members of voice is essential.

In closing, AHCA is committed to making positive change and is dedicated to ensuring that nursing home residents receive consistent high-quality care and remain safe. We are eager to work with Congress, members of this committee, CMS, and other providers so that neither the mothers of Ms. Blank or Ms. Fischer are forgotten.

Thank you for the opportunity to testify today.

The CHAIRMAN. Okay. We will have 5-minute rounds for questions.

[The prepared statement of Dr. Gifford appears in the appendix.]

The CHAIRMAN. Thank you all for staying within your appropriate time to testify. And for the two witnesses who lost loved ones, we are sorry that you had to tell us that story. We thank you for being brave to come here to do it, and probably—as I can tell, it is still troubling you very much to do that because of the ones you love.

I kind of want to get from Ms. Blank and Ms. Fischer some idea what you maybe went through to choose a facility, information that might have been available to you at the time, if you sought any such information, and specifically whether you would rely on the Federal Nursing Home Compare website or the five-star rating system in choosing a facility. I will start with Pat.

Ms. BLANK. Our family did not use that system. It was our home-town nursing home. We knew everyone who worked there. We had a wonderful administrator there for many, many years. He knew every one of the residents, and it was never a question.

It was after he left that things went downhill. But even after my mother's case and the one that you made reference to from Kathy Weaver Arends, the abuse case, that facility still had a five-star rating. So of course, now I definitely would not look at that, and it is not accurate.

The CHAIRMAN. Yes, Maya?

Ms. FISCHER. We did not use that either. We were recommended this nursing home by some friends and family. We did tours of it, talked to other residents' families who lived there in order to gain our information. We did move her in there a number of years ago. So there was not as robust of information on the Internet to do a search at that time. So it was mostly word of mouth and talking to other residents' families who lived there in order to make our decision.

The CHAIRMAN. I am interested in what you were told, whether or not, after you learned that your mother's cases were being investigated, were these cases reported to law enforcement, and if so, do you know who made the report and what challenges, if any, did you face in this process? Pat?

Ms. BLANK. We did not report to law enforcement, but we did talk to the Winnebago County attorney, and we are still currently pursuing criminal charges.

The CHAIRMAN. And you, Maya?

Ms. FISCHER. Yes, in my case one of the nurses did report it to the local police department. They did come and arrest him immediately. The Minneapolis police department and prosecutor's office did an unbelievable job in prosecuting him, but he was taken away and it was reported by the nursing facility.

The CHAIRMAN. At any point in the process, were either one of you contacted by the State's Long-Term Care Ombudsman?

Ms. BLANK. No.

Ms. FISCHER. I don't believe so. No.

The CHAIRMAN. Okay. Thank you.

Now to Dr. Grabowski, I suppose I am going to start out by asking an impossible question. We have quite a few rural communities in Iowa and other States, of course, and when nursing homes close, there might be few options available. Families are torn between traveling long distance to better facilities to visit their family members as they want to, or do they keep them in a lesser facility? What suggestions would you have for families coping with that issue?

Dr. GRABOWSKI. There was a really powerful *New York Times* story, just earlier this week on Monday, that highlighted exactly this issue around rural nursing home closures. This is a really important issue. I would like to say rural nursing homes are like other nursing homes, only more so, and that all the issues we are talking about today, I think, are magnified there: the lack of options, the high dependence on Medicaid, and really the importance of oversight from regulatory bodies.

So I agree with you that that choice you just described is not a good one. Do I go to a substandard nursing home, or do I travel long distances? Oftentimes patients have to travel long distances to a substandard nursing home, so there really is not that kind of choice.

I would hope that we could think about some different policy levers here, like Medicaid payment changes for rural areas. Could we think about additional regulatory oversight in recognition that maybe consumers do not have choice? Can we think about payment and regulations being ways to maybe spur better quality in those rural markets?

The CHAIRMAN. Okay.

Would you answer that question too, Dr. Gifford?

Dr. GIFFORD. We hear and are concerned too about rural facilities. The challenges, I think, as Dr. Grabowski said, are both financial but also workforce. Many people are moving from the rural area into urban areas, so there just are not enough people there. And what we hear and what we recommend today is, we need incentives to get high-quality health-care workers to come in there.

Many of the graduates from nursing school have huge loans, and a loan forgiveness program would be able to go right away to help rectify that situation.

The CHAIRMAN. Senator Wyden?

Senator WYDEN. Thank you very much, Mr. Chairman.

Let me ask you a question, if I might, Dr. Gifford. I think you were here when I said the best nursing homes in this country adhere to a high standard of care. And I took special note of the fact that in Oregon we have a number of our homes working with the unions of service employees and others to improve standards of care.

We have heard, however, really horrendous stories this morning. We heard about an 83-year-old Alzheimer's patient raped. We heard about an 87-year-old patient denied water for weeks. And you said—to your credit—you were very concerned about that.

But I am very troubled about a policy that I believe you advocate. I believe you are in favor of a policy that would take away the option of those families and those patients to secure justice in the legal system. In other words, I believe you are for a policy that would require patients, at least at some facilities, to sign what would be called a pre-dispute arbitration agreement, in effect requiring the families to choose between entering a nursing home of their choice, or waiving their rights if something horrible happened. Now, my understanding is your support for these pre-dispute arbitration agreements is because you think that will keep people out of court and prevent conflicts and the like, a legitimate point.

But tell me why this morning you believe people should be forced to give up their right to secure justice in the legal system, because we heard from two family members about how important that was. Why should people not have the right to have both? If you want to go arbitration, go arbitration. But why should you give up that other right, particularly when these patients and their families are so vulnerable?

Dr. GIFFORD. Senator Wyden, I think that, as you aptly described, the tragedies that they both suffered—there is probably no compensation or any issue that will be able to rectify the situation that occurred.

I do think—and AHCA's position has been—that arbitration is a legal remedy that does allow them to get compensation for any rights and wrongs done out there. So there are two options, which are to either pursue the legal aspect or to pursue an angle through arbitration. And arbitration is often resolved faster and quicker out there. So our position has been, as an association, to allow the pre-dispute arbitration as an option.

Senator WYDEN. But it is the only option for some people. When you talk about supporting pre-dispute arbitration agreements, you in effect support a policy that requires families to choose between entering a nursing home of their choice or waiving their rights if something horrible happens.

I want to move on. I just hope that you all will re-examine this, because I am one who wants to work with facilities that adhere to these high standards of care, and that is why I am pointing out that in Oregon we have some people working very hard to do it. But the idea that those folks over there who have told these stories that ought to shock the conscience of everybody in America should give up their right for legal recourse, I cannot swallow that. It is contrary to everything I have been part of since the days when I represented the public interest on the board of nursing home examiners.

Okay. One other question, if I might, for you, Dr. Grabowski. You are something of an authority on this.

What concerns me—and I very much share the chairman's view on this—is if we are not careful, we are going to lose rural facilities from one part of the United States to another, and we are going to see them just collapse like dominoes and you will not have rural nursing facilities, and rural areas become sacrifice zones.

Last Congress we had a proposal that would have slashed Medicaid with block grants, capped the program. I asked the congressional scorekeepers to analyze this, and they said the Medicaid cuts would reach 35 percent by the end of the first 2 decades. It seems to me if you have something like that—and with Medicaid paying much of the nursing home bill—not only are we going to lose the nursing home guarantee, but we are going to see even more nursing home closures in rural America.

Tell me a little bit about what you see as the ramifications of these kind of cutbacks.

Dr. GRABOWSKI. Absolutely. We are seeing this already. We have had over 400-plus rural nursing home closures. So we are losing, really, the backbone of a lot of these communities in terms of support for older adults. The issue is, once again, as you suggested. It is low Medicaid payment. Many of these nursing homes are almost entirely dependent on the Medicaid program for financing. It is just really hard to continue to operate a high-quality nursing home with the Medicaid rate.

I think the other issue—and Dr. Gifford raised this—is labor, finding workers. That has been a real challenge as well. You might say, well, why don't they just pay more? Well once again, Medicaid is the one reimbursing the care. They are not able to raise wages with low Medicaid payment rates. So we are going to see additional closures. And I think Medicaid is absolutely one way to encourage a healthier rural nursing home sector.

Senator WYDEN. Thank you, Mr. Chairman.

The CHAIRMAN. Let me tell my committee members that this is the way it is going to be for the people who are here now, but remember, with a long list like this, if somebody comes in, you could be cut out of your turn. Senator Scott first, and then Senator Stabenow, and then Hassan, and then Whitehouse.

Senator SCOTT. Thank you, Mr. Chairman, for holding this incredibly important hearing this morning, one that challenges the conscience—as Ranking Member Wyden suggested, shocks the conscience, especially when you listen to Ms. Blank and Ms. Fischer and their testimony. The challenges—I think the whole process of engaging the right place to put your loved one is a difficult process in and of itself, then coming to the decision where you place that loved one, especially in what I consider the sandwich generation— where we have young ones old enough to be on their own, but not necessarily there yet, and folks who are old enough to need our assistance.

So the pain and misery associated with the decision-making process cannot be emphasized enough. And I certainly do not have words to articulate how important this hearing is and how important your testimonies have been. I watched them back in my office, and I will say that it is just a challenge that we need to find ways to root out and to solve.

Abuse and neglect can never be tolerated. So thank you very much for your bravery and your willingness to come forward and be so transparent in a vulnerable way. Our Nation benefits from your testimony, without any question.

In South Carolina, there has been a strong and sustained focus on quality, which I am proud of. The vast majority of our nursing facilities are providing meaningful care to a very vulnerable population in safe and secure settings. There certainly are bad actors, and I do have some questions for Dr. Gifford as it relates to those bad actors.

One of the things that I highlight in South Carolina is that the vast majority of our nursing facilities have either a four- or five- star rating overall, as well as in their staffing levels and the quality of the care. According to a 2017 OIG report, we were one of only 9 States to receive between 0 and 15 complaints for every 1,000 nursing home residents.

That said, listening to your testimonies, we have to do better. And it is incumbent upon us to figure out ways forward. It is vital that we avoid any steps that divert attention and resources away from resident care, away from the actual patients who need and deserve—and frankly are paying for—that type of assistance.

To that end, Dr. Gifford, what changes are necessary from CMS to improve the quality of care in nursing homes, especially taking into consideration what we have heard and, frankly, the contrast with a lot of patients, in South Carolina and many other States, where the level of care is good? How do we improve the engagement with CMS to improve the outcome of the average patient?

Dr. GIFFORD. Well I think, as you have heard today in the testimony by the panelists and the questions, certainly improving five-star is one way to do that, though it is not just about the selecting of homes. I think it is the monitoring of the homes. Certainly one of our recommendations today is, you really need to have the consumer voice added. The fact that we need to have satisfaction on there is something that we have been advocating for for a while. I believe the GAO report on five-star has asked CMS to do that in the past as well. So I think that would help move that in that direction.

I think the other issue is that often the focus of citations, as Dr. Grabowski has talked about in some of his studies, is varied and difficult to understand. And so there is not a consistency there. And when there is greater consistency, they tend to not focus on the broader systems. This is why at AHCA we have really advocated for our members to adopt the Malcolm Baldrige framework.

Senator SCOTT. Yes.

Dr. GIFFORD [continuing]. Because that really focuses on systems. And in those systems, you have to have management with the right training to do the right oversight so that issues when residents have a change in status, like Ms. Blank's mother, or when other State employees are noticed to be not dealing well with residents, that they are notified and then changes can take place before these abuses can occur.

Senator SCOTT. Thank you.

Dr. GIFFORD. That is what we would like to have done.

Senator SCOTT. One last question—I note my time is about up. So how can we ensure that our actions, whether in regulation or enforcement, are targeted at bad actors and avoid increasing the administrative burden for the high-quality facilities across the country that are already placing patients at the center of their attention? Dr. Gifford?

Dr. GIFFORD. Well, I think one of the things we talked about in my testimony is making sure that we have access to the National Practitioner Data Bank at HRSA. I think that will go a long way.

Right now we really only have access to information within the State. As any employees move across State lines or move between provider settings, we do not have access to that information. That would be put into the National Practitioner Data Bank, and we would get access to that. And that is something we could do relatively quickly.

Senator SCOTT. Mr. Chairman, I will just say this in closing, sir. I think it is incumbent upon all of us to take this issue incredibly seriously and perhaps even in our own States take the time to visit some of the nursing homes and see firsthand what may lead to a better experience so that we can avoid as many of the incredible testimonies that we have heard today, if possible.

So I would challenge all of us to make it a priority to visit nursing homes and to become intimately aware of an industry that will be growing, I think, exponentially over the next several years as baby boomers, at 10,000 a day, continue to become a focus of our attention.

Thank you, Mr. Chairman, for this hearing.

The CHAIRMAN. I would back you up, not only to visit the nursing home to see what goes on there and understand it and hopefully encourage more quality care, but it is also a good place to hold a town meeting.

Senator SCOTT. Good thinking, sir. Yes, sir.

The CHAIRMAN. Senator Stabenow?

Senator STABENOW. Well, thank you, Mr. Chairman. First, thank you to you and our ranking member for holding this very important hearing.

Thank you to all of you for being here, and particularly Ms. Blank and Ms. Fischer. I was thinking as you were talking, my mom is 92 years old, and I am blessed because she is doing very well. She is amazing—former nurse—and doing very well. But if that had happened to me, what happened to you—my blood pressure was just going up and up and up thinking about the horror of this. And so, thank you for having the courage to come forward and speak for many people about what happened, and thanks to our other witnesses as well for the good work you do.

And I do want to stress that Medicaid pays for two out of three nursing home residents. And so, when the President's budget comes forward, if it guts Medicaid again, let us be clear, that cuts nursing home care. That makes it harder, Dr. Gifford, to have quality staff that you can maintain. I mean, this is all related, and we need to be serious and understand that as we go forward.

I wanted to speak about transparency, which many of you have talked about. And because we are all at some time going to be looking for a quality nursing home—of which by the way, there are many with dedicated staff and such, but people need to know when there are situations that are not high-quality so you can make the right choices.

So we have talked about the CMS Nursing Home Compare website, which has been around about 20 years in different forms. I actually pulled it up here. As we look at, Ms. Blank, the nursing home that your mom was in, I am assuming that you would want folks to know what happened to your mom in this chapter. Is that a fair assumption?

Ms. BLANK. Absolutely.

Senator STABENOW. Well, it unfortunately is very tough to do when you look at this chapter. And so when we look at this, we see that the nursing home gets a two out of five-star rating, which includes a one out of five inspection rating, four out of five staffing rating, and five out of five quality measure rating.

If you click on health inspections on that tab, you will see three citations in the most recent inspection. August, just months after your mom passed away, they had a "minimal harm or potential for actual harm" and a "few residents affected" category.

And if you go on down to another one, complaint inspections between February of last year and January of this year, it comes up with 9 pages that are extremely hard to figure out for anybody, and I do a lot of work on health policy and work on Medicaid all the time. And this is extremely hard to figure out.

And the first time I read it, I actually missed your mom's case in here because it was listed under level of minimal harm or potential for actual harm. I assume that is not an accurate description in your mind that this was minimal.

Ms. BLANK. Absolutely not.

Senator STABENOW. So what type of information would you want people to have when searching for a nursing home? And how would you recommend we change here from this mass of numbers and so on to actually be able to share information?

Ms. BLANK. Well, just to be able to write it in layman's terms so people can understand, because I read those reports too, over and over again, and I am sure Maya has read those as well—just so that they are understandable so people know what it is and the level of which they are under duress, and, you know, that level was, I think, massive. There were several people there who were under immediate distress, and that is where it needs to be.

The other thing I think—and I am talking a little bit out of turn here, but I think we need to know when they get a fine. That should be reported on there also, because in my mother's case, it was initially $30,000. It was held in suspension. Senator Grassley, with the letter, was able to get it elevated to $77,000. But they get a 35-percent discount if they say, "Okay, we are not going to appeal it."

So why is there a 35-percent discount for that? So that is another thing that is very troubling. So it does not look as bad as it is when it is only a $30,000 fine from a $77,000 fine, which is huge for the State of Iowa. That was a large, large fine for a facility.

Senator STABENOW. Really good points. And by the way, you have to go to the fine print in the back to even find any description of what happened to your mom, as you know.

Ms. BLANK. Yes, ma'am.

Senator STABENOW. Now, Dr. Gifford, you talked about AHCA strongly supporting a mechanism for public reporting on resident and family satisfaction. And you pointed out that nursing homes are the only sector right now where CMS does not require it, and I agree with you completely. I think that is a very important piece of this. And CMS could add this right now, right? They could just add it if they wanted to?

Dr. GIFFORD. It would require setting up a program for everyone to collect it and submit it to CMS, and they would have to issue a rule and regulation, but there is——

Senator STABENOW. But they could. There is nothing that prohibits it.

Dr. GIFFORD. Correct. Yes.

Senator STABENOW. And I hope they will take your recommendation and do that.

Dr. GIFFORD. Thank you.

Senator STABENOW. Dr. Grabowski, do you have other suggestions on improving quality or availability of information so that people can make a good decision? People want to make good decisions; families want to make the right decision. It seems to me that it is all of our collective jobs to make sure they have that information so they can do that.

Dr. GRABOWSKI. Absolutely, and the experience of Ms. Fischer and Ms. Blank not using Nursing Home Compare is actually very typical. Very few residents and their families actually access the website.

So a first step would just be getting individuals to potentially choose their nursing home through the hospital. Are there ways of using hospital discharge planners to mandate that everyone be shown information about the different nursing homes in their area?

Another idea, obviously, is to improve the actual quality of the quality rankings. We heard about nursing homes that maybe are not the best performers getting four or five stars, and we need to make certain those are accurate ratings.

And then the final point is, these ratings really reflect a very narrow part of the entire experience. I think they are very focused on the nursing side of the nursing home experience. They are not very focused on the home. There is very little about the quality of life in the nursing home. There is very little about patient satisfaction, to Dr. Gifford's point.

I often use this line, that I can learn more about the hotel that I stayed in last night here in DC prior to this hearing than I can about any of the nursing homes in this local area. It should not be that way. We should be able to learn a lot more about these nursing homes.

The CHAIRMAN. Senator Hassan?

Senator HASSAN. Thank you, Mr. Chairman. And I want to thank you and the ranking member for holding this hearing.

To all of our witnesses, thank you for being here today, and particularly to Ms. Fischer and Ms. Blank. Thank you for having the strength and courage to talk about something so extraordinary painful in public. Just please know what a difference it makes when you do. And so you have a lot of people out there who are very grateful, and I hope your stories will help a lot of others avoid the harm that your loved ones experienced.

So I want to talk a little bit and follow up really, Dr. Grabowski, with you and maybe, Dr. Gifford, you may also want to talk about it. One of the greatest challenges that you have both mentioned for many nursing homes is staffing. Facilities often have a very difficult time recruiting and training staff. Difficulty finding high-quality workers can obviously impact the health and safety of residents.

I have heard from nursing homes in my State about this problem directly. For example, at one nursing home, the president of the nursing home and all of the non-clinical and administrative staff are cross-trained as licensed LNAs so that they can take on shifts. This nursing home not only pays for staff to receive their licensed nursing assistant training, but also provides a stipend while they attend class because so many people who want to get their LNAs cannot afford to miss work and take the class at the same time. And this nursing home provides on-site daycare to attract employees, but it is still not enough.

Despite all of this, the nursing home is still struggling tremendously with a workforce problem to a point where it affects their census, how many beds they can have, because State regulators are very clear with them, you may not have more patients than you have staff to take care of. So we know that low staffing rates are linked to poor outcomes for patients, so it is absolutely critical we address it.

So let us start with you, Dr. Grabowski, anything you can add. You have already talked a little bit about it, what Congress can do to help support nursing homes with recruitment and retention to ensure that they have the workforce that they need.

Dr. GRABOWSKI. Absolutely. This is a national crisis. Many nursing homes just cannot find the labor out there that they need. I would make one point in addition. I already mentioned payment. I would go, kind of, a little further there and say some States have been very innovative in developing wage pass-through programs where they do not just pay nursing homes more, but they actually put the dollars specifically towards staff. And I think that is really important—not just paying more, but paying more for staff.

And I do think we have seen some important innovations in terms of quality monitoring right now with the Payroll-Based Journal or PBJ data, that now we can actually see who is caring for our loved ones on any given day in these nursing homes.

So I think we have improved data resources to monitor nursing homes. Let us give them the resources now to make certain that we have sufficient staffing on a consistent basis.

Senator HASSAN. Thank you. Dr. Gifford, do you have something to add?

Dr. GIFFORD. I would agree with Dr. Grabowski. I would add that, as we listen to our members—and I listened to just even family members and others who were graduating—the debt of healthcare workers is so big that it is not just a salary issue. And that is why we were proposing the loan forgiveness. We thought—these changes we support may take time. They may be very costly. The loan forgiveness would be easier and I think faster to implement to help meet Senator Grassley's and Wyden's issue to address this quickly.

Senator HASSAN. Thank you.

Ms. Fischer and Ms. Blank, I want to thank you both again for being here today and to add my condolences for the heartbreaking stories that you have shared about truly horrific shortcomings in the nursing homes your loved ones were in. I think we all share the sentiment that nobody should have to share the experiences that your family has had, particularly your loved ones. But I just wanted to give you any additional opportunity to let us know what else is on your mind about what steps Congress can take to ensure that abuse and neglect in nursing homes like the abuse and neglect your mothers experienced never happens again.

Ms. Blank will start.

Ms. BLANK. I would like to say that I know for a fact that at least three of the people who were fired from the facility after this made the front page of our State newspaper very easily got a job across the border in Minnesota. They are all working right in the same kind of facilities again, and there was no—they were never charged with anything. So I am sure they never said, "Well, two people died on the same day in our care facility and one of them made the front page of the newspaper," and they are not going to say that, but yes.

So I think some way to follow that, track that that information is also available to people who are looking to employ. But again, that shortage is one of the reasons why they were happy to have these people who had all of that experience, but they did not know why they were let go.

Senator HASSAN. That is helpful. Ms. Fischer?

Ms. FISCHER. I think again, for me, it is mostly about the transparency. In my situation, the person who raped my mother had been investigated numerous times before. So the fact that, you know, he was continually investigated, and he still kept his job—how can that be? How can that be?

I understand maybe one allegation. I understand these are elderly patients; sometimes they get confused. But when you have an employee who is multiply investigated for sexually assaulting nursing home victims, somebody dropped the ball there. And somebody did not take that seriously, and because of that, my mother was a victim of his.

Senator HASSAN. Thank you.

The CHAIRMAN. Senator Cardin?

Senator CARDIN. Thank you, Mr. Chairman.

I want to thank all of our witnesses. Obviously, in regards to safety, the issues of transparency are extremely important. Staffing issues are well understood, that we have a challenge in finding qualified people in adequate numbers, and those issues have been covered, and I think we have to see what role we can play here in Congress to help in regards to those issues.

Dr. Gifford, I want to cover one other issue that has not been talked about yet, and that is the unnecessary senior hospitalization we see from nursing homes. One of the reasons, of course, is that nursing homes by and large do not have 24/7 medical staff on duty, which is understandable. There have been a couple suggestions that have been made. I have been working with Senator Thune on a way you can get on-site emergency medical care within our nursing facilities. We also have the growing understanding of telehealth and what telehealth can do as far as providing timely information that can help deal with patient care.

So my question to you is, within the industry, is there an understanding that in many cases patients who are in nursing homes are—because there are other options available—sent to an emergency room only to find out that it was really not necessary for them to be sent to the emergency room, but that was the safest option at the time?

Are you looking at ways that you can reduce unnecessary hospitalization?

Dr. GIFFORD. Yes, we have made reducing hospitalizations one of our central focus points for our quality initiative areas. And I would say that, particularly in the rural areas, the promise of telehealth is great, but as you know, telehealth varies all over the map with that.

And I do think that, generally speaking, the nursing home staff I talked to find that when people go to the hospital, they come back usually worse than when they left. The acute illness might be treated. The emergency room may address the issue, but the resident really suffers a lot because, as you have heard, these elderly individuals are very frail and have a lot of complications with them.

So we think it is important to address that and lower it. I think telehealth definitely plays a role in it. We hear from members all the time which ones know how to work it, and there are a lot of different companies out there. So we would be happy to work with you and your staff to figure out how better to do that.

Senator CARDIN. Is this an issue of just not understanding telehealth, not having it available, not having the right staffing needs in order to deal with this? I appreciate the fact that you have acknowledged a problem, and you also acknowledge that, by sending the person to the emergency room, it may not even be in their best interest. It is a costly option, by the way, also to our health-care system. But it may not be in their best health-care interest.

Do we have a regulatory problem that is impeding your ability to deal with this issue? Is it a cost issue on staffing? Is it a lack of understanding on how telehealth works? Are there restrictions on telehealth? Where can we assist in helping you solve these problems?

Dr. GIFFORD. I think there are a number of different ways, and probably, given the time and everything, it would be better if we sit down and talk with your staff on how to do it. But I know that one of the common issues we hear from telehealth is about how they get reimbursed for that time. And I think the current reimbursement system was designed prior to telehealth. And how to incorporate that in is one of the challenges that is out there.

Senator CARDIN. And we have had that issue in regards to other issues. This committee has taken action in regards to opioids, in regards to mental health, in regards to other fields where we have been able to expand telehealth opportunities. So I think this is an underutilized area.

Dr. Grabowski, did you want to comment?

Dr. GRABOWSKI. No. I completely agree. We did a study in Massachusetts where we looked at nursing home telemedicine, and it was found to do exactly what you suggested: it prevented hospital transfers during evenings and weekends when staff were not there. We thought this was a real success.

Of course, right when our study ended, the nursing home chain did away with the technology for exactly the reason that was just suggested. It was about payment. They were paying for the technology, "they" being the nursing home. Medicare was enjoying the savings. And so I think bridging that disconnect between who pays for the service and who actually gets the savings—we can have telemedicine in rural areas, in rural nursing homes, and that can be paid for. But in urban and suburban nursing homes, that is not the case.

So I think bridging that disconnect between who pays and who reaps the savings—and is there a way for Medicare to maybe invest in these programs to enjoy some of the savings?

Senator CARDIN. I look forward to working with you.

Thank you, Mr. Chairman.

The CHAIRMAN. Now we have—Senator Thune has come back. So as I told some of you——

Senator THUNE. You seem disappointed, Mr. Chairman. [Laughter.]

The CHAIRMAN. No. Not at all. It is just kind of hard to referee when people are in and out.

Senator THUNE. I know.

The CHAIRMAN. Go ahead, Senator Thune.

Senator THUNE. Well, thank you, Mr. Chairman, for holding the hearing.

Ms. Blank, Ms. Fischer, so sorry for your experiences, and we appreciate hearing your stories.

I think we can all agree that the stories of egregious abuse and neglect that we have heard today have no place in our society, and that as work continues to improve quality and outcomes and to prevent these types of instances of abuse from happening again, we also need to ensure that access to care remains a priority as our population continues to age. And that is certainly an issue that we deal with in South Dakota.

Dr. Grabowski, in your testimony you referred to a *New York Times* article from this Monday that discussed rural nursing home closures. As a result of the closures referenced, more than 100,000 South Dakotans were displaced, many of whom had few options that were less than 100 miles away from the facilities that closed.

Staffing is one of the top issues that I hear about, but for the benefit of the committee, what other challenges do rural facilities face as they work to provide quality care? We see, as I mentioned, more and more nursing homes in my State of South Dakota are closing.

Dr. GRABOWSKI. Yes, and we are seeing that trend nationally with the closure of rural nursing homes. It is really about resources, the resources to pay staff to operate a nursing home. And so, given that these rural nursing homes are often so dependent on Medicare and Medicaid as a less-generous payer of services, they simply do not have the resources to provide high-quality care and even to stay in business.

So I think adding additional resources for rural nursing homes is really important. That was a really well-written story, and a really powerful story about displacing residents and just the effect that has on their health. It is not just bad for residents to be transferred to the hospital; it is also bad for them to have to transfer nursing homes. And so I hope that we can work on ways to provide rural nursing homes with more resources to continue to be that important source of care for older adults.

Senator THUNE. Yes, and that story did point out the disruption, dislocation, and just the deteriorating physical health of people who are put in that situation. And that is, by the way, a circumstance I think that a lot of South Dakotans can relate to, because there are a lot of small communities with nursing homes, and to find another alternative, you literally have to go tens if not hundreds of miles, and that is an incredible disruption for somebody who is in that age, and in some cases, that state of life.

So would you say that in terms of the rural providers, nursing homes in those rural areas that you talked about, the payer mix— Medicaid represents what, 70–80 percent in a lot of those cases?

Dr. GRABOWSKI. Yes. So nationally, Medicaid pays for about two-thirds of all care. In those communities it can be 80–90 percent. So they can be high-Medicaid facilities. And as I mentioned in my testimony, those are exactly the facilities oftentimes that we are seeing with the worst quality of care problems. These are the lowest-resource facilities with the most issues around neglect and poor quality of care.

Senator THUNE. And is that—I know part of that story; you would attribute that to staffing. But it is also just the overall—do you know what the margin is for a nursing home in operating costs if 70 percent to 80 percent of your payer mix is Medicaid?

Dr. GRABOWSKI. So the estimate that we typically see is that nursing homes make a positive margin, sometimes a very healthy margin, on the Medicare side. Obviously private pay, they set the price and the margins are fine there. But in most States—and it varies State to State—the margins are negative on Medicaid. And so that can be ¥2 to ¥5 percent on Medicaid. And that could even be lower in certain low-payment States. So it is certainly very challenging to be a high-Medicaid nursing home.

Senator THUNE. And I want to come back to something that Senator Cardin referenced, because we have a bill that creates an alternative payment model for nursing homes and facilities that actually will find ways to reduce costs through the use of technology and trying to incentivize more of that. You alluded to—and I think Dr. Gifford as well—something about the barriers to that. And a lot of it has to do with reimbursements, which we have heard about for a really long time.

But it seems to me at least that that is a solution, particularly in these rural areas of the country, that offers great opportunity in terms of delivering care and servicing a population that covers vast distances and has great difficulty traveling.

So I would again just throw that out there and say to you that if you have thoughts or ideas that could add to, or enhance, or improve upon that legislation, I would really like to see us address this issue. And we have been trying for a long time. We make little incremental progress, but technology, telehealth, telemedicine I think, can do remarkable things for delivery of services in rural areas of the country.

Thank you. Thank you, Mr. Chairman.

The CHAIRMAN. No we go to the Senator from Nevada.

Senator CORTEZ MASTO. Good morning.

First of all, let me just say to Ms. Blank and Ms. Fischer, thank you. Thank you for being here. Thank you for continuing to be advocates and tell your stories. And it is not easy.

As I sit here, I reflect on—in southern Nevada where I was born and raised, my grandmother, whom I was named after, had Alzheimer's. And she stopped eating and drinking, and unfortunately, the only place that we could help her was in a nursing home. And it is hard. It is hard on the families.

But I also know that, even though your family is around and you want to be there, you cannot be there 24/7. That is why when I became Attorney General in Nevada for 8 years, I created the unit to enforce and prosecute for elder abuse, neglect, and exploitation.

And that is why I was an advocate for a Medicaid fraud unit within the Attorney General's office that does the same thing. And that is one of the reasons why I am excited and thank the chair and ranking member for this hearing today, because, although there are some good nursing care facilities out there, there are some bad players.

And I am counting on the Association to help us find those bad players, and weed them out, and hold them accountable. I do not think there is a role for the Association to protect everyone. I think there is a role that you can play, and I am looking forward to working with you there.

But let me talk, Dr. Grabowski, about an issue that I saw that I think is of concern. I know I saw it. I think I saw it in some of the testimony today that there is a problem of excessive prescribing in some of our nursing homes, either of drugs or treatment. And Medicare beneficiaries may undergo medically unnecessary procedures that are costly, that are dangerous, or both, simply so that the facilities can bill the government.

Can you speak to the payment incentives that drive that type of behavior, if you would, please? I am curious how we can, here at the Federal level, put systems in place, or rules or regulations, whatever we need to do working with the Association, how we can address this.

Dr. GRABOWSKI. Yes. It is a really important issue. So I am glad you raised it.

We see over-medication and inappropriate medications in a lot of nursing home residents. Of course, most of the payment for medications is done separate from the Medicaid system. This is paid, for those long-staying nursing home residents, through Part D through the Medicare program, or for those short-stay rehab nursing home patients, it is paid through their skilled nursing facility benefit.

So it is Medicare really footing the bill for those medications. And I think we could do two things here. We could do a lot more oversight about this inappropriate prescribing. I will give one example, which there has been a lot of interest in, and that has been the inappropriate prescribing of antipsychotics to nursing home residents with dementia. It has been used as a way to basically restrain these residents. Rather than use a physical restraint, we overmedicate them and sedate them, basically. And it is inhumane. It is a terrible practice, but it has been over-utilized, even following a black box warning by the FDA.

So that is an area where I think your committee could really be helpful in continuing to shine a light on that kind of overuse.

And then I think through the payment system, I think keeping a close eye on how we are reimbursing particular drugs and whether those drugs are actually adding value. We have a lot of polypharmacy here. We have big utilization. I think nursing homes can be a partner in this. Obviously, they are not the ones doing the prescribing, but I think a lot of nursing homes are encouraging, at times, residents to get on some of these medications. And so I think nursing homes can certainly be a partner here along with Medicare in trying to address this issue.

Senator CORTEZ MASTO. But let me also address it this way, because I think they are—do you think there is a component of training, whether it is nursing training, doctor training, whatever it is, the training on the utilization of these drugs when it comes to elder care? I mean that, to me, should be where we start, and then whether or not there is some sort of payment incentive we can address. But to me it starts with the training as well and recognizing that working with seniors may be a little bit different.

Let me give you an example. I have a great aunt who is 94, and she can tell you every President, and she is focused and is there mentally and alert. She broke her hip, which left her in the hospital unfortunately, and she was overmedicated. And I think part of that was because they felt that she was older, she did not know, and so they were trying to help her. But instead, it was making it worse.

And when we figured that out and took her off that medication, she was so much better and more alert. But just assuming she is 90 years old and not going to be all there, there is that assumption. I think part of it is the training. Would you agree with that?

Dr. GRABOWSKI. Training is absolutely important. I am glad you raised the role of the hospital here. We see a lot of medications being picked up when individuals are transferred—we heard about the high rate of emergency department and hospital use earlier. They go to the hospital. They come back on several new medications. And so this is sort of a dynamic issue of trying to hold down all these medications.

Senator CORTEZ MASTO. Thank you. And I know my time is up, but that training is key for the nursing homes as well.

Dr. GRABOWSKI. Yes.

Senator CORTEZ MASTO. For those people whom we are hiring, we want to do the background checks. But also we want to make sure they have the qualifications that are necessary and they understand that interaction as well.

So, thank you. I know my time is up. Thank you.

The CHAIRMAN. The next three will be Casey, Daines, and then Warner. And, Senator Daines, I was told you were going to be good enough to take over for me so I can go to another meeting.

Since you are going to be the second one up, why don't you come up here and take over right now.

Senator Casey?

Senator CASEY. Mr. Chairman, thanks very much, and thanks for having this hearing.

It is, to say the least, an outrage to hear what we have heard over far too long, the stories of abuse and neglect that have gone on, stories that have been on the public record more recently. We have had reporting in Pennsylvania, a series entitled "Still Failing the Frail." That is the name of a story from *PennLive,* a newspaper series in Pennsylvania, that talked about some of the abuses that have taken place.

In this particular series, there were stories of patients with maggots in their feeding tubes, patients with bedsores of course, which we hear about a lot, and patients who died as a result of the neglect that they faced.

This hearing, I think, demonstrates clearly that this is an issue that both parties in both houses have to be concerned about. I have here in front of me a letter that Senator Toomey and I have sent to the Administrator of the Centers for Medicare and Medicaid Services, Seema Verma, dated March 4th, outlining a series of nine questions about these issues.

Mr. Chairman, I would ask consent that this letter from Senator Toomey and I, dated March 4th, to CMS Administrator Verma be made part of the record.

Senator DAINES [presiding]. Without objection. Senator CASEY. Thanks very much.

[The letter appears in the appendix on p. 58.]

Senator CASEY. CMS has a program, the Special Focus Facilities Program, but unfortunately this program is so focused that only a fraction of the facilities that require additional attention are in fact admitted to the program. CMS puts together a list of the facilities in every State that it recommends to be included in the program, and as many here know, over 400 are recommended for additional monitoring, but a minimum of 88 are in fact admitted to the program.

Ms. Blank and Ms. Fischer, we are grateful for your testimony, your presence here. Do you believe that families should have access to this secret list of 350 facilities in need of monitoring before making a decision about where their loved ones receive care?

Ms. BLANK. Absolutely. I would say any information that can be helpful in making the decision of where loved ones would go, or in the case of my mother, after she has passed away, any kind of information that could be made available would be helpful. Absolutely.

Senator CASEY. Thank you.

Ms. FISCHER. I would have to agree with that. I think the more information the consumer gets, it certainly helps them make an educated decision. In my situation, if one were to find out that this particular nursing home has had some issues and there were some investigations of sexual misconduct by employees, I think that might change someone's mind as to whether they are going to pick one nursing home over another.

So I think we need all of this information. It is an extremely difficult decision to make, putting your loved one into a nursing home facility. It is heartbreaking, and so any information that we can get to help us make a more informed decision, I would be all for it.

Senator CASEY. Well, thank you very much.

I wanted to highlight some of the questions in the letter that we have sent to CMS. We ask in the first question about the methodology that CMS uses to determine the fixed size of the facilities, and what numbers there are. Number two, we ask about providing the reasoning for maintaining the program's current size. We ask about whether CMS updates the skilled nursing facility candidate list. We ask CMS whether it engages with State survey agencies. We also ask about the prioritization for skilled facilities, participation in the selected program. So it goes on from there, but we want to make sure that we shine a very bright light on this program and have questions answered about it.

I will have additional questions for the second panel, but, Mr. Chairman, thank you very much.

Senator DAINES. Thank you, Senator Casey.

I guess I will do my round of questions now. I guess it is good to have the gavel occasionally, right? But I think I am in line right after Senator Casey. So I am actually following the batting order here in fairness to my colleagues.

Abuse and neglect, I think we all agree, should never be allowed under any circumstance. We heard it firsthand from a couple of our witnesses here today, and I want to thank you for your courage to come here and share the painful story.

We have over 3,700 Montanans receiving care every day in nursing homes. It is an important discussion to have. I am grateful that the chairman has decided to take on this issue and bring this to light in Washington.

This *New York Times* article about the high rate of nursing home closures in rural parts of the country that was published earlier this week is referenced a couple of times. When you think about Montana, you probably think about rural America, and that is true. In fact, 20 years ago in Montana, we had over 100 nursing homes. Today we have just over 70, while at the same time, just in the last 10 years, our senior population has grown 40 percent. And I am guessing these kind of numbers are probably consistent with what we are seeing across much of rural America.

Dr. Grabowski, you have been asked a couple of questions about rural challenges. You have been asked about telemedicine. From a Federal policy viewpoint, as you think about making a recommendation to this committee, what does HELP look like as well as what we could do here to address the challenge that we see with closing nursing homes in rural America?

Dr. GRABOWSKI. So I have talked about Medicaid, as you said. I talked about the importance of, sort of, the workforce and telemedicine. Maybe to add another part of this, we have this huge fragmentation. It is a national issue across Medicare and Medicaid. And another opportunity for rural nursing homes is potentially to leverage some of that Medicare financing. And that means offering a more integrated product, which we see with the special needs plans under Medicare Advantage. We have seen some States participating in the financial alignment initiative, which is an integrated demonstration for dually eligible individuals.

But most of these Medicaid recipients we are describing in nursing homes are also Medicare beneficiaries. And so there is this opportunity to leverage both the Medicaid long-term care benefit, the nursing home benefit, but also the Medicare benefit and add additional resources.

So I would like to put that out there as another idea. It is one that could apply anywhere, but I think it could be especially fruitful for those rural nursing homes.

Senator DAINES. In looking at the demographic trends in our Nation, this is only going to become increasingly a bigger problem, obviously. And I think this is a good discussion to have today about where do we go next, as we think about the next 10 or 20 years.

I was struck by the comment you made, Dr. Grabowski, in response to one of the Senator's questions about how you could go online and see reviews at the hotel you stayed at last night. When it comes to nursing home or senior care, there is an absence of such.

I spent 28 years in the private sector before coming to Washington, DC. In fact, I spent 12 years in the cloud computing business, and we saw firsthand the power of the consumer, unleashing the power of your crowdsourcing input and holding service institutions accountable by what the consumer is saying.

So I did a little research—and not that I was not fully listening to my Senate colleagues and their questioning, but I was doing a little online research. And I looked at

Yelp, for example. I see that Yelp, in 2015, actually added a platform for nursing homes. If you do a Yelp search of nursing homes, you can find it.

But yet when you take a look at how many comments are there—I just looked at a couple examples. Again, it is a bit anecdotal, but they date back to 2016. There was one comment in 2018—two comments about a very large facility that will remain anonymous here for the purpose of this discussion.

My question is, what power do you see in the consumer having a greater voice? And I am going to ask this question of Ms. Blank and Ms. Fischer as well in terms of what you might have done by putting your comments online so others can see what is going on and shining light and bringing more transparency to what is happening as it relates to the care or the lack thereof in several nursing homes.

Dr. GRABOWSKI. So I think there is both a private and a public role here. The public role is, could we enhance Nursing Home Compare to make it a much broader tool where you actually could learn about resident experiences, some quality of life rankings, or patient satisfaction measures? But some of that could also be vignettes about the care. I think that would be really useful. I would want to learn about Ms. Blank's and Ms. Fischer's experiences.

And then on the private side, we are going to see Yelp, Facebook, and other platforms develop these tools. I hope consumers will use them. I think the initial research suggests they add a very different dynamic or dimension to the quality framework here, but they do not——

Senator DAINES. Every business in America now in the service industry is held accountable by consumers. And I recognize that there is good news and there is bad news here in terms of people sometimes writing reviews that are not accurate and so forth. But I think in the totality, that has been a very good thing.

Dr. GRABOWSKI. There is a signal there.

Senator DAINES. Absolutely. It is democracy in action, people voting and expressing their views here as it relates to just—Ms. Blank and Ms. Fischer, any thoughts you had looking at—would you want more Iowans and others to hear your story so that others who are thinking about the services would know about them?

Ms. BLANK. Absolutely, but I think they are hearing it more through the news media and social media than looking on a website for their loved ones, because some of them are not looking at that until they actually need that service. So in my case, I am also a journalist, so I have also told my story. I have let other journalists tell my story as well. And I think that has been much more effective than putting it on a website somewhere for somebody to read.

Senator DAINES. Okay.

Ms. FISCHER. I would agree, and I guess when I think of something like Yelp—you know, we talked about being able to look up the review of our hotel. I do not know if that is necessarily something that people would think of using when they look to find a long-term care facility for their families.

Do I want people to know about what happened to my mother? Absolutely. But again, as Ms. Blank testified to, there were wonderful people in this nursing home. And there was some fantastic experiences, and my mother had a lot of years in this nursing home where people took fantastic care of her.

How we identify this bad situation and make people aware of it—Yelp or reviews of the nursing home itself as a whole may not be the best way to do that. This was one individual, you know, who was, again, investigated by the Department of Health over and over again, but continued to keep his job.

I do not know if that is something necessarily that could be discussed on Yelp or brought to light. It is by a simple review.

Senator DAINES. Thank you. I am out of time. I want to respect my colleagues here.

Senator Warner?

Senator WARNER. Thank you, Mr. Chairman. I have never seen anybody get to the gavel this quickly on the Finance Committee. So that is pretty darn good. [Laughter.]

I want to pick up, actually, on both your lines of questioning. I am very concerned as well about the rural closures, 440 in a place like the Commonwealth of Virginia, particularly in southwest and southside Virginia. This is an enormous challenge. In many of these communities, the nursing home may be even the largest employer. And the burden on families—obviously, I really appreciate the heart-wrenching stories. We have to improve quality, but we also have to find a way to get the incentives right.

I have a two-part question—probably anybody can comment on this—but probably more for Dr. Gifford and Dr. Grabowski. One, the existing CMS rating system on the five-star scale, my understanding is that is graded purely on a curve. So you are going to have a fixed number of ones and fives regardless of whether they all come out on a curve. And I would like to get your comments on the CMS system, and then I do worry—and I do not know if this question has been fully raised. But when we look at—I say this as a former Governor—the mix and match on the funding streams between Medicare and Medicaid, it is a real challenge.

I know MedPAC estimated that the aggregate margin for Medicare skilled nursing facilities was a little over 11 percent. That is a pretty darn good margin. But when you add in the Medicaid reimbursements, the overall industry average drops to about a half-percent margin.

Now as a former business guy, particularly in an industry where you have as much turnover as you have in this field—so that we can avoid the kind of horror stories that we heard from some of our witnesses—is this a viable business model, particularly in some of these smaller communities, if this margin is this thin?

Dr. GRABOWSKI. I will start with the margins, and this issue is magnified. You described this on a sector-wide basis across all nursing homes. Not every nursing home cares for a similar mix of private-pay, Medicare, and Medicaid. There are a lot of high-Medicaid nursing homes out there that are losing money on every resident. And then you have the—

Senator WARNER. And that is where the whole population migrates to as they run through their other resources?

Dr. GRABOWSKI. Absolutely, and so it really becomes the haves and have-nots among nursing homes. I think that is a big part of the problem. And the reason many quality-of-care issues often happen is that we have this kind of lower tier of facilities.

Towards the ratings question, there are some measures where we use thresholds like staffing, but everything is benchmarked, as you suggest, within States. So they are putting this on a distribution, and we have some number of five-stars down to some number of one-stars. And it is kind of on a normal distribution, yes.

Senator WARNER. Another question for you—the question has been asked—as we think about the funding model, we want to improve quality, but particularly as we are looking at these nursing homes that disproportionately only take Medicaid or have this mixed model, I worry that these 440 rural closings are going to continue to increase as people just find that it is not a viable business model.

Dr. GIFFORD. We share the concern. I mean there are a little over 3,000 counties in the United States. Ninety-three percent of those have at least one nursing home in them. And often they are the largest health-care provider in that community. And they go beyond just providing long-term care, but really are a resource for that community.

So keeping them open and maintaining them, I think, really is a priority. And I think you are starting to see the early effects of the challenges out there running nursing homes in this country.

Dr. GRABOWSKI. It is interesting that you mentioned they are the largest employer in many of these counties. They are a really important employer. There are actually more nursing homes in this country than Starbucks, if you can believe it. So there are a lot of nursing homes, 15,000 to 16,000 facilities. So they are a really important employer in rural America and in other parts of the country.

Senator WARNER. Would either of you like to add anything?

Ms. BLANK. Well, it is almost the only place to work in our community, and so to also address what the sitting hearing chair now had to say—I am sorry. I cannot see you——

Senator DAINES. I am not Chuck Grassley, just so you know. [Laughter.]

Ms. BLANK. I know that well, sir. So just the whole idea that things are—to say that on a rating that terrible thing that happened to my mother, that terrible thing that happened to Ms. Fischer; there are a lot of wonderful people who work there.

I have known those people there for all my life, most of them. And so to put a rating on there and to say that this is a terrible place to have your loved one—no, it was a terrible thing that happened to my mother and some other people who live there, so——

Senator WARNER. Right. We need that accountability. And I guess—I know my time is up—I would like to get maybe for the record though, because I do think we need to expect quality, but we also have to expect a business model that works.

And one of the things on electronic health records, the EHRs, nursing homes are not included in the HITECH Act. I think it, again, it is not a silver bullet, but it ought to be part of the solution set, and I hope that we could consider as we move forward to make sure EHRs from nursing homes are included.

Dr. GRABOWSKI. The majority of nursing homes have some electronic health record, but very few connect to hospitals or physicians. So it is another source of fragmentation in our health-care system. And the exclusion of nursing homes from the HITECH Act, I think, was a mistake in hindsight.

Senator WARNER. Thank you.

Senator DAINES. Thank you. Senator Whitehouse?

Senator WHITEHOUSE. Thank you very much, Mr. Chairman.

Let me first welcome a friend, Dr. Gifford, who was for several years our Health Director in Rhode Island and did a terrific job. And before then he was the chief medical officer for a group called Quality Partners, which had the CMS nursing home quality improvement contract and performed a lot of path-breaking work. So I welcome Dr. Gifford as one of the good guys in this effort who has dedicated an enormous amount of his career to trying to move the ball forward in a very complicated and difficult area.

I want to thank Ms. Blank and Ms. Fischer for bringing their stories. And you have no idea how boring Finance Committee hearings can sometimes get. And the policy debates sometimes obscure the harsh painful facts that should draw our attention. And your testimony has really been important in that regard. So, I want to thank you.

I would like to echo the ranking member's remarks about the importance of not allowing mandatory arbitration to degrade the accountability of these organizations. I think the founding fathers set up courtrooms and juries for a reason. They had a lot of confidence in them. It is a core part of the American system of government, and to simply take that away from people, particularly in ways that they had no real bargained choice with is a grave, grave, grave mistake. And I look forward to working with Senator Wyden to make sure we defend against that.

I would like to ask Dr. Grabowski a question for the record to get back to me on. You do not have to answer it right now, but being from a very urban State, Rhode Island, I am very interested in your comment about the difference between rural and urban on telehealth reimbursement, because I do think we need to address telehealth reimbursement as a significant part of improving care here.

I would like to ask Dr. Gifford now to tell me how clear a signal you believe the various quality reporting requirements that nursing homes are subject to—how clear the signal is that emerges. Sometimes I fear that we demand so much reporting in so many different ways that you end up with a kind of Tower of Babel noise coming out rather than a clear articulable signal that Ms. Fischer and Ms. Blank could go to and see, uh-oh, there is one that is signaling real trouble. And it seems to me that there is a lot of noise in the system that obscures the signal of which ones are in trouble.

I guess for the purposes of my time, is that a real problem that we should pursue—and then through a QFR—what would your group recommend to try to get more signal out of the noise?

Dr. GIFFORD. Senator Whitehouse, yes. That is a challenge and a problem we hear about from law enforcement, from our members, and from State service agencies around the country.

It is a challenging issue, and we are happy to respond to you in the QFR session.

Senator WHITEHOUSE. Okay. Good.

The final question I have has to do more generally with end-of-life care. And as you know, we have made a lot of progress in Rhode Island with trying to make sure that people's choices at that very delicate and special time are honored, that people know what the choices are so that they can be honored, that they are recorded where they need to be.

We have most records so that it is actually in most folks' medical files. But I think there is more progress that we need to make and, in particular, towards the end of life when the system insists that before somebody goes into a nursing home for their final days, they need to have 2 nights or 3 days in a hospital, or whether they insist that for purposes of home caregiver respite care, it is the patient who has to go and be dislocated and ambulanced someplace rather than have a home care worker come in and provide respite to the family member, or whether it is forcing the question of ending curative care before palliative care can be administered.

I think there are just some real mistakes in the system right now. And so I would ask for you to take a look at a bill we are going to send to both of you and get your comments on it, because I think there is a way, by waiver, to solve those problems for communities where they are really taking a look at this population as a focus. And C-TAC and other groups are working on this. So I know there is some attention to it, but I would ask you to have a look at the bill. And with that, I conclude my questioning and yield back. Thank you, Mr. Chairman.

Senator DAINES. Thank you, Senator Whitehouse.

This concludes the testimony of this panel. Thank you for coming, and thank you for sharing your insights.

We are going to switch panels here. Bring the next panel up if you would.

[Pause.]

Senator DAINES. I want to extend a warm welcome to our second panel, which includes both Federal as well as State government witnesses. Testifying first is Dr. Kate Goodrich, who heads the Center for Clinical Standards and Quality at the Centers for

Medicare and Medicaid Services. She also serves as Chief Medical Officer for this agency. Welcome, Dr. Goodrich.

Our next two witnesses are from Senator Portman's home State of Ohio, and he would like to introduce them.

Senator Portman?

Senator PORTMAN. Great. Thank you, Mr. Chairman. I thank you and Senator Grassley—now that you are the chair here—for the hearing. It has been fascinating and troubling in a lot of respects.

You know, all of us care a lot about our nursing homes working. In my case, grandparents on both sides ended up their lives in nursing homes. And it was said earlier by some of the witnesses, there are some great people who work in our skilled nursing and our nursing home facilities.

And then there are issues that arise, and one of the issues, as I see it, is that as unemployment goes down—and this is based on a study that was just done, an economic study—the mortality rates actually go up. And I think a lot of that is because of the staffing challenges we have. So one of the issues that I am glad we got some input on and I want to hear more about is our staffing.

But I am very happy to have the opportunity to welcome two of our witnesses here. The first is Toni Bacon. I saw in all the material—I have it—her real name is Antoinette. I never knew that. I always knew you as Toni. But I am going to use Antoinette today in a more formal way.

But she is right where she needs to be in this issue, because she is a very impressive prosecutor. She looks very nice, I know, but she is really one of the toughest prosecutors in the country, and she has that reputation. She actually took on public corruption in Cleveland, OH and is known as really one of the country's premier corruption prosecutors anywhere. And her work ended up, Mr. Chairman, resulting in a total reform of the Cuyahoga County governmental system.

Now, she is in a position that is really important, because she is—although Assistant U.S. Attorney in Cleveland, she is detailed to the Department of Justice as the Associate Deputy Attorney General and the National Elder Justice Coordinator. And in that position, of course, she has taken a national leadership role on elder abuse cases. So she is a tough prosecutor, and she is right where she needs to be, as I said, to be able to help on this critically important issue that we have talked about a lot today. So welcome, and thank you for your service.

Ms. Mitchell, thank you for being here. Keesha Mitchell is a section chief in charge of the Health Care Fraud Section in Ohio Attorney General Dave Yost's office. I saw earlier that your bio said in Mike DeWine's office and they have not updated it yet, but we are happy to have you still in that job.

She is a true expert. She has devoted over 20 years of her career to identifying payment fraud in our State's Medicaid program and to protecting nursing home patients who fall victim to abuse. So she has a great background. And she has also been president recently of the National Association of Medicare Fraud Control Units and has done a lot of work with them, including some of these global settlements, and been a member of their executive and global case committee—so a true expert who speaks around the country on these issues.

And I am delighted to have this expertise in my home State of Ohio and really glad we are going to get to hear from you all today. Thank you for being here.

Senator DAINES. Thank you, Senator Portman. Dr. Goodrich, you may proceed.

STATEMENT OF KATE GOODRICH, MD, DIRECTOR, CENTER FOR CLINICAL STANDARDS AND QUALITY; AND CHIEF MEDICAL OFFICER, CENTERS FOR MEDICARE AND MEDICAID SERVICES, BALTIMORE, MD

Dr. GOODRICH. Thank you.

So, Chairman Grassley, Ranking Member Wyden, Senator Daines, Senator Portman, and the members of the committee, thank you for the opportunity to discuss CMS's efforts to ensure that every nursing home serving Medicare and Medicaid beneficiaries is meeting Federal requirements to keep its residents safe and to provide high-quality care.

Patient safety is our top priority in nursing homes and all facilities that participate in the Medicare and Medicaid programs. And we appreciate the significant time and effort dedicated to this issue by the members of this committee. Chairman Grassley and Ranking Member Wyden have both been leaders on this issue over the years, and we appreciate the continued interest.

Monitoring patient safety and quality of care in nursing homes requires coordinated efforts between the Federal Government and the States. To participate in Medicare and Medicaid, a nursing home must be certified as meeting numerous statutory and regulatory requirements, including those pertaining to health, safety, and quality. Compliance with these requirements for participation is verified through annual unannounced surveys. They are on-site surveys conducted by State survey agencies in each of the 50 States, the District of Columbia, and the U.S. territories. And to help ensure greater consistency among State survey agencies, CMS recently implemented a new computer-based standardized survey methodology across all States. When a State surveyor finds a serious violation of Federal regulation, they report it to CMS, and swift action is taken.

In cases of immediate jeopardy, meaning a facility's non-compliance has caused or is likely to cause serious injury, harm, or even death, we can terminate the facility's participation and agreement. Other remedies could include issuing civil monetary penalties, providing directed in-service training, or denial of payments. For deficiencies that do not constitute immediate jeopardy, they must be corrected within 6 months or the facility will be terminated from the program.

Facilities are also required by law to report any allegation of abuse or neglect to their State survey agency and other appropriate authorities such as law enforcement or Adult Protective Services. When CMS learns a nursing home has failed to report or investigate incidents of abuse, we take immediate action. For example in 2018, when a State surveyor found that a nursing home did not properly investigate or prevent additional abuse involving two residents, placing other residents on the unit at risk for abuse, the nursing home was cited at the most serious level of non- compliance—immediate jeopardy—and they were assessed a civil monetary penalty of almost $800,000. We can also refer suspected cases of abuse or neglect to our law enforcement partners, including the Department of Justice, and we greatly appreciate their ongoing focus on resident safety and facility compliance with the law.

We expect nursing homes to meet our basic standard of care at all times, even during emergency situations. To further protect residents in 2016, we updated and improved our emergency preparedness requirements. Facilities are now required to address location-specific hazards and responses and must have emergency or standby power systems and ensure they are operational during an emergency, develop additional staff training and implement a communication system, and contact necessary persons regarding resident care and health status in a timely manner.

Surveyors recently began verifying facility compliance with our improvements, and as of February 22nd, 98 percent of nursing homes have been surveyed under the new emergency preparedness requirements. Over 70 percent of those surveyed were found to be in compliance, and those cited for non-compliance deficiencies have made all the necessary corrections to come into compliance with these requirements.

In 2016, CMS issued, for the first time in over 25 years, a final rule updating the requirements for nursing homes and other longterm care facilities. These changes reflected the substantial advances in the theory and practice of service delivery that have been made since 1991, such as ensuring nursing home staff are properly trained on caring for patients with dementia. Given the number of revisions, we have provided a phased-in approach for facilities to meet these new requirements, and we are now in the second phase of the three implementation phases. We are taking a very thoughtful approach to implementation and providing education to providers while holding them accountable for any deficiencies.

Promoting transparency is another key factor to incentivize quality. Our five-star rating system on Nursing Home Compare provides residents and families with an easy way to understand meaningful distinctions between high- and low-performing nursing homes on health inspections, quality measures, and nurse staffing.

And just yesterday, we announced important updates to all three of these areas to reflect more recent and meaningful information about the quality of care that each nursing home is giving its residents. We expect every nursing home to keep its residents safe and provide high-quality care. And as a practicing physician who still makes rounds in the hospital on weekends, many of my patients are frail elderly nursing home residents. So I am personally deeply committed to the care of these patients.

We look forward to continued work with Congress, States' facilities, residents, and other stakeholders to make sure the residents we serve are receiving safe and high-quality care. I look forward to answering your questions. Thank you.

Senator DAINES. Thank you, Dr. Goodrich.

[The prepared statement of Dr. Goodrich appears in the appendix.]

Senator DAINES. Ms. Bacon?

STATEMENT OF ANTOINETTE BACON, ASSOCIATE DEPUTY ATTORNEY GENERAL AND NATIONAL ELDER JUSTICE COORDINATOR, OFFICE OF THE DEPUTY ATTORNEY GENERAL, DEPARTMENT OF JUSTICE, WASHINGTON, DC

Ms. BACON. Thank you.

Good afternoon, Acting Chairman Daines, Ranking Member Wyden, Senator Portman, and distinguished members of the committee.

I am Antoinette Bacon, Associate Deputy Attorney General and the Department of Justice's first National Elder Justice Coordinator. As a Federal prosecutor for the past 18 years, I have witnessed the outstanding work of agents and trial attorneys who are investigating and prosecuting the chilling cases of elder abuse that we heard about in the first panel. And I appreciate the opportunity to appear before you to discuss the Department's ongoing efforts to protect older Americans.

For decades, the Department has been actively engaged in combating abuse and exploitation of our Nation's vulnerable seniors. Since its inception, the Medicare Fraud Strike Force has charged nearly 4,000 defendants for over $13 billion in fraud. Additionally, we have brought numerous cases against nursing homes under the False Claims Act and other statutes for grossly substandard and medically unnecessary services.

Certainly these are laudable accomplishments. But we realize there is so much more work that needs to be done. As our population ages, and as stories of victimization reach our headlines with unfortunate frequency, the Department is continuing to expand its resources in every Federal district to ensure that we are ready to meet the enforcement challenges. Here are some examples of just a few ways in which we are building on our strong foundation to prepare.

1) Experienced leadership—The Attorney General designated senior Department of Justice officials with extensive litigation experience to lead our elder justice efforts.
2) Increased internal collaboration—We formed a working group composed of 12 DOJ components to make sure that we are using all appropriate tools and paths to investigate, prosecute, and importantly, to prevent nursing home abuse.
3) Expanding our nationwide resources—We designated an Elder Justice Coordinator in every single U.S. Attorney's office around the country to work with our State, local, and tribal partners on the most pressing issues facing local communities. And we provided training specifically on nursing home abuse to those coordinators.
4) Supporting local law enforcement—We understand that local sheriffs, local police departments, are critical partners in this effort. And we launched a series of free online training resources available right now to all law enforcement officers, to help identify, investigate, and hopefully, again, stop elder abuse.
5) We expanded our network—We partnered with the USDA to address elder abuse in rural and tribal America. This culminated in a Rural and Tribal Elder Justice Summit in Des Moines, IA last November, and resulted in the formation of an Elder Justice Coordinating Council Working Group specifically to address rural elder justice issues.
6) Supporting victims—We announced $18 million in grants for victims of elder abuse for a wider variety of services than ever before.

And with all these systemic changes, we are still continuing to bring meaningful cases. Just last week, we announced a settlement of a False Claims Act case against a Tennessee nursing home chain for allegedly providing grossly substandard care.

The facts of this case are hard to listen to, but they were even more difficult for the residents affected. Some residents had pressure ulcers down to their bones, others were not given adequate medication if they were screaming in pain in their rooms. One did not have a real shower for 5 months—nearly half a year without a real shower. And sadly, as the first panel mentioned, this was not the only case where our nursing home residents are suffering so greatly.

But in my last minute, I would like to highlight a disturbing trend in nursing home abuse. As Senator Portman mentioned, I am an Ohio resident. And I have seen firsthand the devastation that the opioid crisis is causing to our families and to our communities. Tragically, the epidemic has now reached nursing homes.

The Department is finding that some are exploiting vulnerable patients for profit by giving powerful opioids that are not medically necessary, and we all know the dangers of that. Others are stealing residents' opioids, either for their own use or to sell, which unquestionably is leaving seniors in excessive and preventable pain. That is not acceptable. The Department is collaborating with our partners at CMS, at the State MFCUs, and HHS–OIG to identify these cases and to act swiftly to make sure that residents in nursing homes are getting appropriate medication.

Let me close by thanking you for your leadership on many of these most critical and pressing issues facing our Nation's seniors, especially in the passage of EAPPA, the Elder Abuse Prevention and Prosecution Act. And I am pleased to answer your questions. Thank you.

Senator DAINES. Thank you, Ms. Bacon.

[The prepared statement of Ms. Bacon appears in the appendix.]

Senator DAINES. Ms. Mitchell?

STATEMENT OF KEESHA MITCHELL, DIRECTOR, MEDICAID FRAUD CONTROL UNIT, OFFICE OF THE OHIO ATTORNEY GENERAL, COLUMBUS, OH

Ms. MITCHELL. Thank you, Acting Chairman Daines and Senator Portman. Thank you for the opportunity to appear before you today to discuss the role of State Medicaid Fraud Control Units in investigating and prosecuting patient abuse and neglect in nursing homes. I am Keesha Mitchell, Director of the Medicaid Fraud Control Unit in Ohio Attorney General Yost's office. All State Medicaid Fraud Control Units investigate and prosecute Medicaid provider fraud, fraud in the administration of the Medicaid program, and abuse, neglect, and misappropriation involving the residents of health-care facilities.

Currently, 49 States as well as the District of Columbia, Puerto Rico, and the Virgin Islands all have Medicaid Fraud Control Units. While we all operate under unique State jurisdictional statutes, the MFCU model embraces the use of a strike force team of investigators, prosecutors, fraud analysts, and nurses. This is unlike most traditional law enforcement models where the investigation and prosecution proceed without much input from one to the other. This model is particularly important when investigating allegations of abuse and neglect because we have the expertise when dealing with the competency of our victims and reviewing medical records and plans of care. And by way of example, I would offer two recent cases that our unit has investigated.

The first one we are currently prosecuting is where an Ohio grand jury returned indictments against seven current and former employees and contractors of a facility located in Columbus, OH. The defendants are charged with involuntary manslaughter, gross patient neglect, patient neglect, tampering with records, and forgery. Through our investigation, we were able to establish that the facility employees failed to provide required care and falsified patient medical records to make it appear as though the care had been provided. Our investigation also established that a facility resident died from infected skin wounds because facility employees failed to take appropriate action that would have saved his life. And when I am talking about the infected wound, I am talking about a wound that you could actually reach into up to your elbow.

Another case that we had—we had three employees' recent guilty pleas and a verdict where they were found guilty of one count each of forgery and gross patient neglect. The defendants were employed at this facility on the night of January 7, 2018, when a female resident of the facility wandered outside the facility in sub-zero temperatures and died of hypothermia. Despite the fact that the resident was wearing a WanderGuard device which was designed to alert staff when she travelled past sensors placed throughout the facility and exited the facility through a door with an alarm sensor, the resident was not discovered missing for more than 8 hours when the morning staff was preparing residents for breakfast. The defendants who were supposed to be caring for the resident during the nighttime hours documented in the medical record that they had checked on this resident every 2 hours. Through our investigation, they admitted that they never even looked at the residence room to see if she was there.

In the last 10 years, the Ohio Medicaid Fraud Control Unit has processed nearly 3,300 complaints of abuse, neglect, and misappropriation. Under the best of circumstances, these are challenging cases, and we are tasked with the responsibility to speak for those who often are unable to speak for themselves. While this is extremely rewarding work, our efforts are hampered by a number of factors, and I believe my remarks will expand greatly on each one of these factors. So I will just list them.

In order to effectively investigate incidents of patient abuse and neglect, we must ensure timely referrals from State surveyors to their Medicaid Fraud Control Units when they suspect abuse, neglect, or falsification of records. And this oftentimes should occur while the surveyors are actually in the facility, because there is a great amount of time between the time they are in the facility and they are seeing evidence of this type of action and when we actually see the survey and it is posted.

It is crucial that the State and Federal agencies coordinate their investigations to properly leverage our resources and expertise. We must also require nursing homes to properly report and detail incidents of patient abuse, neglect, and misappropriation or face meaningful penalties. And I outlined several very vague reports which we received which would never have alerted us to go in and look at the particular incident. One short one was where the report said that there was an incident that occurred on the ground. And what actually occurred was the resident had eloped and drowned in a pond on the grounds.

Finally, States must address the real outcomes of not properly incentivizing nursing homes to adequately staff their facilities to achieve quality care.

In conclusion, I would like to thank you again for asking me to speak here today and again underline the vital role State Medicaid Fraud Units play in protecting our Nation's nursing home residents. It is important to include us in taskforces and conversations on how best to protect our long-term care patient population.

Senator DAINES. Thank you, Ms. Mitchell.

[The prepared statement of Ms. Mitchell appears in the appendix.]

Senator DAINES. Senator Portman?

Senator PORTMAN. First, I want to thank all three witnesses for the powerful testimony and the explanation of some of the things that CMS and Justice are doing. They are important, and also some of the suggestions for reforms. I will be submitting questions to all three of you. Thank you.

Senator DAINES. Thank you, Senator Portman.

Senator Wyden?

Senator WYDEN. Thank you. Thank you very much, Senator Daines.

Dr. Goodrich, I want to ask you a question with respect to staffing and the relationship to quality, because to me good staffing is more likely to produce good quality. Quaint idea, like two sides of the same coin.

Last year I wrote to CMS after reports nursing homes were overstating how much staff they had on-site to care for patients. You all responded saying that, yes, the nursing homes overstated how much staff they had on-site, and you also found significant fluctuations in staffing from day-to-day, as well as days when there was no registered nurse reported on-site.

So I think my question to you is, could you tell us what you all are working on now, going forward from this day on, to make sure that we deal with what are the key issues here. Good staffing is a path to good quality, and you all share my concern that nursing homes have overstated how much staff they have. What is going on?

Dr. GOODRICH. Yes, thank you for the question and the opportunity to talk about our work on nurse staffing. I would say we do share that concern, and we are very glad, beginning in 2017, that we were able to pilot and now we have fully in place a new process for assessing staffing of nurses and other types of personnel within nursing homes. This is called the Payroll-Based Journal System, and it is a method by which nursing homes have to report to us every quarter their staffing for a variety of different types of positions, including nurses and nurses' aides for 365 days a year.

Whereas previously, the way this was reported to us was simply a 2-week snapshot of their staffing levels. So we do believe that this Payroll-Based Journal Staffing System is much stronger and is much more accurate, because it has to be auditable.

Senator WYDEN. So this is a pilot project?

Dr. GOODRICH. No, it is not a pilot anymore. We did pilot it first, but it is now fully in place.

Senator WYDEN. And can you give us some summary, a written summary quickly, of how it is faring, because obviously, given some of the quality issues we have heard about today, this is serious business.

Dr. GOODRICH. We would be glad to, and I would be glad to tell you how we are using it, if that is helpful.

Senator WYDEN. How long would it take to get a written report on that?

Dr. GOODRICH. I would say not long at all. We can get you something.

Senator WYDEN. Ten days?

Dr. GOODRICH. Yes.

Senator WYDEN. Okay, great.

Since I only have a couple more minutes, I want to ask you about one other thing that I am very troubled about.

Dr. GOODRICH. Sure.

Senator WYDEN. I put out recently—and we sent it all to you— a report called "Sheltering in Danger" that shows nursing homes are not adequately prepared for natural disasters. And I am concerned that, instead of acting on the report's recommendations, CMS is looking at finalizing a regulatory rollback that would scale back emergency training requirements, allow nursing homes to review emergency plans just once every 2 years, and do away with requirements that nursing homes show their work when it comes to coordinating with emergency first responders.

So the idea of CMS allowing nursing homes to go into emergencies without sufficient preparation and practice is very troubling to me. And climate change is only going to make emergency planning more important.

So my question to you is, will the agency—and I am requesting this—rescind its rollback of emergency preparedness standards?

Dr. GOODRICH. So we published a proposed rule, as you note, last year that covered a variety of topics, including emergency preparedness and all of the proposals that you have mentioned, based upon what we have been hearing from the field around concerns about paperwork. Having said that, we have received hundreds of comments on this proposed rule, including a number of comments, specifically, on this issue as it relates to nursing homes and the concerns around the modifications that we were proposing.

We are taking all of those comments, including the ones that you sent to us, strongly into account as we consider our policies for our final rule.

Senator WYDEN. That is not anything that gives me any guidance on how you are proceeding. I mean, to me, given what we have seen, given the threat with respect to disasters—Senator Daines and I are in the west. You know fires we are seeing in the west are infernos. They are not your grandfather's fires.

It seems to me that we need a smarter strategy with respect to emergency preparedness, and you all are going in just the opposite direction. So I am going to give you one more chance to give me some sense that you all are going to be serious about a problem that we found in our report "Sheltering in Danger" that I have only grown more concerned about since then.

Dr. GOODRICH. So what I will say is that we have reviewed your report very carefully and are considering many of the recommendations that you made.

Senator WYDEN. Okay. Just on that, is there anything in that report that you disagree with?

Dr. GOODRICH. There are some things in the report that we do not have authority over, like assisted-living facilities for example.

Senator WYDEN. Right.

Dr. GOODRICH. But I think that most of the things you have in that report are very common-sense. And we are thinking about how we can incorporate them into our guidance.

Senator WYDEN. That sounds like progress, because I want to work with you. And of course, you know we are focused on nursing homes. You have indicated that you think much of the report makes sense.

That sounds like progress. I hope that you all will work with the staff ahead of time before this comes out, because too often CMS— I learn about CMS from things in the newspaper.

There was an effort, for example, the rollback of part of the Affordable Care Act that I authored—1332—to give States the opportunity to try fresh approaches, and I basically learned about it after there had already been press reports and the like. I hope that we can break from that kind of pattern and that you all will be in touch with us before you take final action.

Dr. GOODRICH. We would be glad to do so.

Senator WYDEN. All right.

Thank you, Mr. Chairman.

Senator DAINES. Thank you, Senator Wyden.

Last year there was a State-run nursing home in Montana that was cited for failing to protect patients from verbal, physical, and sexually abusive behaviors of fellow patients. And in fact, it resulted in over $255,000 in fines. In fact, it was in Lewistown. That is where this happened, in Lewistown, MT.

According to reports, on 13 occasions officials were not notified of incidents that included abuse in the facilities wing which houses dementia patients. As part of the investigation, one staff member said they had not been trained on how to help manage resident behaviors. These kind of reports are saddening. They are concerning, particularly as these patients are some of the most vulnerable Montanans who are receiving mental health and long-term care services.

Dr. Goodrich, could you speak to the role of effective staff training programs to ensure that this abuse in Montana's senior homes would never happen again?

Dr. GOODRICH. Yes. First let me say that abuse of any kind— verbal, sexual, physical—is absolutely not permitted. Our expectation is that nursing homes keep their residents safe and free from abuse. That is an absolute expectation.

We do have regulatory requirements around nursing homes, including that they must report any allegations, and certainly any substantiated cases, of abuse to law enforcement immediately. And when we learn of an incident of abuse, we take very swift action. We send our State surveyors out into the field to the nursing home immediately.

And sometimes what we learn when there are cases of abuse is that staff within the nursing home may not have received appropriate training, as you mentioned. And so we ask, whenever we find episodes of abuse—first of all, we implement certain types of penalties to bring the nursing home swiftly back into compliance. And we require that they submit to us something called a Plan of Correction, and that Plan of Correction can include a number of things, depending upon the circumstances, and oftentimes one of those things that is required is related to ensuring that all staff have training around the issues of abuse.

Senator DAINES. When a loved one gets older, a question that I know that many families face, including our family, is, where is a mom or a dad, a grandfather, a grandmother, where are they going to receive the care as they age? And I know for some, in-home care is an appropriate option. I think of my own grandma, Grandma Daines in Billings, who lived at home well into her 90s and had in-home care.

It allowed her to receive that care in the comfort of her own very modest home in Billings with the support of family and friends and other professional caregivers. In-home care can sometimes enhance the patient experience because it also allows them to be home and can be more cost-effective.

Dr. Goodrich, how can we ensure that patients are receiving the high-quality care that they need and deserve in the most appropriate as well as cost-effective settings?

Dr. GOODRICH. Yes, I think that is an incredibly important issue. My mother, who is 81 years old, lives with me, and we were fortunate to have her at home. And that is, of course, the setting where most people would like to be.

We do have authority over a number of types of facilities and health-care organizations, obviously including nursing homes, but also home health agencies and hospice and so forth. And all of these types of facilities, in order to get paid by Medicare and Medicaid, must adhere to a basic set of health and safety standards.

And we survey for those standards within nursing homes on an annual basis and with other types of facilities about every 3 years or so. So we think that is one very key way to hold facilities accountable and organizations accountable for good quality care.

We also have a number of other levers that we use, including quality measures for payment programs, for example, and making information about the quality of care transparent, whether it be our Nursing Home Compare five-star rating system or our Nursing Home Compare website. We also have a Home Health Compare website and Hospice Compare website. We think transparency is another way that we can really ensure that these facilities are incentivized to improve the quality of care.

Senator DAINES. So, speaking of the five-star rating system, the Montana facility that I referenced earlier that had the $255,000 in fine, currently has a two-star rating from Medicare, which means they are considered to be below average in terms of quality care. But years ago, they received one of the best ratings in the country.

A follow-up on the rating system, Dr. Goodrich: do you believe the star rating system provides an accurate assessment of nursing home quality?

Dr. GOODRICH. We have made a number of changes, including as recently as what we announced yesterday to happen in April. But over the past few years, we have made a number of changes to strengthen the five-star rating system so that it does provide the most accurate picture of quality.

For example, we now have, of course, the Payroll-Based Journal nurse staffing data, which is self-reported but auditable. So it is much more accurate than what we had before for the nurse staffing rating. And we also have quality measures that we are including now on the Nursing Home Compare star rating site that are not self-reported and that are actually higher-weighted than other types of quality reporting measures. For example, readmissions to a hospital or transfers to an emergency department, things that are really important for patients and for providers, now have a higher weight on that site.

So we think that we have strengthened the site overall. We have also increased the threshold. So what it takes to get a four- and five-star we have increased over time in order to better distinguish homes from one another as well as to incentivize improvements.

Senator DAINES. Thank you, Dr. Goodrich.

Senator Cortez Masto?

Senator CORTEZ MASTO. Thank you. Thank all three of you for being here.

Ms. Mitchell, let me start with you. How long have you been the Chief of the Medicaid Fraud Unit?

Ms. MITCHELL. Since 2010 and in the unit since 2003.

Senator CORTEZ MASTO. That is fantastic. Thank you. You probably work with Mark Kemberling in the Nevada office.

Ms. MITCHELL. I was just going to say——

Senator CORTEZ MASTO. Yes, so I am curious, because I think you touched on some of the challenges that I saw. And I think it is perfect that all three of you are at the table together, because I think there is the need for that timely coordination from the State right when their surveyors are out there to immediately reach out. I think the task force is important. I also think that coordination amongst the task force members and the immediacy of it and the response are important.

So let me ask you—the first question I have for you is, what can we be doing to help or improve upon whatever coordination that is necessary, but also to help the States recognize that that immediacy for that survey and that referral is important? What should we be doing at the Federal level?

Ms. MITCHELL. Thank you very much for the question, and it really gets to the heart of the agencies working in tandem, because the State survey agency has the administrative jurisdiction to go in and cite, but they can only cite on what they see in the facility at the time that they go in. If it is a complaint survey, they are going in on the complaint, and they can only interview those people, that staff that is there. They cannot even go out—it is my understanding—and interview the actual perpetrator.

So really, in those situations, we believe that that call should go out to us immediately or law enforcement certainly——

Senator CORTEZ MASTO. But the challenge is, because it is administrative, you literally cannot be with them when they are going through that process.

Ms. MITCHELL. Exactly. But I think we need better coordination so that at least we are aware of the allegation and we can start investigating immediately, because time really is of the essence. In these types of instances from some of the earlier testimony, if there is not enough evidence to cite administratively, we should be going out and looking at those perpetrators to make sure that they are not able to stay in the facility and continue, unfortunately, to perpetrate against additional victims.

So I think that is just critically important. And then certainly, some of the other State jurisdictional task forces—where we see systemic neglect and abuse chain-wide, those are instances where we are really trying to work cooperatively with our task force members.

Senator CORTEZ MASTO. Right, and no offense to CMS, but I know there is a love/hate relationship. And so particularly with the States and sometimes with the Medicaid Fraud Units, I think the intent is to make sure there is more of the love, everybody working together. But there is a challenge at times.

Is there something that we should be aware of or that—now that we have all three of you at the table—is there something else that we should be addressing to make sure that there is that responsiveness, the coordination, and everybody is working together? Are there still challenges?

Ms. BACON. Thank you for the question and for the opportunity to answer that. The case I mentioned in my opening statement, the Vanguard case, was actually a CMS referral. I think that is a wonderful example of the U.S. Attorney's community, the Department of Justice working together with our partners to address these types of issues.

Certainly the goal of the Elder Justice Coordinators, the 94—one in each U.S. Attorney's office—is really to serve that quarterbacking role, Senator, that you are concerned with. And it is so important, as my colleague Ms. Mitchell mentioned, that the Elder Justice Coordinators can be a convening force to bring together the State MFCUs, State Attorney General offices, local prosecutors' offices, the ombudsman, anyone in the ecosystem who might touch on and concern these issues, so, one, people know who to call——

Senator CORTEZ MASTO. Right.

Ms. BACON [continuing]. Where to go, and then who has the appropriate tool to address the appropriate problem at the appropriate time.

Senator CORTEZ MASTO. Okay.

Dr. GOODRICH. The one thing I will add is that we do have requirements around how quickly a facility must report, which is not what you are getting at, but nonetheless, they must report any episode of abuse or injury to law enforcement within 24 hours. Regarding the States, we do oversee the State's performance in their survey activities. So we do work very closely with them. And we have been putting a number of things in place over time to try to really standardize our expectations across all the States.

We, like Vanguard, do have some good examples where we and the State agency and law enforcement have worked well together. One very tragic example—but it was a good example of coordination—was, of course, Hollywood Hills in Florida, which is the nursing home under Hurricane Irma where all the residents passed away from heat exposure. And that was an example where everybody really did coordinate quite well.

But we think there probably could be more standardization, and we are continuing to work with the States on that.

Senator CORTEZ MASTO. Thank you.

I noticed my time is up, but—you are here. Go right ahead. I did not know if anybody else was going to be here. I had one more question, but I will wait for a possible second round.

Senator DAINES. You want to ask one more question?

Senator CORTEZ MASTO. I just have one more question for Dr. Goodrich.

In 2017, the State of Nevada discovered serious systemic quality issues with our residential homes where Medicaid beneficiaries with developmental disabilities were—where they were living. And the State shut down these offenders.

So my question to you is, as States continue to shift their service delivery models to focus on home and community-based services, what sort of obligation does CMS have to protect against abuse and neglect in individuals' homes where Medicaid or Medicare is paying for the services delivered?

Dr. GOODRICH. So we have authorities to hold providers of care responsible for health and safety standards in most, sort of, inpatient settings of care. We really do not within the actual home. What I thought you were referring to at first—maybe you were—were the intermediate care facilities for individuals with intellectual disabilities. Those are long-term care homes for particular populations. And we definitely have authority over the health and safety standards for those homes.

But within a home or an assisted living facility, we do not have authority over those particular types of situations.

Senator CORTEZ MASTO. Okay. Thank you.

Senator DAINES. Senator Menendez?

Senator MENENDEZ. Let me start off by thanking—I think they had to leave—Ms. Fisher and Ms. Blank for coming here today and sharing their families' experiences. Unfortunately, I was on the Foreign Relations Committee, but I did see their testimony.

In New Jersey, we have 11 families who lost their children last fall at the Wanaque Center for Nursing and Rehabilitation due to failures at the facility to identify and contain a viral outbreak. And I want to take a moment and recognize those 11 lives that were lost and their families who suffered the loss of their loved ones. And I will be keeping them in mind as I work with my fellow committee members to improve safety and care at nursing homes.

Dr. Goodrich, are you aware that Medicare had cited the Wanaque facility in New Jersey before the outbreak in 2018 that killed 11 children?

Dr. GOODRICH. Yes, sir.

Senator MENENDEZ. How is it that when the Federal Government is working with States to regulate this industry—where are the gaps in the system that allow facilities with multiple citations to continue accepting patients?

Dr. GOODRICH. Thank you for that.

So whenever a facility is cited for anything with whatever level of severity, we expect them to come back into compliance rapidly, and we have a number of tools at our disposal so that they, hopefully, can do that. Certainly for the most severe deficiencies, what we call immediate jeopardy, we have an expectation that they come back into compliance very rapidly, and they have to demonstrate that they have come back into compliance.

And I am sorry. I do not remember the exact circumstances of Wanaque before all of those tragic deaths and what was found previously. But likely what happened is, they came back into compliance after they were cited for whatever deficiency happened.

Certainly over time, as we see facilities have repeated numbers of citations at increased severity, we have the ability over time if they do have repeated sort of offenses, if you will—to increase the number of penalties that they have or to apply more and more severe penalties to bring them back into compliance. But if they do not come back into compliance, if they cannot demonstrate that they are able to provide safe care for their residents, we will terminate them from the Medicare and Medicaid programs. That is the ultimate penalty.

Senator MENENDEZ. What is the time frame for returning into compliance?

Dr. GOODRICH. So it depends on the citation. So if it is at the immediate jeopardy level, typically they have to come back into compliance within—I believe it is about 23 days. So if it is a less severe penalty, then that time frame is a bit longer than that.

Senator MENENDEZ. Well, that did not work out in this case. What are the gaps in oversight?

Dr. GOODRICH. So I think one of the things that we believe, first of all, is that we do have an expectation that these facilities provide safe care. That is their responsibility, to adhere to our regulations and provide safe care. And our job is to hold them accountable for that.

I think one of the things that we have seen over the years is that there may be some inconsistency across the country in how that oversight is applied, how penalties are applied. So we have taken a number of really important steps over the last couple of years, which we are continuing to work on, to further that consistency so that the expectations are the same across the States, and that we are overseeing the States in their application of the enforcement penalties and in their on-site surveys.

Senator MENENDEZ. If that is the case, why is the administration relaxing regulations at a time when we have tragedies like Wanaque?

Dr. GOODRICH. So we are continuing to hold these facilities accountable in the ways that we have before. What we are looking at is ways in which our paperwork and administrative requirements may be getting in the way of patient care. We are really trying to be very thoughtful about that.

Senator MENENDEZ. In the Obama administration, there were a series of quality standards that were implemented, and yet those standards have been walked away from by your agency.

Dr. GOODRICH. So I would be interested in understanding which ones you are referring to in particular. The quality standards for the long-term care facilities, for nursing homes that we finalized in 2016, they are in place. We are actively enforcing those standards now.

Senator MENENDEZ. Let me ask you one other question. I would be happy to go over them with you at greater length outside of the hearing.

In your testimony, you discuss the emergency preparedness standards that went into effect in 2016. You note that nearly 30 percent of nursing homes are not in compliance. What action does CMS plan to take if they are not compliant by the next time you survey them, and when are you going to survey them?

Dr. GOODRICH. So nursing homes have to be surveyed, by law, every year. So they get annual surveys.

And so we have now surveyed about 98 percent of active nursing homes on the emergency preparedness requirements. As you note, about 70 percent of those facilities were in compliance at the time of the survey. We worked individually with each of the nursing facilities that was not in compliance to bring them into compliance. And they all have come into compliance, but because these facilities are surveyed on an annual basis, there will be ongoing oversight for their adherence to those requirements.

Senator MENENDEZ. I have one last question, if I may, Mr. Chairman.

I often hear that one of the challenges is the inability to retain qualified individuals at these institutions. Have we looked at—is there any proposal as to how we ensure that these institutions have the wherewithal to retain qualified individuals to perform the services necessary?

Dr. GOODRICH. I believe that topic was of great discussion in the last panel. And we certainly heard from the panelists concerns around payment and availability of the appropriate staffing and that sort of thing.

We do have expectations of nursing facilities for having the appropriate staffing for their patient population. And we survey for that on a regular basis to make sure that they have the appropriate staffing. Plus they have to report that to us now every quarter using data that is auditable back to their payroll. So we now have a much more accurate picture of the staffing levels and where there may be gaps and deficiencies in staffing that we just did not have before.

And we are continuing to analyze and review that data so that we can have a much better understanding of what additional actions we may need to take based upon that data to improve those circumstances.

Senator MENENDEZ. Thank you, Mr. Chairman.

I will just say that I think there is a gulf between the expectations and the reality in several of these instances. And we look forward to working with you to bridge the gulf. Thank you.

Senator CORTEZ MASTO. Mr. Chairman, I know I said "no," but can I do one follow-up?

Senator DAINES. You may.

Senator CORTEZ MASTO. Thank you.

I want to follow up on Senator Menendez's—one of his questions. In November of 2017, the Trump administration issued an 18-month moratorium on full enforcement of eight standards of care. And they included baseline care planning, staff competencies, the provision of behavioral health services, antibiotic stewardship, and limiting psychotropic medications. Is that moratorium still in effect?

Dr. GOODRICH. That moratorium ends in May of this year. I would like to be clear about what the moratorium did.

Senator CORTEZ MASTO. Thank you.

Dr. GOODRICH. We still surveyed for all of those things.

Senator CORTEZ MASTO. Okay.

Dr. GOODRICH. And we still cited facilities that were not in compliance with those eight items. The moratorium was around using some of our more severe penalties, enforcement penalties like civil monetary penalties, for just those eight items for 18 months. And instead, the enforcement remedies that we put in place were more educational in nature.

Starting in May of this year, those eight items now will be subject to any of the penalties that we have.

Senator CORTEZ MASTO. Will not be or will be?

Dr. GOODRICH. They will be.

Senator CORTEZ MASTO. So it goes back into effect?

Dr. GOODRICH. Yes.

Senator CORTEZ MASTO. So what was the purpose of the moratorium then?

Dr. GOODRICH. We published our final rule in October of 2016, revising the requirements and participation for the health and safety standards for long-term care facilities. It was a complete overhaul. It was a huge change for the industry.

And so because of that, at that time, we also finalized that we were going to phase in the implementation of those requirements in three phases. Phase two, which was some of the ones that were, quite frankly, a little bit of a bigger lift for facilities, began in November of 2017. And what we had heard was that some facilities, in particular in rural areas, were having difficulty being ready for those particular eight items at the time in November of 2017.

And we felt we could not delay requiring it, but what we could do is take a more educational approach for about 18 months before we had, sort of, the threat, if you will, of civil monetary penalties and termination.

Senator CORTEZ MASTO. Thank you, Doctor; thank you very much.

Thank you, Mr. Chairman.

Senator DAINES. Thank you, Senator.

I want to thank our witnesses for your attendance and participation today. We are grateful to you for traveling here to share your time, your expertise with this committee.

I ask that any member who wishes to submit questions for the record please do so by the close of business on Tuesday, March 20th. And with that, this hearing is adjourned. [Whereupon, at 1 p.m., the hearing was concluded.]

Appendix: Additional Material Submitted for the Record

Statement of Antoinette T. Bacon, Associate Deputy Attorney General, Office of the Deputy Attorney General, Department of Justice

Good morning Chairman Grassley, Ranking Member Wyden, and distinguished members of the Committee. I am Antoinette Bacon, Associate Deputy Attorney General and Department of Justice Elder Justice Coordinator. I appreciate the opportunity to appear before you today to discuss this critical issue of our time, which is the quality of care that our elders receive in our nation's nursing homes and skilled care facilities. We have a legal and a moral obligation as a government to ensure that the elderly members of our society who raised us, guided us, and fought for our freedoms receive quality health care during their nursing home stays, which for many, is at the end of their lives when they are frail and most vulnerable.

The Department of Justice ("Department") has been bringing to justice nursing homes that provide grossly substandard care to their residents for over two decades through its Elder Justice Initiative. We have brought civil and criminal cases against the nation's largest nursing home chains, small regional chains, single facilities, and against nursing home CEOs and executives. As a career prosecutor, I have seen over the past 18 years the devastation and pain caused by these criminals. It can span generations and destroy communities.

And while the Department and our federal, state, local, tribal, and non-governmental partners have done so much great work in this area, there is still much work to be done as our population ages and as stories of victimization of our nation's elders in nursing homes reach our national headlines with unfortunate frequency.

The Department's commitment to nursing home cases spans multiple departmental components and includes actions that the Elder Justice Initiative, the Civil Division Consumer Protection Branch, the Criminal Division, the Civil Rights Division, and our U.S. Attorney's offices have pursued, and are pursuing, to combat abuse in nursing homes across the country. In addition, and significantly, the Department's commitment to nursing home matters is underscored by the infrastructure that the Department has put in place to combat elder abuse both in nursing homes and in community settings.

First, leadership has directed resources across the Department to focus on elder justice, including nursing home quality cases. Specifically, the Department named Marc Krickbaum, U.S. Attorney for the Southern District of Iowa, to Chair the Attorney General Advisory Committee's subcommittee on Elder Justice, which advises the Attorney General on policies and strategies for combatting elder abuse and fraud. Second, he appointed me to serve as the Department's first National Elder Justice Coordinator. I also chair the Department's Elder Justice Working Group, composed of 12 components, which brings together diverse expertise to focus on a variety of threats to America's seniors. Last year, the Department ordered each of the 94 U.S. Attorneys' offices to appoint an Elder Justice Coordinator ("EJC") tasked with fulfilling the Elder Abuse Prevention and Prosecution Act of 2017's ("EAPPA") mandate of: serving as the legal counsel for the federal judicial district on matters relating to elder abuse; prosecuting, or assisting in the prosecution of, elder abuse cases, and particularly focusing on nursing home quality matters; conducting public outreach and awareness activities relating to elder abuse; and ensuring the collection of data required to be collected under the EAPPA. Having an EJC in every federal district allows the Department to work on the most pressing elder justice issues facing those communities, while also collaborating with state, local, and tribal partners to combat all forms of elder abuse and fraud.

The EJCs enhance and broaden the reach of the outstanding work done by the Department's Elder Justice Initiative ("EJI"), which for decades has been a leader in prosecuting nursing home cases and in promoting greater federal, state, and local coordination to resolve cases where nursing homes provide grossly substandard care to their residents. Under EJI's leadership, the Department, in early 2016, enhanced its commitment to nursing home matters by creating ten Elder Justice Task Forces located across the country, including in U.S. Attorney Krickbaum's state of Iowa and in my home state of Ohio. The Elder Justice Task Forces are led by representatives from the U.S. Attorneys' Offices, and most include on their multi-disciplinary teams state Medicaid Fraud Control Units, state and local prosecutors' offices, the Department of Health and Human Services ("HHS"), state Adult Protective Services agencies, Long-Term Care Ombudsman programs, law enforcement, and emergency medical services in their respective communities. The multi-disciplinary teams allow the Task Forces to focus on the most significant problems in their communities to identify needed solutions quickly and efficiently. These Task Force leaders serve as mentors to the EJCs and as a model for other districts to pursue providers that provide grossly substandard care to their residents.

The Department, through its many components, has prosecutors across the nation who are focused on protecting America's elders in nursing homes. We have brought so many cases like the ones that I am going to describe to this Committee. These few examples show the breadth and tragedy of the abuse we have identified. The facts of these cases are hard to listen to but were even harder to experience for the residents affected.

Just last week, the Department announced that it settled a failure of care False Claims Act case against the Brentwood, Tennessee nursing home chain Vanguard Healthcare and several Vanguard companies for $18 million in allowed claims. The United States, partnering with the State of Tennessee, brought to justice this company and its CEO and Chief Compliance Officer for allegedly providing grossly substandard care to its residents on basic care needs such as administering medications as prescribed, providing standard infection control, failing to prevent pressure ulcers, and using physical restraints. Our nation's elderly residents suffered such harm in the Vanguard facilities as residents faced pressure ulcers down to the bone, residents who were not adequately provided with pain medications and as a result were screaming in pain in their rooms, and a resident who only received one real shower in five months.

Another example of the Department's failure of care False Claims Act matters focuses on the alleged overuse of antipsychotic medications such as occurred in a case brought in the Northern District of Iowa. On February 1, 2017, an Iowa nursing facility, the Abbey of LeMars, Inc., its ownership, and its management, agreed to pay $100,000 to resolve allegations that the care provided to their nursing facility residents was grossly substandard. During this time, the nursing facility allegedly overused anti-psychotic medications to numb or sedate residents to keep residents from expressing their needs. Residents were allegedly not given adequate nourishment or bathing care and residents were subjected to physical and chemical restraints rather than other types of interventions.

Given the particularly egregious nature of the resident harm at issue in these types of cases, nursing home defendants frequently enter into Quality of Care Corporate Integrity Agreements ("CIAs") with the Department of Health and Human Services' Office of Inspector General at the same time they settle their False Claims Act liability with the Department of Justice. For example, in 2014, following an extensive federal-state investigation, the Extendicare Health Services, Inc. and its subsidiary Progressive Step Corporation paid the United States $28 million for a civil False Claims Act failure of care settlement, the largest such settlement in the Department's history. The United States alleged that Extendicare failed to have a sufficient number of skilled nurses to adequately care for its residents and failed to prevent resident pressure ulcers. At the same time, Extendicare entered into a 5-year Quality of Care Corporate Integrity Agreement with HHS-OIG. Under this agreement, Extendicare was required to have a comprehensive compliance program with systems in place to address the quality of resident care. Indeed, this CIA had specific staffing provisions and is still in force today.

An additional example, on November 16, 2017, the Department settled a case with Hyperion Foundation, in which the entities and individuals agreed to pay the United States a total of $1.25 million to resolve allegations of false claims to Medicare and the Mississippi Medicaid program for providing grossly substandard care to residents at the Oxford Health and Rehabilitation nursing home in Lumberton, Mississippi. The Department alleged that Hyperion lacked adequate nursing staff, failed to meet the nutritional needs of residents, failed to administer medications to residents as prescribed by their physicians, overmedicated residents, and diverted Medicare and Medicaid funds to other affiliated entities, leaving the facility unable to pay for its basic operations, including food, heat, air conditioning, pest control, and cleaning.

As a result of these care failures, residents suffered immeasurably, including one resident who lost over 14 pounds in the facility over sixty days and developed massive, foul-smelling pressure sores on the resident's buttocks, heels, and legs, and another resident who complained of leg pain only to discover the pain was caused by a live snake wrapped around her leg. The physical plant in which these residents were forced to live was truly horrific. This facility was frequently plagued by filth, mold, insects, snakes, and rodents. Roaches were found on food trays and in the ice machines.

Although the horrific description of neglect of care occurred in rural Mississippi, it is important to shinea light on the fact that our nation's rural elders are particularly vulnerable to abuse in nursing homes. In some rural communities, staff are not as available and people are often further from family members who can visit facilities and check on loved ones. The Trump Administration and this Department recognizes that we have a particular responsibility to ensure that our elderly residents in rural America are cared for in a way that retains their dignity and respect. In November last year, the Department held a Rural and Tribal Summit in Des Moines, Iowa, where we brought together federal, state, local, and tribal governments, as well as subject matter experts, to address, among other things, the health of our rural elder populations. We discussed care in long-term facilities and see this issue as a Department priority.

These cases make clear that the care that these residents suffered is not the care that our elders, our parents, relatives, and friends deserve.

The Department's enforcement reaches beyond false claims act cases. The Civil Rights Division is fully engaged in combatting elder abuse by pursuing relief affecting public and private residential health care facilities, including nursing homes. Civil Rights attorneys conduct investigations to eliminate abuse and grossly substandard care in Medicare- and Medicaid- funded public long-term care facilities, as well as the unnecessary segregation of individuals who require health care supports and services. For example, in 2018, the Department entered into an agreement with the State of Louisiana, whose nursing facilities have long been reported as among the worst for quality of care in the nation, to address its alleged overreliance on nursing facilities to house people with mental illness.

In the most egregious cases, the Department has and will continue to pursue criminal prosecutions. One example is a case prosecuted by the U.S. Attorney's Office for the Eastern District of Missouri, the United States Department of Health and Human Services, Office of the Inspector General, and the Missouri Medicaid Fraud Control Unit. Between 2013 and 2016, John Sells, CEO of Benchmark Healthcare of Festus and a number of long-term care facilities in Missouri, Kentucky, and Tennessee, stole Medicaid funds, which were intended to provide care for the elderly and disabled residents at Benchmark. Because Sells diverted funds to his own use, the residents did not receive medication, food, and needed dietary supplements. On one occasion, the residents were given only a clear bowl of broth soup and a very small cookie, which was not substantial and failed to meet their nutritional needs. The facility's staff resorted to using their own money to buy food for the residents, because in some instances there was little to no food provided by Benchmark. Additionally, the facility was dirty, as trash piled up and flies infested the surrounding area in the absence of pest control services, and due to a lack of routine maintenance and repairs, the facility was also unsafe. In October 2017, Sells was sentenced to 41 months in prison, and ordered to pay over $667,000 in restitution.

Our nation is in the midst of an opioid crisis. Tragically, seniors in nursing facilities are not immune to its devastating effects. In the Fall of 2018, the United States Attorney's Office in the Southern District of Iowa and the Iowa Medicaid Fraud Control Unit ("MFCU"), identified a troubling trend in Iowa nursing homes. MFCU was investigating numerous allegations of nursing care facility employees, ranging from nurses to certified nursing assistants, who diverted controlled substances from elderly patients who had valid prescriptions, to their own illegal use, leaving the patients in pain because their caregivers stole their medication. Six nurses and certified nursing assistants have been indicted, and so far one has pleaded guilty. Let me emphasize that the charges are merely allegations and each defendant is presumed innocent until proven guilty.

The Criminal Division's Medicare Fraud Strike Forces, in conjunction with HHS' Centers for Medicare and Medicaid Services ("CMS") and the Office of Inspector General of HHS ("HHS-OIG"), have been a strong team working together to combat elder abuse. Recently, the team identified a provider unnecessarily prescribing powerful opioids to residents. As part of a guilty plea in January 2018, Yasser Mozeb admitted that he conspired with the owner of the Tri-County Network, Mashiyat Rashid, along with other co-conspirators, to prescribe medically unnecessary controlled substances, which allegedly included oxycodone, hydrocodone, and oxymorphone, to Medicare beneficiaries, many of whom were addicted to narcotics. He also admitted that co-conspirators directed physicians to require Medicare beneficiaries to undergo medically unnecessary facet joint injections in order to obtain prescriptions for the narcotics. Some of these beneficiaries were also then referred to specific third party home health agencies, even though those referrals were medically unnecessary.

It is likely that because of these health care fraud schemes, at least some of these beneficiaries never received the medical attention and treatments they actually needed, or suffered through medically unnecessary procedures. Additionally, some elders in nursing homes are also not receiving the appropriate medication as prescribed by their physicians, because the staff or visiting relatives and friends are instead stealing the medication to sell or to maintain their own addiction. This undoubtedly causes these seniors to be in excessive and preventable pain. This Administration will not tolerate this type of abuse.

While the focus of today's hearing is nursing home enforcement, I would like to expand my discussion of the Department's work done on elder justice issues to focus on the Department's efforts in combatting financial exploitation and bringing scammers to justice. On February 22, 2018, the Attorney General announced the largest coordinated sweep of elder fraud cases in history. With help from our partners at all levels of government and in the private sector, the Department brought civil and criminal actions against more than 250 defendants from around the globe who victimized more than one million Americans, most of whom were elderly. The cases included criminal, civil, and forfeiture actions across more than 50 federal districts, with losses exceeding $500 million.

These scams imperil older adults as they steal their money, life savings, and their pride. Studies show that older adults suffering financial exploitation are more likely to suffer other forms of elder abuse. Sometimes the pain from having been scammed is more than some elders can bear. At last year's Elder Fraud Sweep, we heard from the granddaughter of a victim of multiple financial fraud schemes. The perpetrators were persistent, and eventually defrauded the victim of everything she had. After realizing what had happened, the victim felt embarrassed, and, hopeless, her sense of self-worth at an all-time low, she took her own life. This is a clear example of the tragic effects these crimes can have on an individual. Financial scams can be deadly and at the Department we are pursuing these scams with unparalleled vigor. Because of situations like this, and others, the Department's Office for Victims of Crimes has given $18 million in grants for senior victims this past year and we will continue to support victims while continuing to pursue their perpetrators.

Clearly, elder justice is a Department priority. We are actively engaged in pursuing and combatting abuse and exploitation of our nation's vulnerable senior citizens, and through coordination with our partners, the Department remains committed to using all appropriate tools and paths to investigate, prosecute, and prevent abuse of our nation's elderly in nursing homes. Our many dedicated public servants have elder justice as their daily mission and we support them in their efforts on this priority issue.

Again, thank you for this opportunity to speak before you today. I look forward to further discussions on these issues, and I am pleased to answer any questions you may have.

Questions Submitted for the Record to Antoinette Bacon

Questions Submitted by Hon. Chuck Grassley

Question. Have each of the Elder Justice Coordinators in the field met with each elected District Attorney to find out if they have designated an elder abuse prosecutor? If so, can you highlight areas of the country where this practice has been established? Are there areas in which District Attorneys are not designating an Assistant District Attorney or Attorneys to carry out this function?

Answer. As a general matter, Elder Justice Coordinators in the United States Attorneys' Offices have taken steps to reach out to their State and local counterparts. For example, the U.S. Attorney's Office for the Southern District of California has joined the San Diego County District Attorney Office's Elder Protection Council, a private/public collaboration designed to raise awareness, enhance prevention, and improve protection for San Diego County's elder population. Working together, along with private sector stakeholders, they launched the San Diego County Elder and Dependent Adult Abuse Blueprint, which is designed to highlight best practices for a coordinated law enforcement and community response to elder and dependent adult abuse in order to better prevent, protect, prosecute, and partner on this public safety challenge. Given the sheer number of District Attorney's offices around the country, it would be difficult to catalogue the extent to which each has specifically designated an elder abuse prosecutor. With that caveat, we are not aware of any United States Attorney's Office that has reported an inability to identify individuals to partner with in State and local law enforcement. In addition, the Department itself continues to work closely with the National Association of Attorneys General (NAAG) and the National Association of Medicaid Fraud Control Units (MFCUs) to identify ways to ensure that Federal and State prosecutors are coordinating strategically to stem the tide of elder abuse and financial exploitation in the Districts.

Question. Does each Elder Justice Coordinator interact in a meaningful way with long-term care licensing agencies in each State to encourage sharing of information on all allegations of elder abuse? If so, can you highlight some examples of where this practice has achieved success?

Answer. As part of their training, the Elder Justice Coordinators were provided with a network of State and local agencies that play a role in working with, or monitoring, nursing homes and other long term care providers, including but not limited to federally funded Long Term Care Ombudsmen, State-funded Adult Protective Services agencies, State survey and certification agencies, and State licensing agencies. Many Elder Justice Coordinators have reported communicating or working with those State and local partners as part of their training, outreach and coordination efforts. Some districts, like the Middle District of Tennessee, Eastern District of Pennsylvania, and the Eastern District of Virginia, have regular meetings with their State and local partners as part of their ongoing elder justice efforts.

Question. Do Elder Justice Coordinators encourage strategy sessions with all stakeholders in each judicial district to develop a comprehensive strategy to respond to elder abuse? If so, can you elaborate on where and how this is working successfully? Are there areas where this collaboration can be improved? Please explain.

Answer. Elder Justice Coordinators have reported a variety of working groups that made up of relevant stakeholders, including not only the State and local governmental officials described above, but also other Federal stakeholders (e.g., the FBI, the Department of Agriculture, and the SEC), other governmental stakeholders (such as first responders), and individuals representing various involved community partners, including from the private sector such as financial and nursing home professionals, federally funded Long Term Care Ombudsmen, State-funded Adult Protective Services ("APS"), and Federal and State-funded legal aid lawyers. For example, the District of Oregon hosts a monthly fraud working group that includes participants from the Oregon Attorney General's office as well as APS; one of the primary topics addressed in the working group's meetings is elder abuse. Members of the working group participate in an email list that allows the group members to effectively communicate on elder justice initiatives not just during the meetings, but throughout the month. All of this has allowed stakeholders in Oregon to effectively coordinate on elder justice strategies and identify and implement effective approaches to combating elder fraud and abuse.[1]

---

[1] https://www.justice.gov/usao-dc/pr/us-attorney-liu-announces-initiative-combat-elder-abuse-and-financial-exploitation.

Question Submitted by Hon. Todd Young

Civil Penalties /Exclusion

Question. Nursing homes who receive Federal funding are mandated to report and investigate suspected abuse and neglect in their nursing homes—failure to do so results in civil penalties of up to $300,000 and possible exclusion from participation in any Federal health-care program.

How often do these fines and penalties occur?

Answer. The Department of Health and Human Services would be in a better position to answer this question.

Question Submitted by Hon. Benjamin L. Cardin

Elder Financial Abuse

Question. Elder financial abuse results in financial losses of about $3 billion annually, and is growing as scam artists develop new ways to defraud vulnerable seniors out of their money and possessions. According to a 2010 MetLife study, about 12 percent of reported cases of elder financial abuse originate from a legitimate business such as nursing home administration or an institutional caregiver.

Many more seniors are defrauded or tricked by neighbors or acquaintances who take advantage of their trust while in a nursing home. The Consumer Financial Protection Bureau has published a lengthy manual addressing some of these issues, entitled "Protecting Residents From Financial Exploitation." The goal of this manual is to educate providers about signs that a vulnerable individual is being taken advantage of financially.

What more needs to be done to protect our vulnerable seniors from financial abuse, and does the Federal Government have a role in this?

Answer. The Federal Government is already playing an active role in protecting older Americans from financial abuse. The second historic elder fraud sweep announced March 7, 2019 highlighted the prime importance the Department and its partners place on shielding American seniors from financial fraud. The sweep involved cases of local financial abuse as well as transnational criminal organizations defrauding thousands of victims. The Department is actively investigating and stopping international schemes targeting seniors, like the tech fraud schemes highlighted at the Department's Elder Fraud Sweep in March.

Likewise, the Elder Justice Coordinating Council (EJCC), which is comprised of 14 Federal agencies, is supported by an informal Elder Justice Working Group, with participation of senior staff from each of the 14 EJCC member agencies. The Working Group has established a voluntary dissemination subcommittee that focuses on leveraging Federal resources in order to coordinate Federal governmental information dissemination and to coordinate efforts to raise public awareness of common and developing fraud scams, how older Americans may protect themselves, and on all aspects of prevention and responses to all forms of elder abuse, neglect, and financial exploitation.

Moreover, the Federal Government is actively developing training, information, and resources for responders to elder fraud and abuse—including law enforcement, first responders, prosecutors, and Adult Protective Services workers—to help expand and enhance their capacity to support elder abuse victims. For example, last year the Department launched EAGLE, the Elder Abuse Guide for Law Enforcement, which is a free, on-line resources guide that include evidence collection checklists, tips for interviewing older adults, State and local statutes, and best practices for documenting elder abuse. Additionally, the Department launched the Elder Justice Neighborhood Map, a free, user-friendly webpage that helps people locate elder abuse services in their State.

While the Federal Government has been very active in combating financial fraud, there is always more that can be done. We welcome the opportunity to work with Congress on potential ways to continue advancing our efforts to prevent elder financial exploitation.

Question Submitted by Hon. Catherine Cortez Masto

Question. Ms. Bacon, you explained collaboration on the Elder Justice Task Forces by the U.S. Attorneys' Offices, most of which include State MFCUs, the State Department of Health and Human Services, and State Adult Protective Services agencies among others. How do you make sure that patterns of quality deficiencies identified by this group are flagged and addressed by CMS?

Answer. The Department has a very strong working relationship with the CMS Division of Nursing Homes, among other CMS components The Department works closely with that CMS Division to identify providers that are providing grossly substandard care. In many of those cases, CMS then determines which of its remedies to apply to a particular provider, anywhere from denial of payment for new admissions to termination from Federal health-care programs.

PREPARED STATEMENT OF PATRICIA BLANK, DAUGHTER OF NURSING HOME NEGLECT VICTIM, MARCH 6, 2019

Ladies and Gentlemen, my name is Patricia Olthoff-Blank. I am from Shell Rock Iowa. I want to thank you for allowing me to present testimony this morning on this very important issue. It is personal to me because my mother Virginia Olthoff died as the result of neglect at a nursing home where she had lived for nearly 15 years. As a matter of fact, today marks the one year and one day anniversary of her funeral.

One of the most frustrating parts about how she died is that during her 15 years at Timely Mission Nursing Home in Buffalo Center, Iowa, my family believed she was getting good care. Each time we visited, she seemed comfortable, was dressed in regular clothes not pajamas and seemed to be clean and well groomed. We were familiar with many of the staff including the director of nursing who went to high school with me and my brothers.

There had always been good communication from the staff between my father who lived just three blocks from the facility until his death in 2012 and me as the eldest child and only daughter.

After my father's death, I became the family member responsible for decisions and the administrators called if there were needs. And they called often which I appreciated.

Your mom needs new glasses, she could use a haircut, she needs her toenails trimmed, and she could use some new underwear.

They also contacted me and discussed each time her medication was altered, she had dementia but she communicated with the staff and with us. Although she often just thought we were some nice people who came to visit. I was always invited to attend her yearly evaluation which I did not attend because I live two and a half hours away and it was conducted during the week. But the staff always was available to discuss the report over the phone. Fast forward to February 28th, 2018 at 3am, I received a phone call from the overnight Registered Nurse who told me simply "Your mother is moaning." And she asked me what do you want me to do? "I said, "Give her something for pain."

And the nurse said, "All we can give her is Tylenol," and she asked me again, "What you want me to do?" I said, "I think she needs to go to the hospital." She said ok and hung up.

The next call I got was from an emergency room nurse at a hospital in Mason City who said I had better come quickly because she was not sure my mother would be alive in the hour or so that it would take me to get there.

My husband, brother and I were greeted by the Emergency Room doctor who said my mother was extremely dehydrated and had sodium levels that were so elevated that she likely had suffered a stroke. He also said quote" this did not just happen." "I believe she has been without water or any type of fluid for at least 4 or 5 days." He also told us he is a mandatory abuse reporter and he was going to report this. (I heard the doctor say this but I wasn't sure what it meant because I was so surprised that she was this ill and was likely going to die soon).

My mother was given morphine for extreme pain, and we transferred her back to Timely Mission where she passed away a few hours later.

We held her funeral on March 5th and found it odd that no one from the nursing home where she had lived for 15 years attended the funeral. The church is just four blocks away. The director of nursing sent a beautiful bouquet of roses, but we received no sympathy cards from anyone on the staff which is unusual in a small town. Many of them knew my mother before she developed dementia and often told me stories about her when I would come to visit.

After the funeral, I went on my life grieving my mother especially in April because we shared a birthday, it was my first one without her, she would have been 88.

In July, I got a phone call from Clark Kauffman, a reporter for the Des Moines Register who said he was sorry for my mother's death and wanted to know if I had any comments about a Department of Inspections and Appeals Report. I had no idea what he was talking about but remembered what the emergency room doctor had said so it was now making sense.

The report read like a horror story. According to numerous staff members, my mother had been eating very little and drinking almost nothing for almost 2 weeks. Where was my call? The report also said she had been crying out in pain often, where was my phone call?

She did have a Do Not Resuscitate order but she wasn't having breathing or cardiac issues. The DNR states that she is to be made comfortable with an IV for fluids, oxygen and morphine or something for pain. NONE of that happened. The DIA report also mentioned her doctor who noted that my mother had lost a considerable amount of weight. Again where was my phone call?

The DIA report also showed that there were several certified nursing assistants who frequently notified their supervisors of my mother's condition but nothing was done.

I want to thank the CNAs, nurses and others who work in care facilities and do their jobs right. The facilities are often under staffed and these people work for much less money than they should be paid. Please thank those people if you have a loved one in nursing care. I also want to thank the Emergency Room doctor who reported the neglect and I especially want to thank Clark Kauffman and other journalists who take time to read these lengthy reports and write stories about these inspections, so perhaps something can be done about the current situation. I have more ideas that I will address in the comment section if there is time. Thank-you

Letter Submitted by Hon. Robert P. Casey, Jr., a U.S. Senator from Pennsylvania, United States Senate, Washington, DC 20510, March 4, 2019

The Honorable Seema Verma
Administrator
Centers for Medicare and Medicaid Services
Washington, DC

Dear Administrator Verma:

We are writing on behalf of the 80,000 Pennsylvanians who call a nursing facility home. Recently, select nursing homes in the Commonwealth were the subject of an in-depth investigation into patient neglect and understaffing.[2] Given this chapter, we are writing to request additional information on the Special Focus Facility (SFF) Initiative, a statutorily required Centers for Medicare and Medicaid Services (CMS) program[3] intended to enhance care quality and foster improvement among nursing facilities that persistently under perform.

We are proud of our State's high-quality nursing facilities, which benefit from dedicated leadership and staff members devoted to their residents' health, flourishing and overall wellbeing. Recent reporting suggests, however, that there are facilities that fall short of the care standards that we should expect of every one of our Nation's nursing homes. As detailed in these reports, despite recent changes in ownership and prior investigations,[4] some of our older constituents and people with disabilities residing in these homes experienced significant harm, including insect infestations, improper wound care, unsanitary conditions, supply shortages, and more.

Neglect and abuse of this nature is altogether unacceptable and through a robust system of competition, monitoring, oversight, technical assistance and enforcement, it should be entirely avoidable. Among the many vital elements of this system, we understand that CMS works alongside the Pennsylvania Department of Health (DoH) to administer the SFF program. Indeed, three of the nursing facilities featured in the aforementioned investigation are current participants in the program.

We are interested in learning more about the program's operations, scope and overall effectiveness. In continuation of our engagement on these issues, we ask that CMS provide answers to the following questions about the SFF program and the facilities eligible for and/or participating in this initiative:

1) There are more than 15,570 nursing homes in the U.S.[5] Less than 1 percent (0.6 percent) participate in the SFF program and less than 3 percent (2.8 percent) are eligible for the candidate list. What methodology did CMS use to determine the fixed size of the following:
   a) Total SFF participants nationally (88 facilities);
   b) Total candidates nationally (435 facilities);

---

[2] Daniel Simmons-Ritchie, "Still Failing the Frail," *PennLive,* November 2018, *http://stillfailingthefrail.pennlive.com/.*

[3] 42 U.S.C. 1395i–3; 42 U.S.C. 1396r.

[4] Daniel Simmons-Ritchie and David Wenner, "Failing the Frail," *PennLive,* August 2016, *https://www.pennlive.com/news/page/failing_the_frail_part_1.html.*

[5] CMS, "Provider Info," *Data.Medicare.Gov,* accessed on February 12, 2019, *https://data.medicare.gov/Nursing-Home-Compare/Provider-Info/4pq5-n9py.*

c) Total required participants per State (ranging from 1–6); and d. Total candidates per State (ranging from 5–30);[6]

2) CMS guidance[7] indicates the number of candidates and required SFF participants have not been updated since May 2014. Please provide the agency's reasoning for maintaining the program's current size (both candidates and participants), as well as the total number of SFF participants and candidates nationally for each year since 201O;
3) How frequently does CMS update the SFF candidate list? In addition, please provide information on how long a facility typically remains on the candidate list before selection in the SFF program;
4) What process does CMS engage in with State Survey Agencies (SA) to determine which candidates to select for the SFF program? Does CMS require or encourage the SA to take into consideration the scope and severity of deficiencies cited in prior surveys? Does CMS require or encourage the SA take into account any State action that has been taken against a facility?
5) Are there are any circumstances where a facility is prioritized for SFF participation or selected for the program outside of the rolling selection window (e.g., before a slot becomes available upon a participating facility's graduation or termination)?
6) Please indicate what, if any, surveying and oversight actions are taken with respect to candidates *not* selected by SAs for participation in the SFF program;
7) Please provide information on the frequency with which facilities cycle on and off the candidate list and what, if any, surveying, oversight and enforcement actions are taken if those repeat candidates are not selected for the SFF program. Please provide the average length of time a facility remains in the SFF program until graduation and /or termination of Federal participation, as well as details on outliers (least amount of time, most amount of time, etc.). Please also provide information on facilities that exit the program without graduating or being terminated from Federal participation;
8) CMS makes the list of selected SFF facilities publicly available on a monthly basis; however, the list of potential candidates is provided only to the candidates themselves. Please provide the most recent candidate list and the agency's reasoning for not previously releasing this list to the public; and
9) Pennsylvania's SFF participation includes a minimum of 20 candidates and 4 participants. Please provide the name, address, and length of candidacy for each of the Pennsylvania facilities on the SPF candidate list.

---

[6] CMS, Center for Clinical Standards and Quality/Survey and Certification Group, "Fiscal Year (FY) 2017 Special Focus Facility Program Update," March 2, 2017, *https://www.cms.gov/ Medicare/Provider-Enrollment-and-Certification/SurveyCertificationGenInfo/Downloads/ Survey-and-Cert-Letter-17-20.pdf.*

[7] *Ibid.*

Please provide answers to these questions by March 27, 2019 as well as a briefing for our staff members. Thank you for your consideration and we look forward to your response.

Sincerely,
Robert P. Casey, Jr.
U.S. Senator

Patrick J. Toomey
U.S. Senator

Statement of Maya Fischer: Daughter of Sonja Fischer, Nursing Home Rape Victim

Chairman Grassley, Ranking Member Wyden, and members of the Committee, thank you for the opportunity to be here today on behalf of my mother, Sonja Fischer.

My mother, suffering from advanced Alzheimer's, was a Medicare patient at Walker Methodist Health Center in Minneapolis. On December 18, 2014, at 4 a.m., a nurse walked into her room and witnessed a male caregiver, George Kpingbah, raping my mother.

My mother had suffered from Alzheimer's for twelve years. She was totally immobile, unable to speak and was fully dependent on others for her care.

When I saw the nursing home's number on caller ID, I prepared myself for the worst, that my mother had passed away. I was not prepared for what I heard. A nurse informed me that my mother had been sexually assaulted and was being transported to the hospital. And just like that, my mother became another statistic in the shocking reality of nursing home abuse. My mother was so much more than a statistic, so please allow me to tell you about her.

My mother was born in Jakarta, Indonesia in 1931. In 1942, the Japanese army invaded the Indonesian islands. In the horror of war, soldiers were raping and killing women and young girls. My grandparents were left with no option but to flee their homeland with their twelve-year-old daughter.

My mother ended up in the United States, became a US Citizen, and built a life for herself in this country. She was a testament to the American Dream. In this country, she was happy and safe—a world removed from the horrors of her youth. It was impossible to imagine that at the end of her life, when she had no ability to fend for herself, she would suffer the very same horror her parents had had fled their home to protect her from.

At 83 years old, unable to speak, unable to fight back, she was more vulnerable than an infant when she was raped. The dignity which she always displayed during her life, which was already being assaulted by her disease, was dealt a further devastating blow by her caregiver.

I received the phone call that this unthinkable act had been committed against my mother during the week of Christmas in 2014. This news was devastating not only for its immediate shock but how it has affected the memories we had of my mother and Christmases past.

Now and for the rest of my life, when I think of my mother at Christmas, I think of the horrifying shock of that call.

The sense of helplessness I felt, trying to comfort her while she had a rape kit performed will remain with me always. As will the nine hours I spent in the emergency room with her and the fear she must have felt with the bright lights and the scary noises of monitors going off. I will remember the pain she went through having an IV drip to make sure that at 83 she didn't contract a sexually transmitted disease.

My final memories of my mother's life now include watching her bang uncontrollably on her private parts for days after the rape, with tears rolling down her eyes, apparently trying to tell me what had been done to her, but unable to speak. I still feel the guilt of not being able to take care of her myself and having to entrust her care to others only to have her subjected to this unthinkable assault.

I remember the difficult decision we had to make when we realized that we could no longer care for her at home. We understood this meant we had to select a nursing home. We did everything we could to find the best place for her.

We assured my mother that she would be safe: she would not suffer. I can never overcome the guilt of realizing that these promises were not kept: She was not safe, she was raped.

Could this rape been prevented? It is my understanding that other residents had previously complained of sexual misconduct while Mr. Kpingbah worked there. I have learned that the Department of Health investigated these prior complaints, did nothing, and then kept them hidden. I can't help but wonder how my mom's, my family's, and my life would have been different had the Department not kept these allegations hidden.

Families struggling to care for their loved ones, do everything they can to find the best possible care. To make the best decision possible, we rely on the information provided by the Department of Health. We must have access to all important information to help us make these difficult decisions.

Please consider what I have shared with you today, how this crime has changed our lives forever, how it stole away the last shred of my mother's dignity and tarnished the memory of a decent and loving woman who had already suffered enough.

Thank you for allowing me to tell my mother's story.

Testimony of David Gifford, MD, MPH, Senior Vice President of Quality and Regulatory Affairs American Health Care Association

Chairman Grassley, Ranking Member Wyden, and distinguished members of the Committee, I'd like to thank you for holding this important hearing. My name is Dr. David Gifford, and I am a geriatrician and currently Senior Vice President of Quality and Regulatory Affairs at the American Health Care Association (AHCA). Previously, I served for six years as Director of the Rhode Island State Department of Health. Prior to that, I was the Chief Medical Officer for Quality Partners of Rhode Island, while also serving on the faculty at Brown University. In addition, I've been a medical director in a number of nursing homes in Rhode Island. Throughout my career, I have been asked to participate on numerous federal expert panels, including the Centers for Medicare and Medicaid Services' (CMS) panel to develop the Quality Assurance & Performance Improvement Program for nursing homes and the Center for Disease Control's Infection Control Panel. On behalf of AHCA and its members, I would like to thank the committee for the opportunity to participate in this morning's hearing.

I would like to begin this written statement by saying that Ms. Virginia Olthoff and Ms. Maya Fisher's mother were entrusted into the care of nursing homes. Quite simply and regrettably, these nursing homes not only failed them; they failed and tragically impacted the lives of their families and friends, as well. Families and residents who are often at their most vulnerable and in need of care and support should never have to worry about their physical safety, let alone experience what Ms. Olthoff and Ms. Fisher's mother endured. As a physician who has committed my career to the improvement of care for the elderly and as a son of two elderly parents, on behalf of AHCA, I am appalled and disgusted by the two devastating incidents we will discuss here today. Chairman Grassley and committee members, thank you for making sure that they are not forgotten.

Before I turn to a discussion of some proposed strategies to address abuse in nursing homes, I would like to briefly provide some important context about the industry as a whole. AHCA is the nation's largest association of long term and post-acute care providers representing nearly 10,000 of the 15,000+ nursing homes in the country who routinely provide high quality care to over a million residents and patients every day. We represent nearly half of all not-for-profit facilities, two-thirds of proprietary skilled nursing facilities (nursing homes), and half of government facilities.

Our mission is improving lives by delivering high quality care. While there are tragic stories like the ones presented today, and this hearing is rightfully focused on how to prevent these tragedies in the future, I also want to remind you and the American public that there are also countless heartwarming accounts of nursing home staff caring for residents as if they were their own family members. One of the privileges of my job is to travel the country and meet nurses, nursing assistants and nursing home staff from around the country who dedicate their lives to the care of the elderly. Today, I hope that we focus on solutions to prevent these unconscionable incidents in the future and limit using too broad a brush to castigate the countless, hard-working, committed staff caring for elderly residents in nursing homes around the country. Staff such as the more than 200 employees at the Good Samaritan Society in Florida who left their families at home during Hurricane Irma to stay with their residents over several days, make preparations for the storm, and ensure the residents' safety.

Let me also tell you about the staff in a Colorado nursing home who cared for Jeraldine. After her husband passed away, she was prescribed an off-label antipsychotic and became depressed and socially withdrawn while in her home. This led to her admission to a Colorado nursing home. Over time, the dedicated team of certified nursing assistants (CNAs), nurses, and other caregivers got to know her and realized they could safely remove her from all psychotropic medications. Today, Jeraldine has experienced dramatic improvements. She is one of our most active residents, serving as a key member of the residents' council and, as she puts it, is "a different person" today than when she arrived. This turnaround in Jeraldine's quality of life was a direct result of the actions taken by the caring staff – something that is also going on around the country every day for the millions of residents for which our members care.

Quality Improvements in America's Nursing Homes

I am proud to report to you, Chairman Grassley and Ranking Member Wyden, that in the last seven years, both the quality of care and caregiving methods used in our nursing homes have improved dramatically. We need to build off of this success to address the complex issues raised today.

In early 2012, AHCA launched the Quality Initiative, a member-wide challenge to meet specific, measurable targets in areas including hospital readmissions and the off-label use of antipsychotic medications and to adopt the Department of Commerce's Malcom Baldrige framework of health care excellence. Our members stepped up to that challenge.

Since the launch of this Initiative, our members have demonstrated significant qualitative and quantitative improvements in the care provided to nursing home residents. For the first time in the history of Baldrige program, an AHCA member in Idaho won the Department of Commerce's prestigious national Malcom Baldrige award for health care over all other health care providers.

First and most importantly, nursing homes over the past seven years have demonstrated improvement in 18 of the 24 quality outcomes measured and publicly reported by CMS. The data demonstrates further that:

- Fewer residents are returning to the hospital from the nursing home. An important measure of nursing home quality is the number of residents who return to a hospital because their condition has deteriorated during their nursing home stay. Today, that indicator of quality has changed for the better. Since 2011, the number of residents returning to the hospital after a nursing home stay has declined 11.6 percent.

- Fewer residents are receiving antipsychotic medications. Today, less than one in seven nursing home residents are receiving antipsychotic medications. This is a significant decline from 2011 when 25 percent of all residents received an antipsychotic.
- Staff are spending more time than ever before with residents. Remarkably, 75 percent of nursing homes received three out of five stars or better from CMS for staffing. In fact, in 2018, three out of every four nursing homes had more registered nurses and clinical staff caring for residents than what CMS projects they should have based on the type of residents in the facility. This is a significant improvement even compared to just two years ago when 18 percent had staff greater than what CMS expected based on the facility's residents. At the same time as described below we are facing serious staffing challenges.
- Nursing homes provide more person-centered care today than ever before. Only one in 18 nursing home residents report experiencing pain compared to one in eight in 2011. Moreover, since 2011, common ailments among nursing home residents have steadily declined. For example, we can document a 20 percent decrease in pressure ulcers, a 61 percent decline in urinary tract infections, and a 35 percent decline in depressive symptoms. And, as Jeraldine's story demonstrates, nursing homes have trained staff to better understand and care for residents with dementia without medications and replace antipsychotic medications with robust activity programs, social workers, and resident councils so that residents can be mentally, physically, and socially engaged.

Improvements Have Been Made, but Challenges Remain

The dramatic improvements described above are the result of the unrelenting commitment of AHCA members dedicated to improving the care provided for their nursing home residents. It also from AHCA's decision to identify and concentrate on root cause issues. However, from time to time, we fall short – sometimes terribly short.

Let me state for the record loudly and unequivocally: the cases of neglect and abuse like those we heard about today are inexcusable and should not happen – ever. The trust the elderly and their families place in us should never be violated.

AHCA is committed to preventing, not just reducing, future cases of neglect and abuse. Indeed, as AHCA's Senior Vice President of Quality and Regulatory Affairs, having spent my career working to improve nursing home quality, incidents like these are painful to hear, horrific and should never have happened to these individuals or to anyone else.

So how do we prevent something like what happened to Ms. Olthoff and to Ms. Fisher's mother from happening in the future?

As a representative of AHCA who is a primary care physician and former public health official, I think about prevention efforts in two important ways. First, how to prevent a disease from of adverse event from happening in the first place, which would be referred to as primary prevention – versus the second type, how do you treat and prevent a disease from getting worse – so called secondary or tertiary prevention. Both are effective strategies but need to be done in concert since neither alone are effective in preventing disease. Let me use the flu as an example. Primary prevention efforts would include the use of the influenza vaccine to prevent the influenza before it happens. When the vaccine is not effective, secondary and tertiary strategies are needed such using an oral antiviral medication such as Tamiflu, to treat individuals who have already developed the flue in order to prevent complications or the spread of the infection.

Using these public health principles as an analogy, currently, most CMS regulations and enforcement actions to address abuse would be classified as secondary or tertiary prevention efforts (that is steps and actions taken after an allegation of neglect or abuse). There is less focus on steps to prevent instances of abuse, or so-called primary prevention. For example, CMS already has extensive and broad regulations in place,[8] and there are criminal laws and penalties about elder abuse. CMS regulations clearly state that residents shall not suffer from any abuse and require immediate reporting to law enforcement and the state licensing agency within two to 24 hours of any allegation of neglect or abuse; posting and notification of residents' rights; procedures on how to report allegations/concerns; and steps on reporting and investigating any allegations, as well as mandated employee education about abuse and reporting requirements. All of these are steps to be taken after neglect or abuse has occurred.

These regulations do not stand alone. Rather, they are augmented by CMS' vast authority to enforce and mandate penalties upon those nursing homes that are non-compliant after the abuse or neglect has occurred. For example, CMS must apply civil monetary penalties (CMP) up to $21,393 per day upon a nursing home when cited for abuse or neglect that harms a resident. The per diem CMP remains in effect until the problem leading to abuse or neglect is corrected. Additionally, CMS can limit admissions to a nursing home, deny payments to that same facility, terminate a facility from Medicare and Medicaid, and report those individuals involved in a violation to the state professional licensing boards. In addition to requiring the nursing home to submit a plan of correction, CMS can also mandate remedies to fix the situation, including mandatory staff training, the transfer of at-risk residents to other facilities, hiring of an external manager/consultant, hiring of an external monitor, or any other remedy it determines necessary to remedy the problems found during their onsite inspections.

[8] See F-tags 600 through 610 in the State Operating Manual at https://www.cms.gov/Regulations-and-Guidance/Guidance/Manuals/downloads/som107ap_pp_guidelines_ltcf.pdf.

So as one can see, there is no shortage of regulations addressing abuse and neglect and the penalties are severe.

It is AHCA's position that neither the number of pages of regulations nor the amount of penalties imposed (secondary and tertiary prevention efforts) will stop bad actors from engaging in bad activities. Rather, we would recommend focusing on primary prevention strategies to prevent neglect or abuse before it happens. In order to develop effective primary prevention strategies, another tenant of public health efforts and quality improvement strategies to prevent disease and adverse events is to focus on the underlying root causes.

To identify potential causes, we have spoken with members and considered the abuse and neglect citations. After reviewing these specific citations of abuse and neglect to a resident, we make the following recommendations:

1) Expand federal programs that attract healthcare workers to the nursing home industry.
2) Strengthen federal regulations around reporting and sharing of information about employees who have engaged in abuse.
3) Make ratings of resident and family satisfaction with Nursing Home care publicly available.

First, as we examine these cases and discuss this issue with members, it is AHCA's position that one of the causes for many of the incidents cited by CMS for neglect frequently lies in part with a nursing home's ability to hire, engage, and retain skilled, talented, and suitable staff to care for this frail and vulnerable population. Unfortunately, there is a national workforce shortage, which is even worse in the rural areas. When we do identify or train high quality staff, they often take jobs in the hospital or resign from a nursing home to accept positions in a hospital. We are in desperate need of a program to attract and retain more nurses, aides, and health professionals, such as social workers and activities coordinators. To this end, we would recommend expanding on other successful federal programs that use loan forgiveness to attract health care workers in needed areas, including nursing homes.

Second, we need to a much stronger process to prevent people who are at risk of inflicting abuse or neglect from working in nursing homes. Presently, the federal government prohibits nursing homes from hiring direct-care employees who will care for resident that have been:

- "Found guilty of abuse, neglect, exploitation, misappropriation of property, or mistreatment by a court of law," or

- "Had a finding entered into the State nurse aide registry concerning abuse, neglect, exploitation, mistreatment of residents or misappropriation of their property," or
- "Have a disciplinary action in effect against his or her professional license by a state licensure body as a result of a finding of abuse, neglect, exploitation, mistreatment of residents or misappropriation of resident property."

Currently, CMS, in its guidance to nursing homes, states that "facilities must be thorough in their investigations of the histories of prospective staff. In addition to inquiry of the State nurse aide registry or licensing authorities, the facility should check information from previous and/or current employers and make reasonable efforts to uncover information about any past criminal prosecutions." AHCA strongly supports this guidance.

Additionally, states can require nursing homes to complete a criminal background check on employees prior to hiring. Many providers also choose to implement more stringent hiring policies than what is mandated by law. In this regard, AHCA routinely advises members on best practices and model policies for employee background screening. After all, the safety and security of patients, residents, and families begins with recruiting staff of the highest integrity. However, we hear from members across the country repeatedly that this is one of the most difficult challenge they face.

In addition to checking state registries, CMS also requires facilities to "report to the State nurse aide registry or licensing authorities any knowledge it has of actions by a court of law against an employee, which would indicate unfitness for service as a nurse aide or other facility staff." However, this is only required staff found unfit by a court of law. The court systems take time, and other actions are not reported.

In addition, when a negligent staff member moves to another state, their history of abuse or neglect does not consistently make it into the next state's registry. AHCA proposes that to ameliorate this situation, nursing homes require easier access to and participation in the national practitioner data bank maintained by the Health Resource and Services Administration (HRSA). This data bank currently collects information from hospitals, health plans, and state licensing boards for all health care professionals, including any terminations by providers who participate in the data bank. It is AHCA's position that the national practitioner data bank must be available to all Medicare and Medicaid certified providers for the purposes of background checks of prospective employees. This will significantly improve the profession's ability to root out bad actors before they are hired.

Third, AHCA strongly supports a mechanism for public reporting on resident and family satisfaction. Nursing homes are the only sector without a CMS reporting requirement on satisfaction. Making consumer satisfaction information available to families and future residents will go a long way toward enhancing transparency regarding the operation of a nursing home. Often, staff involved in abuse and neglect were identified early on as being "rough" or "difficult" with residents. Having the resident's and families report their satisfaction with the care and staff can help detect concerns to avoid tragic events like those described today.

Finally, AHCA would be remiss if it did not address the relationship between the safety and security of patients, residents, and families and the ability of its member homes to recruit and retain staff of the highest caliber. We have already established that our members are struggling to find the right staff. It is also a challenge to offer competitive salaries and benefits to staff. In its March 2018 Report to Congress on Medicare Payment Policy, the Medicare Payment Advisory Commission (MedPAC) reported that nursing homes have no extra room to increase costs compared to the reimbursements they receive from Medicaid and Medicare, which cover three-fourths of residents in nursing homes. The cost of more regulation that focuses on paper documentation, allegations requiring investigations, and reports of cases redirects limited resources and staff away from providing care to residents. This is unsustainable, and efforts to further improve nursing home care must be considered within this context.

Conclusion

One of the most important concerns before AHCA – in addition to ensuring that we never again experience incidences like Virginia Olthoff and Maya Fisher's mother – is how to continue and sustain the improvements in care that we have seen since 2012. This is why we encourage nursing homes to have strong systems in place. Over the past several years, we have supported and strongly encourage members to adopt CMS' Quality Assurance and Performance Improvement (QAPI) program, despite the fact that these regulations do not go into effect until November 2019. Our members who have adopted this approach consistently have better clinical and workforce outcomes and significantly fewer citations for abuse or neglect.

AHCA is committed to continuing to strive for complete elimination of all instances of abuse and neglect. We are committed to working with this committee and others to achieve that goal. We believe the answers will largely be found, not in adding to an already broad and expansive set of regulations and penalties that fall into the secondary or tertiary prevention category, but in developing and strategies such as those proposed today, that will help prevent these tragic incidents from happening.

Quality care in America's nursing homes has come a long way, and it remains our focus, our passion, and our commitment. We continue to challenge ourselves to improve and enhance quality, as demonstrated by both the data and the experiences of Jeraldine and our dedicated staff who overcome myriad obstacles to make sure our residents remain safe and properly cared for. This is especially true as we prepare for the increased demand for long term and post-acute care in the future as baby boomers begin to reach the age of 85.

AHCA stands ready to work with Congress, members of this committee, CMS, and other health care providers to continue its mission to improve lives by delivering common sense solutions for quality care so that neither Virginia Olthoff nor Maya Fisher's mother are forgotten. Thank you for the opportunity to testify today.

Prepared Statement of Kate Goodrich, M.D., Director, Center for Clinical Standards and Quality; and Chief Medical Officer, Centers for Medicare and Medicaid Services

Chairman Grassley, Ranking Member Wyden, and Members of the Committee, thank you for the invitation and the opportunity to discuss the Centers for Medicare & Medicaid Services' (CMS's) ongoing efforts to ensure that Americans in nursing homes receive high quality care. For vulnerable Medicare and Medicaid beneficiaries residing in nursing homes for long stays, these institutions are much more than healthcare facilities – they have become homes. Every nursing home serving Medicare and Medicaid beneficiaries is required to keep its residents safe and provide high quality care. We have focused on strengthening requirements for nursing homes, working with states to enforce statutory and regulatory requirements, increasing transparency of nursing home performance, and promoting improved health outcomes for nursing home residents.

Across our efforts, we work to make sure the focus remains where it should be – on the patient and their family. By reducing administrative burden through our Patients Over Paperwork initiative,[9] CMS is allowing clinicians to spend more time with their patients, which is particularly important in a nursing home setting where residents have more complex care needs, and care decisions are sometimes directed by family members. Reducing provider burden can also lower administrative costs, allowing facilities to dedicate their resources to other areas such as improving patient care. Our Meaningful Measures framework,[10] launched in 2017, helps make sure providers are held accountable for the quality of care they provide by identifying high priority areas for patient-centered, outcome-based quality measurements in all health care settings. For example, "make care safer by reducing harm caused in the delivery of care" is one of the six Meaningful Measures domains, and includes measures such as avoiding complications like bed sores and preventing healthcare-associated infections.

We appreciate the significant time and effort dedicated to this issue by Chairman Grassley and Ranking Member Wyden, and we look forward to working with this Committee and Congress as we continue to enhance our efforts to improve both the quality of services received and the quality of life experienced by nursing home residents.

---

[9] https://www.cms.gov/Outreach-and-Education/Outreach/Partnerships/PatientsOverPaperwork.html.

[10] https://www.cms.gov/Medicare/Quality-Initiatives-Patient-Assessment-Instruments/QualityInitiativesGenInfo/MMF/General-info-Sub-Page.html.

We also greatly appreciate the work of the Government Accountability Office (GAO), the Department of Health and Human Services Office of Inspector General (HHS-OIG), and the Department of Justice (DOJ), including their recommendations and ongoing assistance to ensure resident safety and facility compliance.

Strengthening Nursing Home Requirements

Every nursing home resident has the right to be treated with dignity and respect, and we expect every nursing home to meet this expectation. All long-term care facilities that seek to participate in Medicare and Medicaid must comply with basic health and safety requirements set forth in statute[11] and regulation,[12] including requirements for infection control, quality of care, nursing services, the unnecessary use of psychotropic medications, and many others. Compliance with these requirements is determined through unannounced, annual on-site surveys conducted by state survey agencies in each of the 50 states, the District of Columbia, and the U.S. territories. To prevent facilities from being able to predict the occurrence of their next survey, annual surveys are conducted at varying time intervals. The statewide average interval between surveys must be no greater than 12 months, but individual facilities may experience a gap of up to 15 months between annual surveys.[13] Nursing homes must remain in substantial compliance with these requirements, as well as applicable Federal, state, and local laws, and accepted professional standards, to continue as a Medicare or Medicaid participating provider.[14]

In 2015, CMS issued a revised regulatory proposal for public comment based on the findings of a comprehensive review of our existing regulations. This review focused on ways to improve the quality of life, care, and services in long-term care facilities, optimize resident safety, reflect professional standards, and improve the logical flow of the regulations.

This process resulted in CMS issuing – for the first time in over 25 years – a final rule[15] updating the requirements for nursing homes and other long-term care facilities. These revisions are an integral part of our efforts to hold nursing homes accountable for improved health outcomes, while at the same time minimizing administrative burden for providers. The changes also reflect the significant innovations in resident care and quality assessment practices that emerged over the previous three decades, as the population of long-term care facilities has become more diverse, more clinically complex, and more has been learned about resident safety, health outcomes, individual choice, and quality assurance and performance improvement.

---

[11] Sections 1819 and 1919 of the Social Security Act.

[12] 42 C.F.R. part 483, subpart B.

[13] Sections 1819(g)(2)(A)(iii) and 1919(g)(2)(A)(iii) of the Social Security Act.

[14] 42 C.F.R. §483.70(b).

[15] Available at https://www.federalregister.gov/documents/2016/10/04/2016-23503/medicare-and-medicaid-programs-reform-of-requirements-for-long-term-care-facilities.

Of particular note, the final rule made a series of changes that resulted in a more streamlined regulatory process, aligning program requirements with current clinical practice standards to enhance resident safety and improve the quality and effectiveness of care delivered to residents.

Among other provisions, the 2016 rule finalized changes intended to:

- Ensure that facilities provide residents with the necessary care and health services including behavioral health, based on a comprehensive assessment, to attain the highest practicable physical, mental health and psychosocial well-being.
- Require all long-term care facilities to develop, implement, and maintain an effective comprehensive, data-driven quality assurance and performance improvement program that focuses on systems of care, outcomes of care, and quality of life.
- Ensure that long-term care facility staff members are properly trained on resident's rights, properly caring for residents including caring for residents with dementia, and in preventing elder abuse.
- Ensure that long-term care facilities take into consideration the health of residents when making decisions on the kinds and levels of staffing a facility needs to properly take care of its residents.
- Improve care planning, including discharge planning, for all residents with the involvement of the facility's interdisciplinary team and consideration of the caregiver's capacity, which will give residents information they need for follow-up after discharge, and ensure that instructions are transmitted to any receiving facilities or services.
- Expand protections for residents from the use of inappropriate drugs, including expanding requirements for those who use psychotropic drugs or who have not previously used psychotropic drugs, including antipsychotics.

We have since reviewed these changes with a focus on reducing administrative burden while prioritizing resident safety and have begun enforcing and monitoring implementation. In response to public comments and to ensure facilities have time to make these important, longterm changes, CMS is implementing this rule in three phases based on the complexity of the revisions and the work necessary to revise interpretive guidance and survey processes. The schedule for the three phases is:

- Phase 1: Beginning in November 2016, the implemented rules included provisions that did not impose additional requirements on facilities or were straightforward to implement.
- Phase 2: In November 2017, a revised survey system incorporating the new requirements was introduced.

- Phase 3: Starting in November 2019, this phase will include requirements that will take longer for nursing homes to implement, such as such as including a new compliance and ethics program.

A key component of the requirements for participation in the Medicare and Medicaid programs are emergency preparedness standards for the planning, preparing, and staff training for potential emergency situations. CMS issued a final rule[16] in September 2016 updating and improving upon the emergency preparedness requirements for nursing homes and other providers and suppliers participating in Medicare and Medicaid to add additional requirements to safeguard residents and patients during emergency situations. For example, CMS now requires facilities to use an "all-hazards" risk assessment approach in emergency planning to identify and address location-specific hazards and responses.[17] In addition, facilities are now required to develop and maintain an emergency preparedness training and testing program for new and existing staff, along with a communications system to contact appropriate staff, patients' treating physicians, and other necessary persons in a timely manner to ensure continuation of patient care functions.[18]

The new emergency preparedness standards became effective on November 15, 2016, and state surveyors began to evaluate compliance with the new requirements as part of the certification and recertification survey process on November 15, 2017. As of February 22, 2019, 98 percent of the 15,581 active nursing homes have been surveyed under the new emergency preparedness requirements, and over 70 percent of these were found to be in compliance. We expect all certified nursing homes to be surveyed for compliance with these new requirements by the end of this month. All facilities that have been cited for noncompliance deficiencies under these requirements have made the necessary corrections to come into compliance with the emergency preparedness requirements.

Earlier this year, we issued clarifying manual interpretative guidance for nursing homes and state survey agencies on emergency preparedness.[19] The instructions included adding emerging infectious disease threats to the current definition of all-hazards approach and clarifying standards for alternate source power and emergency standby systems.

Working with States to Enforce Nursing Home Requirements

Monitoring patient safety and quality of care in nursing homes serving Medicare and Medicaid beneficiaries requires coordinated efforts across the Federal Government and

---

[16] Available at https://www.gpo.gov/fdsys/pkg/FR-2016-09-16/pdf/2016-21404.pdf.

[17] 42 C.F.R. §§483.73(a)(1).

[18] 42 C.F.R. §§483.73(c), (d).

[19] Available at https://www.cms.gov/Medicare/Provider-Enrollment-and- Certification/SurveyCertification GenInfo/Downloads/QSO19-06-ALL.pdf.

states. In addition to meeting Federal statutory and regulatory requirements, nursing homes must also meet state licensure requirements, which vary by state. Because the state survey agency is usually the same agency responsible for both state licensure and Federal surveys, these on-site surveys are typically performed by the same state team at the same time, with the state and Federal findings identified separately: one for state licensure purposes and one for Medicare and Medicaid compliance purposes. The state survey agencies also manage the intake of complaints and conduct investigations accordingly.

To help ensure greater consistency among state survey agencies, in November 2017, CMS implemented a new computer-based standardized survey methodology across all states. This new resident-centered survey process provides surveyors with more information on quality of care issues at that facility and allows surveyors more flexibility to ensure the quality of care issues and concerns they identify through resident observation and interviews are addressed. CMS makes results of these surveys available through our Nursing Home Compare website[20] and through datasets on our Quality, Certification, and Oversight Reports database[21] and the Medicare data website.[22] In April 2018, CMS began distributing monthly performance feedback reports to CMS Regional Offices and state survey agencies, identifying reporting issues such as inconsistencies with Federal processes. CMS Regional Offices meet quarterly with state survey agencies in their region to discuss survey outcomes and issues, and CMS meets monthly with a panel of state survey agency directors to discuss survey issues.

Addressing Suspected Abuse and Neglect in Nursing Homes

Abuse and mistreatment of nursing home residents is never tolerated by CMS, and the agency takes any allegation of these types of incidents very seriously. CMS requires nursing homes to report allegations of abuse, neglect, exploitation, or mistreatment, including injuries of unknown source and misappropriation of resident property, immediately to their state survey agency.[23] When we learn a nursing home failed to report or investigate incidents of abuse, CMS takes immediate action against the nursing home. For example, in 2018, when a state surveyor found that a nursing home did not properly investigate or prevent additional abuse involving 2 residents, placing other residents on the unit at risk for abuse, the nursing home was cited at the most serious level of noncompliance (immediate jeopardy) and assessed a civil monetary penalty of approximately $798,679. In addition to issuing civil monetary penalties, CMS can, and under certain circumstances must, deny payments or terminate a facility's Medicare and Medicaid participation agreements when appropriate.

[20] https://www.medicare.gov/nursinghomecompare.
[21] https://qcor.cms.gov/main.jsp.
[22] https://data.medicare.gov/.
[23] 42 C.F.R. §483.12(c).

State survey agencies can conduct complaint surveys at any time, and anyone can file a complaint, including residents, family members, nursing home staff, and anyone else who has reason to suspect abuse or neglect is taking place. CMS's Nursing Home Compare website[24] includes links and other helpful information to help patients and families determine when and how to file a complaint. Nursing homes are required to post similar information on how to file complaints and grievances in their facilities.[25]

When state surveyors identify noncompliance with Federal certification requirements, including abuse, they document this for the facility and, in cases where the facility is not in substantial compliance, refer the case to CMS for enforcement. To continue to participate in Medicare and Medicaid, the facility is required to address identified issues and develop a corrective action plan.[26] When immediate jeopardy to resident health and safety exists, meaning that the provider's noncompliance with one or more requirements has caused, or is likely to cause, serious injury, harm, impairment, or death, CMS and the State Medicaid Agency may terminate the facility and/or install temporary management in as few as two calendar days, and up to 23 calendar days,[27] after the survey which determined immediate jeopardy exists. Civil monetary penalties can also be assessed up to approximately $20,000 per day until the immediate jeopardy is removed and substantial compliance is achieved, as well as other remedies. A facility's removal of the conditions that caused the immediate jeopardy may, at CMS's discretion, result in the rescission of the termination if the facility demonstrates substantial compliance with all requirements during an unannounced re-survey.

For deficiencies that do not constitute immediate jeopardy situations, remedies could include directed in-service training, denial of payments, or civil monetary penalties. While CMS has the authority to terminate Medicare participation of all providers (including nursing homes) and suppliers because of noncompliance with the applicable statutory or regulatory requirements, State Medicaid Agencies have the authority to terminate Medicaid providers and suppliers in their state. State Medicaid Agencies are also required to deny or terminate the enrollment of any provider that has been terminated for cause under Medicare or another state's Medicaid or CHIP program, in accordance with relevant regulatory provisions. Nursing facilities that do not achieve substantial compliance within six months are terminated from Medicare and Medicaid participation.

When a provider's certification has been terminated from the Medicare program and we see signs of potential fraud or abuse, CMS may refer this information to the HHS–OIG and potentially the DOJ based on the facts and circumstances surrounding the termination.

---

[24] https://www.medicare.gov/NursingHomeCompare/Resources/State-Websites.html.

[25] 42 C.F.R. §483.10.

[26] https://www.cms.gov/Regulations-and-Guidance/Guidance/Manuals/downloads/som107c07.pdf.

[27] 42 C.F.R. §§488.410, 488.456(c), 489.53(d)(1) and 489.53(d)(2)(ii).

Special Focus Facilities

The Special Focus Facility initiative was developed to address those nursing homes that would be identified as providing substandard quality of care, having more problems or more serious problems than other nursing homes, or having a pattern of serious problems that persisted over a long period of time. Often, these nursing homes would institute enough improvements to address the presenting problems in order to come into compliance and continue to receive Medicare payments, but then significant problems would re-surface by the time of the next survey, leading them to be identified as providing substandard quality of care again. Such facilities with a "yo-yo" or "in and out of" compliance history rarely addressed underlying systemic problems that were giving rise to repeated cycles of serious deficiencies. Nursing homes designated as a Special Focus Facility are inspected by survey teams twice as frequently as other nursing homes and must recommend progressively stronger enforcement actions in the event of continued failure to meet the requirements for participation with the Medicare and Medicaid programs. For example, the Regional Office could impose a higher civil money penalty or add a Denial of Payment for New Admissions if consecutive surveys find problems.

The Special Focus Facility program provides a mechanism for state survey agencies and CMS Regional Offices to provide additional attention and resources to these facilities for the purpose of improving their quality of care and protecting residents. CMS has strengthened the Special Focus Facility program over the past several years to ensure that homes either improve so that they can graduate from the program, or they are terminated from Medicare and Medicaid participation. The objective of all enforcement remedies is to incentivize swift and sustained compliance in order to protect resident health and safety. Within 18-24 months after CMS identifies a facility as a Special Focus Facility nursing home, we expect that the facility would make significant, lasting improvements and graduate from this program, be terminated from the Medicare and Medicaid programs, or show promising progress but be permitted to continue as a Special Focus Facility for some additional time.

Our efforts are designed to help facilities come back into compliance, as well as prevent future noncompliance, without requiring a termination from the Medicare and Medicaid programs that would lead to disruptions in patient care. Nevertheless, our primary obligation is to ensure that all nursing home facilities are safe and can meet resident needs, and we will terminate facilities that do not appropriately correct deficiencies.

Increasing Transparency of Nursing Home Performance

Promoting transparency is a key factor to protecting patient safety and holding facilities accountable for the health outcomes of their residents, and CMS is committed to empowering patients and their families by providing access to the information they need to support their health care decisions for long-term care facilities. Through our Nursing Home Compare website,[28] consumers and families have the ability to compare facilities' performance in key areas. This transparency of performance information also serves as a strong, market-based motivator for facilities to make continuous improvements to the quality of care they provide.

Nursing Home Compare and Nursing Home Five-Star Quality Rating System

CMS first created the Nursing Home Compare website in 1998 and has regularly increased the amount of information available to beneficiaries and their families about the quality of care in nursing homes participating in the Medicare and Medicaid programs. In 2008, we introduced a quality rating system that gives each nursing home a rating of between 1 and 5 stars. CMS's Nursing Home Compare website contains information for more than 15,000 Medicare and Medicaid nursing homes around the country.

CMS bases the ratings of the Nursing Home Five Star Quality Rating System on an algorithm that calculates a composite view of nursing homes from three measures: results from their annual surveys; performance on certain quality measures, such as re-hospitalizations and unplanned emergency visits; and staffing levels. Copies of the detailed annual survey reports, along with results from complaint surveys, are available on the Nursing Home Compare website.

CMS continues to work to improve Nursing Home Compare and the Five Star Quality Rating System. In 2016, CMS expanded the number of quality measures included in Nursing Home Compare and the Five Star Quality Rating System. In April 2018, we took steps to improve the accuracy of the staffing information by using Payroll-Based Journal data, and, most recently, in October 2018, we added new measures on hospitalizations, falls, and care planning for functional ability. The survey information on Nursing Home Compare and the Five Star Quality Rating System is typically updated on a monthly basis, and quality measure and staffing information is typically updated quarterly.

Tracking Nursing Home Staffing Data through the Payroll Based Journal

CMS has long identified staffing as one of the vital components of a nursing home's ability to provide quality care. Current law[29] requires facilities to electronically submit direct care staffing information (including agency and contract staff) based on payroll and other auditable data. In 2015, CMS developed the Payroll-Based Journal system, which allows all facilities to submit their staffing data each quarter. The data, when combined with resident census information, is then used to calculate the level of staff in each nursing home.

---

[28] https://www.medicare.gov/nursinghomecompare.
[29] Section 1128I(g) of the Social Security Act and 42 C.F.R. §483.70(q).

This new staffing information is calculated using the number of hours facility staff are paid to work each day in a quarter, instead of the previous method of calculating staffing information using the total number of hours facility staff worked over a two-week period as self-reported by the facility, and submitted about once a year. Importantly, unlike the previous data source, the new data are auditable back to payroll and other verifiable sources.

In April 2018, CMS began using data from this system to post staffing information on the Nursing Home Compare tool. The Payroll-Based Journal data provides unprecedented insight into how facilities are staffed, which can be used to analyze how facilities' staffing relates to quality and outcomes. Already, the new data has helped us identify issues, such as days with no registered nurse reported onsite. We are deeply concerned about these issues and are working to address them. For example, we started in July 2018 to adjust the Nursing Home Compare ratings by assigning a one-star staffing rating to facilities that report seven or more days in a quarter with no registered nurse. Last November, we announced three updates to the Payroll-Based Journal reporting program. CMS will now use frequently-updated payroll-based data to identify and provide state survey agencies with a list of nursing homes that have a significant drop in staffing levels on weekends, or that have several days in a quarter without a registered nurse onsite. State survey agencies are required to conduct surveys on some weekends based on this list. If surveyors identify insufficient nurse staffing levels, the facility will be cited for noncompliance and required to implement a plan of correction. We have also updated the Payroll-Based Journal Policy Manual to provide clarification on how nursing homes should report hours for "universal care workers" and deduct time for staff meal breaks, and providing facilities with new reports to ensure they are submitting data accurately and in a timely manner. In the future, we anticipate using this data to report on employee turnover and tenure, which impacts the quality of care delivered.

Promoting Improving Outcomes and Quality of Care in Nursing Homes

Making sure residents receive high quality care – and making sure we are meaningfully measuring the quality of care they are provided – is critical to our efforts to improve patient safety. Patient harm resulting from inadequate staffing or the prescription of unnecessary medication can be just as serious as harm resulting from abuse or neglect, and we have several initiatives in place to help facilities improve patient outcomes and the quality of care provided.

National Partnership to Improve Dementia Care in Nursing Homes

In 2012, in response to quality and safety concerns related to the use of antipsychotic medications among a growing number of residents with dementia, CMS launched the National Partnership to Improve Dementia Care in Nursing Homes. The Partnership uses a multidimensional approach that includes public reporting, state-based coalitions, research, provider and surveyor training, and revising surveyor guidance to optimize the quality of care for all residents, especially those with dementia, by reducing the use of antipsychotic medications and enhancing the use of non-pharmacologic approaches and person-centered dementia care practices.

Since the launch of the Partnership, there have been significant reductions in the prevalence of antipsychotic medication use in long-stay nursing home residents. Between the end of 2011 and the end of the second quarter of 2018, the national prevalence of antipsychotic use in long-stay nursing home residents was reduced by 38.9 percent, decreasing from 23.9 percent to 14.6 percent nationwide. The Partnership continues to work with state coalitions and nursing homes to reduce the rate even further. In October 2017, to build on that progress and demonstrate the Partnership's renewed commitment to improving quality of care in nursing homes, CMS encouraged facilities with low rates of antipsychotic medication use to continue their efforts and maintain their success, and set a new goal for those with higher rates to decrease antipsychotic medication use by 15 percent for long-stay residents by the end of 2019.[30] Among these specific facilities, the prevalence of antipsychotic use among long-term residents decreased by 11.7 percent between the end of 2011 and the second quarter of 2018, indicating that we are making significant progress towards meeting this 15 percent goal.[31] We continue to look for opportunities to strengthen both the survey process and enforcement efforts to ensure that nursing homes consider non-pharmacologic approaches when appropriate and that residents are not receiving unnecessary medications.

National Nursing Home Quality Care Collaborative

CMS also leads the National Nursing Home Quality Care Collaborative with the Quality Innovation Network-Quality Improvement Organizations. The Collaborative launched in April 2015 with the mission to improve care for the 1.4 million nursing home residents across the country; currently, over 78 percent of the nation's nursing homes participate.[32] The Collaborative works to rapidly spread the practices of high performing nursing homes nationwide with the aim of ensuring that nursing home residents receive the highest quality of care. Specifically, the Collaborative strives to instill quality and performance improvement practices, eliminate healthcare-acquired conditions, and dramatically improve resident satisfaction by focusing on the systems that impact quality, such as staffing, operations, communication, leadership, compliance, clinical models, quality of life indicators, and specific, clinical outcomes. For example, CMS and the Quality Innovation Network National Coordinating Center released an All Cause Harm Prevention in Nursing Homes Change Package on November 28, 2018, highlighting the

30 https://www.cms.gov/newsroom/fact-sheets/data-show-national-partnership-improve-dementia-care- achieves-goals-reduce-unnecessary-antipsychotic.

31 https://www.nhqualitycampaign.org/files/Late_Adopter_Report.pdf.

32 All Cause Harm Prevention in Nursing Homes Change Package, available at: https://qio program.org/sites/default/files/editors/141/C2_Change_Package_20181226_FNL_508.pdf.

successful practices of high-performing nursing homes. The Change Package covers a wide range of strategies and actions to promote resident safety and describes how the nursing home leaders and direct care staff at chosen sites shared and described their efforts to prevent, detect, and mitigate harm.[33]

Skilled Nursing Facility Quality Reporting Program and Value-Based Purchasing Program

In recent years, we have undertaken a number of initiatives using payment reforms to promote higher quality and more efficient health care for Medicare beneficiaries. Implementing programs like the Skilled Nursing Facility Quality Reporting Program and the Skilled Nursing Facility Value-Based Purchasing Program is an important first step towards transforming Medicare from a passive payer of claims to an active purchaser of quality health care for its beneficiaries.

The goal of the Skilled Nursing Facility Quality Reporting Program is to use quality measures and standardized data to promote interoperability and give post-acute care providers access to longitudinal information so they can better facilitate coordinated care, improved outcomes, and overall quality comparisons. Measures reported under the program include functional status, skin integrity, medication reconciliation, and major falls. In addition, several measures are calculated using claims data, meaning facilities do not have to submit additional data for these measures. Under the program, skilled nursing facilities and all non-critical access hospitals swing-bed rural hospitals that fail to submit the required quality data to CMS are subject to a two percentage point reduction to their skilled nursing facility payments for that fiscal year.

As required by law,[34] the Skilled Nursing Facility Value-Based Purchasing Program will apply either a positive or negative incentive payment adjustment to skilled nursing facilities based on their performance of the program's readmissions measure. The program's incentive payments began on October 1, 2018, and aim to improve individual outcomes by rewarding providers that take steps to limit the readmission of their patients to a hospital. Also as required by law, CMS will make publicly available facilities' performance under the program, specifically including each skilled nursing facility's performance score and the ranking of skilled nursing facilities for each fiscal year.[35]

Moving Forward

Every nursing home resident has the right to be treated with dignity and respect, and we expect every nursing home to meet this expectation. While nursing facilities have made progress towards these goals, there continues to be a strong and persistent need for

---

[33] All Cause Harm Prevention in Nursing Homes Change Package, available at: https://qioprogram.org/sites/default/files/editors/141/C2_Change_Package_20181226_FNL_508.pdf.

[34] Section 1888(h) of the Social Security Act.

[35] Available at: *https://www.cms.gov/Medicare/Quality-Initiatives-Patient-Assessment-Instruments/Value-Based-Programs/Other-VBPs/SNF-VBP.html.*

ongoing improvement efforts around patient safety and quality of care in nursing homes. CMS remains diligent in our duties to monitor nursing homes participating in Medicare and Medicaid across the country, as well as the state agencies that survey them, and we look forward to continuing to work with Congress, states, facilities, residents and other stakeholders to make sure the residents we serve are receiving safe and high quality health care.

Testimony of David C. Grabowski, PhD, Professor, Department of Health Care Policy Harvard Medical School, Boston, MA

Chairman Grassley, Ranking Member Wyden, and distinguished members of the Committee my name is David Grabowski and I am a Professor of Health Care Policy at Harvard Medical School. I want to thank you for inviting me to testify today on the important issue of protecting older Americans from abuse and neglect in nursing homes.

On a given day, roughly 1.5 million individuals receive care from approximately 16,000 nursing homes nationwide. These individuals have high levels of physical and cognitive impairment and often lack family support and financial resources. As such, these are among the frailest and most vulnerable individuals in our health care system. We spend roughly $170 billion on nursing home care annually. This sector is heavily regulated. Yet, quality issues persist in many U.S. nursing homes.

Here is a section from a US Senate Special Committee on Aging report. In this chapter, the Committee identified the following nursing home abuses:

> Lack of human dignity; lack of activities; untrained and inadequate numbers of staff; ineffective inspections and enforcement; profiteering; lack of control on drugs; poor care; unsanitary conditions; poor food; poor fire protection and other hazards to life; excessive charges in addition to the daily rate; unnecessary or unauthorized use of restraints; negligence leading to death or injury; theft; lack of psychiatric care; untrained administrators; discrimination against minority groups; reprisals against those who complain; lack of dental care; advance notice of state inspections; false advertising [1].

If this chapter does not sound familiar to the Senators and their staff, it's because it was published in 1974. I would acknowledge that the nursing home sector has made important improvements over the past 45 years. For example, the use of physical restraints in nursing homes has dropped. The rate of unnecessary hospital admissions and readmissions has also fallen. And, it is important to note certain nursing homes are providing innovative care. For example, a few nursing homes have begun to offer small house nursing home models that offer a less-institutional, more resident-focused living environment.

Some important changes have occurred in the nursing home sector since the 1974 report. First, today's residents have much greater acuity and medical complexity, suggesting their needs are much greater relative to residents even 10 or 20 years ago. Second, nursing homes today still deliver chronic care services for long-stay residents but they also care for post-acute patients following a hospital stay. Post-acute Medicare payments keep facilities afloat financially, especially in the context of expanded home and community options, lowered occupancy rates, and parsimonious Medicaid payments.

Third, nursing homes continue to be largely for-profit owned, but the sector has experienced a great deal of private investment entry and corporate restructuring [2-4], Fourth, the nursing home sector has become much more regulated over time. In particular, the Nursing Home Reform Act was passed as part of the Omnibus Reconciliation Act of 1987 (OBRA '87) [5]. The extensive standards established by OBRA '87 were resident-focused and outcome-oriented, emphasizing quality of care, resident assessment, residents' rights, and quality of life. Finally, many market-based approaches have been implemented to encourage better nursing home quality of care including report cards and value-based payment.

In spite of all these changes, many of the issues identified in the Senate report in 1974 persist today. In my testimony, I would like to take on two issues. First, I will review the state of nursing home quality today. Second, I will identify why we have been focusing on this issue for nearly five decades. What are the underlying issues that lead to persistent low nursing home quality?

The State of Nursing Home Quality

Nursing home quality of care continues to be an important public policy issue in spite of prolonged public outcry [6-9] and government commissions [10-12]. Often the number of nurses per resident is low and the staff turnover rate is high [13]. Residents may develop new health problems after admission from physical restraints and missed medications [14, 15]. There are a number of studies documenting mistreatment of older adults in nursing homes [16]. Amenities that are common within a nursing home – including the food, activities and public spaces – are too often sub-standard [17]. The quality of life in many US nursing homes is inadequate and large numbers of residents suffer from isolation and loneliness [18].

Staffing

Labor is the dominant input into the production of nursing home care, accounting for roughly two-thirds of nursing home expenditures. Nursing homes are predominantly staffed by registered nurses (RNs), licensed practical nurses (LPNs) and certified nurse aides (CNAs). Higher nursing home staffing has generally been found to be associated with better quality of care [13, 19]. Nursing homes with low staffing levels, especially low RN levels, tend to have higher rates of poor resident outcomes such as pressure ulcers, catheterization, lost ability to perform daily living activities, and depression. Staffing standards may also improve working conditions, which would increase job satisfaction and reduce nursing turnover and burnout. Nursing home staff, especially CNAs, have very high turnover [20, 21]. It is not uncommon for nursing homes to have their entire set of CNAs change multiple times within a calendar year. Research has found that nursing homes with higher staff turnover have worse quality [13, 21-23].

Primary care physicians have been termed "missing in action" in the nursing home setting [24]. Some nursing homes have a nurse practitioner onsite [25], but typically, a group practice covers primary care in the nursing home [26]. These physicians are rarely onsite at the nursing home. For urgent issues, the physician may come visit the resident at the nursing home, but after hours and on weekends, this is often the exception rather than the rule. In these instances, it is more likely that the physician transfers the resident to the emergency room. Very few nursing homes have invested in innovative off-hour clinical delivery models like telemedicine [27].

Poor Care Practices

In the context of staff shortages, nursing homes often use labor-saving practices to deliver care [28]. These labor-saving practices are typically associated with a greater risk of morbidity and mortality. For example, managing incontinence may be labor-intensive, through regularly scheduled toileting and bladder rehabilitation, or labor-saving through urethral catheterization [29]. Urethral catheterization places the resident at greater risk for urinary tract infection and long-term complications including bladder and renal stones, abcesses, and renal failure. Nursing homes face similar decisions with respect to feeding residents (hand feeding versus feeding tubes), and in monitoring and controlling residents' behavior (monitoring by staff versus physical or chemical restraints). Although antipsychotics are not appropriate for the majority of nursing home residents with dementia, nursing homes often use antipsychotics to "manage" behavioral symptoms associated with dementia [30, 31]. Feeding tubes can result in complications including self-extubation, infections, aspiration, misplacement of the tube, and pain. Immobility resulting from physical restraints may increase the risk of pressure ulcers, depression, mental and physical deterioration, and mortality [29]. Inappropriate use of antipsychotic medications may also result in mental and physical deterioration [32].

Poor Outcomes and Adverse Events

Researchers have identified a range of poor nursing home outcomes that could have been prevented such as falls and pressure ulcers or delayed such as functional decline and mortality. Many of these outcomes are reported as quality measures on the federal Nursing Home Compare website. The transfer of nursing home residents to the emergency room and hospital has emerged as an important area of interest for policymakers. These transfers are known to be frequent [33, 34], costly [35], often preventable [36] and potentially associated with negative health outcomes such as iatrogenic disease and delirium [37]. Although the rate of avoidable hospitalizations has declined in recent years, analyses by CMS suggested it was still 15.7% in 2015 [38].

Safety

Many nursing homes are not safe environments to live. A large research literature documents both staff-on-resident [39, 40] and resident-on-resident [41] abuse in nursing homes. Deficiency citations are given to nursing homes that are in violation of Medicare/Medicaid regulations in four specific areas (abuse; neglect by staff; criminal screening investigating and reporting; and, abuse prevention and policy development and implementation). 20% of facilities received one of these citations in 2007 [42]. Nursing homes can also be cited for deficiencies related to overall safety. In 2007, 33% of nursing homes were cited for environmental safety issues (e.g., "lighting levels"; "handrails"), 47% for care safety issues ("medication error rate"; "availability of physician for ER care"), and 60% for Life Safety Inspection issues (e.g., "fire alarm systems"). It should be noted that some of these deficiency citations can be for relatively minor events.

Nevertheless, 16% of nursing homes were found to have at least one of the most severe deficiency citations from 2000 through 2007. These deficiency citations are for actual or potential for death or serious injury.

One important nursing home safety issue involves emergency preparedness. This issue received increased scrutiny following the deaths of eight nursing home residents in Hollywood, Florida in September 2013 following Hurricane Irma [43]. A facility lost electricity during the hurricane and didn't have a generator capable of powering the air-conditioning. A Kaiser Health News investigation suggested many nursing homes fail to plan for even basic contingencies:

> In one visit last May, inspectors found that an El Paso, Texas, nursing home had no plan for how to bring wheelchair-dependent people down the stairs in case of an evacuation. Inspectors in Colorado found a nursing home's courtyard gate was locked and employees did not know the combination, inspection records show. During a fire at a Chicago facility, residents were evacuated in the wrong order, starting with the people farthest from the blaze [44].

According to the article, nursing home inspectors issued 2,300 violations of emergency-planning rules over the prior four years, but they labeled only 20 as serious enough to place residents in danger. Although a third of nursing homes were cited for failing to inspect their generators each week or test them monthly, none of these violations was categorized as a major deficiency. This raises the important issue of whether current safety standards are being effectively enforced.

Low Quality of Life

Due to the fact that patients often spend long periods in nursing homes relative to most health institutions, quality of life is an important aspect of a resident's nursing home experience. Historically, there has been much greater emphasis on the "nursing" rather than "home" part of the nursing home experience. Quality of life may be thought of as generally corresponding to those characteristics of nursing home care that affect the resident's sense of well-being, self-worth, self-esteem, and life satisfaction. It's about how the resident is treated: for example, "having one's privacy respected by others' knocking before entering a bathroom, or having one's dignity maintained by not being wheeled down a hallway scantily covered en route to the shower" [18].

Measures such as resident or family satisfaction are important indicators of nursing home quality. Unfortunately, many nursing homes fall short on this domain. Nobody wants to go to a nursing home: In a survey of community-dwelling elders, almost one-third indicated they would rather die than enter a nursing home [45]. And once there, many individuals, especially family members, report low levels of satisfaction with the care delivered [46, 47].

Traditional nursing homes fall short in several domains [18]. Care is often directed by the facility rather than the resident. Ideally, residents should be offered choices about issues personally affecting them like what to wear and when to go to bed. Many nursing homes are quite institutional with long hallways with a nurse station at one end, linoleum floors and two residents to a room. These nursing homes feel more like a hospital than a home. The staff structure at these facilities is often quite hierarchical with very little empowerment of direct caregivers. Nursing homes are not just suboptimal places to live, they are also often difficult places to work. CNAs tend to be paid at or near the minimum wage and many workers may view retail establishments and fast food restaurants as a better opportunity at that wage [48]. A more participatory management structure that engages CNAs in the decision-making process would help with staff turnover and performance.

Why Is Nursing Home Quality Such a Persistent Problem?

The U.S. nursing home market has a series of features that lead to persistent low quality. The way in which we regulate and oversee care quality, how we pay for nursing home services, how we regulate the supply of providers, and the inability of many residents to oversee and monitor their care all may contribute to low quality.

Payments Are Often Low and Fragmented

When it comes to nursing home care, as the old saying goes, we get what we pay for. Due in part to the exclusion of long-stay nursing home services from the Medicare benefit, Medicaid is the dominant payer of nursing home services, accounting for 50% of revenues and 70% of bed-days. Medicaid payment rates are typically 70-80% of private-pay prices. In many states, the average "margins" for Medicaid residents are negative, suggesting the cost of treating Medicaid residents exceeds the amount that Medicaid reimburses for their care [49].

The nearly 15 percent of U.S. nonhospital-based nursing homes that serve predominantly Medicaid residents have fewer nurses, lower occupancy rates, and more health-related deficiencies [50]. They are more likely to be terminated from the Medicaid/Medicare program, are disproportionately located in the poorest counties, and are more likely to serve African-American residents than are other facilities. Low or negative margins for a substantial portion of a nursing home's population strongly incentivizes facilities to prioritize the labor-saving care delivery approaches described previously in an effort to lower the costs of care. Moreover, a high-Medicaid census is likely to lead to nursing home closures, which can also put seniors at risk. A *New York Times* article from earlier this week suggested 440 rural nursing homes have merged or closed over the past decade [51]. The article suggests many rural facilities are "losing money as their occupancy rates fall and more of their patients' long-term care is covered by Medicaid, which in many states does not pay enough to keep the lights on."

Another payment issue is the fragmentation in coverage of nursing home and medical services for long-stay nursing home residents [52]. Many of these individuals are dually eligible in that Medicaid covers their nursing home care while Medicare covers all their health care including physician and hospital services. This "silo" based payment structure introduces strong incentives for nursing homes to transfer sicker patients to the emergency department and hospital in order to limit the burden on their staff and also improve their potential standing with surveyors. As the saying goes in many US nursing homes, "when in doubt, ship them out."

The fragmented Medicaid-Medicare coverage of long-stay nursing home residents also serves as a barrier to developing programs to prevent unnecessary transfers [52]. Nursing homes that invest in models and staff to safely reduce the likelihood of hospital transfers predominantly generate savings for Medicare, while Medicaid often must pay for the increased cost of long-stay care in the nursing home. Thus, state Medicaid programs have little incentive to invest in policies to discourage transfers from the nursing home setting.

Quality Regulations Are Extensive but Oversight Inconsistent

To date, the primary approach to addressing low quality has been regulation (see Figure 1). Regulations are extensive and the sanctions, when enforced, can be severe, ranging from fines to probation to closure. In particular, OBRA '87 has shaped oversight for the past 30+ years. The OBRA '87 standards overhauled nursing home regulation and sought to hold nursing homes to a higher standard. Specifically, it strengthened existing quality standards, elevated quality of life and residents' rights to be of equal importance with traditional quality of care standards, required collection of detailed assessment data

(Minimum Data Set), consolidated Medicare/Medicaid requirements, and expanded the range of available sanctions. OBRA '87 spurred many improvements in that it reduced physical restraints, catheter use, psychotropic medication use, and pressure ulcers. It also increased discussions between residents and care providers about care plans, end-of-life, etc., while increasing staffing levels overall. As noted in the prior section however, cracks are very clearly evident in the current quality assurance framework. Recent investigative reports have documented substantial lapses in oversight processes across multiple states [53-55]. Importantly, states are largely responsible for implementation of oversight responsibilities and many of the identified gaps have been state specific.

The Trump Administration has proposed to scale back oversight and enforcement of nursing home rules as part of their broader movement to reduce bureaucracy, regulation and government intervention in business. In particular, new guidelines discourage regulators from levying fines in some situations, such as if an incident were a "one-time" event rather than evidence of a broader problem [56]. The new guidelines would also likely result in lower fines for many facilities. The administration has also proposed relaxing rules around emergency preparedness [57].

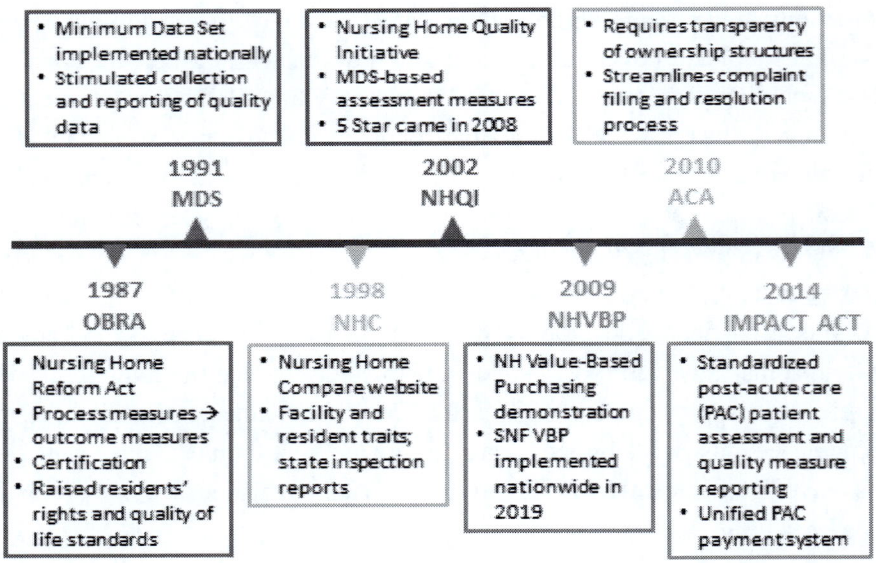

Figure 1. Nursing Home Quality Timeline.

Certificate-of-Need Regulation Impede Innovation

Certificate of need is an oft-used strategy to constrain health care spending [58]. It rests on what is termed "Roemer's law," which states "a built bed is a filled bed is a billed bed." The logic goes something like this: if a state can hold the total number of nursing home beds down, then it will constrain the number of Medicaid beneficiaries in those beds, which ultimately lowers overall state Medicaid spending on nursing homes. 34 states still have nursing home certificate-of-need laws on the books.

Research has been fairly clear: nursing home certificate-of-need laws lower access and quality of care, while increasing private-pay prices [59-61]. Certificate of need has even distorted the size of nursing homes [62]. The average number of beds in a nursing home is roughly 110 in states without a certificate-of-need law and 131 in states with a law.

Certificate-of-need laws also discourage innovation in a sector badly in need of modernization. Many recent culture change quality initiatives, such as the Green House and other small house models, have highlighted the importance of capital investment towards improving nursing home quality of care [63]. Although data on the capital stock in the nursing home industry are sparse, one estimate suggests the average age of nursing home structures is about 30 years [64]. Many older nursing homes lack private rooms and have an institutional, less home-like environment.

Lack of Quality Transparency

Although nursing home care is fairly non-technical in nature, monitoring of care can often be difficult for residents and their families. Given the high prevalence of dementia in the nursing home population, the resident is often neither the decision-maker nor able to easily evaluate quality or communicate concerns to family members and staff.

Furthermore, the elderly who seek nursing home care are disproportionately the ones with no family support to help them with the decision process [65]. When residents did not have family member visit during the first month of care, one study found a greater likelihood of dehydration and urinary tract infection in for-profit nursing homes [66].

The Centers for Medicare and Medicaid Services produces the Nursing Home Compare tools on the Medicare.gov website to facilitate better consumer choice by providing data and summary rankings on the quality of care delivered by all eligible providers [67]. Although Nursing Home Compare was designed to facilitate easy comparisons across facilities on meaningful characteristics, evidence suggests that it is coming up short.

The Nursing Home Compare tool lacks information on many of the provider features that may be of the greatest importance to residents and their families. For example, the website gives no information about the amenities provided by a facility, the physical setting where care is delivered and a patient resides, the culture and care philosophy of the nursing home, the ability of the facility to coordinate with acute and primary care providers, and the availability of physicians and nurse practitioners on site. Accessing these "data" in the current environment likely requires an in-person visit to a facility, a time-consuming endeavor that requires a proactive family support system, or a word-of-mouth recommendation from a trusted source without competing incentives, which may not exist.

Staffing is an important quality measure used to profile nursing homes on the federal Nursing Home Compare website. Since staffing data were first reported on the website in

1998, Nursing Home Compare relied on data that were self-reported by facilities based on average levels over a two-week lookback period and rarely audited [68, 69]. Many researchers have questioned the completeness and accuracy of these facility-reported staffing data [68, 70, 71].

In October 2014, President Obama signed into law the Improving Medicare Post Acute Care Transformation Act of 2014 (IMPACT Act), which provided funding to implement Section 6106 of the Affordable Care Act requiring that nursing homes use the Payroll Based Journal (PBJ) system to submit auditable staffing and resident census data [72]. Using the PBJ platform, nursing homes were required to begin submitting payroll-based staffing data in July 2016 on a quarterly basis. In April 2018, the Centers for Medicare and Medicaid Services (CMS) began using payroll data as the source for staffing information in Nursing Home Compare and the Five-Star Quality Rating System. Daily staffing data are now available for all U.S. nursing homes.

Policymakers are already beginning to use the payroll data in their oversight and monitoring of facilities. CMS used the payroll data to lower the quality star ratings at 1-in-11 facilities on Nursing Home Compare, both because of low RN staffing and failure to submit data [73]. In the wake of a New York Times story documenting discrepancies between payroll and administrative data [55], Senator Wyden issued a letter demanding that CMS fully implement the transition to using payroll data and pursue increased protections for nursing home residents [74]. Similarly, the Office of the Inspector General has announced it will monitor CMS collection of the payroll data and enforcement of related staffing standards [75].

Beyond shortcomings in the Nursing Home Compare tool itself, more work is needed to actually get this information into the hands of consumers. We know that in its current form, Nursing Home Compare has had limited effects on patients' actual choices [76], and available evidence indicates that a considerable portion of this limited impact could stem from a general lack of awareness, on the part of both patients and discharge planners, that the tool even exists [77, 78]. Furthermore, it appears that when hospital case managers are aware of the tool and its accompanying quality rankings, they are reluctant to share such information with patients for fear of violating patient choice regulations [79]. Patients and providers alike need to know that help is available, and barriers to accessing this website during the potentially stressful and hectic time of choosing a nursing home need to be minimized.

The lack of quality transparency makes it difficult for patients and their families to "vote with their feet" by choosing better quality facilities and avoiding the lowest quality ones. In turn, nursing homes may not face sufficient market pressure to improve care quality or develop new models of care that better match resident preferences. Even if residents and their families are unable to use report card information at times of crisis, greater quality transparency could still factor into government oversight activities and have a positive influence on care.

Summary

We have made important progress towards improving nursing home quality over the past few decades since the 1974 US Senate report [1]. I would assert, however, that the nursing home sector is *better but still not well*. We have a lot of work left to do. Significant quality of care problems persist at many US nursing homes. However, these problems are not isolated to particular facilities or patients. These problems are related to system level issues in how we pay for care, how we regulate providers, and the inability of residents and their advocates to monitor and oversee care. Unless we address these broader issues, we will be discussing poor nursing home quality for another fifty years.

References

[1] U.S. Senate. *Nursing home care in the United States: Failure in public policy, Supporting Paper No. 1. The Litany of Nursing Home Abuses and Examination of the Roots of the Controversy.* Senate Special Committee on Aging, Subcommittee on Long-term Care. Washington, D.C.: U.S. Government Printing Office; March 1, 2019 1974.

[2] Stevenson D, Grabowski D, Coots L. *Nursing Home Divestiture and Corporate Restructuring: Final Report*: *Prepared for Office of Disability, Aging and LongTerm Care Policy, Office of the Assistant Secretary for Planning and Evaluation, U.S. Department of Health and Human Services, Contract #HHS- 100-03-0033.; 2006.*

[3] Fowler AC, Grabowski DC, Gambrel RJ, Huskamp HA, Stevenson DG. Corporate Investors Increased Common Ownership In Hospitals And The Postacute Care And Hospice Sectors. *Health Aff. (Millwood).* Sep 1 2017;36(9):1547-1555.

[4] U.S. Government Accountability Office. *Nursing Homes: Complexity of Private Investment Purchases Demonstrates Need for CMS to Improve the Usability and Completeness of Ownership Data* (GAO-10-710). 2010; http://www.gao.gov/new.items/d10710.pdf. Accessed November 25, 2014.

[5] Hawes C. *Assuring Nursing Home Quality: The History and Impact of Federal Standards in OBRA-87.* New York, NY: The Commonwealth Fund;1996.

[6] Vladeck BC, Twentieth Century Fund. *Unloving care: the nursing home tragedy.* New York: Basic Books; 1980.

[7] Mendleson MA. *Tender Loving Greed*. New York: Alfred A. Knopf; 1974.

[8] Institute of Medicine. *Improving the quality of care in nursing homes*. Washington, D.C.: National Academy Press; 1986.

[9] Institute of Medicine. *Improving the quality of long-term care*. Washington, D.C.: National Academy Press; 2001.

[10] U.S. Government Accountability Office. *Nursing Homes: Despite Increased Oversight, Challenges Remain in Ensuring High-Quality Care and Resident Safety* GAO-06-117;2005.

[11] Office of Inspector General. *Psychotropic drug use in nursing homes.* Washington, DC: US Dept. of Health and Human Services. Report No. OEI 02-00-00490;2001.

[12] U.S. Senate. *Nursing home care in the United States: Failure in public policy.* Senate Special Committee on Aging, Subcommittee on Long-term Care. Washington, D.C.: U.S. Government Printing Office;1974.

[13] Collier E, Harrington C. Staffing characteristics, turnover rates, and quality of resident care in nursing facilities. *Res Gerontol Nurs.* Jul 2008;1(3):157-170.

[14] Castle NG, Mor V. Physical restraints in nursing homes: a review of the literature since the Nursing Home Reform Act of 1987. *Medical Care Research and Review.* Jun 1998;55(2):139-170; discussion 171-136.

[15] Gerety MB, Cornell JE, Plichta DT, Eimer M. Adverse events related to drugs and drug withdrawal in nursing home residents. *J Am Geriatr Soc.* Dec 1993;41(12):1326-1332.

[16] Lindbloom EJ, Brandt J, Hough LD, Meadows SE. Elder mistreatment in the nursing home: a systematic review. *Journal of the American Medical Directors Association.* Nov 2007;8(9):610-616.

[17] Miller SC, Cohen N, Lima JC, Mor V. Medicaid capital reimbursement policy and environmental artifacts of nursing home culture change. *The Gerontologist.* Feb 2014;54 Suppl 1:S76-86.

[18] Koren MJ. Person-centered care for nursing home residents: the culture-change movement. *Health affairs (Project Hope).* Feb 2010;29(2):312-317.

[19] Bostick JE, Rantz MJ, Flesner MK, Riggs CJ. Systematic review of studies of staffing and quality in nursing homes. *J Am Med Dir Assoc.* 2006;7:366-376.

[20] Munroe DJ. The influence of registered nurse staffing on the quality of nursing home care. *Res. Nurs. Health.* Aug 1990;13(4):263-270.

[21] Thomas KS, Mor V, Tyler DA, Hyer K. The relationships among licensed nurse turnover, retention, and rehospitalization of nursing home residents. *The Gerontologist.* Apr 2013;53(2):211-221.

[22] Lerner NB, Johantgen M, Trinkoff AM, Storr CL, Han K. Are nursing home survey deficiencies higher in facilities with greater staff turnover. *Journal of the American Medical Directors Association.* Feb 2014;15(2):102-107.

[23] Castle NG, Engberg J. Staff turnover and quality of care in nursing homes. *Medical care.* Jun 2005;43(6):616-626.

[24] Shield RR, Wetle T, Teno J, Miller SC, Welch L. Physicians "missing in action": family perspectives on physician and staffing problems in end-of-life care in the nursing home. *J Am Geriatr Soc.* Oct 2005;53(10):1651-1657.

[25] Intrator O, Feng Z, Mor V, Gifford D, Bourbonniere M, Zinn J. The employment of nurse practitioners and physician assistants in U.S. Nursing homes. *Gerontologist.* Aug 2005;45(4):486-495.

[26] Katz PR, Karuza J, Intrator O, et al. Medical staff organization in nursing homes: scale development and validation. *J Am Med Dir Assoc.* Sep 2009;10(7):498-504.

[27] Grabowski DC, O'Malley AJ. Use of telemedicine can reduce hospitalizations of nursing home residents and generate savings for Medicare. *Health Aff. (Millwood).* Feb 2014;33(2):244-250.

[28] Cawley J, Grabowski DC, Hirth RA. Factor substitution in nursing homes. *J. Health Econ.* Mar 2006;25(2):234-247.

[29] Zinn JS. The influence of nurse wage differentials on nursing home staffing and resident care decisions. *Gerontologist.* Dec 1993;33(6):721-729.

[30] Stevenson DG, Decker SL, Dwyer LL, et al. Antipsychotic and benzodiazepine use among nursing home residents: findings from the 2004 National Nursing Home Survey. *Am. J. Geriatr. Psychiatry.* Dec 2010;18(12):1078-1092.

[31] Grabowski DC, Bowblis JR, Lucas JA, Crystal S. Labor Prices and the Treatment of Nursing Home Residents with Dementia. *International Journal of the Economics of Business.* 2011;18(2):273-292.

[32] Harrington C, Tompkins C, Curtis M, Grant L. Psychotropic drug use in long-term care facilities: a review of the literature. *Gerontologist.* Dec 1992;32(6):822-833.

[33] Intrator O, Grabowski DC, Zinn J, et al. Hospitalization of nursing home residents: the effects of states' Medicaid payment and bed-hold policies. *Health Serv Res.* Aug 2007;42(4):1651-1671.

[34] Brownell J, Wang J, Smith A, Stephens C, Hsia RY. Trends in Emergency Department Visits for Ambulatory Care Sensitive Conditions by Elderly Nursing Home Residents, 2001 to 2010. *JAMA Intern Med.* Oct 28 2013.

[35] Grabowski DC, O'Malley AJ, Barhydt NR. The costs and potential savings associated with nursing home hospitalizations. *Health affairs (Project Hope).* Nov-Dec 2007;26(6):1753-1761.

[36] Saliba D, Kington R, Buchanan J, et al. Appropriateness of the decision to transfer nursing facility residents to the hospital. *Journal of the American Geriatrics Society.* Feb 2000;48(2):154-163.

[37] Ouslander JG, Weinberg AD, Phillips V. Inappropriate hospitalization of nursing facility residents: a symptom of a sick system of care for frail older people. *Journal of the American Geriatrics Society.* Feb 2000;48(2):230-231.

[38] Brennan N, Engelhardt T. Data Brief: Sharp reduction in avoidable hospitalizations among long-term care facility residents *CMS.gov Blog* 2017; https://www.cms.gov/blog/data-brief-sharp-reduction-avoidable-hospitalizations-among-long-term-care-facility-residents. Accessed March 1, 2019.

[39] Castle N, Ferguson-Rome JC, Teresi JA. Elder abuse in residential long-term care: an update to the 2003 National Research Council report. *Journal of applied gerontology: the official journal of the Southern Gerontological Society.* Jun 2015;34(4):407-443.

[40] Hawes C. Elder Abuse in Residential Long-Term Care Settings: What Is Known and What Information Is Needed? In: Bonnie RJ, Wallace RB, eds. *Elder Mistreatment: Abuse, Neglect, and Exploitation in an Aging America*. Washington, DC: National Academies Press; 2003.

[41] Lachs MS, Teresi JA, Ramirez M, et al. The Prevalence of Resident-to-Resident Elder Mistreatment in Nursing Homes. *Ann. Intern. Med.* Aug 16 2016;165(4):229-236.

[42] Castle N. Nursing Home Deficiency Citations for Abuse. *Journal of applied gerontology : the official journal of the Southern Gerontological Society.* Dec 2011;30(6):719-743.

[43] Gabler W, Fink S, Yee V. At Florida Nursing Home, Many Calls for Help, but None That Made a Difference. *New York Times*2017.

[44] Rau J. Nursing Home Disaster Plans Often Faulted As 'Paper Tigers'. *Kaiser Health News*2017.

[45] Mattimore TJ, Wenger NS, Desbiens NA, et al. Surrogate and physician understanding of patients' preferences for living permanently in a nursing home. *Journal of the American Geriatrics Society.* Jul 1997;45(7):818-824.

[46] Bolt SR, Verbeek L, Meijers JMM, van der Steen JT. Families' Experiences With End-of-Life Care in Nursing Homes and Associations With Dying Peacefully With Dementia. *Journal of the American Medical Directors Association.* Feb 1 2019.

[47] Fosse A, Schaufel MA, Ruths S, Malterud K. End-of-life expectations and experiences among nursing home patients and their relatives – a synthesis of qualitative studies. *Patient Educ. Couns.* Oct 2014;97(1):3-9.

[48] Institute of Medicine. *Nursing Staff in Hospitals and Nursing Homes: Is It Adequate?* Washington, D.C.: National Academy Press; 1996.

[49] Medicare Payment Advisory Commission. *Report to the Congress: Medicare Payment Policy.* Washington, DC March 2018.

[50] Mor V, Zinn J, Angelelli J, Teno JM, Miller SC. Driven to tiers: socioeconomic and racial disparities in the quality of nursing home care. *Milbank Q.* 2004;82(2):227-256.

[51] Healy J. Nursing Homes Are Closing Across Rural America, Scattering Residents. *New York Times.* March 4, 2019.

[52] Grabowski DC. Medicare and Medicaid: conflicting incentives for long-term care. *Milbank Q.* 2007;85(4):579-610.

[53] Office of Inspector General. Early Alert: The Centers for Medicare & Medicaid Services Has Inadequate Procedures To Ensure That Incidents of Potential Abuse or

Neglect at Skilled Nursing Facilities Are Identified and Reported in Accordance With Applicable Requirements (A-01-17-00504) 2017; https://oig.hhs.gov/oas/reports/region1/11700504.pdf. Accessed March 4, 2019.

[54] US. Government Accountability Office. *Nursing Home Quality: Continued Improvements Needed in CMS's Data and Oversight.* Washington, DC2018.

[55] Rau J. 'It's Almost Like a Ghost Town.' Most Nursing Homes Overstated Staffing for Years. *The New York Times*2018.

[56] Rau J. Trump Administration Eases Nursing Home Fines in Victory for Industry. *New York Times.* December 24, 2017.

[57] Centers for Medicare & Medicaid Services. *Fact sheet: Medicare and Medicaid Programs; Proposed Regulatory Provisions to Promote Program Efficiency, Transparency, and Burden Reduction* 2018; https://www.cms.gov/newsroom/fact-sheets/medicare-and-medicaid-programs-proposed-regulatory-provisions-promote-program-efficiency-0. Accessed March 4, 2019.

[58] Grabowski D. Nursing Home Certificate-Of-Need Laws Should Be Repealed. *Health Affairs Blog*2017.

[59] Harrington C, Swan JH, Nyman JA, Carrillo H. The effect of certificate of need and moratoria policy on change in nursing home beds in the United States. *Med. Care.* Jun 1997;35(6):574-588.

[60] Nyman JA. The Effects of Market Concentration and Excess Demand on the Price of Nursing Home Care. *Journal of Industrial Economics.* 1994;42(2):193-204.

[61] Grabowski DC, Angelelli JJ. The relationship of Medicaid payment rates, bed constraint policies, and risk-adjusted pressure ulcers. *Health Serv. Res.* Aug 2004;39(4 Pt 1):793-812.

[62] Rahman M, Galarraga O, Zinn JS, Grabowski DC, Mor V. The Impact of Certificate-of-Need Laws on Nursing Home and Home Health Care Expenditures. *Medical care research and review: MCRR.* Feb 2016;73(1):85-105.

[63] Zimmerman S, Bowers BJ, Cohen LW, Grabowski DC, Horn SD, Kemper P. New Evidence on the Green House Model of Nursing Home Care: Synthesis of Findings and Implications for Policy, Practice, and Research. *Health Serv. Res.* Feb 2016;51 Suppl 1:475-496.

[64] Lewis RJ. SNFs need to 'tough it out' for the first part of 2005. *Long Term Living.* 2005;54:62-64.

[65] Norton EC. Long-Term Care. In: Culyer AJ, Newhouse JP, eds. *Handbook of health Economics*. Amsterdam: Elsevier Science, North-Holland.; 2000:955-994.

[66] Chou SY. Asymmetric information, ownership and quality of care: an empirical analysis of nursing homes. *J. Health Econ.* Mar 2002;21(2):293-311.

[67] McGarry BE, Grabowski DC. Helping Patients Make More Informed Postacute Care Choices. *Health Affairs Blog* 2017.

[68] Feng Z, Katz PR, Intrator O, Karuza J, Mor V. Physician and nurse staffing in nursing homes: The role and limitations of the Online Survey Certification and Reporting (OSCAR) system. *J Am Med Dir Assoc.* Jan-Feb 2005;6(1):27-33.

[69] Harrington C, Zimmerman D, Karon SL, Robinson J, Beutel P. Nursing home staffing and its relationship to deficiencies. *J Gerontol B Psychol Sci Soc Sci.* Sep 2000;55(5):S278-287.

[70] Kash BA, Hawes C, Phillips CD. Comparing staffing levels in the Online Survey Certification and Reporting (OSCAR) system with the Medicaid Cost Report data: are differences systematic? *Gerontologist.* Aug 2007;47(4):480-489.

[71] Straker JK. *Reliability of OSCAR Occupancy, Census and Staff Data: A Comparison with the Ohio Department of Health Annual Survey of Long-Term Care Facilities.* Oxford, OH: Scripps Gerontology Center, Technical Report 3-01; 1999. Report No.: Technical Report 3-01.

[72] Centers for Medicare and Medicaid Services. *Electronic Staffing Data Submission Payroll-Based Journal: Long-Term Care Facility Manual*2015.

[73] Rau J, Lucas E. Medicare Slashes Star Ratings for Staffing at 1 in 11 Nursing Homes. *New York Times*2018.

[74] Wyden R. 2018; https://www.finance.senate.gov/imo/media/doc/081418% 20SNF%20Staffing%20Quality%20Letter.pdf.

[75] U.S. Office of Inspector General. *CMS Oversight of Nursing Facility Staffing Levels.* 2018; https://oig.hhs.gov/reports-and-publications/workplan/summary/wp-summary-0000319.asp. Accessed November 7, 2018.

[76] Werner RM, Konetzka RT, Polsky D. Changes in Consumer Demand Following Public Reporting of Summary Quality Ratings: An Evaluation in Nursing Homes. *Health Serv. Res.* Jun 2016;51 Suppl 2:1291-1309.

[77] Konetzka RT, Perraillon MC. Use Of Nursing Home Compare Website Appears Limited By Lack Of Awareness And Initial Mistrust Of The Data. *Health Aff. (Millwood).* Apr 2016;35(4):706-713.

[78] Castle NG. The Nursing Home Compare report card: consumers' use and understanding. *Journal of aging & social policy.* Apr-Jun 2009;21(2):187-208.

[79] Medicare Payment Advisory Commission. *Chapter 5: Encouraging Medicare beneficiaries to use higher quality post-acute care providers.* Washington, DC: Report to the Congress: Medicare and the Health Care Delivery System.; June 2018.

Prepared Statement of Hon. Chuck Grassley, a U.S. Senator from Iowa

Good morning. I want to welcome everyone to our hearing on an extremely important topic, elder abuse, and thank our witnesses for joining us today.

Elder abuse—and nursing home abuse in particular—has been a topic of ongoing concern to me for the last 2 decades. As the former chairman of the Senate Aging Committee, for example, I conducted oversight of the nursing home inspection process and convened hearings focused on enhancing standards and compliance across the nursing home industry.

More recently, I sponsored the Elder Abuse Prevention and Prosecution Act, a new Federal law that calls for training of elder abuse investigators, collection of data on elder abuse, and collaboration among Federal officials tasked with combating seniors' exploitation. Its enactment was a top priority for me as Judiciary chairman in the 115th Congress.

But Congress's work in this area isn't done. Hardly a week goes by without seeing something about nursing home abuse or neglect in the national news. Every family has a loved one—a mother, a father, or a grandparent—who may someday need nursing home care. That makes this a topic of enormous concern to every American.

And today, two such Americans are here with us to share their heartbreaking experiences. They are both the daughters of former nursing home residents who were victims of abuse or neglect. First, we'll hear from a constituent and friend of mine, Pat Blank, whose mother Virginia died in an Iowa nursing home due to horrific neglect. This facility was fined for the mistreatment of Virginia as well as another Iowan, Darlene Weaver. Second, I want to welcome Maya Fischer, whose 87-year-old mother, an Alzheimer's patient, was brutally raped by a nursing aide. In each of these cases, the victim's trust was betrayed by the very individuals who were en- trusted to care for and protect them.

Sadly, these are not isolated cases. They could happen to anyone. According to the Inspector General, a whopping one-third of nursing home residents experienced harm while under the care of their federally funded facilities. And in more than half of these cases, the harm was preventable.

Two years ago, the Inspector General also issued an alert, warning the public about deficiencies cited at nursing homes in 33 States. A significant percentage of these cases involved sexual abuse, substandard care, and neglect.

It is our job to protect America's most vulnerable citizens, and to prevent them from becoming victims. Many, like the elderly mothers of Maya Fischer and Pat Blank, cannot speak for themselves. Some rely on wheelchairs and walkers just to get up from their beds. Others have mental or cognitive disabilities that prevent them from communicating wrongdoing. We depend on nursing homes to render the skilled nursing care that many of our loved ones cannot provide on their own.

As chairman of the Senate Finance Committee, I'll continue to make it a top priority to ensure our most vulnerable citizens have access to quality long-term care in an environment free from abuse and neglect. I intend for today's hearing to shed light on the systemic issues that allow substandard care and abuse in America's nursing home industry and to help lead the way to reforms.

I hope to hear from our expert witnesses, for example, about why some nursing home abuse and neglect cases never get reported to law enforcement, as required by law. I hope to hear that we've fixed the weaknesses in the five-star rating system, and that we've cracked down on social media abuse. Every American listening today can be sure I will continue shining the public spotlight on this issue for as long as it takes to fix these problems. It's my hope that the oversight work of this committee will prevent elder abuse from claiming more victims, so that we won't need to call more witnesses to testify about the horrible abuse their mom or dad experienced in a nursing home. Thank you all for joining us. I look forward to your testimony.

Prepared Statement of Keesha Mitchell, Director, Medicaid Fraud Control Unit, Office of the Ohio Attorney General

Introduction

Mr. Chairman and Members of the Committee, thank you for the opportunity to appear before you today to discuss the role of the state Medicaid Fraud Control Units ("MFCUs") in investigating and prosecuting patient abuse and neglect in nursing homes. I am Keesha Mitchell, Director of the Medicaid Fraud Control Unit in Ohio Attorney General Dave Yost's Office.

The Medicare-Medicaid Anti-Fraud and Abuse Amendments enacted by Congress in the 1970s established the state Medicaid Fraud Control Unit Program, and provided the states with incentive funding to investigate and prosecute (1) Medicaid provider fraud, (2) fraud in the administration of the Medicaid program, and (3) abuse, neglect, and misappropriation involving the residents of health care facilities. Currently forty-nine states, the District of Columbia, the U.S. Virgin Islands, and Puerto Rico have MFCUs. MFCUs are usually located in the state Attorney General's office, although some units are located in other state agencies with law enforcement responsibilities, such as the state police or the state Bureau of Investigation. While we all operate under unique state jurisdictional statutes, the MFCU model embraces the use of a "strike force" team of investigators, prosecutors, fraud analysts, and nurses.

When Congress created the MFCUs, it did so not only because of the evidence of massive fraud in the Medicaid program, but also because of the horrendous tales of nursing home abuse and neglect. The MFCUs are the only law enforcement agencies in the country that are specifically charged with investigating and prosecuting abuse and neglect of residents in nursing homes. By way of example, I offer:

Whetstone Gardens and Care Center

An Ohio grand jury recently returned indictments against seven current and former employees and contractors of Whetstone Gardens and Care Center, a nursing facility located in Columbus. The defendants are charged with Involuntary Manslaughter, Gross Patient Neglect; Patient Neglect; Tampering with Evidence; and Forgery. Through the use of a covert video surveillance camera, we were able to establish that facility employees failed to provide required care and falsified patient medical records to make it appear as though the care had been provided. Our investigation also established that a facility resident died from infected skin wounds because facility employees failed to take appropriate action that would have saved his life. This investigation is on-going, and we've received more than thirty-five additional complaints regarding care in this facility since this story aired.

Hilty Mennonite Community Nursing Home

In another case, three employees of Hilty Mennonite Community Nursing Home pled or were found guilty of one count each of Forgery and Gross Patient Neglect. The defendants were employed at Hilty Mennonite Community Nursing Home on the night of January 7, 2018, when a female resident of the facility wandered outside the facility in subzero temperatures, and died of hypothermia. Despite the fact that the resident was wearing a WanderGuard device, which was designed to alert staff when she travelled past sensors placed throughout the facility, and exited the facility through a door with an alarm sensor, the resident was not discovered missing for more than eight hours, when the morning staff was preparing residents for breakfast. The defendants, who were supposed to be caring for the resident during the nighttime hours, and documented that they checked on the resident every two hours throughout the night, admitted that they never even looked in the resident's room to see if she was there.

As you may know, Medicaid is the primary payer source for most certified nursing facility residents, with more than six in ten residents (about 832,000 people) covered by Medicaid as their primary payer in 2016. In the last ten years, the Ohio MFCU has processed nearly 3,300 complaints of abuse, neglect, and misappropriation, and posted 241 criminal convictions resulting from those complaints. Under the best of circumstances, these are challenging cases, and we are tasked with the responsibility to speak for those who are often unable to speak for themselves. While this is extremely rewarding work, our efforts are hampered by a number of factors.

Surveys

While we accept complaints from any and all sources, the majority of our complaints originate with our state survey agency, the Ohio Department of Health ("ODH"), and take the form of either surveys or Self-Reported Incidents. The survey agency conducts both annual and complaint surveys which, as the name would imply, are initiated in response to specific complaints. In either case, the surveyors do not conduct investigations, per se; they make determinations regarding violations based on records, on-site interviews, and on-site observations. They rarely interview staff members not present during their visit, even if they were involved in the incident. They base their citations on what they see, what they are told, and what they review. This can be problematic for various reasons. As we have confirmed in numerous investigations, facility staff are often not truthful with surveyors, the administration encourages falsification of information, and facility administrator's ramp up staffing during the survey to give the appearance of readily available staff.

There is a real need for a prompt referral to state MFCUs if the surveyors see evidence of falsification of records or have real concerns regarding neglect or abuse of residents in the facility. Currently we see a survey report after it is complete and after ODH has exited the facility. The survey and the facility response to their citations are available to the public but only several weeks after the survey. We would like to see better collaboration between the state survey agency and MFCUs throughout the country.

Underreporting

The survey agency also responds to Self-Reported Incidents which originate with the facilities themselves. As in many states, we experience problems with prompt and accurate reporting. The law requires that care facility operators promptly report to the survey agency and law enforcement any reasonable suspicion of a crime committed against a resident of the facility, including patient abuse, patient neglect, and misappropriation. Unfortunately, the manner in which the incident is reported by the facility often minimizes the seriousness of the offense or omits relevant facts which might otherwise cause a referral to the MFCU. By way of example, I offer:

Example #1

In one example, a facility reported only that a female resident had fallen from a wheelchair during transportation in a facility van. The report indicated that the driver of the van had swerved to miss a deer in the road, and that the "effect on the resident" was that the resident said: "My behind hurts." Our investigation revealed that the resident was airlifted to a hospital with two fractures in her neck, one fracture in her lower back, and fractures of both knees. The resident died days later as a result of her injuries. During a subsequent interview with the Nursing Home Administrator, she admitted that she was intentionally vague in reporting the incident, at the direction of the facility's attorney.

Example #2

In another example, a facility reported an "injury of unknown origin" resulting from an "Incident [which] occurred outside of building." Our investigation revealed that the facility resident had eloped and drowned in a pond on the facility grounds.

In both of these examples, the facilities knew exactly what had happened to their residents, but omitted relevant facts from their reports. We can only speculate as to why certain facilities under-report, but it seems reasonable to assume that they are attempting to avoid a criminal investigation by law enforcement, a complaint survey, or a potential civil action.

It is also worthy of note that as part of a MFCU's performance standards, we are required to report convictions to HHS-OIG for their provider exclusion list. Not all prosecutorial agencies are required to do this, which magnifies the importance of involving MFCUs in the prosecution of nursing home employees. While Medicaid funded care facility providers in Ohio are prohibited from employing excluded individuals, all care facilities, regardless of how they are funded, are precluded from employing individuals identified on Ohio's Nurse Aide Registry and individuals with disqualifying criminal convictions. We would recommend that all care facilities also be prohibited from employing individuals identified in the following:

1) The Abuser Registry, Ohio Department of Developmental Disabilities
2) The Sex Offender and Child Victim Offender Database, Ohio Attorney General
3) The U.S. General Services Administration System for Award Management Database
4) The Database of Incarcerated and Supervised Offenders, Ohio Department of Rehabilitation and Corrections.

Reimbursement

Finally, the "elephant" in the room is staffing; both the quantity and quality of staff and the way we reimburse nursing homes. Current funding models often incentivize facilities to maximize profit by increasing the relative complexity of care required by their patients which in turn increases their reimbursement. The policy underlying this model anticipates that the nursing home will then have to increase staff to meet the needs of their patient population. However, there still remains a financial incentive to decrease direct care staffing levels to lower operating costs, regardless of the acuity level of a nursing home's patient population. While it is important to employ quality staff over a set number of staff, our investigations have shown time and again that quality staff will leave an understaffed facility due to an inability to provide required care and fear for their licensure. Additionally many problematic facilities employ temporary agency staff who are not familiar with the patient's ongoing care. Let us be plain: If we want adequate staffing and quality of care, we are going to have to pay for it. This will likely mean more funding for long term care, and an overhaul of the Medicare and Medicaid reimbursement models.

Autumn Healthcare of Zanesville

Autumn Healthcare of Zanesville, Inc. and Steve Hitchens were convicted on January 9, 2017. The corporation was convicted of one count of Engaging in a Pattern of Corrupt Activity; one count of Medicaid Fraud; two counts of Telecommunications Fraud; two counts of Tampering with Evidence; nine counts of Forgery; and one count of Theft. Hitchens, the owner, was convicted of one count of Tampering with Evidence; one count of Tampering with Records; and one count of Forgery.

This investigation started with covert video surveillance cameras placed in residents' rooms, followed by a detailed comparison of the care evidenced on the video with the care memorialized in the residents' medical records. The investigation found that Autumn Health Care of Zanesville, through its owner and many of its managers, habitually altered official documents to falsely make it appear that it was regularly providing adequate care for its residents. Although the records reflected a high level of care, the investigation found that several patients missed treatments and were given therapy that they didn't need in order for the company to make more money. The corporation was ordered to pay restitution totaling $167,640.10, and Hitchens was sentenced to three years community control and 100 hours of community service.

Collaboration with Federal Law Enforcement Partners

State MFCUs also actively participate with our federal counterparts on Elder Justice Task Forces. We believe through joint investigations, sharing information, and regular meetings, we strengthen our efforts nationally to protect the most vulnerable of our population who reside in our nursing homes and other care facilities. These task forces allow us to leverage the resources and expertise of the states and the federal government, particularly where we see chain-wide systemic patient neglect. Working together has allowed us to focus our efforts nationally on nursing home chains for failure to provide services in violation of certain essential requirements that the state Medicaid programs expect skilled nursing facilities to meet. Examples of these failures have included an insufficient number of skilled nurses to adequately care for residents, inadequate catheter care for residents, and inappropriate care to prevent pressure ulcers or falls.

Conclusion

State Medicaid Fraud Control Units play a vital role in protecting our nation's nursing home residents. In order to effectively investigate incidents of patient abuse and neglect we must ensure timely referrals from State Surveyors to their MFCUs when they suspect abuse, neglect or falsification of records. We must also require nursing homes to properly report and detail incidents of patient abuse, neglect and misappropriation or face meaningful penalties. It is crucial that state and federal agencies coordinate their investigations to properly leverage our resources and expertise. Finally, states must address the real outcomes of not properly incentivizing nursing homes to adequately staff their facilities to achieve quality care.

Prepared Statement of Hon. Ron Wyden, a U.S. Senator from Oregon

Generations ago, with Social Security, America closed the door to the era of impoverished seniors living out their last years in almshouses and poor farms. Decades later, with Medicare and Medicaid, it guaranteed that seniors would have access to health care. To continue that hard work, one of the challenges this country faces today is ensuring that seniors in nursing homes are safe and well cared-for. Our best nursing homes meet a high standard of care, but tragically, not all do.

Seniors in nursing homes are among the people most vulnerable to the life-threatening consequences of abuse and neglect. Across this country, that vulnerability is being exploited in unimaginably cruel ways in nursing homes that are unsafe, under-staffed, and uninterested in providing even the most basic, humane level of care. This morning the committee will hear stories of seniors being sexually and physically abused, starved, dehydrated, and left for dead. These stories, unfortunately, are too common around the United States.

Last November, I released a report, "Sheltering in Danger," examining the tragic deaths of 12 residents at a nursing home in Florida when nursing home managers and staff failed to evacuate them after Hurricane Irma.

Just this week, a news report from Ashland, OR told the story of an elderly nursing home resident who was found with mold, ulcers, and infections after she went a week without bathing. A nurse was allegedly stealing her pain medication, and, even after a trip to the hospital to treat her infections, the person who was charged with her care continued to steal her medicine until she died 17 days later. So as the committee examines these issues today, there are a few specific matters that need investigation.

First, the Trump budget is coming out next week, and it's a safe wager it'll include another draconian attack on Medicaid. That program helps cover costs for two out of three seniors in nursing homes. I'll fight this cut with everything I've got, because it would turn back the clock on the effort to improve care, and it would inevitably lead to more nursing homes closing their doors.

Second, at a time when the Federal Government ought to be raising standards and rooting out harmful, substandard care and those who provide it, the Trump administration and CMS are going in the wrong direction.

The basic regulations on nursing homes date back 3 decades. Since then, a 2003 study found 20,000 complaints of exploitation, abuse, and neglect. Reports from the

National Center on Elder Abuse and a State agency in New York found that only a slim fraction of cases get reported. A 2014 report from the HHS Inspector General found that a third of Medicare beneficiaries were harmed within a matter of a few weeks of entering a nursing home.

That's why there was an effort in 2016 to update the basic rules for nursing homes. The update required nursing homes to develop plans to prevent infections. It mandated concrete policies and procedures to prevent abuse, neglect, mistreatment, and theft. It said that nursing homes shouldn't pump residents full of psychotropic drugs unless they are necessary to treat a specific, diagnosed condition.

It banned the practice of forcing seniors to sign away their legal rights with prearbitration contracts as a precondition of admission to a nursing home. It established tougher financial penalties for nursing homes that harm residents or fail to meet safety standards.

Come 2017, under the banner of deregulation, the Trump administration decided to roll back those changes and more. Other examples, related to recommendations in my "Sheltering in Danger" report: I'm worried Trump rollbacks will mean nursing homes are underprepared for natural disasters in the future. And there is still no Federal rule mandating that nursing homes have emergency power generators. So whenever I hear the Trump administration throw around the phrase "patients over paperwork," I think of how they're letting criminals and substandard caregivers off the hook when they hurt vulnerable seniors.

Next, it's time for a hard look at the way the Federal Government rates nursing homes. At a hearing in the Aging Committee years ago, I pointed out that it was easier to get accurate reviews of washing machines than of nursing homes.

After that hearing, the Centers for Medicare and Medicaid Services created a new rating system that should have been a powerful tool for seniors and their families to sort out the good homes from the bad. It hasn't turned out that way.

Too much of the information that goes into the rating system is self-reported. It is not a reliable indicator of quality. For instance, one of the witnesses coming before the committee today will tell us about how her mother passed away after suffering extreme neglect at a facility in Iowa. That home got top marks for quality: a five-star rating. This hearing must accelerate fixes to this system.

I'll close with this final point. I know in Oregon there are homes and labor unions working together to set higher standards and raise the quality of care. As a young man, I was the co-director of the Oregon Gray Panthers, an advocacy group for older Oregonians. I also served on the State Board of Examiners of Nursing Home Administrators, even though the industry got State legislators to vote to keep me off it.

I spent a lot of time visiting people who lived in sordid conditions, who needed a lot of help just to get through the day, who were victims of scams and abuse. For me, those memories still serve as a reminder that the job of working to ensure sen- iors have a dignified retirement is never complete.

So I'm pleased the chairman has brought this hearing together. There's a lot to be done on this issue, and I look forward to working with both sides of the com- mittee on it.

COMMUNICATIONS

AARP
Washington, DC

March 5, 2019

The Honorable Chuck Grassley
Chairman
Committee on Finance
United States Senate
Washington, DC

The Honorable Ron Wyden
Ranking Member
Committee on Finance
United States Senate
Washington, DC

Dear Chairman Grassley and Ranking Member Wyden:

AARP appreciates the attention you are giving to the quality of care and quality of life of our country's nursing home residents, the federal standards for nursing homes, and their enforcement. Thank you for holding the March 6, 2019 hearing entitled, "Not Forgotten: Protecting Americans from Abuse and Neglect in Nursing Homes." AARP, with its nearly 38 million members in all 50 States, the District of Columbia, and the U.S. territories, is a nonpartisan, nonprofit, nationwide organization that helps people turn their goals and dreams into real possibilities, strengthens communities and fights for the issues that matter most to families such as healthcare, employment and income security, retirement planning, affordable utilities and protection from financial abuse.

AARP has been deeply concerned over recent reports and evidence of dangerous conditions in nursing homes across the country. Ensuring the health, well-being, quality of care and quality of life, and safety of nursing home residents is critically needed.

AARP is concerned with regulatory and administrative actions taken by the Centers for Medicare & Medicaid Services (CMS) over the last couple of years, as well as potential future actions under consideration, that could weaken the quality of care and quality of life for our country's approximately 1.3 million nursing home residents.

In 2016, CMS issued a final regulation that provided the first comprehensive review and update for the Medicare and Medicaid conditions of participation for skilled nursing facilities (SNFs) and nursing facilities (NFs) (collectively "nursing homes") since 1991.

CMS received thousands of comments, including from AARP. The final rule provides additional emphasis on person-centered care and addressing residents' individual needs and preferences; improved protections against abuse, neglect and exploitation; better planning for resident care; and stronger protections against evictions, among other benefits. Recognizing the comprehensive nature of the regulatory revisions, CMS provided for implementation of the requirements in three phases over three years.

While many nursing homes provide quality care, media coverage and investigations continue to document the devastating cases of potential abuse, neglect, poor care, and even death that are too common in nursing homes. The Department of Health and Human Services Office of Inspector General (OIG) issued an August 2017 early alert finding that "CMS has inadequate procedures to ensure that incidents of potential abuse or neglect of Medicare beneficiaries residing in SNFs are identified and reported"[36] to law enforcement in accordance with applicable requirements. The OIG also found that CMS was not using available tools to enforce the requirement that skilled nursing facilities report potential abuse to law enforcement. In a September 2017 data brief, the HHS OIG also found that overall, "states received one-third more nursing home complaints in 2015 than in 2011" and that states "prioritized more than half of nursing home complaints into the most serious categories – "immediate jeopardy" and "high priority."[37]

Unfortunately, these findings coincide with a disturbing trend of CMS actions to undermine federal oversight and enforcement of nursing home quality standards. In November 2017, CMS established an 18-month moratorium on imposing certain enforcement remedies – specifically civil money penalties (CMPs), discretionary denials of payment for new admissions, and discretionary termination – for specific Phase 2 requirements under the nursing home conditions of participation final rule, such as baseline care plans and behavioral health services.[38] CMS would instead focus on provider and nursing home surveyor education during this time. Regulations need effective enforcement in order to be meaningful, and this delay in enforcement amounts to an additional delay in implementation. CMS has also issued guidance that reduces the amount of CMPs, such as by making *per instance* CMPs the default, rather than the higher *per day* CMPs, for noncompliance that existed before a nursing home survey.[39]

---

[36] https://oig.hhs.gov/oas/reports/region1/11700504.pdf.

[37] https://oig.hhs.gov/oei/reports/oei-01-16-00330.pdf.

[38] https://www.cms.gov/Medicare/Provider-Enrollment-and-Certification/SurveyCertificationGenInfo/Downloads/Survey-and-Cert-Letter-18-04.pdf.

[39] https://www.cms.gov/Medicare/Provider-Enrollment-and-Certification/SurveyCertificationGenInfo/Downloads/Survey-and-Cert-Letter-17-37.pdf.

In the case of making per instance CMPs the default for noncompliance before a nursing home survey, AARP notes that such a change conflicts with the enforcement provisions in the Social Security Act that provide for the imposition of CMPs for "each day of noncompliance." Given this, AARP has asked CMS to withdraw the directive making this change and to notify its Regional Offices as well as State Survey Agency Directors that they again have discretion to impose per-day CMPs for past noncompliance as the Nursing Home Reform Act and its implementing regulations provide.[40] Both of these examples weaken federal enforcement of federal nursing home quality standards.

Any weakening of the federal nursing home regulations will negatively impact nursing home residents. For example, a state may defer enforcement of nursing home violations to the federal government, whereby the state assesses the greater of the federal or state penalty, but not both. Thus, if a federal penalty is greater and then federal penalties and enforcement are weakened, this lowers the bar, further jeopardizing the health and safety of residents, including in states that may already have more nursing homes providing poor quality care. AARP state offices in a number of states, including Texas, Minnesota, Louisiana, Oklahoma, Arizona, Georgia, Illinois, Kansas, and South Dakota have also taken action to improve the quality, safety, rights, and protections for nursing home residents and their families or improve enforcement of standards for nursing homes.

CMS also issued a proposed rule in 2017 to reverse the existing prohibition on the use of pre-dispute, binding arbitration agreements in nursing home admission contracts.

AARP filed comments on this proposed rule and joined other organizations and individuals in opposing this proposed rule. Pre-dispute binding arbitration is not appropriate where abuse and neglect are at issue. As outlined in our comments, we were alarmed that the provisions of the proposed rule would very likely have dangerous and harmful impacts on nursing home residents, as well as their families, and place them at even greater risk than they faced before CMS addressed this issue its 2016 nursing home conditions of participation final rule. AARP has urged CMS to retain the prohibition on pre-dispute arbitration provisions in long-term care facility admission contracts. In the alternative, AARP urged CMS to simply rescind the sections of the final regulation entitled "Reform of Requirements for Long-Term Care Facilities" (81 FR 68688) which addressed arbitration, rather than adopting the proposed rule. If this proposed rule was finalized as proposed, it would remove an enforcement tool that nursing home residents and their families can use to hold nursing homes accountable for providing quality care. The Office of Management and Budget (OMB) is currently reviewing this final rule.

OMB is also currently reviewing a proposed rule that CMS is planning to issue to "reform the requirements that long-term care facilities must meet to participate in the

---

[40] https://www.aarp.org/content/dam/aarp/politics/advocacy/2019/01/aarp-letter-to-cms-about-cmp- changes-final-10219.pdf.

Medicare and Medicaid programs, that CMS has identified as unnecessary, obsolete, or excessively burdensome on facilities."[41] While the upcoming proposed rule has not yet been released, the description of the proposed rule raises questions and concerns about whether it will reverse or undo important protections and standards for current and future nursing home residents, including those more recently added to the current nursing home conditions of participation. In November 2017, AARP joined other organizations and individuals in strongly opposing current and proposed efforts to revise the nursing home requirements of participation and delay their implementation. We also requested that CMS retain the regulations as issued in October 2016 and implement and enforce these requirements according to the originally outlined schedule. We are pleased that since then you and other leaders of Congressional committees of jurisdiction have raised questions and/or concerns regarding CMS' oversight and enforcement of nursing home quality of care standards and protection of nursing home residents.

CMS should maintain strong federal nursing home quality standards, oversight, and enforcement to protect nursing home residents' rights, health, safety, and well-being. We appreciate the Committee's efforts to protect nursing home residents from abuse and neglect, including this hearing and any future investigative or other work. We look forward to working with you and your staff on these critical issues for our nation's nursing home residents and their families.

Sincerely,
David Certner
Legislative Counsel & Legislative Policy Director
Government Affairs

ALTARUM
Washington, DC

Statement Submitted by Anne Montgomery, Program to Improve Eldercare, Altarum

Use of Data and Enhanced, Coordinated Monitoring and Enforcement to Decrease Abuse and Neglect in Nursing Homes

Thirty-two years after passage of the Omnibus Budget Reconciliation Act of 1987 (COBRA 1987), the quality of care in many of our nation's skilled facilities (SNFs) and nursing facilities (NFs) remains extremely uneven.

[41] https://www.reginfo.gov/public/do/eAgendaViewRule?pubId=201810&RIN=0938-AT36.

Changing this longstanding pattern requires a more comprehensive strategy that includes close monitoring and full use of available data about organizations and individuals who own and/or exercise significant influence over the finances and operations of individual nursing homes and chains. Information about owners and "additional disclosable parties" is available in the Provider Enrollment, Chain, and Ownership System (PECOS). In addition, safety and quality of care for frail elders with complex medical conditions and ongoing need for daily assistance and supports demands robust, well-trained direct care staffing. Oversight must include closer attention to whether staffing levels and types of staff actually meet expert recommendations issued by CMS 18 years ago (U.S. Centers for Medicare and Medicaid Services, Abt Associates Inc. Appropriateness of Minimum Nurse Staffing Ratios in Nursing Homes. Report to Congress, 2001). Reliable, auditable staffing data are available in the Payroll-Based Journal (PBJ) database administered by the Centers for Medicare and Medicaid Services (CMS). The PBJ data, together with information from state oversight of SNFs and NFs on their compliance with federal safety and quality standards from the survey and certification inspection program, quality data derived from resident assessments and complaint investigations submitted by residents, provide state and federal officials with powerful tools which they can use to profile and carefully analyze—on an ongoing basis—which facilities and chains are showing signs of poor performance that threatens residents' safety.

Homes that demonstrate, through these data, that they are unwilling and/or unable to address core problems of compliance with routine safety and quality standards and understaffing can be dealt with more forthrightly, through stepped-up oversight and coordinated enforcement by CMS, the HHS Office of Inspector General (HHS–OIG) and the Department of Justice (DOJ), in partnership with Medicaid Fraud Control Units (MCFUs) and other state enforcement officials. Poor management of facilities that causes obvious safety and quality of care problems, and abuse, harm and neglect of residents, should not be allowed to continue once it is discovered. Changing this pattern may necessitate more frequent deployment of some of the tougher available remedies—provider exclusion by the HHS OIG and termination of funding by CMS, in concert with DOJ and in coordination with state law enforcement officials. Congress can also exercise closer oversight of poor-performing homes and chains through oversight hearings, investigative letters that raise concerns and request timely information from agencies, SNFs and NFs, and ongoing audits by the Government Accountability Office (GAO) and the HHS–OIG.

With regard to rationale, little could provide more compelling evidence of the significant need to improve SNF care quality than the facts that lie at the center of the Manorcare, Skyline, Hyperion, and Vanguard cases. In a recent *Washington Post* article (cited in the Background Section), residents at Manorcare suffered drug overdoses, pressure ulcers, broken bones and broken lives, even as they tried to cope with a filthy, roach-infested environment. With regard to Skyline, after the owner stopped providing funding for basic care and in some cases for staff salaries, 122 facilities were closed, which left 5,700 residents in Nebraska, Arkansas, South Dakota, Kansas, Pennsylvania, Tennessee, Massachusetts, Florida, Kentucky, and New Jersey with no organized alternatives to continue the care they required.

Such stories of substandard care illustrate a longstanding trend of poor-quality care in a significant minority of nursing homes. This was highlighted by the HHS– OIG in a February 2014 report, which found that an estimated 22 percent of Medicare beneficiaries experienced adverse events[42] during their SNF stays (HHS–OIG 2014 Report). That report, which was referenced to by Senator Grassley at the March 6th hearing, documented a pattern of common adverse events, including medication-induced delirium, exacerbation of pre-existing conditions resulting from an omission of care, and surgical site infection associated with wound care. An additional 11 percent of Medicare beneficiaries experienced temporary harm events during their SNF stays, such as pressure ulcers and falls or other trauma with injury associated with poor resident care.

Available Data and Its Use in Identifying Nursing Homes That Provide Poor Quality Care

As highlighted above, publicly available data can provide investigators and regulators seeking to take action to address poorly performing SNFs and NFs with a wealth of data to target individual nursing homes and chains that may warrant closer scrutiny. These data reside in: (1) the PECOS database; (2) the Nursing Home Compare website; (3) the PBJ database; and (4) ProPublica's "Data Store" resource.

PECOS provides data on ownership and "additional disclosable parties," and ownership data are also available on Nursing Home Compare. The 2008 "Nursing Home Transparency and Improvement Act" championed by Senator Grassley and many others requires that owners and "additional disclosable parties"—"any person or entity who exercises operational, management or financial control over a facility" or "leases or subleases real property to the facility"—to report their identities. It also requires reporting of the organizational structures of various types of entities that are linked to facilities, including the members and managers of LLCs.

CMS' Nursing Home Compare website has summary data from annual inspections of nursing homes that are funded by Medicare or Medicaid and monitored by the survey and certification program. Nursing Home Compare can be searched by facility and by state and contains key quality data about the rate of pressure ulcers, falls, antipsychotics, reported pain and other metrics. The website also contains data about inspection results

[42] The HHS–OIG Report defines "adverse events" as harm to a resident that is the result of medical care, including failure to provide needed care. Adverse events include medical errors but they also include more general substandard care that results in resident harm, occurring in the areas of medication administration, resident care, and infections. (HHS–OIG 2014 Re- port).

and specific deficiencies that are cited during inspections, and data on staffing. These data can be used to assess whether individual homes and homes that are part of chains—including facilities that are owned, managed, or otherwise controlled under various types of contractual business arrangements— have staffing that meets the minimum standard recommended by CMS' 2001 report—4.1 hours of nursing care per resident per day.

Finally, ProPublica's datasets allow investigators to search "Statements of Deficiencies," including identifying patterns of deficiencies in nursing homes across a given state, and to search by categories of deficiencies, e.g., "falls" or "sexual abuse," to find homes with particular quality problems.

In summary, federal and state agencies responsible for regulating nursing homes and for enforcement have access to excellent information with which to hold nursing homes accountable.

Enforcement Remedies That Agencies Currently Have Available to Hold Nursing Homes Accountable

At the federal level, the primary agencies with jurisdiction over nursing homes are: (1) CMS, (2) HHS–OIG, and (3) DOJ. When data or surveys show that a nursing home has poor quality care, CMS has several remedies. The agency can deny payment for new admissions; deny additional admissions until safety and care problems are resolved; put a temporary manager in place, as occurred in the Skyline case; or terminate funding and close a facility, as in the Vanguard case. CMS may also enroll a facility in the "Special Focus Facility" program, which means that a nursing home is subjected to a survey every 6 months, and penalties for continued poor survey results increase. If these homes do not improve, they can be fined more heavily and ultimately terminated.

HHS–OIG has several remedies available as well, which include civil monetary penalties, quality Corporate Integrity Agreements (CIA) that typically extend for five years, and exclusion of providers from federal funding. The HHS–OIG has a graduated series of enforcement tools and penalties that are designed to bring a home or SNF corporation into quality compliance. For example, the HHS–OIG can levy financial stipulated penalties that are enumerated in CIAs on homes that are found to be non-compliant with the monitoring and quality improvement terms and targets featured in these agreements. Following the expiration of, and even during the pendency of a CIA, a second level of enforcement that CMS could operationalize is to require a nursing home to develop and execute specific plans of correction in areas where the SNF has experienced documented problems. If those plans of correction fail to result in measurable, improved quality within an agreed time frame, CMS could move to impose a denial of payment for new admissions (DPNA). Further, in the event that quality of care in a post-CIA SNF remains significantly problematic, CMS, working with DOJ prosecutors that focus on nursing homes providing grossly substandard care, could move to have a temporary receiver or state manager appointed to run the home. The agency could also terminate payment and close the facility. Finally, if the quality of care in multiple homes that are part of a group or chain is extremely poor, HHS–OIG, relying on the evidence developed by DOJ and state MCFU attorneys, could explore whether to exclude the entire chain from participation in federal healthcare programs.

Issues to Consider

In view of the availability of these data, which can be combined to identify poorly performing organizations and individuals who can be aggressively monitored, CMS and DOJ can take additional steps to discourage individuals and organizations from treating nursing homes as if they were merely investment opportunities for private gain. CMS' authority to terminate funding is not very frequently used; and the HHS–OIG's authority to exclude providers is also not often used. DOJ has the authority to bring cases, but doing so can take years. If, in addition, the culture of collaboration and cooperation between CMS, the HHS OIG and DOJ were strengthened to more rapidly identify the "bad apples" for increased scrutiny and possible termination and exclusion, enforcement could be better targeted and more effective. Today, too many poor performing homes are sanctioned lightly, and many continue operating at taxpayer expense for years.

Moreover, in the wake of Skyline, state regulators should strengthen their due diligence in order to probe more thoroughly into what prospective owners, operators, buyers and investors know about the care of frail elders nearing the end of their lives, the depth of their knowledge of applicable quality of care standards, and their understanding of compliance requirements.

Additional Answers and Potential Solutions: Improved Agency Coordination

Another important improvement strategy may be to set up an Interagency Coordinating Task Force among the relevant agencies at CMS, HHS–OIG, DOJ, and a representative from the state MFCUs. That Task Force would develop and guide the implementation of processes that assure integration of the tools that each agency has, so as to identify, target, and remedy poor quality care in SNFs across the spectrum. The Task Force would establish protocols and strategies for nursing homes that require intervention under particular circumstances, and results of this collaboration could be reported back to the Committee at regular intervals.

Additionally, mandatory background checks based on CMS' National Background Check Program (NBCP) should be required for all long-term care workers, administrators, and those who exercise operational, financial or management control over a facility or chain. More than half of all states have now accessed funding through the NBCP to improve, streamline and modernize their background check systems. Comprehensive checks across all states would decrease the risk of horrific crimes of sexual abuse, among others, that were discussed at the Senate Finance hearing on March 6, 2019.

The motivation and background of individuals and organizations wishing to acquire, operate and manage groups of homes and chains warrants closer scrutiny. Arguably, the chaos resulting from Skyline Healthcare's demise did not have to cascade across entire states if regulators exercised stronger due diligence as the owner rapidly acquired facilities across many states, including Kansas, Nebraska, Pennsylvania and New Jersey.

A purely transactional approach to nursing home ownership, which are home to many very frail people who are nearing the end of their lives, may put them at unnecessary risk of abuse and neglect. Keeping certain operators out of the industry in some cases may be the most prudent course. More monitoring is also critical as well as deeper analysis of available data and improved use of a variety of sanctions available to different agencies that can be used more strategically to improve the industry's overall performance and decrease the harm experienced by residents living in poor-performing homes.

Background Articles

https://www.washingtonpost.com/business/economy/opioid-overdoses-bedsores-and-broken-bones-what-happened-when-a-private-equity-firm-sought-profits-in-car-ing-for-societys-most-vulnerable/2018/11/25/09089a
4a-ed14-11e8-baac-2a674e91502b_story.html?utm_term=.7ec34c5f42a7.

https://www.keloland.com/news/investigates/company-with-history-of-financial-probl ems-puts-d-seniors-at-risk_20180816012013816/1374
257644.

https://skillednursingnews.com/2018/05/eight-former-skyline-nursing-homes-pa-sold-new-owners/.

https://www.seattletimes.com/nation-world/arkansas-regulators-want-takeover-of-2-skyline-nursing-homes/.

https://www.northjersey.com/story/news/watchdog/2018/04/16/thousandsnursing-home-patients-could-affected-fast-growing-nj-nursing-home-company-trouble-nebraska/493643002/.

https://www.kcur.org/post/state-kansas-takes-control-15-financially-troubled-private-nursing-homes.

https://www.omaha.com/livewellnebraska/chain-of-nebraska-nursing-homes-placed-in-receivership-after-missing/article_013a2693-60af-5359-b258-c99a6325e30c.html.

https://www.mcknights.com/news/skyline-payroll-issues-force-kansas-to-seek-its-largest-ever-nursing-home-takeover/.

Statement Submitted by Kathy Arends

My Mother Darlene Weaver was diagnosed with Parkinson's and the onset of dementia in 2014. She became a resident at Timely Mission Nursing Home in Buffalo Center, Iowa in July of 2015.

The decision was made as a family, including Mom, for her to go to Timely Mission. Mom knew most of the residents and staff at the facility, her Aunt was a resident there as well. Buffalo Center was her hometown, and more importantly we trusted Timely Mission Nursing Home to care for our Mother.

Shortly after admission there were medication errors. Mom had been prescribed the Exelon patch for her dementia. The instructions were clear, apply one new patch every 24 hours and remove the old patch. The new patch was to be applied in a different location to avoid skin irritation.

One evening when I went to visit, I was helping her get ready for bed when I noticed two Exelon patches on her. I brought it to the attention of the nurse that night and then called the director of nurses right away the following morning and expressed my concerns. I was reassured she would take care of the problem.

It continued to happen, sometimes Mom would have two patches on, sometimes three and at times none. Every time this happened, it affected Mom mentally and physically in a negative way. Each time I noticed the mistake, I made the nurse on duty aware and then would tell the director of nurses.

After I became upset because of the constant problem the director of nurses decided to have the nurse applying the new patch, take the old one off and put it on a separate piece of paper in hopes it would help them to remember to remove the old one. That didn't help, we still had problems.

Mom was prescribed Sinemet for her Parkinson's. It was prescribed three times a day, at specific times, on an empty stomach before meals. This medication was important to Mom, giving her the ability to walk without "freezing up" and for her to stand up from a sitting position. We had problems with this medication not being given at the prescribed times.

When the medication errors kept happening, I went to talk to a board member. He told me he didn't want to hear my complaints and walked away. I tried to talk to another board member, she told me the board didn't have anything to do with the way the nursing home was run.

I contacted the Ombudsman for Timely Mission regarding the constant problems with medication errors. I was told the nursing home had a two-hour window to administer medication. Either two hours before the prescribed time, or two hours after the prescribed time. My Mom was prescribed medication, at a specific time for a medical reason. When this medication was not given as prescribed, this also affected Mom mentally and physically.

Mom complained to me about a CNA that would refuse to help her when she needed it. This CNA would be verbally disrespectful to Mom and it upset her. I contacted the administrator and the director of nurses, informed them of the problem and told them this CNA was not allowed to work with Mom, nor be in her room. The administration ignored what I had asked and still allowed her in Mom's room.

I kept complaining about the CNA and the medication problems to the director of nurses. She told me I was welcome to take Mom to another facility. Other family members complained about problems with their loved ones and they were told the same, they were welcome to move their loved one to another facility. Some families lived in fear and wouldn't complain about problems they were having. The CNA eventually quit and went to work in Minnesota.

There were numerous times I went to visit Mom and she had green discharge from her eyes running down her face. When I had the nurse come in, they told me they hadn't noticed the discharge. It took the facility days to get Mom on antibiotic drops for her eyes.

Mom's hygiene was at times not good. Some of the staff wouldn't clean her false teeth and I would find them covered with black. Her glasses were always dirty, her toenails never got cut unless I did them and the food Mom always complained about.

I was told Mom couldn't have candy or homemade baked items in her room because of ants. My Mom loved to snack! Dehydration and UTIs were a problem and when I complained about Mom not getting enough fluids and asked the nursing home staff to offer them to Mom, they told me if the pitcher in her room was filled with water that is all they were required to do.

Mom started getting upset in the evenings wondering if the CNA that had refused to help her and had been mean to her was working. I asked some of the other staff and they told me the CNA had been fired from her job in Minnesota and came back to work at Timely Mission, working the overnight shift. I again made calls to the administrator, the director of nurses and I talked to the MDS coordinator and informed all of them this CNA was not allowed to work with Mom, and I told them how upset Mom was at night worrying about it and that she would cry.

In April of 2017 I received a phone call from the nursing home to tell me Mom had a fall. I asked if she was hurt and they told me she hurt her left shoulder, but she had full range of motion and they were certain she was fine. An hour later they called to tell me they were going to take Mom to the clinic to have it x-rayed just to be sure it was ok. They called to tell me it showed no injuries.

Mom was in a great deal of pain that evening when I went to see her. I asked the nurse if she had been given Tylenol and she told me no, that if Mom wanted Tylenol, she had to ask for it. When I helped Mom get ready for bed, I found a duplicate Exelon patch on her left shoulder, the shoulder she had injured. She had two patches on again.

She needed a lot of assistance to get into bed, to go to the rest room and to get out of bed that night when I was there. I told the nurse when I was leaving that Mom needed help with everything and asked her to please make sure Mom got help.

In the morning I called the director of nurses about the duplicate patches and told her Mom needed help with everything because she was in so much pain from her fall. I asked her to have a call button necklace put on and she agreed to do it. Every time I went over to see Mom, she didn't have the call button on. The nurses kept taking it away from Mom because they said they didn't have time to answer it every time she pushed it—she still wasn't getting assistance like she needed.

The pain in Mom's shoulder continued, she wasn't eating well, and she was in bed a lot. When I expressed my concern about her not eating and the fact that she was losing weight, the MDS coordinator told me she hadn't lost weight. Two days later the social worker called me to tell me they were going to increase Mom's supplement drink because she had lost a significant amount of weight.

Mom developed a cough the middle of May and by the end of May it had gotten worse. I told the director of nurses Mom needed antibiotics because she sounded terrible. She did nothing. I called Mom's doctor numerous times about the cough, each time I was told the director of nurses told the doctor that Mom didn't have a fever, her lungs were clear, and Mom said she felt fine.

June 12, 2017, the nursing home called to tell me Mom had another fall. Again, I asked if she was hurt and the nurse told me she was okay and was resting in bed. I got another call shortly after that and they told me they were taking her to the clinic just to make sure her shoulder was okay. I got in my car and went to the clinic they took her to; I didn't tell anyone I was going to the clinic.

I walked through the clinic door and my Mom was sitting in a wheelchair holding her left arm with her right hand, shaking and crying, sitting there all alone. As I sat there with her, I noticed her left foot was on the floor and not on the wheelchair foot rest. I asked her to pick up her foot and put it up so when I pushed her back to see the doctor, I wouldn't hurt it. She looked at me sobbing and told me she couldn't move her leg, it hurt too bad.

The doctor at the clinic knew they would not be unable to get Mom out of the wheelchair because of her injuries. He called the ambulance to have her transported to the hospital. When they moved her from the wheelchair to the stretcher, her pain was excruciating.

In the emergency room the doctor came to tell us the result of Mom's x-rays. Broken left shoulder, broken left upper arm where a massive black and blue mark was that went all the way around her arm, broken left hip and other injuries. My Mom looked at me with tears running down her face and said, "No more, Kathy. . . . I can't do it any more."

She was admitted to Hospice the next day and passed away June 18, 2017 from her injuries and pneumonia in both lungs. The hospice doctor told me he wanted the medical examiner to come in when Mom passed away. When the medical examiner was done examining Mom's body, she ordered a complete autopsy. The results of the autopsy were devastating. I immediately filed a complaint with the Department of Inspections and Appeals, as I had done prior about other complaints.

A 63-page report dated 09/01/2017 found the nursing home guilty of many violations. Sadly, some of the violations in this chapter were repetitive ones that occurred starting in January 2007. Timely Mission Nursing Home had approximately 65 violations after the Department of Inspections and Appeals completed investigations during this time period.

Had Timely Mission Nursing Home been held accountable years ago, maybe lives could have been saved, maybe my Mom's life could have been saved, maybe Virginia Olthoff could have been saved.

Timely Mission Nursing Home failed my Mom, the Department of Inspections and Appeals failed her, the broken elderly care system failed my Mom. She lost her life while the individuals that should have been held accountable, went on with their lives, getting jobs in different states working with the elderly.

Darlene Weaver, a mother of three, a grandmother of six and a great grandmother of eight, we will never forget her.

Kathy Arends

Letter Submitted by Jeanette Armstrong

U.S. Senate
Committee on Finance
Dirksen Senate Office Bldg.
Washington, DC

RE: Hearing "Not Forgotten: Protecting Americans From Abuse and Neglect in Nursing Homes," held on March 6, 2019

March 13, 2019
Subject: Experiences with overmedication of my husband.

Many years ago, my husband, a brilliant space scientist, began showing signs of dementia. I now identify it as Frontal Lobe dementia based upon his symptoms such as changes in personality and behavior problems. When care of him in the home became unsafe and exhausting, our family made the decision to move both of us to a senior living facility which had a dementia treatment component. We moved the end of March 2017. By May 2017, he was moved to the site for dementia patients. Actually I was told by the facility administrator that he was not in a safe situation with me, and if I did not move him, I could be charged with elder abuse.

I believe he was overmedicated including with over the counter drugs. For example, he had trouble with diarrhea. To me, it made common sense to reduce or remove the stool softeners and laxatives from the array of drugs he was taking but I felt that my input had no effect.

He had many trips to hospitals. During one trip to the hospital, his blood pressure was slightly elevated and the hospital doctor put him on medicine to lower his blood pressure. He had never had a blood pressure problem, and while in the hospital and upon returning to health care at home, all blood pressure results were normal or below. I could not convince them to consider looking at removing that medication or to lower the dose. One of the side effects of low blood pressure is falling which is a side effect of several of the other medicines he was on and, of course, he fell and went through periods when he could not walk.

He had 2 stays at St. Johns in Leavenworth in the Senior Behavioral Health section. I understand the purpose was to regulate medications. I was given the feeling if I did not consent to his going there, I would have to find a new place immediately.

It seemed as if when a new drug was added, nothing was reduced or taken away. In December, 2017, he fell and could not get up. We spent the first 3 weeks in December in the hospital trying to "detox" him and get him up and walking again. On the day of release, December 23, I wondered about the delay in the release papers. In talking with the discharge nurse, I discovered the hospital was told that the facility where we were living would not take him back unless he came back on all the medications he was on when he left. They were waiting for the Doctor to get out of a meeting to write the prescriptions.

I was very upset. I had already found another care facility where I could move him, but they could not take him until the 26th of December because of already committed holiday staff schedules. At a point, I thought that we were going to have to live in the hospital lobby or a motel, as I refused to take him back to Facility One. The issue was finally resolved because the nurse, who I believe did not have the authority to make the medication decisions, was no longer a member of the staff. She is on the staff of another nursing home in the area.

He did go back to Facility One and I was able to get him moved to Facility Two within a couple of months. He died June 2, 2018 in the second facility.

Another practice of both homes that I thought was marvelous to begin with but now I am beginning to doubt, is that both homes had their own doctor. Transporting a dementia patient to a doctor's office, waiting in the waiting room and the treatment room is not a pleasant experience. Facility One doctor was in Topeka and every two weeks his nurse came around, evaluated the patients and, as I understood, reported back to doctor and prescription changes were made. I never met this doctor. Facility Two had a local doctor who did actually come into the facility and evaluate patients. I did meet and talk with this doctor several times.

I tried to keep up on the drugs they were giving him, the dosages and side effects and the interactions. Not being a medical doctor, I had to assume the facilities, nurses and doctors knew what they were doing. I regret that assumption, but dementia is a hard disease to treat and I am not sure what other path our family could have taken.

California Advocates for Nursing Home Reform et al.

www.canhr.org

California Advocates for Nursing Home Reform, Center for Medicare Advocacy, Justice in Aging, Long Term Care Community Coalition, National Association of State Long-Term Care Ombudsman Programs, and National Consumer Voice for Quality Long-Term Care

The above organizations would like to thank Chairman Grassley and Ranking Member Wyden for holding the March 6 hearing, "Not Forgotten: Protecting Americans From Abuse and Neglect in Nursing Homes." No one who heard Patricia Blank recount the extreme dehydration and subsequent death of her mother in an Iowa nursing home and Maya Fischer talk about the brutal rape of her mother in a Minnesota facility during this hearing will ever forget their stories. The horrific suffering of both nursing home residents and that of others calls for a serious examination of how to combat and end nursing home abuse and neglect. As consumer advocates representing the experiences and interests of nursing home residents nationwide, we take this opportunity to offer recommendations for preventing or addressing abuse and neglect of residents and to respond to statements and testimony made during the hearing.

Abuse and neglect of nursing home residents occurs far too often. They are at increased risk due to the prevalence of dementia and dependency on caregivers for personal care. The systems designed to protect residents and hold facilities and perpetrators accountable have not been as effective as they should be.

Strong, clear actions need to be taken immediately to protect residents and prevent others from suffering the same indignities and fate as the mothers of Patricia Blank and Maya Fischer. To that end, we offer the following recommendations.

Recommendations

1) Congress should oppose any weakening of resident protections by urging the Centers for Medicare and Medicaid Services (CMS) to retain the Requirements of Participation for Long-Term Care Facilities as issued in October 2016.

In October 2016, CMS published revised federal nursing home regulations that had been developed over a four-year process of listening to consumers, nursing home providers, and health care experts, including formal notice and comment.[43] These regulations include important new standards that better protect vulnerable individuals and reduce the likelihood of resident harm, such as robust requirements for staff training and prevention, reporting and responding to abuse, neglect and exploitation.

CMS has indicated its intention to change these already revised and improved nursing home regulations in order to reduce the supposed burden on nursing home operators. This would be a mistake; the protections in the current regulations are sorely needed. Nursing home residents as a whole are more vulnerable than when the nursing home regulations were first released in 1991. Residents' acuity level has increased, and the majority have some form of dementia. The increased prevalence of physical and cognitive impairments makes residents more at risk of abuse and neglect, as evidenced by the CNN investigative report that exposed widespread sexual assault in nursing homes across the country, including the rape of Maya Fischer's mother.[44] In addition, poor care, abuse, and neglect continue to be a problem nationwide as documented by studies and reports.[45]

The 2016 rules respond to these issues and safeguard residents. For instance, as noted above, there are stronger protections related to abuse, neglect and exploitation. In addition, facilities must annually assess the needs of residents and determine what resources, including numbers, types and competency levels of staff, are necessary to provide the required care and services.

2) Congress should call on CMS to: (1) reverse the decision to set per-instance, rather than per-day, Civil Monetary Penalties as the default financial remedy for violations; and (2) end the persistent under-identification of resident harm in nursing homes.

During the hearing, Dr. Goodrich testified that there are a range of enforcement sanctions, including Civil Monetary Penalties (CMPs) which CMS can impose when a facility is not in compliance or serious abuse has been verified. However, although CMS theoretically has a wide range of enforcement remedies, actual use of these remedies has been relatively narrow. One of the major reasons for inadequate enforcement is the failure to appropriately assign "scope and severity" levels. Most deficiencies are assigned a "no harm" severity level. In fact, in 2015 only 3.4% of all health violations were

---

[43] Federal Register, Vol 81, No. 192, October 4, 2016, 42 CFR Parts 405, 431, 447, 482, 483, 485, 488, and 489.

[44] Blake Ellis and Melanie Hicken. Sick, Dying and Raped in America's Nursing Homes. CNN Reports. February 22, 2017.

[45] *Adverse Events in Skilled Nursing Facilities: National Incidence Among Medicare Beneficiaries* (Feb. 2014) OEI-06-11-00370. *Nursing Facilities, Staffing, Residents, and Facility Deficiencies, 2009-2015*. Prepared by: Charlene Harrington, Ph.D. Helen Carrillo, M.S. University of California San Francisco and Rachel Garfield Kaiser Family Foundation.

identified as having caused any harm to a resident, despite the documented evidence on survey reports frequently showing otherwise.[46] The scope and severity levels are critical because they determine the enforcement remedies that can be imposed – and a no-harm level rarely leads to any enforcement action, let alone a meaningful enforcement action.

Inadequate nursing home oversight is further weakened by policy changes that CMS has already implemented. Many of these changes correspond to requests from the nursing home industry and were made without public notice or comment. In November 2017, CMS placed an 18-month moratorium on major enforcement of several key regulations that became effective that same month. Other changes lead to lower and less frequent fines. Examples include:

- Making per instance CMPs the recommended remedy rather than per diem fines in all but a few limited circumstances. The result is generally lower penalties imposed for noncompliance.
- Allowing CMPs to be optional instead of mandatory when Immediate Jeopardy does not result in serious injury, harm, impairment, or death.
- Changing how remedies are selected and factors to consider giving CMS Regional Offices (ROs) discretion. For instance, ROs can take into consideration whether the cited noncompliance is a one-time mistake or accident.

These changes are counterproductive. The threat of fines is a critical deterrent to abuse and substandard care, particularly when they are large enough to impact a facility's actions. Yet policy revisions are already having an effect: the average fine is now $28,405 compared to $41,260 in 2016.[47]

3) Congress should pass legislation requiring a minimum staffing standard of at least 4.1 hours of direct care nursing time per resident per day.

The relationship between staffing levels and quality of care has been well established. When there is not enough staff, residents suffer physically. They experience painful pressure ulcers, malnutrition, dehydration, infections, preventable hospitalization, injuries, and more. Severe lack of staff, when combined with stress and burnout, are factors that can lead to neglect and abuse.[48]

Insufficient staffing occurs because federal law requires no minimum staffing standard for nursing homes. Medicaid and/or Medicare certified facilities must have

---

[46] Safeguarding NH Residents& Program Integrity: A National Review of State Survey Agency Performance, LTCCC (2015).

[47] Jordan Rau. Trump Administration Cuts the Size Of Fines For Health Violations In Nursing Homes. Kaiser Health News. March 15, 2019.

[48] Catherine Hawes, Ph.D. Elder Abuse in Residential Long-Term Care Settings: What Is Known and What Information Is Needed? National Academy of Sciences 2003.

"sufficient staff" to meet residents' needs, but this provision is vague and ambiguous. The lack of specificity means that the decision about staffing levels is up to individual nursing homes. Facilities often cut staffing to maximize profits.

A 2001 study by the federal government determined that a nursing home resident needs at least 4.1 hours of care per day: 2.8 hours from nursing assistants, 0.55 hours from licensed practical nurses, and 0.75 hours from registered nurses.[49] This is the minimum amount of care needed to prevent common quality of care problems like pressure ulcers, dehydration, and losing the ability to carry out daily tasks like eating, dressing, and walking. *As of December 2018, U.S. nursing homes provided an average of only 3.5 total care staff hours per resident per day, significantly below the recommended 4.1 hours.*[50]

4) Congress should ban the use of pre-dispute arbitration agreements in nursing homes.

A pre-dispute arbitration agreement in a nursing facility is signed by a resident during the admissions process, when he or she will know nothing about any future dispute that may be subject to the arbitration agreement. Generally, residents or their family members sign these agreements because they feel that they have no choice, and during times of great stress and confusion.

Pre-dispute arbitration agreements are inherently unfair and dangerous for consumers. They lessen nursing facility accountability by forcing residents into secret proceedings when seeking redress. This hides allegations of abuse, neglect and poor care from the public and regulators, which diminishes the consequences of negligent care by providing cover for poorly performing facilities. Fewer consequences can allow substandard care to continue, leading to more, not fewer, injuries, and greater costs to taxpayer-funded programs like Medicare. Civil court cases help deter bad actors, thereby protecting residents.

Congressional action is needed. The 2016 regulations include a provision barring pre-dispute arbitration, but the government declined to appeal preliminary injunctive relief in a Mississippi federal court that barred the enforcement of the regulation.[51] Subsequently, CMS proposed a regulation that not only would allow pre-dispute arbitration agreements but would, for the first time, explicitly permit nursing facilities to require pre-dispute arbitration agreements as a condition of admission.[52]

---

[49] Abt Associates for U.S. Centers for Medicare and Medicaid Services, "Appropriateness of Minimum Nurse Staffing Ratios in Nursing Homes." December 2001.

[50] Long Term Care Community Coalition News Alert: Latest Data Indicate Low Staffing Is Persistent & Pervasive. February 2019.

[51] Am. Health Care Ass'n v. Burwell, 217 F. Supp. 3d 921 (N.D. Miss. 2016).

[52] 82 Fed. Reg. 26,649 (2017).

5) Congress should (1) update minimum funding and maintenance of effort provisions for the State Long-Term Care Ombudsman Program in the reauthorization of the Older Americans Act (OAA) to reflect the most current fiscal year; and (2) increase the current OAA Title VII State Long-Term Care Ombudsman Program authorized funding level to $35 million.

Under the federal Older Americans Act (OAA), every state is required to have a State Long-Term Care Ombudsman Program (LTCOP) that addresses complaints and advocates for improvements in the long-term care system. Each state has an Office of the State Long-Term Care Ombudsman, headed by a full time State Long-Term Care Ombudsman who directs the program statewide. Trained individuals designated as ombudsman representatives by the State Ombudsman directly serve residents.

Among other duties, long-term care ombudsmen investigate and seek to resolve complaints made by or on behalf of residents of long-term care facilities. This includes complaints about abuse. Ombudsmen are directed by what the resident wants and must adhere to strict confidentiality laws. Depending on the situation and resident consent, ombudsmen may make a referral to the appropriate protective service, regulatory, or law enforcement entity and/or pursue a range of advocacy strategies with the goal of doing as much as the resident wants them to be do. Ombudsmen may also provide training to facility staff on abuse prevention.

The LTCOP, in many states, struggles to provide residents with regular access to help due to insufficient funding. LTCOPs are stretched so thin because funding has not increased significantly in the last decade. Many programs have not recovered from funding cuts that occurred beginning in 2008. This means that many residents cannot receive the advocacy, assistance and support they need to obtain quality of care and quality of life.

6) Congress should: (1) request a GAO study into the financing of long-term care facilities, specifically looking at how federal funds are used; and (2) pass legislation requiring (a) audits of cost reports, (b) transparency through detailed financial reporting that includes disclosure of finances regarding related-party companies and owners, (c) limits on how much money in administrative costs a nursing home can claim and how much profit they can make from those public funds, and (d) any additional dollars allocated for Medicare and/or Medicaid funding for nursing homes be spent on direct care only.

Under the Nursing Home Reform Law, one of the duties of the Secretary of Health and Human Services is to "promote the effective and efficient use of public moneys."[53]

---

[53] 42 U.S.C. § 1395i–3(f)(1).

Yet neither the Secretary, government officials nor the public know whether Medicare and Medicaid dollars are being spent appropriately and responsibly. Medicare does not audit financial cost reports, and financial reports do not reveal the hidden profits, such as inflated payments for management, pharmacy, staffing and therapy services made to other companies owned by the same persons or entities who own the facility.

In addition, there are no requirements for how nursing homes spend federal funding. Some nursing home operators disproportionately use public dollars to pay for salaries, administrative costs, and other non-direct care services.[54] For instance, the New York State Attorney General recently filed a complaint against an operator, alleging that the operator diverted Medicaid funds away from residents and "paid such monies for their own benefit through companies they owned or controlled."[55] An article in *The New York Times* reports that related-party transactions have become a "common business arrangement, [as] owners of nursing homes outsource a wide variety of goods and services to companies in which they have a financial interest or that they control."[56]

7) Congress should pass legislation regarding corporate accountability that requires CMS to: (1) establish minimum federal criteria for assuming ownership or management of Medicare and/or Medicaid funded nursing homes; and (2) deny or revoke a facility's Medicare enrollment if an owner is affiliated with a previously revoked facility.

There is a growing number of acquisitions/mergers/deals in which large numbers of nursing homes are taken over by corporations, with little to no scrutiny of the corporations' financial capacity or experience and/or history of providing care.

- Nursing home chains can sell their homes to companies with a track record of poor care. This is exactly what happened when Avante, a Florida-based nursing home chain, sold its North Carolina nursing facilities to SentosaCare. SentosaCare had a history of substandard care, with large numbers of violations.[57]

---

[54] Medical Loss Ratios for Nursing Homes: Protecting Residents and Public Funds. Joint Statement from the Center for Medicare Advocacy and the Long Term Care Community Coalition.

[55] Ex-owners of nursing home face felony charges. The Daily Star. Denise Richardson. June 7, 2018.

[56] Care Suffers as More Nursing Homes Feed Money Into Corporate Webs. New York Times. Jordan Rau. January 2, 2018. Christopher H. Schmitt. The New Math of Old Age: Why the nursing home industry's cries of poverty don't add up. Investigative Report. U.S. News & World Report. September 30, 2002.

[57] Richard Craver, "Avante plans to sell six NC nursing homes, including three in Triad," *Winston-Salem Journal* (Apr. 18, 2018).

- Corporations buying facilities may have no previous experience in running nursing homes. Skyline was considered an "unknown firm," while the *Philadelphia Inquirer* noted the general lack of information about the company.[58]
- Owners with a seriously troubled history are permitted to start a new company and repeat the history. For example, in the mid-1990s, there had been bankruptcy and sudden closings in facilities owned by Jon Robertson.[59] However, in 2006 he started a new company, Utah-based Deseret Health Group, which went on to experience the same problems.[60]
- Owners are allowed to buy or sell nursing homes even if they are in financial distress. When Skyline took over 18 nursing homes in South Dakota, it was already struggling to pay its bills in other states. In Kansas where Skyline had 15 facilities, the executive director of the Kansas Health Care Association stated, "I honestly don't believe the Skyline people had a year's worth of working capital."[61]

The failure to assess whether owners and managers are qualified and competent is harming residents, who may have to relocate if their facilities are forced to close following bankruptcy. The resulting transfer trauma experienced by many residents can lead to physical, mental, and emotional decline, and sometimes even death. The federal government needs to establish standards to ensure that individuals and companies who have such an impact on resident health and safety are capable and fit to do so.

8) Congress should make the National Background Check Program mandatory.

Current background check systems do not adequately protect nursing home residents from exploitation and abuse. A 2011 report by the Office of the Inspector General (OIG) found that 92 percent of nursing facilities employed at least one individual with at least one criminal conviction.[62] Additionally, nearly half of nursing facilities employed five or more individuals with at least one conviction.[63] Most convictions were for property crimes (e.g., burglary, shoplifting, writing bad checks), and an alarming number of convictions were for crimes against persons, including sex crimes. The same report found that only ten states require both an FBI and a statewide criminal background check for

---

58 Maggie Flynn. Troubled Skyline Highlights Problems with Under-the-Radar Skilled Nursing Operators. Skilled Nursing News. April 12, 2018.

59 Eric Slater, "Entrepreneur Fades From View as Empire Collapses; Business: Critics say owner of shuttered nursing homes, including one in Reseda, lived lavishly amid unpaid bills," *Los Angeles Times* (Oct. 23, 1997).

60 H.B. Lawson, "Nursing home faces closure; Deseret Health Group closing facilities in several states, Saratoga facility put on chopping block Friday," *The Saratoga Sun* (May 6, 2015).

61 Kelsey Ryan and Andy Marso. How a small company above a N.J. pizza parlor put Kansas nursing home residents at risk. The Kansas City Star. April 15, 2018.

62 Department of Health and Human Services, Office of the Inspector General, *Nursing Facilities' Employment of Individuals with Criminal Convictions* (2011).

63 Ibid.

prospective employees. This means that in many states, prospective employees' out-of-state convictions go undetected and those with records of abuse are often hired by nursing facilities.[64]

The National Background Check Program (NBCP) was created to address these problems. It is a *voluntary* program that provides non-competitive grants to states in order to help them implement and improve employee background check systems in long-term care facilities. The program is administered by the Centers for Medicare and Medicaid Services (CMS) in consultation with the Department of Justice (DOJ) and the Federal Bureau of Investigation (FBI).

A 2016 DHS report found that 25 states have participated in the program. It also found that the NBCP screened out 30,025 individuals with a history of patient abuse or a violent criminal background through September 30, 2014.[65] Congress should build on this program's success and make it mandatory so residents in all states receive this important protection.

Response to Witness Testimony

In addition to the above recommendations, we find it necessary to comment on issues raised by some of the witnesses and their answers to questions during the hearing. Specifically:

Medicaid Reimbursement

During the hearing, Dr. David Grabowski testified that the Medicaid rate was too low and "you get what you pay for." He indicated that rural nursing homes were closing because the Medicaid reimbursement rates were inadequate and cited the *New York Times* article[66] that focused on the closing of Mobridge Care and Rehabilitation Center in South Dakota.

Before concluding that the Medicaid rate is too low, we urge Committee members to consider three points. First, as noted earlier, the amount of money nursing homes allocate to administrative costs and profits, instead of care, is not known. This could mean that the problem may be how nursing homes choose to spend their Medicaid dollars, rather than lack of sufficient money. For this reason, we urge Congress in recommendation #5 to request a GAO study into the financing of long-term care facilities, specifically looking at how federal funds are used.

Second, more money does not necessarily mean better quality care. Despite Medicare reimbursement rates of approximately $550 or more per day, a Department of Health and Human Services Office of Inspector General investigation found that 1/3 of Medicare

---

[64] Ibid.

[65] Department of Health and Human Services, Office of the Inspector General, *National Background Check Program for Long- Term-Care Employees: Interim Report* (2016).

[66] Jack Healy. Nursing Homes Are Closing Across Rural America, Scattering Residents. The New York Times. March 4, 2019.

beneficiaries receiving skilled nursing facility services experienced harm within 16 days of admission, and almost 60% of that harm was determined to be preventable.[67]

Third, Skyline's takeover of Mobridge and the corporation's subsequent failing may have been a significant factor in the closing of the facility. At the beginning of 2017, Mobridge was bought by Skyline Healthcare Inc. By April 2018, a divisional vice president in charge of Skyline facilities in South Dakota sent emails to the South Dakota Department of Health stating that employees across the group in the state had not been paid, and the facilities only had enough housekeeping and laundry supplies for four more days of operation, and food for residents for five more days.[68] In May, the state put a receiver in place, but by November the receiver petitioned for Mobridge's closure, claiming significant and unsustainable losses.[69] A similar pattern could be seen in Skyline facilities elsewhere, for example in Nebraska and Kansas, where states sought court-approved receiverships or otherwise took over the nursing homes in order to assure that residents would continue to receive food, medicine and care.[70]

Nursing Home Compare and the Five-Star Rating System

We are concerned that the many comments and questions about the accuracy of Nursing Home Compare and the Five-Star Rating system at the hearing indicate an over-reliance on data in consumer selection of nursing homes.

While improvements are needed, Nursing Home Compare and the Five-Star Rating System are not a fool-proof indication of a nursing home's quality. Consumers must be encouraged to use other factors, such as onsite visits, whenever possible in evaluating a facility. Conditions in long-term care facilities can change so rapidly that the information reported may already be out-of-date, particularly if there has been a change in the administrator or director of nursing, or if the facility has recently been bought by a corporation.

Additionally, when CMS implemented a revised survey process on November 28, 2017, the agency imposed a freeze on health inspection data used to calculate the health inspection star rating. As a result, the most recent inspection has not been included in the five-star rating system. While the freeze is scheduled to end in April 2019, prospective residents and their family members researching facilities during this time period have received incomplete information.

[67] *Adverse Events in Skilled Nursing Facilities: National Incidence Among Medicare Beneficiaries* (Feb. 2014) OEI-06-11-00370. *Nursing Facilities, Staffing, Residents, and Facility Deficiencies, 2009-2015*. Prepared by: Charlene Harrington, Ph.D. Helen Carrillo, M.S. University of California San Francisco and Rachel Garfield Kaiser Family Foundation.

[68] Bart Pfankuch, Wave of SD nursing home closures hitting hardest in rural small towns. The Brookings Register. March 17, 2019.

[69] Ibid.

[70] Toby Edelman. Buying and Selling Nursing Homes: Who's Looking Out for the Residents? Center for Medicare Advocacy.

Unfortunately, too many consumers have such limited choices of nursing homes that information about quality is often moot. Consumers and families seeking a nursing home after hospitalization are frequently given very limited time to decide about a long-term care facility, and/or may be directed towards a facility with which there is a referral arrangement with the hospital. Additionally, a growing number of consumers in Medicaid managed care plans have little to no choice of nursing homes (as of 2017, 24 states had Medicaid Long-Term Services and Supports programs[71]), while others are limited by geographical or other constraints.

Improvement in Quality Care

In his testimony, Dr. David Gifford said that the quality of nursing home care has improved dramatically. Nevertheless, the following data show that quality is still elusive for too many nursing facilities:

- Almost 21% of nursing homes received a deficiency at the level of harm or immediate jeopardy[72]
- 42% of nursing homes had either a one-star or two-star rating for health inspections[73]
- 42% of nursing homes had chronic deficiencies three years in a row[74]
- 20% of nursing home residents - approximately 250,000 individuals - are administered antipsychotic drugs that are life-threatening[75]
- 7.5% of nursing home residents - approximately 95,000 individuals - have unhealed pressure ulcers even though research shows that almost all pressure ulcers are preventable[76]
- A 2014 US Office of Inspector General (OIG) report found that 33% of Medicare residents experienced adverse events or harm within 16 days of admission to a skilled nursing facility. Almost 60% of the harm was determined to be avoidable.[77]

---

[71] Elizabeth Lewis, Steve Eiken, Angela Amos, Paul Saucier. The Growth of Managed Long-Term Services and Supports Programs: 2017 Update. January 29, 2018. Truven Health Analytics.

[72] Charlene Harrington, Ph.D., Helen Carrillo, M.S. University of California San Francisco. Rachel Garfield, MaryBeth Musumeci, Ellen Squires, Kaiser Family Foundation. Nursing Facilities, Staffing, Residents and Facility Deficiencies: 2009-2016. April 2018.

[73] CMS Provider data, Processing date: February 1, 1019.

[74] Chronic Deficiencies in Care: The Persistence of Recurring Failures to Meet Minimum Safety & Dignity Standards in U.S. Nursing Homes. Long Term Care Community Coalition. 2017.

[75] Long Term Care Community Coalition News Alert November 2018: Latest Data on Nursing Home Antipsychotic Drugging. 2018Q2 MDS Data (N0410A: Medications - Medications Received – Antipsychotic).

[76] Safeguarding NH Residents& Program Integrity: A National Review of State Survey Agency Performance, Long Term Care Community Coalition. 2015.

[77] Adverse Events in Skilled Nursing Facilities, DHHS OIG, February 2014.

Nursing Home Regulations

Since January 2017, CMS has systemically worked to rollback resident protections through proposed revisions of current regulations. Dr. Kate Goodrich stated in her testimony that this relaxing of rules was aimed at "paperwork and administrative requirements" that "may be getting in the way of patient care."

The changes CMS is pursuing cannot be characterized as focused just on "paperwork." In addition to reversing the ban on arbitration agreements described earlier, here are examples of what the agency is targeting:

- *Development of care plans for residents within 48 hours of admission.* Nursing home residents have significant care needs, and appropriate care must be provided from the first day. To protect residents during their vulnerable first days in the facility, the federal government in 2016 strengthened care planning regulations. Elimination of these requirements could lead to poor care, injury and death.
- *Reporting serious bodily injury due to abuse or neglect within 2 hours.* Delayed reporting reduces the chances of providing prompt assistance to abuse victims and finding forensic evidence. The 2016 regulations addressed this problem by mandating that severe harm be reported within two hours. However, this timeframe for reporting may now be extended. Permitting additional time before severe harm is reported means residents may not get help quickly enough and preserving vital evidence in an investigation may be jeopardized. Lessening any requirements related to abuse reporting leaves residents at greater risk of abuse.
- *Protections against evictions.* Across the country, nursing homes are discharging residents against their will and sending them to inappropriate and unsafe settings, such as homeless shelters. Residents who are kicked out like this can experience harm and may never recover. To better protect residents from improper evictions, the 2016 regulations require nursing homes to notify local ombudsman programs whenever a nursing home moves to evict a resident. Long-term care ombudsmen are advocates for nursing home residents. When ombudsmen are notified, they can contact the resident and/or representative and provide assistance if requested. Most of the time ombudsmen are successful in resolving a problem or concern that has triggered the proposed discharge, thereby reducing inappropriate discharges. This notification requirement may be eliminated or modified, leaving residents without much needed assistance.

Conclusion

The organizations listed at the beginning of this statement thank the Committee for bringing attention to the care and treatment of our country's nursing home residents, who, too often, feel as if they are invisible and forgotten. The failure to address long-standing problems, and current and possibly future rollbacks of protections, are sending a strong message to residents that they are also being abandoned. We stand ready to help the Committee ensure that residents are not forgotten, and that nursing home safety and oversight are strengthened, not weakened.

Letter Submitted by Linda S. Carlsen

Committee on Finance
Washington, DC

This letter is meant to highlight what I believe is most important to residents and their families for all nursing homes and extended care living facilities. If each resident could be afforded the dignity of having a safe place, adequate staff, the best health and supportive care available and the freedom to make his or her own choices whenever possible, we would have a place for our loved ones where their living conditions were better than they are now. There are so many concerns that these needs are not being met and haven't been met for a very long time.

I have a personal story that I would like to share because it changed my life and to some extent, the lives of my family members. My step-father was a dentist for 50 years in Illinois where he had his own practice. After he retired, he moved to Arkansas where he stayed until he was too sick to be alone and away from his family. I was his only living relative and I felt the need to move him to Kansas where he could be with us and I could take care of him.

I promised him I would never put him in a nursing home but he didn't want to live with us, so when an extended living facility opened up, I jumped at the chance to get him an apartment with the understanding that I would visit him every day and that our family would see him as often as they could. Unfortunately, he was in the hospital because of heart problems more than his apartment and it became clear that I needed more care for him. My promise of not putting him into a nursing home had to be amended to finding the best nursing home for him.

Years before I had been on a community project that looked at all aspects of care for our aging population. I was the chair of the subcommittee on nursing homes in our area and I personally visited all the nursing homes in Johnson County. My stepfather had no signs of dementia and together we visited the nursing homes that I thought might work for him and he was a part of the process every step of the way. After tours and talking to the administrative staff, we decided on a place where we hoped he would get the support he needed. Honestly, I was most interested in the staff and the location whereas he wanted the best "'bricks and mortar."

He could come and go if he felt like it but as time went by, he didn't leave the nursing home. He didn't want to talk about his days in the nursing home and I knew there was something more going on than he was letting me know. He was hiding the fact that he didn't always get his medication, that his bed was dirty much of the time, that his food came any time of the day and that no one was there to help him at night. Every day after work, I would visit him and I began seeing more bruising on his body. Bruising of the skin is natural for an older man in his 80s but this was more than normal bruising of the thin skin of his arms and legs. I started looking for bed sores and other signs of neglect. I believe he was afraid to tell me how he got the bruises. When I questioned the staff about what my stepfather had told me, they denied everything he said but told me I could take him someplace else if I wasn't happy with their services. But the catch was, I didn't know where else to take him. I began coming more than once a day so that I could make sure he got his medications, had a clean bed and ate something. That worked for a while but everything changed one day when I visited him as usual after he had been at the nursing home for one month.

He was in bed and had a back brace on and told me that he had gotten up to go to the bathroom at night and he had fallen and had been given the back brace. The head nurse suggested that I take him to the hospital for x-rays. I was not notified when the accident happened or I would have had him transported by ambulance to the hospital. He had fractured vertebrae, broken ribs and more bruising. The back brace was of no help!

That incident along with the other red flags of neglect prompted me to move him to another facility. I quit my job and spent most of the day with him at the new facility, taking over the jobs the staff should have been doing.

He had had rheumatic fever when he was in dental school and he lived much longer than his doctors ever expected him to live but after the fall, he was incapacitated and I believe that hastened his death. Had proper intervention occurred, he might have had a more comfortable ending.

I have been a board member of Kansas Advocates for Better Care for eleven years because I know we make a difference. I can't change what happened to my loved family member but I can help others know that there is help for them through Kansas Advocates for Better Care and other limited resources.

Sincerely, Linda Carlsen

Center for Fiscal Equity
Rockville, Maryland

Statement Submitted by Michael Bindner

Chairman Grassley and Ranking Member Wyden, thank you for the opportunity to present our comments on this vital issue. We will omit the restatement of our usual four-part tax reform proposal, but will mention that we propose that all Medicare, Medicaid, Affordable Care Act and Health Insurance Exclusion funding will be through our proposed Net Business Receipts/Subtraction Value-Added Tax (NBRT or SVAT).

Our income and inheritance surtax (which taxes cash disbursements from estates and sale of estate assets as normal income), will fund withdrawals from the Medicare Trust Fund, which should be phased out when Baby Boomers have all retired.

Care for the sick and elderly was provided by families prior to the establishment of Social Security. Extended families provided shelter, income and health care because they had to. Allowing seniors to live independently freed the nuclear family to move without taking everyone with them. This led to a crisis in health coverage for those seniors left behind.

The logic of social insurance led to both Social Security, Medicare and Medicaid. This provided care for everyone regardless of accidents of birth or death. Without it, families with no surviving parents or grandparents would pay nothing, where only children might have to pay for both parents and their in-laws. This inequality still happens with housing and it strains many marriages.

Nursing home care is currently provided outside of Medicaid for the wealthy who can self-finance (although this does not necessarily guarantee quality if children or conservators get greedy), by spending down assets or through Medicaid once the assets are gone. Catastrophic insurance can be used as an alternative to spending down assets, although this is usually on available to wealthier individuals.

For most of us, nursing home care can be provided by state facilities, for profit facilities and religious (mainly Catholic) health systems.

Public facilities are being overcome by privatization efforts and often are dependent on local budgets. They are a big ticket item that seems easier to cut, although this is often penny wise and pound foolish, resulting in bad care and spurring privatization.

Private facilities can be good or bad, depending upon rates charged and the quality of the staff. Sometimes one does not imply the other and Medicaid limits may lead to cutting corners, especially in staffing. Often, it takes a great deal of oversight by families to provide decent care, although they may just be witnesses to profit driven care which abuses their loved ones rather than being able to correct it.

Religious care is better because it usually lacks a profit motive and can, along with Medicaid funding, provide better care, although this may also lead to using members of the order who are not as well trained as professional staff. This meets the needs of many seniors, especially in rural states. Indeed, religious care holds a monopoly in some areas are for profit facilities close. Sadly, some systems in urban areas have the same bias to highly paid CEOs and lower paid staff.

In all systems, the need to save can lead to attempts to bust unions or to negotiate for substandard nursing wages or use of lower-skilled staff. Governmental oversight helps matters, but budget cuts can leave such units understaffed with unreasonable caseloads.

The choice between care for patients and oversight is a continual balancing act for CMMS and states.

Medicare for All would provide an ever growing pool of beneficiaries with Medicare benefits at Medicaid prices, with the difference being paid by either a payroll tax (employee employer) or with an NBRT/SVAT, which would tax both labor and profit, as above. This is a change in funding, not a guarantee of quality. Cooperative health care, however, can provide better care for less money.

In the long run, employers, especially ESOPs and cooperatives e could replace health care services for both employees, the indigent and retirees and opt out of Medicare for All and receive an offset for NBRT/SVAT levies. This would allow them to hire their own doctors and arrange for hospital and specialist care with an incentive to cut cost and the ability to do so.

Expanding the number of employee-owned companies and cooperatives could be established with personal retirement accounts. Accounts holding index funds for Wall Street to play with will not help. Accounts should instead hold voting and preferred stock in the employer and an insurance fund holding the stocks of all such firms. NBRT/SVAT collections, which tax both labor and profit, will be set high enough to fund employee-ownership and payment of current beneficiaries.. All employees would be credited with the same monthly contribution, regardless of wage. The employer contribution would be ended for health care at all levels.

ESOP loans and distribution of a portion of the Social Security Trust Fund could also speed the adoption of such accounts. Our Income and Inheritance Surtax (where cash from estates and the sale of estate assets are normal income) would fund reimbursements of the Trust Fund.

Thank you again for the opportunity to add our comments to the debate. Please contact us if we can be of any assistance or contribute direct testimony.

Center for Health Information and Policy (CHIP)

Introduction

Statement of Dr. David E. Kingsley

It is disconcerting that a half century after passage of Medicaid, it is necessary for the U.S. Senate to hold yet another hearing regarding pervasive abuse and neglect in the nursing home system. Throughout the decades of Medicaid-funded skilled nursing care, celebrated cases of abuse and neglect have driven Senate hearings, reform legislation, and salacious stories in newspapers and other media. And yet scandals in nursing homes continue unabated.

The efficacy of one more hearing on nursing home abuse is questionable. Not much will change unless elected officials and advocates recognize the systemic and structural factors causing substandard care. In this testimony, I will discuss three major characteristics of the U.S. nursing home system responsible for the lack of acceptable care in America's nursing homes: (1) privatized, for profit care, which is becoming increasingly financialized, (2) the welfare medicine philosophy underlying the system, i.e., Medicaid, and (3) devolution of much of the responsibility for funding and quality to the states.

A profit oriented medical care system combined with means-testing and state control have created intractable problems for attempts at major reform of government funded long-term care. Indeed, history suggests that senators' criticism and even outrage expressed at senate hearings have only minor impact on the structure and functioning of the overall nursing home system. For instance, less than 10 years after Medicaid began to fuel the growth of a private, for-profit, long term care industry, the Senate Subcommittee on Long-Term Care held hearings for the purpose of determining what the nation was receiving for the billions of dollars of federal support for long-term care.[78]

The committee's report concluded that public policy failed to "produce satisfactory institutional care—or alternatives—for chronically ill older Americans." Furthermore, it stated that "this document—and other documents to follow—declare that today's entire population of the elderly, *and their offspring,* suffer severe emotional damage because of dread and despair associated with nursing home care in the United States today."

When considering the state of the U.S. nursing home system in 2019, one is struck by the subcommittee's statement in 1974 and its similarity to today's nursing home system:

> Efforts have been made to deal with the most severe of problems. Laws have been passed; national commitments have been made; declarations of high purpose have been uttered at national conferences and by representatives of the nursing home industry.
>
> *But for all of that, long-term care for older Americans stands today as the most troubled, and troublesome, component of entire health care system.*[79]

The conclusion was that the taxpaying citizens were not getting what they deserved and what they were paying for. Despite billions spent, the system was rife with abuse, neglect, and scandal. It still is. In fact, taxpayers are no longer funneling mere billions of dollars into the nursing home system, they are paying hundreds of billions in taxes for care which appears to make few people satisfied with what they are getting. Poor care and a dehumanizing environment in a large proportion of skilled nursing facilities are practically the norm.

---

[78] U.S. Senate, Special Committee on Aging, Subcommittee on Long-Term Care (1974), "Nurs- ing Home Care in the United States: Failure of Public Policy." Washington, DC: U.S. Govern- ment Printing Office.

[79] U.S. Senate, *Op. Cit.,* page III.

However, day-to-day abuse and myriad examples of low-quality care are symptoms. The underlying systemic and structural causes of low-quality care must be recognized and addressed. Indeed, in the following I will elaborate on each of the three structural problems and how they negate minor reforms and tweaks. Without recognition of systemic causes of low-quality and dehumanizing care, results of wellmeaning advocacy on the part of legislators and nursing home advocates will be resisted and evaded by the industry.

Privatization, Profit, and Increasing Financialization

As Dr. Grabowski indicated in his testimony regarding the public's view of nursing homes, "a third of people surveyed would rather die than be placed in one." Preferring death or not, hardly anyone wants to spend any of his or her old age in a nursing home. Why, after channeling hundreds of billions of taxpayers' funds into the nursing home industry each year, are taxpayers so dissatisfied with what they are receiving for such a huge expenditure?

Because of the primacy of earnings and ROI, it is not surprising that the nursing home system in the United States is reviled by the citizens who pay for it. In a capitalistic enterprise, the primary duty of management is to shareholders. This is appropriate in other sectors of the economy but of necessity in a profit-oriented medical system the quality of care must be reduced for the sake of marketing, return on investment, and high executive/managerial salaries.

Given that managers at the operations level are discharged with the responsibility to take care of shareholders and optimize return on investment, a portion of tax funds intended for patient care will be diverted to satisfy expectations of suppliers of capital. Therefore, managers are naturally pressured to maintain an understaffed, low-skilled, and low-paid workforce.

The quality of food, facilities, and supplies is determined by either the patients' ability to pay or by the level of state and federal government reimbursement (see my discussion of means tested, lower-tier, welfare-medicine below).

It is common for advocacy groups to press state legislatures to more closely monitor facilities and to force them to enhance quality of care. Industry lobbyists, resisting such attempts, commonly point to inadequate reimbursement and plead hardship at legislative hearings. Perhaps because of the treatment of Medicaid as lower tier medicine and therefore not worthy of higher reimbursement the industry has a case.

On the other hand, the industry's case is weakened by its opaqueness and increasingly complex legal and financial corporate structures. It is difficult for advocates and legislators to rebut hardship pleas without access to corporate financial information. As the industry has adopted increasingly complex financial and legal structures, transparency has become an even bigger problem.

Indeed, the only real innovations in the industry since 1950 pertain to financial restructuring benefitting the industry—often with a negative effect on care. No significant changes have emerged in the design of facilities, management of patients, and organization of care. The total institution remains the paradigm for arranging the daily life of patients. Patients are regimented and dehumanized through rigid, uniform schedules, tasteless institutional cuisine, and mind-numbing boredom in sterile, impersonal surroundings. The total institution is conducive to the economies and efficiencies essential for the highest profit and the lowest costs.

From inception of the nursing home industry in 1950 when amendments to the Social Security Act allowed for reimbursement to vendors providing medical services, a "bottom-line" mentality was set in place and has become a primary feature of the nursing home system. Because federal and state reimbursements were mostly for care of the poor, the spend down became a major structural feature of the U.S. nursing home industry. As the system has developed, the spend down has become a major transference of middle-class assets to wealthy corporate owners and investors. Welfare medicine as exemplified by Medicaid, drives middle-class assets up to wealthier classes—increasing the disturbing trend in wealth concentration in the top one percent.

Following passage of Medicaid, major financial innovations significantly impacted the U.S. economic system. Two innovations, the limited liability corporation and the private equity firm have affected the nursing home industry in a major way.

Embedding a single facility within a network of LLCs is a widespread practice. Typically, in these networks, the operation is an LLC owned 100% by another LLC. Direct ownership in the parent LLC can include one or several owners with a direct interest. Indirect ownership often includes a complicated network of entities and individual investors. Property is often owned by a commercial real estate firm or an REIT.

A nursing home in a small Kansas community illustrates the complex and opaque nursing home legal and financial structures found throughout the United States.

MCPHERSON OPERATOR, LLC

MCPHERSON, KS

Ownership: For profit—Corporation

Legal Business Name: MCPHERSON OPERATOR LLC

Owners and Managers of MCPHERSON OPERATOR, LLC

5% OR GREATER DIRECT OWNERSHIP INTEREST

KANSAS OPERATOR LLC (100%), since 02/25/2015

5% OR GREATER INDIRECT OWNERSHIP INTEREST

BARRES, LLC (NO PERCENTAGE PROVIDED), since 02/26/2015

T AND C CAPITAL ASSETS, LLC (NO PERCENTAGE PROVIDED), since 02/26/2015

WINDWARD HEALTH PARTNERS LLC (NO PERCENTAGE PROVIDED), since 02/26/2015

CRINO, BRYAN (NO PERCENTAGE PROVIDED), since 02/26/2015
FEUER, SCOTT (NO PERCENTAGE PROVIDED), since 02/26/2015
LINDEMAN, STUART (NO PERCENTAGE PROVIDED), since 02/26/2015
PASSERO, JOSEPH (NO PERCENTAGE PROVIDED), since 02/26/2015
OPERATIONAL/MANAGERIAL CONTROL
MISSION HEALTH COMMUNITIES LLC, since 02/26/2015
BORZUMATO, ANDREW, since 02/26/2015
FARRIS, SHARMIN, since 02/26/2015
RUSSELL, RICHARD, since 02/26/2015
OFFICER
LINDEMAN, STUART, since 02/26/2015
RUSSELL, RICHARD, since 02/26/2015[80]

The indirect owners listed above include a private equity firm (Winward Health Communities, LLC), which includes in its portfolio the company shown as the operational/managerial control entity (Mission Health Communities LLC). Mission Health Communities holds itself out as the company operating nearly 30 facilities in Kansas. However, it doesn't appear in the list above as having any direct or indirect ownership. Stuart Lindeman, the CEO of Mission Health Communities is, according to the information provided by CMS, an owner. Bryan Crino, Scott Feuer, Joseph Passero are principles in Skyway Capital Partners, a private investment firm.

The intricate web of entities and the legal arrangements: reduce risk of investors for neglect and abuse leading to lawsuits. Furthermore, complicated accounting procedures render the return on the capital of investors indecipherable and unknowable. With knowing who benefits and how they benefit from depreciation allowances, interest deductions, and other forms of tax accounting, the low profit of margin claims of industry lobbyists is meaningless.

Who Is Responsible? Who Is Making Money? And How Much Are They Making?

In the 1950's, low-interest FHA real estate loans to proprietary interests fueled a commercial real estate component of nursing home system, which attracted investors with no interests in caring for the disabled and frail elderly. Trading in real property and exercising generous tax subsidies through depreciation allowances and deductions for interest on borrowed capital, is as salient a feature of the nursing home industry as is the care for patients in facilities.

[80] Source: *https://www.medicare.gov/nursinghomecompare/ownership-info.html#ID=175437.*

By becoming increasingly financialized,[81] the industry has mirrored the larger macro-economic trend of the U.S. economy over the past few decades. To the detriment of operations and productive activities, nursing home corporations are increasingly driven to enhance return on investment through financial channels. Shadow banking has increasingly replaced traditional banking as a source of financing for the growing number of buyouts, mergers, and acquisitions. When global capital markets drive investment and managerial behavior, the moral and ethical perspective of medical care is separated from the purpose of the enterprise. In the age of global capital flows, the idea of home-town banks lending to local enterprises in the business of providing care to the elders of the community becomes something of a cherished memory.

Shadow banking in the nursing home industry can be illustrated by a nursing home in the tiny rural community of Cherryvale, Kansas. The following ownership information was derived from the Nursing Home Compare website:

CHERRYVALE NURSING AND REHABILITATION CENTER
CHERRYVALE, KS
Ownership: For profit—Corporation
Legal Business Name: CHERRYVALE MANAGEMENT, LLC
Owners and Managers of CHERRYVALE NURSING AND REHABILITATION CENTER
5% OR GREATER DIRECT OWNERSHIP INTEREST
CHERRYVALE MANAGEMENT, LLC (NO PERCENTAGE PROVIDED), since 05/14/2007
CORNERSTONE GROUP HOLDINGS INC (NO PERCENTAGE PROVIDED), since 09/01/2018
NOVOTNY, MICHELLE (NO PERCENTAGE PROVIDED), since 09/01/2018
NOVOTNY, WILLIAM (NO PERCENTAGE PROVIDED), since 09/01/2018
5% OR GREATER INDIRECT OWNERSHIP INTEREST
PATTERSON, CHARLES (50%), since 09/01/2018
OPERATIONAL/MANAGERIAL CONTROL
CHERRYVALE MANAGEMENT, LLC, since 05/14/2007
NEW PARADIGM SOLUTIONS INC, since 09/01/2018
OFFICER
NOVOTNY, MICHELLE, since 09/01/2018
NOVOTNY, WILLIAM, since 09/01/2018

---

[81] For a definition of financialization, see: Krippner, Greta (2005), "The financialization of the American Economy." *Socio-Economic Review,* 3, p. 174: "I define financialization as a pattern of accumulation in which profits accrue primarily through financial channels rather than through trade and commodity production. Financial here refers to the provision (or transfer) of liquid capital in expectation of future interest, dividends, or capital gains."

MANAGING EMPLOYEE
RITCHEY, OLGA, since 09/01/2018

Four entities are shown by CMS to have direct ownership in the facility. One entity, Cornerstone Group Holdings, Inc., is the Family Office of the super-rich, McCloskey family, which is most certainly unfamiliar with either Cherryvale, Kansas or Cherryvale Nursing and Rehabilitation Center.

The website for Comer Group Holdings[82] describes the financial institution as follows:

> Cornerstone Holdings is a private investment company backed by the Family Office of Tom and Bonnie McCloskey. Its mission is to create long-term wealth for the family by making selective investments into operating businesses and real estate ventures. Due to its discretionary capital, Cornerstone is incredibly opportunistic and capable of being very flexible in how it structures its investments.

It is unlikely that Tom and Bonnie McCloskey have any idea that the facility has the lowest possible Nursing Home Care rating (1 on a scale of 1 to 5). A family office is an investment firm set up to manage the money of a single, super-rich family. It is discharged with responsibility for as high an ROI as is possible, not with high quality nursing home care.

As another example of financialization and shadow banking involvement in the nursing home industry, since 2000, private equity firms have been taking over major chains in leveraged buyouts. In a 2010 report, the General Accounting Office noted that of the ten largest nursing home chains in the United States, nine had been bought out by private equity firms in leveraged buyouts. The buyout of Golden Living by Fillmore Capital and the buyout of HCR ManorCare by the Carlyle Group have proven disastrous for these two chains (2nd and 3rd largest in the U.S.) as well as for the states in which they are located. Worst of all, the patients and their families suffer when hot capital flows in and out of large nursing home businesses.

It is not uncommon for P.E. firms to load up the companies they take over with the debt incurred in leveraging the buyout. A minor portion of the purchase is leveraged with P.E. firm equity but they are intent on recouping that investment while leaving debt owed to suppliers of capital on the books of their target. It is the P.E. philosophy that costs can be reduced through "improved" management practices. Typically, this has meant that operations can be squeezed through cuts in staff, food quality, and so forth. Among those who have a professional interest in the nursing home system, it is well-known that it is not unusual for operations to operate at a bare bones minimum.

---

[82] *http://cstoneholdings.com/.*

The Fillmore Capital and Carlyle Group buyouts left a trail of insolvent facilities in several states. Through a series of financial maneuvers such as selling off property and setting up untenable leaseback arrangements, both P.E. firms were able to funnel enough money out of the chains to recoup their equity and provide a return to investors. The CEO of the bankrupt HCR ManorCare left the company with a $116.7 million golden parachute.[83]

These Golden Living and HCR Manorcare bankruptcies left a string of insolvent facilities for states to grapple with. A large proportion of these were taken over by a New Jersey couple without a track record in the nursing home industry. Within a couple of years, the couple's business, known as Skyline, was insolvent with nearly 100 facilities nationwide unable to meet payroll and buy food and other supplies. In the state of Kansas alone, approximately 30 facilities were taken over by the state due to insolvency.

The state of Kansas has turned a large number of these facilities over to Mission Health Communities, which is in the portfolio of a P.E. firm. At this time, it is not known what proportion of capital invested in the nursing home industry is flowing from P.E. and other shadow banking sources. However, it is likely that small, medium-sized, and large chains will be bought out by P.E. firms. This does not bode well for the quality of care and the on-going problem of abuse and neglect.

Welfare Medicine and State Control

As chair of the powerful House Ways & Means Committee, Congressman Wilbur Mills engineered a welfare medicine component to accompany passage of Medicare in 1965. Mills and his fellow Southern Democrats knew that a universal Medical program such as Medicare would have great potential for expansion to the rest of the population. For a variety of reasons they feared the impact of such a powerful federal program on states rights and the rigid racial hierarchy undergirding Southern culture and the plantation capitalist system.

The deal Mills made with Johnson insured that Medicare would pass with some post-hospital nursing care. However, he insisted on what he called a "three-layer cake:" Medicare would include hospitalization (Part A) and a voluntary component for physician care (Part B). The "indigent" needing hospitalization, physician services, and long-term care would be required to prove they were poor enough to receive government provided medical care.

Nursing home care was not shunted off into Medicaid as an afterthought. States, especially Southern states, desired to retain considerable control over monitoring and funding of what they surely knew would become a massive industry. Southern Democrats knew that facilities owned and operated for the most part by private enterprise with a major proportion of funding and regulation at the state level could be expected to

---

[83] (https://www.toledoblade.com/business/2018/03/05/Former-ManorCare-CEO-nets-116-mil- lion-in-bankruptcy-deal/stories/20180305146).

maintain cultural expectations regarding race and class. This was the best deal the Southern Democrats could hope for in their zeal to maintain a segregated, strong, states-rights culture and economy.

Medicaid is medical care for the deserving poor. Unfortunately, in U.S. medical care, the care the poor deserve is of a lesser quality than that provided to patients with health insurance or have the means to pay out of pocket for their care. The lower tier nature of Medicaid was built into the nursing home system. Welfare is stigmatized as government assistance to individuals who are not responsible enough to save and plan for their senior years.

These attitudes toward welfare are deeply embedded in American culture. The philosophical underpinnings of the Elizabethan Poor Laws were imported to the North American continent prior to the founding of the United States. These include the notion that minimal or subsistence care at the lowest level possible prevents the poor from becoming too comfortable on the dole. Although it makes absolutely no sense—especially for the frail elderly in long-term care—the idea was imported into contemporary government medicine. There could be no other explanation for the lower reimbursement for Medicaid than for Medicare. It sends a message regarding the worth of a Medicaid patient versus that of a private pay patient.

Devolving a considerable amount of responsibility for funding and regulating nursing homes to the states places financial stress on state budgets that must be balanced. Furthermore, states are diverse in their fiscal capabilities and ideologies. Like welfare and recipients of assistance in general, Medicaid and its beneficiaries are stigmatized. In some state cultures, the poor are particularly singled out for opprobrium. Anti-welfare ideologies along with anti-tax, anti-government sentiments, has led to draconian cuts in Medicaid in many states.

State legislatures and stage agencies have been subject to capture by the industry. The AHCA has staff and members in all 50 states. A revolving door between the industry and state employment is common. With the resources for campaign contributions and lobbying, the industry has an asymmetrical relationship with advocates for residents.

Politics is about who gets what, when, and how. And who gets what, when, and how depends on who has power. In the United States, especially lately, money is the most potent form of power. Very few states have nursing home advocacy organizations with paid staff. Even if they were able to raise funds for political contributions, they would be prohibited from doing so since they are typically 501(c)(3) nonprofit organizations. Even the funds the existing advocacy organizations have to devote to legislature pales in comparison to the industry's resources.

If ongoing abuse and neglect are to become problems of the past, funding and regulation must be a federal responsibility. The federal government has a constitutional duty to promote the general welfare. Furthermore, with the capability of creating debt and financing programs and infrastructure, the federal government has the resources to create the type of nursing home facilities and care that promotes end-of-life dignity.

Summary

Decade after decade, legislators and advocates have attempted to reform the nursing home system. Failure to address structural/systemic causes of poor-quality care has resulted in maintenance of built in causes such as privatization, means-testing, and state level power while the industry has moved toward increasingly sophisticated, complex financial structures. The flow of capital from the shadow banking system along with the opaque nature of financial and legal networks operating increasingly throughout the nursing home industry will further destabilize a wide number of enterprises operating long-term care facilities.

It appears as though ultra-high-net worth individuals and families have been investing in nursing homes as a means of protecting their assets from taxes and inflation. This is a classic example of shadow banking in a business sector that is becoming increasingly financialized. Unfortunately, innovations accompanying financialized systems allow for secrecy and opaqueness of financial information.

As the nursing home industry becomes increasingly financialized, the purpose of caring for the elderly as a corporate mission becomes less salient in the business of operating skilled nursing facilities. One might say that the business of making money from money with elderly patients as the underlying commodity is emerging as the purpose of the business.

The financial complexity and veil of secrecy characterizing contemporary structures and modus operandi of nursing home corporations presents serious difficulties for advocates and legislators attempting reform. It is difficult to obtain the information needed to determine the amount of taxpayer funds siphoned from care into return to investors. Without that knowledge, the industry's excuse for deplorable conditions, i.e., low reimbursement cannot be evaluated. Nor can legislators and the public understand, advocate for, and plan for the appropriate level of reimbursement.

Given the professional care necessary for a patient with dementia or needing intense care with toileting, turning over in bed, the question becomes: "what should the level of reimbursement be for meeting the needs of the patient in such circumstances?" We also should ask, "what amount of funding is required to create a real 'home-like environment' in what are now dehumanizing, total-institutions?"

The federal government cannot leave these questions to the states. The taxing and budgeting problems of state government will override any significant reform of the nursing home system. Only the federal government can research, plan, and fund public policy necessary for ending the shameful system now in place for the care of frail elders.

Finally, the welfare philosophy of "medical indigence" and means-testing must be ended so that middle-class families are not required to descend into poverty and the stigma of welfare in order to receive long-term care. Indeed, the stigmatizing nature of welfare medicine serves as a psychological barrier to support on the part of the broader society for increased funding.

Statement Submitted by Kendra Cooper, Attorney at Law

Woburn, MA
www.kendracooperlaw.com

Senator Grassley, Ranking Member Wyden, and members of the Finance Committee, thank you for tackling the difficult subject of the ongoing, widespread abuse of elders in nursing homes and long-term care facilities. Over the past 20 years, I have witnessed elder financial exploitation and abuse through the mechanisms of powers of attorney, guardianships, conservatorships and the court system. While some dismiss such abuse and exploitation as rooted in "family" problems, I see from a different perspective, with families of elders targeted and manipulated by a wide range of trusted parties and entities, including some in the nursing home industry. Those with real property to liquidate are particularly valued.

Abusers and exploiters come in many forms. Sadly, they may be doctors, lawyers, court officials and judges. They also may be administrators and their long-term care facilities who are charged with assisting families and the elderly through their twilight years, yet all the while profiting from the eider's vulnerability. Private pay elders in facilities are particularly prized and, while money may not be exchanged directly for bringing an elder to a facility, rewards may be realized in other ways for abusers. Financial institutions, hospital staff, social workers, medical personnel, ministers, deacons and realtors may also profit when elders lose their civil rights and the legal system takes control.

To improve the treatment of elders, it must be admitted and acknowledged that some parties collectively collude and racketeer to further their own self interests. These abusers work against the interests of the elderly and their families, spending down an eider's assets until those assets are gone and the eider's "usefulness" as a private pay resident has ended. Elders with nothing more to be taken are in danger of quietly suffering an untimely death.

In one particularly well-documented Massachusetts/Maine interstate "granny snatching" abuse and exploitation case, an elderly, legally blind woman was taken from her home in Massachusetts to a facility hundreds of miles away in Maine. She then was misdiagnosed with dementia by a speech pathologist whose determination was then relied upon by the medical doctor who signed the guardianship application. Though a doctor's evaluation of capacity was required by Maine law for the guardianship proceeding, that medical doctor never actually examined the elder to determine her incapacity. Court documents show the speech pathologist later claimed he was unaware the elder was legally blind when he evaluated her.

The Maine Supreme Judicial Court (SJC) in its Memorandum of Decision declined to hear the elderly woman's case. The SJC considered the Appeal of the guardianship appointment "untimely," allowing the court to bypass the substance of the Appeal and avoid making a ruling that may affect other similarly flawed guardianship appointments. The elder in question, penniless and no longer a private-paying resident, died within months of this Memorandum, her legal options exhausted. Doctor's Notes obtained after her death revealed a methodical effort on the part of the elder's guardian and the attending nursing home physician to progressively drug (using morphine) the legally blind elder to death, beginning shortly after the SJC Decision.

Over a 5-year period, the elder was isolated in three Maine facilities and her phone access and mail tightly controlled. Though the elder received services from Mass Eye and Ear Infirmary while living in her Massachusetts home, Maine services for her blindness were declined by the guardian (according to nursing home administrator testimony). The elder was kept in the dark and never allowed to return to Massachusetts alive.

Few are concerned about the circumstances of an elder's death. Abusers and exploiters know elder deaths tend not to be investigated and, in the case of this elderly woman, the Maine medical examiner's office refused to conduct an autopsy, claiming it was unnecessary "due to age" and the fact the elder died in a care facility.

Georgia passed a law (HB 72) in 2015 making it a felony for groups of people and entities to collude and racketeer to financially exploit an elder. However, if cases are not acknowledged and investigated properly at the lowest levels, it is unlikely abusers will ever be prosecuted.

In 2015, the Maine Attorney General released a *Task Force Final Report on Financial Exploitation of the Elderly.* Acknowledged in the report is "a pervasive lack of training for all professionals in the system, including law enforcement, prosecutors, judges and court personnel" and adult protective services (APS) on how and when to report to law enforcement.

Unfortunately, Maine is not an anomaly among our states and little effective change has occurred. In October 2014, a Massachusetts Special Commission Report on Elder Protective Services also warned of a lack of training of investigators in financial exploitation and cautioned against the screening out of abuse complaints without adequate investigation of exploitation. That report expressed a need for better abuse prevention protocols among law enforcement, district attorneys, Elder Protective Services (EPS) workers and the implementation of Financial Abuse Specialist Teams (FAST).

While the national Elder Abuse Prevention and Prosecution Act 2017 (EAPPA) is a start, the provisions for training prosecutors only touch the surface of the problem. Financial exploitation of elders is commonplace throughout the country and, when elders are transported across state lines by perpetrators who "venue shop" for a willing Probate judge to help isolate the elder, families often face insurmountable obstacles. Unlike kidnapped children, the court too often takes a dim view of the value of elder lives and it is not a priority to return them to their homes and make them whole. Few people are willing to help the elderly and even fewer are willing to fight to protect their assets. In far too many situations, the elderly can be drugged, misdiagnosed with dementia and eliminated. Such cases also may be profitable for pharmaceuticals and the nursing homes.

Greater Federal oversight is needed on how guardianships are obtained and retained, along with increased scrutiny of every step that takes away elder civil rights, whether powers of attorney, guardianships or conservatorships. Abuse and exploitation can happen to anyone, poor or rich, average or exceptional. Wire transfers of assets can occur in minutes but recovery of stolen elder assets is rare. We need better training in the patterns of financial exploitation, especially for law enforcement, protective services, prosecutors, judges and court officers. When abuse in facilities is reported, there needs to be action taken by states and the Center for Medicare and Medicaid (CMS) and the records of their findings should be made readily available to reporters of the abuse.State and federal agencies and the courts should not be allowed to obstruct and withhold access to records to conceal nursing home abuse from families of loved ones.

Abusers and exploiters know the flaws and gaps in the protections of elders. As the ranks of the "baby boomer" generation swell in retirement age, financial abuse and exploitation of elders is a lucrative, growing industry that demands Federal oversight and accountability, not the least of which is the nursing home/long-term care business where elders and their families are most vulnerable to exploitation.

Thank you for this opportunity to raise some of my concerns with your committee.

Letter Submitted by Margaret A. Farley, Attorney at Law, P.A.

Lawrence, Kansas

March 19, 2019
U.S. Senate
Committee on Finance
Dirksen Senate Office Bldg.
Washington, DC

Dear Senators:

I am writing to submit my statement for the record regarding the March 6, 2019 Senate Committee on Finance hearing, "Not Forgotten: Protecting Americans from

Abuse and Neglect in Nursing Homes." I am fairly certain that the goal embodied in the title of the hearing was not met.

I have been advocating and working for a better standard of quality of care of nursing home residents in Kansas for almost 40 years. I have a BSN and I am a practicing attorney. My job as a discharge planning RN in a Kansas City area hospital in the late 1970s and early 1980s was to refer patients to local nursing homes if necessary when they were ready to leave the hospital. That was when I learned first-hand how bad nursing homes could be. Several individual families I referred to one nearby nursing home which always had openings returned to me to complain about the poor care. I organized a meeting of local nursing homes at the hospital, called it a quality of care committee, and warned the nursing homes if I had repeated complaints from families about the care of their loved ones, I would not refer discharged patients to them. It was a mere drop in the ocean towards quality care.

While I was at the hospital because I felt I had a duty to do so as a licensed nurse, I searched for enlightenment and help on the appalling problem of poor nursing home care which I had discovered. I learned about Kansans for Improvement of Nursing Homes (KINH—founded in 1975) and found that organization and two of its co-founders, Petey Cerf and Harriet Nehring, operating out of a closet, a hopeful starting point for a solution to the problem of poor nursing home care. KINH later changed their name to Kansas Advocates for Better Care (KABC). I found that I was not alone: that other people found nursing home care appalling and wanted to work for better care for this forgotten population.

Petey Cerf, on behalf of KINH, delivered written testimony on more than one occasion which became a part of the Congressional record, when extensive testimony on the hazards of life in U.S. nursing homes was given during the late 1970s and early 1980s. Those hearings were substantive and in depth. Petey's work over several years, "Inside Kansas Nursing Homes" allowed probably a hundred or more families a voice for the trauma their loved ones suffered due to nursing home abuse and neglect. Petey recorded and then transcribed their stories.

Over the years KINH, a/k/a for the last 20 years or so, KABC, now under the leadership of Executive Director Mitzi McFatrich, has provided informed testimony on bills, introduced new bills, commented on state and federal regulations, held statewide public meetings for the public and for nursing home nurses, administrators and social workers, worked in conjunction with the University of Kansas Medical Center in Kansas City, Kansas on annual professional workshops, urged new regulations, served on statewide committees, provided education to nursing home staff, pleaded with the state legislature for increased staffing, increased quality of staffing, etc. We have made significant progress but it is not enough.

As a nurse and attorney from Kansas, I have been an activist and advocate, joining the voices of thousands of others who care about nursing home residents over the past almost 40 years. I served as a board member of KINH in the early 1980s, the executive director of KINH (now known as Kansas Advocates for Better Care) from 1990–1996, the president of the board of directors of KABC, the president of Consumer Voice from 1998–2000, and currently serve as secretary of the board of KABC. I am also a practicing attorney, representing persons who have been injured, abused, neglected or killed by nursing facility or assisted living or rehabilitation/ SNF care for the last 20 years.

I respectfully ask that this Committee at least identify and reference the long ago congressional reports in the 1970s and 1980s and 1990s and 2000s or combine them with the record for this hearing. It will serve as a truer timeline and status report on whether we actually have forgotten or not over the years. The conclusion is irrefutable. While the quality of care may tick up or down a bit, we are, in so many ways, right back where we started.

Senator Grassley, be aware that I recently visited a friend in an Iowa nursing home and it was as appalling as any I have ever seen. So although I sat on the stage with you in the 1990s at a Consumer Voice conference in DC, I have to say your passion about poor nursing home care is not working even in Iowa. Have you given up? Is that why such a half-hearted effort for a hearing on nursing home abuse and neglect? When I was visiting in Iowa, I observed open verbal abuse against two separate individuals between a group of residents and another individual—taunting/ denigrating/humiliating; no staff member intervened; residents were sitting in the dining room waiting for dinner to be served for over an hour. Residents had to beat each other to the table they wanted. A cold grilled cheese sandwich and cold green beans were served on a Saturday night for dinner. My friend couldn't stomach the food. No one from the staff offered her different food about what I say, including the twinkling unanswered call lights. I could go on. I felt as though I had stepped back in time to nursing home care in the 1970s portrayed by Mary Adelaide Mendelson in her ground breaking book, "Tender Loving Greed."

Women and men raped in nursing homes; confused old people are abused and neglected and dropped and thrown and ignored and told to wait to go to the bathroom when everyone in the facility knows that they cannot or will not follow such commands, or they are told to go in their diapers, or their bed; they become dehydrated because no water is available—often visible but impossible to reach—they suffer fractures and untreated UTIs and decubitus ulcers and are drugged for "bad behaviors," etc. But if they are not cognitively capable to report what happened and what the harm was (did she know she was being raped—what's the harm?) crimes go uncharged and civil cases are dismissed or reduced before juries or in settlements.

Most residents in nursing homes have cognitive disorders. Almost no training on dementia is provided to persons entering the workforce, CNAs, CMAs.

I was very disappointed that there was no representation at all from consumer advocacy organization at the national level or even state level. This committee gave the nursing home industry association a voice (the American Health Care Association) but gave no voice whatsoever to the national consumer association (Consumer Voice) or any state associations or the Ombudsmen also resident advocates, or statewide consumer advocacy organizations which comprise the membership of the Consumer Voice. I feel for the two women who gave heart wrenching articulate and real life testimony and whose family members suffered intolerable care. But the scales were grossly unbalanced. That wasn't fair was it? Was that intentional? Clearly there were too few witnesses and the breadth of the experience and expertise of the witnesses far too limited. Also AMOA, the Society for Post Acute and Long Term Care Medicine, physicians who serve as treating physicians and medical directors, could have enlightened the Committee. Where were the associations who represent nurse aides (who do most of the daily work of nursing home care by far)? Where were rehabilitation therapists? The mental health specialists (Do you know how common depression is in nursing homes? Where were the long term care RNs and LPNs?

If you want additional anecdotal testimony: At least two of my family members, my father (within the last 5 years) and my paternal grandfather (about 25 years ago) were injured or killed by poor nursing home care. Both suffered falls due to negligent care resulting in serious injuries. My father died as a result. My grandfather never walked again. Preventable falls kill many people living in nursing homes. This is always caused by insufficient numbers of staff who may be undersupervised or undertrained. Why do I say that? Because if someone was there in attendance and properly trained and supported, that person would not have fallen. We freely allow people to fall in nursing homes and ruin the rest of their lives, as major fractures in late life mostly do. We all look the other way.

The industry says Medicaid doesn't pay enough. I think there is some truth to that—but let's test the theory. Have them open all of their books and let's examine them. After all, the federal government is paying for a big chunk of the care they provide. Testimony from the industry at your hearing was that negative margins are experienced on the Medicaid side but 12% margins are common on the Medicare side. And the big players in the nursing home industry have gamed the system for years. Many make money through layers of corporations and through REITs. And the rates for private pay residents are completely uncontrolled. People actually think they will get better care for more money. It's a myth. And guess what happens to people who have been gouged into poverty on their private pay rates and still aren't dead yet? They go on Medicaid. Wouldn't it make better sense to reasonably regulate private pay rates since we all pay for Medicaid care once the money runs out?

To inform the Committee I suggest you ask the American Association for Justice to provide examples of the cases which their members have brought on behalf of nursing home residents. Not just two people: thousands of people. And for the sake of all that is sacred, drop the Trump-renewed burden of arbitration on people injured by nursing home care. Other than to further upset the balance of power between consumers of nursing home care, there is ZERO reason to allow nursing home corporations to extract agreements for pre-dispute arbitration as a condition of entry into a nursing home. Give an old person and their sorrowful family a fighting chance at least.

Better staffing, better training and better supervision will fix most of the problems of poor care. Despite consumer advocates' demands for reasonable staffing standards for almost 50 years, no standards have been implemented other than the requirements for RN and LPN coverage in the Nursing Home Reform Law. Only in the last few years has the public been privy to pay stub info. Always before, the information has been unauditable self-reports. When KABC has introduced bills to increase staffing—the Kansas industry representatives have said that they already staff at the levels we promote in our bills; the very next day they say they cannot do it because of a staffing shortage. The workloads for many nurse aides are almost abusive. They and their charges carry the weight of understaffing. Who wants to work under such conditions for low pay?

My last point in this running monologue: Assisted living type facilities are in fact nursing facilities of yesterday without the protection of the federal nursing home reform law. There is big money there and we don't regulate them at the federal level, and we barely do at the state level. That has to change or we are just inviting further unnecessary injury and suffering and death.

Respectfully submitted, Margaret A. Farley, JD, BSN

Letters Submitted by Molly Flowers, R.N.

"Have Your Family and Friends Involved: Family and friends can help make sure you get good quality care." *From*—"Your Rights and Protections as a Nursing Home Resident" *(Medicare.gov; downloads.ems.gov)*

If you don't have family or friends you don't get "good quality care." The Government website suggests family and friends are a necessity to getting "good quality care" in nursing homes. Aren't nursing homes paid to give care? Do we think they get paid to give poor quality care? Are residents without family and friends left sucking hind teat because they have no one who "can help make sure [they] get good quality care." This statement is an admission that you will be neglected unless you have an outside advocate. And it shows the depth of our acceptance that nursing homes' employee staff who seemingly are beyond anyone's control neglect and abuse old, weak and dependent ones.

Molly Flowers, RN

From: Molly Flowers

Date: Wednesday, August 2, 2017

Subject: Substandard and Discriminatory Nursing Care in Dallas County Nursing Homes

To: webmaster <webmaster@bon.texas.gov>

Dear Texas Board of Nursing (BON) Board Member, Mrs. Patti Clapp,

The mission of The Board is to protect the public. And the public needs protecting! As a human being and native of Dallas County who was raised by sacrificial parents I am sickened by what I have observed in Dallas County's Nursing Homes. As a Registered Nurse I am disgusted! We subject our weak, old and broken ones to conditions that are deplorable and reprehensible. We permit a level of nursing neglect that would get acute care's doors closed. We wait for Austin and Washington to pass laws. We discuss reimbursement and staffing (which, by the way, are NOT the problems). We determine what healthcare we'll avail to immigrants, indigents, homeless, jailed, pediatric, maternity, and HIV clients. Yet we completely ignore the neglect with which we care for our old, broken, defenseless and weak ones?

Why do we tolerate this substandard (by practice standards) and discriminatory (by demographics and treatment goals) nursing care in Dallas County Nursing Homes? Why do we consistently pitch it off to State, or Ombudspeople. Why do we put up with this third-world-country of nursing in Dallas??

My parents stayed in four different Dallas nursing homes from September 2009, through November 2016. During their stays I visited nearly daily for four years, then daily for three years. I witnessed firsthand through the eyes of a registered nurse and daughter this substandard and discriminatory nursing care.

I have emailed and /or discussed my concerns with Texas Board of Nursing, Am Nurses Association and various other nursing entities, Dall as County Hospital District, two DCHD Board of Managers members, DADS Regional Director Paul Campbell, Senator Cornyn, Senator Huffines, and Rep Marchant. In 2014, I met with Susana Sulfstede of The Senior Source to tell her about the starvation and dehydration and neglect I was witnessing. In 2014–2015, I wrote thirteen complaints to DADS against one nursing home. And when that nursing home expelled my parents I wrote a fourteenth complaint. In 2015, I participated in a conference call with CMS, Senior Source ombudsmen, and State Liaison to address starvation and dehydration. I met with local Office of Inspector General to report Medicaid fraud, waste, and abuse in the form of care reimbursed, but not given. In April I filed a complaint with the ACLU for Violation of the Older Americans Act of 1965, Title 1, Section 101, Paragraphs 2 and 4 by Dallas County Nursing Homes. I sent a letter similar to this one to each of Dallas County's four County Commissioners and Commissioners Court Judge Clay Jenkins. I asked my commissioner for a resolution that Dall as County will not tolerate substandard and discriminatory nursing care and medical care in its nursing homes. I asked for a citizens' task force with Commissioner backing for traction and credibility to describe the problems, identify fixes, plan, implement and review.

We MUST work to make Texas nursing homes safe! We MUST bring them up to the same standards in nursing practice that we have in acute care. Investigate for yourself these and all of Texas' nursing homes on DADS' website. Research the owners, the money behind them, and the neglect with which some owners manage these homes. Read the citations and reviews and ask yourself, is this what I would want?

I am told today's substandard nursing care is because nurses today do not know the Nursing Practice Act, their standards of nursing, and the rules that govern their practice. I don't recall excuses ever being any part of any nursing plan of care. Whatever the cause, the buck's destination is always the same: the nurse!

I was NEVER going to put my precious beloved parents Mom (92 years old when she died November 2016) and Daddy (93 years old when he died November 2015), he a dentist for fifty years across from SMU, co-founder of the Dallas Chapter LSU alumni club, lifetime member of SERTOMA International, precinct chairman and volunteer on five medical missionary trips to Honduras, into nursing homes. But, God had other plans. And what I saw of nursing made me sick; MAKES me sick to this day.

Additionally, families are robbed of an invaluable commodity in the form of time meant to be spent in the presence of our loved ones being spent on nursing duties. I'll say that again: time meant to be spent in the presence of our loved ones is stolen away from us as we spend it to do the work of the nurses- over and over and over again. We must spend time meant to be spent in the presence of our loved ones to track down staff to change Mother, or to put Daddy to bed, or to give pain medication. Or, we must spend time meant to be spent in the presence of our loved ones to complain to DADS about nursing neglect. We must spend time meant to be spent in the presence of our loved ones to talk on the phone with administration, or meet with them in person about one nursing problem or another. We must spend time meant to be spent in the presence of our loved ones to teach a director of nurses about the respiratory care of the post pneumonia geriatric patient!

As families, our jobs are to love our loved ones. Our jobs are to sit with them, to comb their hair, to paint their nails, to watch movies or football games with them, or to look at photos, or share meals. Nursing homes have stolen countless hours from us by requiring us to provoke their nurses into doing their jobs! We will never get those hours back.

Finally, I can tell you there is nothing in place now in the complaint mechanism of the Board of Nursing to protect the public. I can report a nurse (IF the home will give me the last name of the nurse). The nurse will blame the Certified Nurse Aide (CNA). The CNA will blame the resident (he/ she refused, had a visitor, was asleep, said 'not now'). And the BON will find no fault.

What's it going to be for Dallas County Nursing Home residents? STOP the neglect, the starvation, the dehydration, and the deprivation in these heinous places. STOP the substandard and discriminatory nursing care in Dallas County Nursing Homes. Require that all Dallas County Nursing Home Nurses, RN's and LVN's, practice according to the same standards as acute care nurses, that is, according to the Nursing Practice Act and Standards of Practice for Professional Nursing in the State of Texas.

Most Sincerely,

Molly Flowers, R.N.

From: Molly Flowers
Date: Thursday April 27, 2017
Subject: Nursing Homes
To: Charles.Schwertner@senate.texas.gov

Why do Dallas County Nursing Homes hire staff who can't speak English, medical directors who don't see residents, nurses who can't do basic assessments, administrators who don't leave their offices? Why are they owned by corporations who don't allocate funds for hot water tanks, for instance, and ample supplies for bedside care?

Why do families have to fight for decent care? And why don't they sue for back wages for doing the facilities' work? Why don't nurses and CNAs feed residents? Or hydrate them? Why don't med aids know what they're giving? Why doesn't OIG have more fraud cases of Medicaid/Medicare dollars buying care not given? Five things acute care has that long term care hasn't. Why not?

1) Vigorous staff recruitment and retention in the form of competitive reimburse package: benefits+salary+tuition reimbursement (don't squeal to me about facility reimbursement; these owners are loaded)
2) Vigorous relationship with the outside world (medical students, nursing students, therapy students, advanced degree students (MBA, MHA, MPH), researchers, Joint Commission, families, volunteers, churches, do-gooders, special projects/certifications/studies/grants)
3) Just Culture
4) Vigorous in-house compliance, ethics, safety, clinical training
5) Progressive discipline leading to termination of long term care is discriminatory and substandard. It is healthcare we would not tolerate for maternity, trauma, pediatric, or AIDS patients.

Shame on Us. Molly Flowers, R.N.

Subject: List emailed to CMS Investigator Susanna Cruz, RN, MSN at her request August 13, 2015—names changed

Good afternoon, Miss Cruz.

Thank you for your time this morning. This is to re-cap the highlights of the conversation that took place on the telephone between Joyce, private duty sitter for my father, you and me. Mother has been in nursing home 7 years: XYZ facility, 2009-2012, ABC facility, 2012 to present. Father has been in ABC facility going on 8 months.

I am in ABC facility daily M–F evening through bedtime and weekends by 4pm until after 8pm—sometimes as much as 10 hours each Saturday and Sunday.

ABC facility has been without hot water since Thursday, August 6. Father has not been bathed since Wednesday August 5th. Hot water lack began July 29th, but prior there were periods when it was off, then on, then off, then on, for some weeks.

Issues and concerns have for many months been reported, documented and addressed to administration, state, DON, staff nurse, CNAs and outside agencies.

It has become routine for CNAs to state to resident/family/sitter that they are "short staffed" and therefore unable to assist resident as requested for toileting, getting out of bed, getting dressed in a timely manner. Privately paid sitters must routinely remind staff to refresh Mother's empty O2 canisters.

Privately paid sitter routinely helps a blind resident at lunch because facility staff do not help, nor come to table to inquire of him if he needs help.

I told DON and Administrator that 2 CNAs stood Mother from wheelchair to bed when it was ordered and stated on her room door that she uses total lift to stand. Administrator and Regional Clinical Director (on conference call) had me come to meeting (DON broke down on icy roads) and told me perhaps mother is not a fit for the facility and perhaps I should move her to another nursing home. Both CNAs continued to work with Mother and Father. Administrator said CNAs felt I was investigating their work with my mother and I should check my approach.

Mother did not receive a bath for over 2 weeks. I asked the Unit Manager if Mother could change to morning bath schedule, she said sure and Mom started routinely getting bathed. Peter, CNA told me recently, "No, we're short-staffed" when I asked if Mom got a bath.

Joyce, private duty for Father x5 years, M–F 8a–4p said when State comes in all staff run around, show-up in the dining room, but when state leaves, they go back to not doing what they should do.

I asked repeatedly for months for Daddy to be allowed to get up at his request in the very early morning (6am) as per his preference and lifetime habit. DON and night nurse said that's fine. CNAs on nights and ones coming in at 6 refused, telling him, "there is nothing going on, stay in bed" so it never happened until recently a 7p–7a private sitter had enough of my complaining to them and started bugging CNAs to death so they would do it and they did. I have prevented MANY falls being in the dining room while Florence and Tami and Wilson sit at the nurse's station, no CNAs present.

Mom is a choke risk has been for all the time she has been there, yet Wednesday, August 5th, she ate alone at table with a couple residents in dining room, no staff in dining room at 7 p.m. having gotten out late from beauty shop. I told veteran CNA she is choke risk and needs to be supervised, she said oh, she did not know . . . that's another thing, CNAs aren't kept abreast of tx care plans and changes.

In 4 years I have never seen supervisor, DON nor Administrator in the evening. No oversight, supervision. No leadership ever checks on what the nurses are doing.

Currently there are 3 residents who wander and go in and out of residents' rooms. CNA Lucy told me, what can you do? They wander . . . I complained to Wilson, nurse he went and retrieved one. A resident recently punched out one of the roamers.

Sitter recently had laundry personnel get Patient X a different wc because hers was caked with stool, food and urine. Sitter sits for another resident but has known Patient X for a long time.

Joyce reported observing a female resident fall out of her wheelchair onto the footrests and wound nurse said, "Man down," and nurse Chris picked her up and put her back in her wheelchair and then pushed her back to the table in the dining room.

I report things to State. There is more I can send you if you are interested. Molly Flowers, R.N.

Letter Submitted by Paul Greenwood

U.S. Senate
Committee on Finance
Re: March 6, 2019 Full Committee Hearing
"Not Forgotten: Protecting Americans from Abuse and Neglect in Nursing Homes"

To the committee members:

My name is Paul Greenwood. I am a licensed attorney in California and also am qualified as a lawyer in the United Kingdom. Last March I retired from the San Diego District Attorney's Office after working as a deputy district attorney for 25 years.

In January 1996 I was asked by my office to begin an elder abuse prosecution unit and I served as lead prosecutor in that capacity for the next 22 years until my retirement. I now spend much of my time teaching and training others around the nation on elder abuse investigations and prosecutions.

I have been involved in the prosecution of over 750 felony cases of elder abuse and neglect including homicides, sexual assaults, neglect, physical and emotional abuse and financial exploitation. California has an excellent statute, namely Penal Code section 368 which defines two types of victims—elders aged 65 years or older and dependent adults aged 18–64 with either a physical or mental disability.

I am pleased that this committee has seen fit to take a closer look at the problem of elder abuse and neglect in nursing homes. However, I would urge the committee to broaden its scrutiny to include not only skilled nursing homes but also assisted living and unlicensed facilities.

One of my major frustrations is the fact that our office received very few investigative reports of abuse and neglect in an institutional setting. The majority of the cases that I prosecuted originated from a community setting. Therein lies the biggest challenge for this committee—how do we get such incidents that occur in nursing homes to be channeled to law enforcement.

In the last four years of my assignment we were able to make some impact in redressing the lack of referrals from assisted living facilities. The initiative was inspired by a series of articles that appeared in our local newspaper, the San Diego Union Tribune in September 2013 entitled "Crimes go uninvestigated at care homes." As a result our County Board of Supervisors gave our office additional monies that allowed us to hire additional investigators and allocate another prosecutor to our elder abuse unit. I spent a year developing a protocol with the local office of the California Attorney General (AG) and with the Department of Social Services Community Care Licensing (CCL) which is the state agency responsible for the licensing of assisted living facilities. As a result CCL began to share reports by e-mail with my office and with the Attorney General.

The arrangement that we established was to designate my office or the local Attorney General's office as the lead prosecutor agency in alternate months for any CCL referrals that rose to the level of criminal abuse or neglect. The three agencies would meet on a regular basis to discuss cases and apportion resources and as a result there has been a welcome increase in the number of successful prosecutions.

Unfortunately we have not been able to replicate a similar system with the state agency that oversees licensing of skilled nursing facilities.

Having been involved in elder abuse and neglect prosecutions for many years I am convinced that the only effective approach is through the use of multi disciplinary teams.

Here are some issues that I have encountered that I believe are barriers to protecting residents of long term care facilities from abuse and neglect:

- Local law enforcement is rarely called to a facility to investigate allegations of neglect or abuse.
- The Long Term Care Ombudsman's office is heavily dependent on volunteers and is often conflicted because of a resident's insistence that nothing be done to report the abuse or neglect.

- The state agencies responsible for "investigating" violations in nursing homes are not proactive enough to share their findings in a timely fashion with law enforcement or the county prosecutor's office.

And here are some recommendations that I respectfully submit could have a positive impact on the protection of residents:

- Each State agency that has oversight on issuing and revoking licenses for nursing homes be mandated to share reports of alleged abuse and neglect in a timely fashion with local law enforcement, the County Prosecutor's office and with the State Attorney General's office.
- Counties in every state should develop a multi disciplinary task force to discuss ways to share information and develop protocols for investigation and prosecution of abuse and neglect. Such task force members should include at a minimum a representative from local law enforcement, the County prosecutor's office, the state Attorney General's office, the Ombudsman, Adult Protective Services, the state licensing agency referenced above and regional medical facilities.
- Develop training for all first responder EMTs, paramedics and hospital triage staff so that when a resident is admitted with indicia of abuse or neglect there is a protocol for an immediate referral to local law enforcement.
- If the state has mandatory reporting laws, to encourage prosecutors to consider prosecuting a facility that has willfully failed to make a timely report of such abuse or neglect to the appropriate authorities.
- Each county or region should develop a blueprint along the lines of the San Diego County blueprint that we developed last year and which is attached.
- Establish training for local law enforcement and prosecutors on how to investigate and prosecute cases of resident neglect.

In conclusion I strongly feel that the key to protection from abuse and neglect is to be found at the county level. The challenge is for us to create protocols all over this country that provides for a timely referral to local law enforcement, the County prosecutor's office and the state Attorney General's office to ensure that investigations are conducted. In regions where resources on the ground are stretched, I hope that the U.S. Attorney's elder justice coordinator can provide some assistance in suggesting additional support.

I urge this committee to invite the director of each of the 50 state agencies that issues and revokes licenses for long-term care facilities to submit a report outlining what arrangements are currently in operation for sharing their findings of abuse and neglect violations with local law enforcement. Getting that data (or lack of it) will give the committee insight into what I see as the most pressing issue for reform.

Paul Greenwood
Retired elder abuse prosecutor
Consultant and trainer

San Diego County Elder and Dependent Abuse Blueprint 2018

Coordinated, Caring, Community Response

History

In the summer of 2017, San Diego District Attorney Summer Stephan began a formal planning process to coordinate San Diego's community response to elder abuse. Because of a rise in elder abuse prosecutions, as well as the impending explosion of the elder population, the District Attorney brought together countywide stakeholders on November 3, 2017 for a first-ever "think-tank" of experts, including professionals from all disciplines that serve as touchpoints for elder and dependent adults. Those experts identified gaps and needs in our community, and set goals for the future. District Attorney Stephan then convened a larger Elder and Dependent Abuse Summit on March 1, 2018, where this Blueprint was unveiled and endorsed. For the first time, our county has a formalized written set of goals and guidelines to enable us to utilize best practices as we collectively serve our elders and dependent adults.

Mission Statement and Values

This Blueprint commits San Diego County to a coordinated community response to Elder and Dependent Adult Abuse. We are committed to thoughtful, prompt, thorough and effective services to the victims we serve. We will strive to utilize best practices in our fields, as well as to cooperate, collaborate, communicate and train with others dedicated to this mission.

Need for a Countywide Blueprint

The United States Census Bureau reports that by 2050, the world's population aged 65 and older will increase to almost 1.6 billion people. One in six people will be 65 or older in 2050. In San Diego County, almost 23% of the population is projected to be over age 65 by the year 2050, which is a 10% increase from 2015. The County of San Diego's Adult Protective Services data is consistent with these predictions, as there has been a 17.1% increase in new cases assigned for investigation compared to fiscal year 2007–2008. In fiscal year 2015–2016, there were a total of 13,755 reports of suspected abuse. San Diego community partners will prepare for this growth and strategize how best to serve our seniors.

Our civilization will be judged on how we treat our youngest and our oldest members

—Summer Stephan, San Diego County District Attorney

Necessary Definitions

Elder: any person 65 years or older (CA Penal Code section 368(g), Welfare and Institutions Code section 15610.27)

Dependent Adult: any person between the ages of 18 and 64 who has physical or mental limitations that restrict his or her ability to carry out normal activities or to protect his or her rights. (PC 368(h), W&I 15610.23(a)) a position of trust with, an elder or dependent adult, whether paid or not. (PC 368(i))

Dispatcher Response

Dispatchers are an integral part of the community response to elder abuse because they are a first touchpoint to the abuse. Dispatchers should continue their education on signs of abuse and receive ongoing training on Alzheimer's and other related dementias.

Patrol Response

Responding peace officers play a crucial role in creating successful outcomes for Elder and dependent adult victims. Patrol officers and deputies in San Diego County will strive to do the following when feasible:

- Become educated about various elder and dependent adult abuse, and penal code sections accounting for physical and financial abuse, as well as neglect. The most relevant code sections are contained in ADDENDUM A.
- Request Emergency Protective Orders when legally appropriate in order to best protect elder victims.
- Treat elder and dependent adult citizens with dignity and respect.
- Follow interview guidelines in ADDENDUM B for interviewing elders and dependent adults.
- Recognize that elder or dependent adults may have difficulty narrating events, appear to be poor historians, or lack short term memory, which adds to their vulnerability.
- Document the scene using the San Diego Countywide Elder and Dependent Adult Abuse Supplemental contained in ADDENDUM C.
- Cross-Report to Adult Protective Services (APS) by calling 1–800–510–2020 (from within San Diego County area codes) or 1–800–339–4661 (from area codes outside San Diego County) and follow-up by sending a written report of documented suspected abuse within two working days, or reporting through the

Aging and Independence Services Web Portal at *www.aiswebreferral.org,* which does not require any follow up written report. (W&I 15640(c) and 15658.)

- Obtain a signed medical release from potential victims.
- Interview caregivers separately. In some situations, the caregiver may be the abuser.
- Recognize victim cooperation is not always necessary for prosecution. Each dispatched call or case should be investigated on its own evidentiary merits.
- Consult with a supervising Elder Abuse Deputy District Attorney or Deputy City Attorney to determine whether the case is more than simply "civil" in nature.
- Physical Abuse/Endangerment Cases: Document all injuries, obtain statements from each elder or dependent adult and document the demeanor of the elder or dependent adult. Photograph or videotape the suspected crime scene, and document any physical evidence and the general appearance of the residence. Seize any objects used to injure the elder or dependent adult and document any medications present at the scene and any pertinent medical history or conditions. Interview the medical personnel available. Reports: (1) Prepare an initial crime report in all cases of suspected physical abuse or endangerment and (2) Cross report to APS (see section below titled, "cross reporting requirements.")
- Financial Abuse: Determine the identity of the reporting party, any relationship between the reporting party and the elder or dependent adult, and why the reporting party notified law enforcement. Determine the dates of economic loss, how the loss was discovered, and who discovered the loss. Obtain sample signature of the elder or dependent adult. Identify and interview, when feasible, all witnesses who may have relevant information. Interview any caregivers to determine their duties and responsibilities, including any financial agreements or loans provided to a caregiver by the elder/dependent adult. Obtain written consent to request bank records, credit statements, real estate loan documents all accessible financial documents pertaining to the suspected financial abuse.
- Neglect cases: Neglect occurs when a caretaker or custodian fails to act with a degree of care that a reasonable person would have used when caring for an elder or dependent adult. Officers should do their best to document all physical evidence and consider videotaping the living conditions.
- Special Considerations/Circumstances with Domestic Violence involving the Elderly: On occasion domestic violence offenders may be elderly or extremely infirmed. In some cases it may be possible to establish that an elderly offender is not competent, not aware of their actions and/or was previously diagnosed by a physician or Adult Protective Services (APS) of not being competent to make their own decisions as a result of dementia or a related disorder of cognitive decline. It is important to be aware that some offenders present a significant health risk due to the shock of incarceration and or removal from their normal

place of residence as a result of their advanced age or significant medical condition or diagnosis of Alzheimer's or other related dementia. In addition to investigating/documenting the domestic violence incident as outlined in the San Diego County Law Enforcement Domestic Violence protocol, some or all of these options may be applicable based on the individual set of circumstances as alternatives to arrest/booking:

- Obtaining an Emergency Protective Order (EPO) and ensuring family members can keep the victim and offender in separate locations
- Evaluate for 5150 W&I and if feasible/and or appropriate, commit offender to either an LPS designated hospital or CMH
- Contact/request local or available PERT (Psychiatric Emergency Response Team) team
- Complete an arrest report indicting the offender was released pursuant to Penal Code section 849(b) or taken into custody and released thereafter to a competent third party who will assure the safety of both the victim and the offender
- Contact the duty Adult Protective Services/Aging and Independent Services representative (1–800–510–2020) for additional resources to keep the victim safe and separated from the offender if the offender cannot be incarcerated/booked.
- Cross-Report to APS (see ADDENDUM G)

Investigation Response

Follow-up investigations are necessary in many elder abuse cases, as first responders may not be in the best position to gather all existing evidence. Follow-up investigations in San Diego County when feasible should include:

- Determining the victim is safe and whether there is a need for emergency housing.
- Cross-reporting to APS.
- Making contact with the assigned APS social worker, Ombudsman or Department of Justice for the possibility of joint investigation or sharing of information when appropriate and if necessary.
- Obtaining any prior APS referrals if they exist.
- Verifying that the initial investigation by patrol addressed all elements of the reported crime.
- Obtaining and viewing all available evidence, including medical information, photographs, bank, checking and financial records.
- Determining if more evidence should be collected or obtained.

- Follow-up interview of victim as soon as possible, preferably videotaped, and outside the presence of caregiver or others present in the home.
- Attempting to interview the suspect when legally appropriate, preferably videotaped.
- Attempting to make appropriate law enforcement notifications if suspect remains unidentified.
- Taking advantage of other countywide resources if needed, including those listed in ADDENDUM D.
- Obtaining a signed medical release from victim if not already received by patrol.
- If victim is conserved, obtaining conservator-signed release, along with paperwork that documents the conservatorship.
- Interviewing the victim's treating physician or other medical professionals that interviewed the victim.
- Conducting follow-up interviews with neighbors, family members, or others that may have information or evidence about the incident.
- Conducting a recorded pretext call if necessary, reasonable, and warranted.
- Executing warrants for electronics that may contain relevant evidence.
- Collecting dispatch 911 recordings for current incident and any past incidents.
- Sharing and preserving body-worn camera evidence.
- Collecting physical or documentary evidence related to the crime.
- Obtaining handwriting samples from the victim and the suspect. Have the suspect sign his/her name, as well as the victim's name.
- Documenting the suspect's access to victim's financial information.

Prosecution Response

The San Diego City Attorney's Office and the San Diego County District Attorney's Office will dedicate specially trained prosecutors to handle elder abuse cases vertically. Prosecutors are strongly encouraged to do the following when feasible and legally appropriate:

- Become familiar with best-practices in the field of Elder and Dependent Adult Abuse prosecution.
- Participate in outreach to elevate awareness and education in the community about elder and dependent adult abuse.
- File Penal Code section 368 crimes either as misdemeanors or as felonies.
- Request Criminal Protective Orders.
- Oppose case continuances due to the vulnerable nature of elder victims and witnesses when legally appropriate.

- Conduct conditional exams of elder or dependent adult victims in order to preserve their testimony.
- Treat all victims and witnesses in a trauma-informed way with dignity, respect, and care.
- Use experts including handwriting analysts, forensic accountants, wound care experts, civil attorneys, geriatricians, geriatric psychologists, psychiatrists, and deputy medical examiners to provide evidence related to necessary elements of the elder abuse crimes.
- Be familiar with the "San Diego County Prosecutor Elder and Dependent Adult Case Preparation Checklist" attached in ADDENDUM E.
- Use a prosecutor-checklist to enhance collection of evidence and have consistency in case preparation such as the one attached in ADDENDUM E.
- Make efforts to secure victim restitution as early as possible in the criminal process.
- Elicit victim testimony with full-cross examination as soon as possible after charging, due to *Crawford v. Washington* 6th amendment concerns.
- Participate in ongoing training and education in the field of Elder and Dependent Adult Abuse.
- Achieve consistency and uniformity when possible in case issuance, handling, and resolution.

Restraining Orders

Restraining orders are one of the most important public safety tools we have to protect elder and dependent adults. All criminal justice system partners should familiarize themselves with the available restraining order options available in ADDENDUM F, obtain restraining orders for victims if appropriate, and enforce restraining orders according to the Penal Code. (Penal Code sections 836(c)(1); 13701; 13710 136.2; 1371(c); 136.2(h)(2).) Criminal Protective Orders in elder or dependent adult cases may be valid for up to 10 years. (Penal Code section 368(l).) Officers shall enforce out of state protective orders or restraining orders that are presented to them if (1) the order appears valid on its face, (2) the order contains both parties' names, and (3) the order has not yet expired. "Out of state orders" include those issued by U.S. Territories, Native Tribes, and military agencies. (Full Faith and Credit Provision of the Violence Against Woman Act, Family Code sections 6400–6409.) This protocol should be read in conjunction with the San Diego County Domestic Violence and Children Exposed to Domestic Violence Law Enforcement Protocol adopted in 2015.

Psychiatric Emergency Response Team (PERT)

The Psychiatric Emergency Response Team consists of specially trained officers and deputies who are paired with licensed mental health professionals. Together, they respond on-scene to situations involving people who are experiencing a mental related crisis and have come to the attention of law enforcement. The PERT team is a tremendous resource for law enforcement in the response to elders who may have Alzheimer's or other related dementias. PERT teams are encouraged to continue collaboration and cooperation with law enforcement and participate in cross-training with community partners so PERT teams can best support law enforcement and elderly perpetrators/victims.

Cross-Reporting

Depending on the location of the abuse, the type of abuse, and whether the suspect is a licensed health practitioner, law enforcement, adult protective services, and the local ombudsman are required to cross-report incidents of abuse, and report the results of their investigation of referrals or reports of abuse to the respective referring or reporting agencies listed in ADDENDUM G (W&I 15640).

Mandated Reporting

Welfare and Institutions Code sections 15630–15632 mandate that certain individuals must report any abuse or suspected abuse to elders or dependent adults. Mandated reporters shall make a report whenever the mandated reporter:

- In his/her professional capacity or within the scope of his/her employment;
- Has knowledge of or observes abuse or neglect;
- Is told by an elder or dependent of abuse or neglect; or
- Reasonably suspects abuse or neglect. (W&I 15630.)

What Happens if a Mandated Reporter Does Not Report?

A mandated reporter who fails to report an incident of known or reasonably suspected elder and dependent abuse or neglect is guilty of a misdemeanor, and can be fined or sentenced to jail time. (W&I 15630(h).)

Who Is a Mandated Reporter? (W&I 15630(A).)

- Any person who has assumed full or intermittent responsibility for the care or custody of an elder or dependent adult, whether or not he or she receives compensation.
- Administrators, supervisors and any licensed staff of a public or private facility that provides care or services for elder or dependent adults.
- Elder or dependent adult care custodian.

- Health practitioner.
- Clergy member.
- Employee of the Adult Protective Services agency.
- Law enforcement.
- All officers and employees of financial institutions.

When and How Must a Mandated Reporter Make the Report?

Mandated reporters shall report by telephone or the confidential internet reporting tool immediately or as soon as practicably possible. If reported by telephone, a written report shall be sent, or an internet report shall be made within two working days.

Telephone Call: Immediately or as soon as practically possible, call Adult Protective Services at 1–800–510–2020 (from within San Diego County area codes) or 1–800–339–4661 (from area codes outside San Diego County).

If abuse occurred in long-term care facility call Long Term Care Ombudsman at 1–800–640–4661.

Written or confidential internet report: Within two working days, fill out form SOC 341 or SOC 342 (financial institutions).

Online Submissions: *www.AISWebReferral.org* Mandated reporters can register ahead of time and be approved to submit non-emergent reports 24/7 and no paper SOC 341/342 is required with this method.

Can a mandated reporter be civilly liable for reporting abuse? No. Mandated reporters shall not be civilly or criminally liable for any report made. (W&I 15634.)

Confidentiality of mandated reporter: The reports made pursuant to W&I sections 15630, 15630.1, and 15631 shall be confidential and may be disclosed only to persons or agencies who legally are entitled to the information, such as Adult Protective Services, a local law enforcement agency, the office of the District Attorney, the office of the City Attorney, the office of the Public Guardian, the Probate Court, members of multidisciplinary teams who use the information for prevention, identification or treatment of abuse or elderly or dependent persons, and all others listed in W&I 15633.5.

Ombudsman Reporting Requirements

The Long Term Care Ombudsman will ask all victims or authorized representatives if they want law enforcement or the Bureau of Medi-Cal Fraud involved. If the victim or victim's authorized representative consents, the Ombudsman shall cross-report known or suspected criminal activities to local law enforcement or to the Bureau of Medi-Cal Fraud & Elder Abuse as soon as possible and must follow up with a written report within two working days. (W&I 15640(d).) If the Ombudsman's office learns of any instance of neglect occurring in a health care facility that has seriously harmed any patient or reasonably appears to present a serious threat to the health or physical well-being of a patient in that facility, it shall immediately report by phone and in writing within two working days to the bureau. If the victim or potential victim of the neglect withholds consent to being identified, the report shall contain circumstantial information about the neglect but shall not identify the victim or potential victim. (W&I 15640(d).)

Suspected Sexual Abuse of an Elder or Dependent Adult

When sexual abuse is suspected, efforts should be made by all community partners to treat the elder victim with dignity and care, with the recognition that many victims delay in their disclosure of sexual abuse for reasons including but not limited to fear, shame, embarrassment, and self-doubt. Ideally, repeated interviews should be kept to a minimum, and all criminal justice and community partners involved should do their best to communicate and collaborate with one another in a search for the truth. Victims should be notified that they have the right to a support person of their choosing pursuant to Penal Code sections 679.04 and 264.2. Crime reports and cross-reports should be made pursuant to the sections in this protocol titled "Cross-Reporting." Documentation of the physical evidence and crime scene is important, as are any injuries to the victim. Coordination with and dispatch of the Sexual Assault Response Team, according to department policy, should be done as quickly as reasonably possible to ensure any appropriate examination can be conducted with consent of the elder victim, or with consent from the victim's legal guardian, conservator, or attorney in fact for health care. Exams are activated by calling 760–739–2150 (business hours) or through the 24-hour phone line at 888–211–6347 (holidays, weekends, after business hours). Recorded interviews should be made for suspects, and documentation made of all statements made by suspects. When taking a suspect into custody, law enforcement should follow any department policies regarding collection of evidence or performing a standard rape kit on the suspect.

Aging and Independence Services

Aging and Independence Services (AIS) provides services to older adults, people with disabilities, and their family members, to help keep clients safely in their homes, promote healthy and vital living, and publicize positive contributions made by older adults and persons with disabilities. AIS operates a call center that provides aging and disability resource information for the community as well as serves as the hotline for reporting elder and dependent adult abuse. AIS commits to continued collaboration and partnership with criminal justice agencies dedicated to serving the elder population and dependent adults.

Adult Protective Services

AIS operates Adult Protective Services, which serves adults 65 and older and dependent adults 18 and older, who are harmed or threatened with harm, to ensure their rights to safety and dignity. APS investigates elder and dependent adult abuse, including cases of neglect and abandonment, as well as physical, sexual and financial abuse. APS commits to partner and collaborate with other criminal justice agencies dedicated to the prevention of and response to elder and dependent adult abuse. APS further commits to involvement with the San Diego Elder and Dependent Adult Death Review Team, which reviews elder and dependent adult deaths in the County of San Diego to determine if system-wide changes or improvements should be made.

Long Term Care Ombudsman

The County of San Diego's Long Term Care Ombudsman (LTCO) program is a part of AIS. LTCO advocates for residents in long term care facilities, such as nursing homes, as well as investigates abuse in other licensed facilities. An Ombudsman listens to concerns, provides information and assistance when requested, and will investigate and resolve complaints related to care or personal rights. The Long Term Care Ombudsman commits to partner and collaborate with criminal justice agencies dedicated to the prevention of and response to elder and dependent adult abuse.

Office of the Public Administrator/Public Guardian/Public Conservator

Within the Office of the Public Administrator/Public Guardian/Public Conservator, the Public Administrator serves as the administrator of decedent estates and attends to their final affairs, at times involving issues of abuse and neglect of older adults and adults with disabilities. The Public Guardian serves as the legally-appointed conservator for persons found by the Probate Court to be substantially unable to attend to their own care needs and /or effectively manage their assets, particularly where no other person is able and available to reasonably act on their behalf. Frequently, Public Guardian conservatees are frail, residing in skilled nursing facilities, and previously the victims of abuse and/or neglect. The Public Conservator serves as the legally-appointed Lanterman-Petris-Short (LPS) conservator for persons struggling with grave disability due to a mental illness and therefore acts to secure stabilizing treatment services and evaluate the need for conservatorship reestablishment on an annual basis. The Office of the Public Administrator/Public Guardian/Public Conservator commits to partner and collaborate with other criminal justice agencies dedicated to the prevention of and response to elder and dependent adult abuse.

California Department of Social Services, Community Care Licensing Division, Senior Care Program Office

Community Care Licensing (CCL) commits to continue their existing collaboration with the Office of the Attorney General as well as the San Diego District Attorney's Office and San Diego City Attorney's office to best protect elders and dependent adults residing in Assisted Living facilities and community care facilities. CCL will continue to be a valued partner in the assisted living facility coordinated program sponsored by

County Supervisor Dianne Jacob and refer suspicious cases to the Attorney General, the District Attorney, or the City Attorney when appropriate.

Attorney General's Office

The Attorney General's Bureau of Medi-Cal Fraud and Elder Abuse (AG) serves as a valued community partner in the Assisted Living Facility program sponsored by County Supervisor Dianne Jacob, as well as a partner with the San Diego District Attorney's office sharing jurisdiction to investigate and prosecute elder and dependent adult abuse in other institutional settings, including nursing homes and hospitals. The AG will continue to collaborate with other stakeholders to best protect elders and dependent adults.

Suspicious Death/Homicide

An unexplained or suspicious elder or dependent adult death should be treated as a homicide until a complete investigation including autopsy has been performed. Do not presume that all elder deaths are natural simply because of the age or physical limitations of the deceased.

Removal of Firearms from Those Legally Prohibited to Possess Them

Law enforcement should be familiar with the laws surrounding firearm relinquishment of those individuals who cannot legally possess them. (Penal Code section 18100 et. seq.) When law enforcement verifies that a restraining order has been issued, the officer shall make reasonable efforts to determine if the restraining order prohibits the possession of firearms and/or requires the relinquishment of firearms. If the order prohibits firearms possession, when feasible and reasonable, the officer will make reasonable efforts to:

- Inquire whether the restrained person possesses firearms (ask the restrained person or the protected person).
- Query through the California Law Enforcement Telecommunication Systems (CLETS) and the Automated Firearms System (AFS) to determine if any firearms are registered to the restrained person.
- Receive or seize prohibited firearms located in plain view or pursuant to a consensual or other lawful search. (PC 18250(a).)
-

Elder and Dependent Adult Death Review Team

The County of San Diego Elder Death Review Team meets quarterly to review suspicious elder and dependent adult deaths occurring in San Diego County. The goal of the multidisciplinary team is to identify risk factors associated with these deaths, maintain statistical data, facilitate communication between involved investigative agencies, and identify any system improvements that could have been made surrounding the suspicious death. Information gathered by the Elder Death Review Team and any recommendations made by the team are used to develop education, prevention, and if necessary, prosecution strategies that will lead to improved coordination of services for families and the elder population. This Blueprint serves as a re-commitment by community partners to continue participation and support of this important multidisciplinary team and routinely provide data to the public in a report.

Emergency Medical Technicians and Paramedic First Responders

First responding Emergency Medical Technicians (EMT), Paramedics (PM) or EMT/PM firefighters play a crucial role in creating successful outcomes for elder and dependent adult victims. First responders in San Diego County strive to do the following when feasible:

- Become educated about physical, financial and neglect elder abuse.
- Treat elder and dependent adult with dignity and respect.
- Request law enforcement response when Elder abuse is suspected by or reported to EMS/Fire personnel.
- Follow applicable guidelines in ADDENDUM B when assessing elder and dependent adults for a medical complaint or injuries.
- Recognize that elder or dependent adults may have difficulty narrating events, appear to be poor historians, or lack short term memory, which adds to their vulnerability as potential victims.
- Document the scene and all injuries using electronic patient care record (ePCR).
- Cross report to APS by calling 1–800–510–2020 and follow up by sending a written report of documented suspected abuse within two working days, or complete an AIS Web Referral. (W&I 15640(c).)
- Interview caregivers separately. In some situations, caregiver may be the abuser.
- Neglect cases: Neglect occurs when a caretaker or custodian fails to act with a degree of care that a reasonable person would have used when caring for an elder or dependent adult. First responders should do their best to document all physical evidence and consider keeping EKG monitor on for entire incident.

Concluding Commitment

San Diego Community Partners and Stakeholders have come together to collaborate on this important protocol. This Blueprint signifies our ongoing commitment to a coordinated community response to elders, seniors, and dependent adults so they are served with dignity, compassion, and the highest quality of care.

Addendum A: Relevant Penal Code Sections: Elder and Dependent Adult Abuse

Acquiring Access Cards Without Consent	484e
Battery on an Elder	243.25
Caretaker Defined	368(i)
Dependent Adult Defined	368(h)
Dissuading a Witness from Contacting the Police	136.1
Domestic Violence	273.5
Elder Defined	368(g)
Elder Abuse False Imprisonment	368(f)
Elder Abuse Physical Felony	368(b)(1)
Elder Abuse Physical Misdemeanor	368(c)
Elder Abuse Financial, Caretaker Felony > $950	368(e)
Elder Abuse Financial, Non-Caretaker Felony > $950	368(d)
Forgery	470
Forging Access Cards	484f
Grand Theft Felony > $400	487
Fraud or Embezzlement: Two or more related felonies	186.11(a)
Loss exceeds $100,000	186.11(a)(3)
Loss exceeds $500,000	186.11(a)(2)

Sentencing Enhancements

Physical Abuse Causing GBI	368(b)(2)
Victim under 70 years old + 3 years	368(b)(2)(A)
Victim 70 years or older + 5 years	368(b)(2)(B)
Physical Abuse Causing Death	368(b)(3)
Victim under 70 years old + 5 years	368(b)(3)(A)
Victim 70 years or older + 7 years	368(b)(3)(B)
Committing any felony & Causing GBI + 3 years	12022.7
Repeat Offenders, Victim is 65 or Over	
Generally + 1 year	667.9
Anal or Genital Penetration with Foreign Object + 2 years	667.10

Addendum B: Suggestions for Interviewing Elders and Dependent Adults

Special Concerns When Interviewing Older Victims

Interviewing older victims requires special care and patience. Simple measures such as treating the person with respect and asking permission to enter the home or to be seated can help the victim to feel less anxious. Other strategies include:

- Speak slowly and clearly, and be patient in waiting for a response.
- Keep your weapon out of sight—a weapon can be frightening.
- Address the victim by name, but do not use first names as this is considered disrespectful by many elderly persons. You might ask, "Is it okay if I call you Mrs. Smith?"
- Tell the victim you are there to help.
- If the person is having difficulty remembering when an event occurred, offer memory cues like "At the time of the event, what television program were you watching?"
- For hearing impaired persons, eliminate as much background noise as possible and use visual cues. Speak directly to the victim, looking at them when you speak.
- Allow the victim to describe the incident in his or her own words.
- Be patient and reassuring. Some older people, particularly, those in crisis, may need time to collect their thoughts and may need to take frequent breaks.
- Acknowledge the victim's anxiety and try to discern its cause. For example, you may say, "You seem anxious. Is there anything in particular you are worried about? Are you concerned that your relative will find out that you have talked with me?"
- Keep questions short and simple.
- Ask open-ended questions that encourage further discussion.
- Even if the victim appears to be somewhat confused, do not discount the information.
- Make every effort to obtain the fullest possible response before relying on information from others.
- Do not discount a complaint because the victim is unwilling to cooperate.
- Assess the likelihood of retaliation. If a threat is present, arrange for protection.
- Determine whom the victim first told about the abuse/neglect/fraud.
- Show the victim records or other documents that suggest abuse. Record his or her response to each one that is in dispute.
- Conclude the interview in such a fashion that the victim feels free to contact the investigator again.
- Ensure that the victim is capable and has the means for follow-up contact. If not, take measures to facilitate follow-up with the victim.
- Determine whether the witnesses are likely to be intimidated, made to feel guilty, or threatened with reprisal for providing testimony.

Victims with Dementia or Diminished Capacity

When interviewed patiently, persons with dementia, Alzheimer's disease or other illnesses that diminished capacity, can often provide useful information. A sensitive approach to interviewing the person with diminished capacity may yield valuable results. Following are some strategies that may make the police interview more productive:

- Keep the interview area quiet and as free as possible from environmental distractions (e.g., TV or open window with traffic noise).
- If possible, conduct the interview in the morning, to avoid the effects of "sundowning."
- Begin the interview with orienting information, such as the purpose of the interview and what you would like to accomplish.
- Offer a few words of reassurance.
- Relax and be yourself. Your degree of calmness is quickly sensed, just as any anxiety will be sensed.
- Acknowledge the person's feelings. It shows your concern and that you are trying to understand his or her point of view.
- Speak slowly and in a soothing tone, without infantilizing the individual.
- Give the person with diminished capacity ample time to respond.
- Repeat questions as needed, using simple and concrete words.
- Remember that what has been asked may take longer to be understood.
- Give simple directions, one step at a time.
- Distraction or redirection may help to calm and refocus an individual who is upset.
- Document non-verbal reactions. For example, if the individual becomes agitated, frightened, or mute when asked about a certain person or situation, there may be a reason.

Cultural Issues

Our community is diverse. Cultural factors may inhibit the reporting of elder abuse crimes or cooperation with the police in some cases. It is important to have an understanding of the cultural factors that might influence the victim or the victim's family. Cultural norms of perseverance, silent suffering and quiet endurance are valued in many communities. These qualities are also associated with victimization. Consequently, elders may deny or minimize problems, or refuse to cooperate with authorities.

Some cultures place great value on family interdependence and multi-generational households. They may fear the social consequences of bringing shame to the family. Some cultures believe that maintaining community or family honor is more important than the interests of the individuals and that the authorities should not be involved in what they consider "family matters."

Laws and customs in some countries forbid intervention in family affairs without the family's permission. Elders who are immigrants may also have fears in relation to police based on experiences in their country of origin. They may not know they have rights in this country regardless of their immigrant status. They may fear deportation if the police get involved. Empathy and reassurance can help to reduce these fears.

Good cross-cultural communication begins with respect. As you would with any older victim/witness, begin by addressing a person formally, using his or her last name. Cultural beliefs often emerge during interviews. While a gentle touch on the shoulder may be comforting to some elderly victims, in some cultures this is considered an intrusion or offensive.

In some cultures it is considered disrespectful to make eye contact with an authority figure such as a police officer, while in others it is rude not to make eye contact. Some victims may be reluctant to reveal injuries that are covered with clothing due to cultural customs of modesty or religious beliefs. Be careful not to interpret an unwillingness to show injuries as an indication that there are no injuries.

While culture does play a significant role in shaping a person's behavior, it should not be seen as an automatic predictor of how a given victim will respond. Each case is unique and should be assessed keeping relevant aspects of culture in mind.

Language

Many elders who live in insular ethnic communities do not speak English. In these situations it is important to use an impartial interpreter. Avoid using a family member, friend or neighbor to communicate with the victim or with the suspected offender. This is likely to bias the translation. The interpreter may be involved in the abusive situation or may give an inaccurate translation due to their personal bias. The victim may also be reluctant to speak honestly in front of an acquaintance or family member.

Fears the Victim May Have

Victims may fear retribution, such as isolation or emotion/verbal abuse. The abuser may be an adult child or grandchild. It may be very difficult for a parent to testify against a child. The abuse may cast doubt on their ability to live alone and they will be placed in a nursing home. The abuser may be a spouse of many years.

Suggested Interview Questions: Financial Abuse

Background Information

- What is your name?
- Do you have any close relatives? (Identify nature of relationship, names, addresses, phone numbers of any relatives)
- Who are some of your close friends? (Identify names, addresses, phone numbers and length and nature of relationship)
- Are you close to any of your neighbors? (Identify names and addresses)
- Does anyone visit you on a regular basis?
- When is the last time you saw a doctor? Who is your doctor? Who took you to your last doctor's appointment?
- Have you been diagnosed with any medical condition?

Housing Questions

- Where do you live?
- Do you own your home? How long? Who is on the title of the house?
- How long have you lived in your current residence?
- Does anyone live with you? (Identify names and relationships) Do they pay rent?
- Do they provide any services for you in exchange for staying there?

Caretaker

- Do you have a caretaker?
- How long has caretaker been involved with your care?
- Does caretaker get paid? If yes, how much?
- Who takes care of bills or finances?
- Who signs the checks?
- Do you drive? (Who takes elder to appointments, shopping, etc.)
- When did you stop driving?
- Does anyone other than the suspect provide any services for you? If so, describe.

General Finance Questions

- Who handles your finances?
- Who writes the checks?
- Who pays the bills?
- Who does your taxes?
- What is your monthly income? (Amount and sources of income)
- What are your monthly expenses? (Describe some of them)
- Have you ever given anyone permission to sign your name? Use your credit card?
- Place their name on any of your banking accounts?
- Have you signed any documents lately? If so, what were they?
- What are the balances on your bank accounts? Credit card accounts?
- Do you have investment accounts? With whom?
- Do you have a will or trust? Does anyone have a valid Power of Attorney for you?
- Do you have an attorney? (Name and phone number, if available)

Suspect Related Questions

- How long have you known the suspect? How did you meet the suspect?
- Does the suspect provide any services for you? If so, describe. Who hired the suspect?
- How is the suspect compensated for any services provided?
- Did you ever give the suspect any loans or gifts (monetary or otherwise)?
- Does the suspect owe you any money?
- Do you owe the suspect any money?
- Is there anyone else who can do the things the suspect currently does for you?

Case Specific Questions

- Do you recognize these documents?
- Do you recognize these signatures?
- Why did you agree to the transaction(s)?
- Who spoke to you before you agreed to the transactions(s)?
- What was your understanding of the agreement?

Interview Suggestions for Neglect or Physical Abuse

Background Information

- Name.
- Do you have close relatives? Who are some of your closest friends?
- Are you close to any of your neighbors?
- Does anyone visit you on a regular basis?
- Do you get meals brought in with "Meals on Wheels" or another agency?

Housing

- Where do you live?
- Do you own your home? Who has title to the house?
- How long have you lived there? Does anyone live with you? Do they pay rent?
- Does anyone provide you any services in exchange for living with you (*i.e.,* take you to appointments, clean your house, etc.)

Caretaker

- Do you have a caretaker? For how long have you had this caretaker?
- Does the caretaker get paid? If yes, how much?
- Who takes care of bills or finances?
- Who signs the checks?
- Do you drive? When did you stop driving?

Financial

- Who handles your finances?
- Who writes the checks?
- Who pays the bills?
- Who does your taxes?
- Do you have a will or trust? Does anyone have a valid Power of Attorney for you?
- Do you have an attorney?
- How long have you known the suspect?
- How did you meet the suspect?
- Who hired the suspect?

- Does the suspect provide any services to you?
- How is the suspect paid for any services provided?
- Did you ever give the suspect any loans or gifts?
- Does the suspect owe you any money?
- Do you owe the suspect any money?
- Who is generally responsible for taking care of you?
- How long have they been taking care of you?
- When was the last time you saw a doctor?
- Will you sign a medical release form? (If yes, have elder/dependent adult sign the form, or if Power of Attorney, ask that individual to sign)

Physical Abuse

- Did you have any physical injuries before this incident?
- Were those injuries reported? If not, why not?
- What happened to you during the current incident?
- Who did this to you?
- When did this happen?
- Did the person tell you why he/she did it to you? What specifically did the suspect say?
- Did you see a doctor regarding the injury?
- What doctor?
- Obtain consent for medical release from victim or person with Power of Attorney over victim.

Techniques for Interviewing Suspects in Elder or Dependent Adult Cases

- Advise the suspect of his or her Miranda rights if conducting a custodial interrogation.
- Encourage the suspect to relate the incident in her or his own words.
- Note the suspect's attitude or demeanor during the interview.
- Determine the relationship between the suspect, victim, and witnesses.
- Look for behavioral indicators of abuse.
- Note statements that are inconsistent with other findings and evidence.
- If handwriting is an issue, collect handwriting samples (financial crimes).
- Show the disputed documents to the suspect one at a time, and then record his or her response to each one.

- If the suspect admits to abuse, ask him or her to specify precisely what he or she did and record it.
- Do not communicate hostility or disbelief.

Suggested Questions for Caretakers Who May Also Be Suspects

Background Questions

- Name.
- Address.
- DL Number.
- Contact Information.

Relationship with the Victim

- How do you know the victim? For how long?
- Who lives with the victim?
- Do you live here? If yes, for how long?
- Do you pay rent or do you receive room and board in exchange for services you perform for the victim?
- Are there any other relatives living in the area? Do they visit and how often?

Current Medical Care

- Is the victim currently under a doctor's care?
- What is the doctor's Name?
- When was the last time the victim saw a doctor?
- Did you take the victim to the doctor? If not, who did?

Medical History

- Is there any recent or past history of accidents, illness, disease, or mental health issues regarding your relative?
- Explain details and dates of any medical diagnosis.
- Does the victim take any medications? If yes, how often and how much?
- Where is the medication stored?
- Who gives the victim their medication(s)?

- Describe the victim current mental state. Is he/she slow, forgetful, trusting, easily influenced?

Legal Issues

- Is the elder conserved? If so, when and by who?
- Does anyone have valid Power of Attorney over the elder?
- Does the elder have a will or trust? If so, who are the beneficiaries and have there been any recent changes made to it? Who is the trustee? Successor trustee?
- Who is the elder's attorney? Name and contact information.
- Are you the victim's conservator? If so, since when?
- Do you have a valid Power of Attorney over the victim? If so, since when?

Background on Becoming the Caretaker

- How did you get to be the caretaker?
- Who hired you?
- What was your training for this job?
- How long have you been the caretaker?
- How are you coping with the caregiving responsibilities?

Current Duties

- Are you the only caretaker?
- Who, if anyone, assists you in caring for the victim? What is his/her name? What does he/she do specifically?
- What are your duties as it relates to:
  - Medication?
  - Toilet assistance?
  - Cooking/cleaning services?
  - Shopping?
  - Paying bills?

Elder/Dependent Adult's Financial Situation

- What is the elder's monthly income and from what sources? (Social Security, pension).
- What are the elder's monthly expenditures?
- Is the elder in debt or at financial risk?

- Where does your relative bank and is anyone joint on the accounts?
- Does anyone else have access to the elder's bank accounts, ATM, credit cards, etc. and why?
- What are the current balances on the victim's banking & credit card accounts?

Suspect's Involvement with Victim's Finances

- What are you paid? How are you paid? How often are you paid?
- Does the victim owe you any money? If so, how much and what for?
- Who is responsible for the victim's finances/bills? Who pays the bills?
- If you pay the bills, how long have you been doing so? Does anyone else help?
- Do you make any deposits of your own money into the elder's account? If so, why, how much and how often?
- Do you have access to the victim's savings or checking accounts? Money market accounts? Investments? Is your name on any of these accounts? If so, why?
- Do you have access to the victim's credit cards? Have you ever had permission to use the victim's credit card?
- Have you or someone else withdrawn money from any account or financial institution on behalf of the elder? If so, why, what for, did you have permission and was it paid back?
- Have you or the elder singed any documents recently? (i.e., loans, deeds, promissory notes, Power of Attorney, etc.)
- Have you written any checks for the elder and had them sign the check?
- Have you ever had permission to sign the victim's name?
- Who writes the checks (to pay the victim's expenses)?
- Who, if anyone, do you talk to before making a financial decision on behalf of the victim?
- Has the victim given you any gifts, money or loans?
- Do you have any promissory notes showing loans to you from the victim or from the victim to you?

Suspect's Current Financial Situation

- Are you employed anywhere else? Where and how long?
- Do you have any bank accounts? How many and where?
- Is the victim joint on any of your accounts?
- Have you received an inheritance recently or won any money?
- Have you or anyone else taken a trip or vacation with the elder or at the elder's expense? If so, who, when, where, and how much did it cost?

- What are your sources of income? What are the total amounts per month? Any recent inheritances, unusual winnings?

Ask Specific Questions About the Current Case

- Obtain as many details as possible.
- If appropriate, show the suspect any documents to verify signatures.

Concluding Questions

- Have you ever been arrested? If so, what for and are you currently on probation or parole? If so, name of probation officer/parole agent.
- If needed, what is the best way to contact you in the future?
- Is there anything else you think I should know or want to say about this case?

Suggested Questions for Suspects Who May Be Contractors, Landscapers, Handyman, etc.

Background Questions

- Name.
- Address.
- DL Number.
- Contact Information.

Background on Suspect's Business

- How long have you been in business? Are you a sole proprietor or incorporated? Number of employees?
- Have you entered into any type of verbal or written contract for services or home repairs with the elder? If so, describe the dates, necessity of work and pay received. Obtain copies of contract or receipts.
- Do you have a valid state contractor's license for the work performed? If so, contractor's license number and bonding company.

- Has any disciplinary action ever been taken against your license? If so, when, where and what for?
- Do you maintain separate financial accounts for your business? (i.e., a business checking or savings accounts versus personal banking accounts)
- Do you maintain a business office or work from your home? Obtain a business card and /or document all contact information.
- Is your business the only source of income? If not, what is your secondary source of income and how much does that source contribute to your finances?

Information on the Current Case

- How were you contacted for the job? (i.e., through neighborhood solicitation, phone book, word of mouth, or friend)
- Was a building permit obtained prior to beginning the job? Obtain copies.
- Did you sub-contract work out to another party or person? If so, is that person licensed, was the work completed and did you pay them?

Addendum C: San Diego Countywide Elder and Dependent Adult Abuse Supplemental

CASE #:	**Reporting Officer & ID#:**
PRIMARY VICTIM	**RELATIONSHIP OF SUSPECT TO VICTIM**
☐ Elder (65 years and older) ☐ Dependent adult (18-64 years) **Dependent adult has physical or mental limitations which restrict his or her ability to carry out normal activities or to protect his or her rights, including, but not limited to, persons who have physical or developmental disabilities or whose physical or mental abilities have diminished because of age.*	**If Domestic Violence, use DV Supplemental form* ☐ Adult child of victim ☐ Minor child of victim ☐ Other family member ☐ Caregiver/care custodian (not related by blood or family) ☐ Friend ☐ Acquaintance ☐ Stranger ☐ Self ☐ Other
VICTIM	**SUSPECT**
VICTIM NAME (Last, First, Middle)	**SUSPECT NAME** (Last, First, Middle)
DATE OF BIRTH: **M** ☐ **F** ☐	**DATE OF BIRTH:** **M** ☐ **F** ☐
EMOTIONAL DEMEANOR UPON ARRIVAL	**EMOTIONAL DEMEANOR UPON ARRIVAL**
☐ Upset ☐ Crying ☐ Fearful ☐ Calm ☐ Angry ☐ Nervous ☐ Not at Scene ☐ Flat Affect	☐ Upset ☐ Crying ☐ Fearful ☐ Calm ☐ Angry ☐ Nervous ☐ Not at Scene ☐ Flat Affect

Reported Types of Abuse (Check all that apply)

Physical: ☐ Assault ☐ Battery ☐ Constraint ☐ Sexual ☐ Restraint ☐ Chemical ☐ Medication (over or under dosing) ☐ Other

Neglect: ☐ General: Malnutrition/clothing/shelter ☐ Isolation ☐ Abandonment ☐ Medical ☐ Sexual ☐ Fiduciary ☐ Other

Financial: ☐ Theft ☐ Misuse of funds or property ☐ Extortion ☐ Duress ☐ Fraud

Mental Suffering: ☐ Verbal assaults ☐ Threats ☐ Fear ☐ Unaddressed mental health challenges ☐ Unaddressed cognitive challenges/crisis

Self-Neglect: ☐ General: Malnutrition/clothing/shelter ☐ Unmet medical needs ☐ Unpaid bills ☐ Unkempt ☐ Suicidal
☐ Unaddressed mental health challenges ☐ Unaddressed cognitive challenges/crisis

INJURIES

☐ Report of pain ☐ Bruise(s) ☐ Abrasion(s) ☐ Head injury

☐ Laceration(s) ☐ Possible broken bones ☐ Soreness

☐ Other:____________________

Explain:____________________

☐ No visible or reported injuries

☐ Draw location of injuries in diagram below

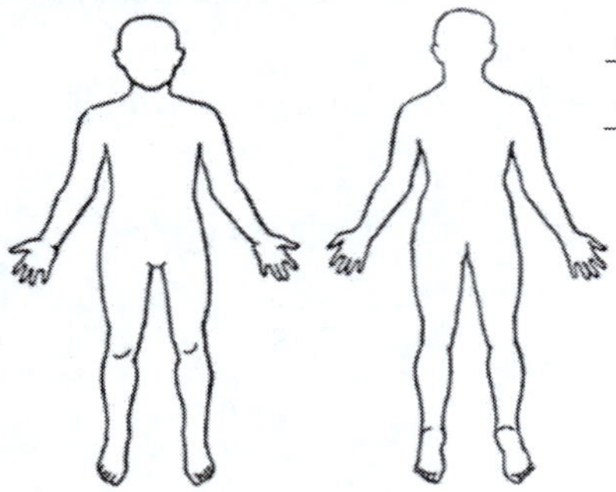

HT: ________

WT: ________

INJURIES

☐ Report of pain ☐ Bruise(s) ☐ Abrasion(s) ☐ Head injury

☐ Laceration(s) ☐ Possible broken bones ☐ Soreness

☐ Other:____________________

Explain:____________________

☐ No visible or reported injuries

☐ Draw location of injuries in diagram below

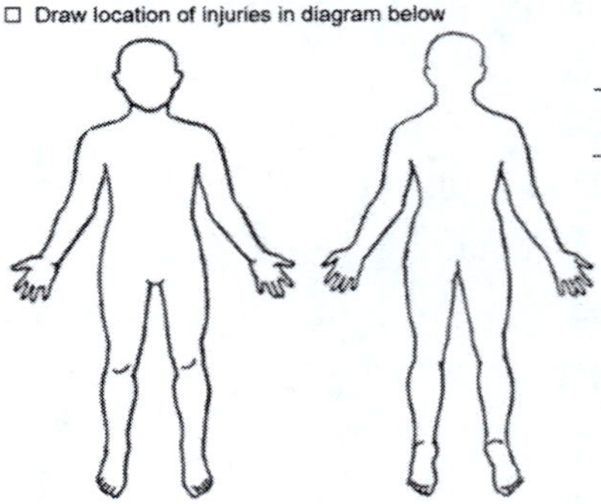

HT: ________

WT: ________

MEDICAL

☐ Death ☐ First Aid Provided

Medications and chronic conditions or current diagnoses::
____

List any limitations on activities of daily living: ____________________

Medical treatment: ☐ None ☐ Declined Medical Aid ☐ Will Seek Own

Does Victim have Medical Insurance? ☐ Yes ☐ No

☐ Paramedic Response ☐ Transported to Hospital

☐ Hospital /Medic Unit: ____________________

☐ Medical Release Signed by Victim?

MEDICAL

☐ Death ☐ First Aid Provided

Medications and chronic conditions or current diagnoses:
____

List any limitations on activities of daily living: ____________________

Medical treatment: ☐ None ☐ Declined Medical Aid ☐ Will Seek Own

Does Suspect have Medical Insurance? ☐ Yes ☐ No

☐ Paramedic Response ☐ Transported to Hospital

☐ Hospital /Medic Unit: ____________________

☐ Medical Release Signed by Suspect?

SUBSTANCE ABUSE

Possible influence of:
☐ Alcohol ☐ Drugs ☐ Both ☐ None

☐ Symptoms observed: ____________________

History of Substance Abuse by Victim? ☐ Yes ☐ No

Sample Taken By: ____________________

Requested Preservation (Sample Taken at Hospital): ☐

SUBSTANCE ABUSE

Possible influence of:
☐ Alcohol ☐ Drugs ☐ Both ☐ None

☐ Symptoms observed: ____________________

History of Substance Abuse by Suspect? ☐ Yes ☐ No

Sample Taken By: ____________________

Requested Preservation (Sample Taken at Hospital): ☐

STRANGULATION

Did the suspect strangle or "choke" the victim ☐ Yes ☐ No ***If yes, complete the Countywide Strangulation Documentation Form.***

FIREARMS/DEADLY WEAPONS OWNED/USED/IMPOUNDED

Firearm(s)/deadly weapon(s) used during the incident? ☐ Yes ☐ No List/describe weapon(s) used: ____________________

Does suspect have access to firearms? ☐ Yes ☐ No List/describe: ____________________

Firearm(s)/deadly weapon(s) impounded per PC 18250? ☐ Yes ☐ No List/describe weapon(s) impounded: ____________________

FIREARMS/DEADLY WEAPONS OWNED/USED/IMPOUNDED		
Firearm(s)/deadly weapon(s) used during the incident?	☐ Yes ☐ No	List/describe weapon(s) used:
Does suspect have access to firearms?	☐ Yes ☐ No	List/describe:
Firearm(s)/deadly weapon(s) impounded per PC 18250?	☐ Yes ☐ No	List/describe weapon(s) impounded:

HISTORY OF ABUSE

Prior history of abuse/neglect from this suspect? ☐ Yes ☐ No Was this prior abuse/neglect documented by law enforcement? ☐ Yes ☐ No

Approximate number of prior incidents: ________ Case Number(s): ________

Investigating Agency(s): ________

WITNESSES

Witnesses present during incident? ☐ Yes ☐ No All witness statements taken? ☐ Yes ☐ No

Witness info listed in crime report? ☐ Yes ☐ No ***Include witness statements in Report***

CROSS REPORT TO ADULT PROTECTIVE SERVICES

Peace officers are mandated per 15630 (b)(1) W&I to report suspected elder and dependent abuse and neglect

Cross report to APS filed? ☐ Yes ☐ No Adult Protective Services: 800-510-2020

EVIDENCE COLLECTED

Physical Evidence Collected (e.g. torn clothing, broken objects)? ☐ Yes ☐ No

Location Collected: ☐ Crime Scene ☐ Hospital ☐ Other: ________

Photographs Taken? ☐ Victim ☐ Suspect Photographs Of: ☐ Crime Scene ☐ Physical Evidence ☐ Witness(es) ☐ Other: ________

RESTRAINING ORDERS

TRO/RO on record? ☐ Yes ☐ No If Yes, Issuing court:: ________ ☐ TRO/RO No. ________

Emergency Protective Order Issued? ☐ Yes ☐ No

VICTIM RESOURCES PROVIDED

☐ Incident or Crime Case Number ☐ Victim Advised of Right to Support Person ☐ If Regional Center client, did you advise the victim to contact their Case Manager or offer to contact Case Manager on victim's behalf?

☐ Elder & Dependent Adult Abuse Resource Guide ☐ Victim Advised of Right to EPO

Addendum D: San Diego County Resource Guide

Elder and Dependent Adult Abuse and Neglect

Adult Protective Services (800) 510–2020	
Adult Protective Services (APS) investigates reports of abuse and neglect. Trained professionals assist elder and dependent adults who are harmed or threatened with harm. This may include physical, sexual, and financial abuse, mental suffering, neglect or abandonment by another, and self-neglect. Anyone can report elder and dependent adult abuse.	
Law Enforcement	
For emergencies, call 911.	Non-emergency numbers:
Carlsbad Police Department	(760) 931–2197
Chula Vista Police Department	(619) 691–5151
Coronado Police Department	(619) 522–7350
El Cajon Police Department	(619) 579–3311
Escondido Police Department	(760) 839–4722
La Mesa Police Department	(619) 667–1400
Oceanside Police Department	(760) 435–4900
National City Police Department	(619) 336–4411
San Diego Police Department	(619) 531–2000, (858) 484–3154
San Diego Sheriff's Department	(858) 565–5200

(Continued)

Your local Sheriff and police and departments investigate crimes against elders and dependent adults based on the jurisdiction where the incident occurred. According to California State Penal Code 368 P.C., the State of California considers those persons age 65 and older to be elders. Persons 18–64 years old who have physical and/or mental limitations that restrict their ability to carry out normal activities or to protect their rights are considered dependent adults. Information on Elder Abuse Crimes: *www.sdsheriff.net/elder* and *www.sdcda.org.*	
San Diego County District Attorney's Office and San Diego City Attorney's Office	
These offices are committed to the successful prosecution of those committing crimes against elders and dependent adults. Victim advocates are also available to assist with safety planning, support, referrals, court accompaniment and processing of Victim Compensation and restitution applications. San Diego City Attorney's Office, Victim Services Coordinators: (619) 236–6220 San Diego County District Attorney's Office, Victim Assistance Program: Central (619) 531–4041, East (619) 441–4538, South (619) 498–5650, North (760) 806–4079	
ORDERING POLICE REPORT(S)	
Victims have a right to one free copy of their police report. Contact the responding law enforcement agency in the jurisdiction in which the incident occurred. Requests for reports can be made to most jurisdictions through the mail or in-person. The following information is necessary to request a report copy: name of the parties involved, date and location of incident, and the report number if available. Bring identification if you go in-person to pick up your report.	
RESTRAINING ORDERS	
Victims of Elder and Dependent Adult Abuse may file for a civil restraining order at no cost. There are free clinics available to assist you in the application process: *www.sdcourt.ca.gov* and select the "Civil" tab and then select "Harassment Restraining Order." *Arrive early. Be prepared to spend a minimum of one-half of a day to a full day at the court to obtain your restraining order. Arrive a minimum of two hours before the clinic closes.* Things to bring with you when you complete your paperwork, if available: Address of the person you would like restrained; date of birth for the person you would like restrained; physical description of the person you would like restrained; photographs of any injuries (if applicable); and a copy of the police report(s) if any.	
OTHER LOCAL RESOURCES	
Senior Mental Health Team (800) 510–2020	Assesses and initiates appropriate actions for older adults age 60+ with mental health issues. Currently serving East County, Central, and North Coastal areas.
Long Term Care Ombudsman (800) 640–4661	Investigates reports of abuse in nursing homes and residential care facilities, and advocates for residents' rights.
Public Guardian (858) 694–3500	May be appointed conservator by the Probate Court when it is determined that someone is unable to care for himself/herself physically and/or financially and no family members or alternates are available.
Public Administrator (858) 694–3500	Performs estate administration for people who have died with no family member or other person to handle their affairs.

Public Conservator (858) 694–3500	A mental health conservator can be court ordered for people who are gravely disabled as a result of a mental disorder.
Meals on Wheels (800) 573–6467	Nutritious meals delivered to homes by caring volunteers. *www.meals-onwheels.org*
Methamphetamine Hotline (877) 662–6384	24 hour hotline for treatment information and to report criminal activity related to meth use in San Diego County.
NATIONAL WEBSITES	
Elder Justice Coalition	*www.elderjusticecoalition.com*
National Adult Protective Services Association	*www.napsa-now.org*
National Center on Elder Abuse	*https://ncea.acl.gov*
National Clearinghouse on Abuse in Later Life	*www.ncall.us*
National Committee for the Prevention of Elder Abuse	*www.preventelderabuse.org*
National Organization for Victim Assistance	*www.trynova.org*
U.S. Department of Health and Human Services, Administration on Aging	*www.hhs.gov/aging/index.html*

ADDENDUM E: SAN DIEGO COUNTY PROSECUTOR ELDER AND DEPENDENT ADULT CASE PREPARATION CHECKLIST

Victim Name ____________________

Prosecutor ____________________

Case Number ____________________

Date ____________________

Interviewing Strategies

- Privacy: Speak in private, away from family members and suspects, especially if unsure whether family members will be witnesses and/or defendants.
- Advocate: Consider having an advocate present.
- Remove distractions: Turn off cell phones and find a quiet room.
- Make the meeting accessible: Meet with older persons at their home, whenever possible.
- Address any needs, questions or concerns that the victim may have: Prior to starting the interview, including physical and medical ones. If unable to address these needs, connect him/her with a professional who can assist.
- Develop rapport: Develop a relationship and him/her feel comfortable. A few ways are to ask about his/her family, life, career or other interests. Avoid being

patronizing or fraternizing (e.g., using first name without permission, raising your voice, physical contact, talking down, baby talk).

- Be Patient: Ask the victim questions one at a time and allow him/her time to respond. Older adults may need more time to process the questions and their responses, so be patient.

Preparing for Court

- Identify Needs and Arrange Accommodations: Inquire with the victim about needs pertaining to mobility, language and communication (e.g., translators, interpreters, assistive devices), oxygen, medication, nutrition, hydration, and other medical treatment. Incorporate accommodations into all parts of the criminal justice process including court-room appearances and pre-trial meetings.
- Transportation: Work with the victim and Victim Witness staff to determine travel arrangements and transportation needs for attending meetings and hearings. Ensure that someone other than he suspect or the suspect's allies provide the transportation.
- Tour the Courtroom: Arrange a tour in advance for the victim through Victim Witness and court staff. Review where the victim will sit and the court process.
- Waiting Room: Identify a comfortable place, away from the court room, for the victim wait,
- Scheduling: Consider the victims medical and other special needs when scheduling. Select the times for court appearances and testimony of the victim at times/days that work best for him/her. One victim is present, avoid delays.

Evidence Collection	**√ Complete?**
Psychological/psychiatric evaluation of victim * If capacity, consent or undue influence may be an issue	
Victim deposition or testimony with full-cross examination, as soon as possible after charging (Crawford)	
Videotape the victim at the early stage of the investigation to include:	
Victim's perception of time, place or place	
Facts: Consent	
Facts: Perpetrator's identity	
Facts: Review docs/evidence. Ask victim to sign his/her name in the video	
Facts: Impact of crime. Include a walk-through video of abuse or neglect crime scene if possible	

Medical Evidence	
Medical Records of current and underlying conditions from emergency room, nursing facilities, treating physicians, dentist, pharmacy, others	
Specific medical documents including lab reports, x-rays, nurses' notes, social worker's notes	
Medications—Include actual bottles/containers for prescriptions to show physician and pharmacy, possession and full/empty status given recommended dosage over time from the date of the last refill	
Adult Protective Services records of current and prior contacts	
Evidence Collection	√ Complete?
Law enforcement contacts with involved parties and witnesses including 911 tapes, arrest reports, and criminal histories	
Jail records including phone calls and visitor logs by or on behalf of the suspects	
Other	
Financial Records	
Credit card reports	
Investment account records	
Credit reports	
Victim's bank records	
Evidence Collection	√ Complete?
Checkbook registers	
Suspect's bank records	
Other	
Legal Documentation	
Powers of attorney	
Prior civil cases	
Court/protection orders	
Property deeds	
Wills and trusts	
Advanced directives/living wills	
Conveyances	
Guardianship/conservatorship documents	
Other	
Consultation with Experts	
Forensic accountants	
Handwriting analysts Geriatricians	
Geriatric psychologists and psychiatrists	
Medical Examiner	
Wound care experts	
Civil attorneys	
Other	
Interviews	
Witness who can describe the victim's condition, level of functioning, activities, and interaction with the defendant at the time of the incident and before.	
Evidence Collection	√ Complete?
Include a description of changes over time.	
Medical providers (prior and current)	

(Continued)

Family and friends	
Banking/financial	
Hair stylists/barbers	
Local businesses	
Faith community	
Acquaintances/social	
Neighbors	
Adult day care services	
Adult Protective Services	
Civil attorneys	
Social services (Meals on Wheels, etc.)	
Payees for expenses the suspect paid with the victim's money	
Physical Evidence	
Photo and video documentation:	
Crime scene, including if relevant, the contents of the refrigerator, cupboards, and medicine cabinets (including actual bottles/containers for prescriptions to show physician and pharmacy, possession and full/empty status given recommended dosage over time from the date of last refill)	
Suspect's living area	
Victim's living area	
Major new purchases by the suspect	
Victim's body—injuries over time	
Victim's body—signs of neglect	
Clothing victim was wearing at time if incident (include adult diapers if applicable)	
Bedding	
Writing/journals/letters	
Locks on outside of doors	
Photos and videos related to conduct	
Defendant's and victim's ISP records	
Evidence Collection	√ Complete?
Legal file for victim's civil attorney	
Nutritional supplements	
Medications and supplies	
Restraints and bindings	
Assistive devices (or lack thereof)	
Defendant's computer, flash drives, etc.	
Checkbooks, check registers	

Adapted from the Prosecuting Elder Abuse Cases: Basic Tools and Strategies by the National Center for State Court, Williamsburg, VA.

Addendum F: Protective Orders and Restraining Orders

Protective Orders and Restraining Orders

There are many different forms of protective and restraining orders. Sometimes your case will involve Elder Domestic Violence. Peace officers should refer to the Countywide Domestic Violence and Children Exposed to Domestic Violence Law Enforcement Protocol for more information specific to Domestic Violence restraining orders.

If the case involves Elder Domestic Violence (intimate partner abuse between elders, or when an elder is the victim of intimate partner abuse), peace officers should consider the general policies and statues below:

I. GENERAL POLICY:

Enforcement officers. This includes orders from other states. (PC 13701, PC 836(c)(1).)

II. MANDATORY ARREST POLICY:

PC 13701(b) states that law enforcement shall arrest an offender, absent exigent circumstances, if there is probable cause that a DV restraining order/protective order has been violated. (PC 13701(b).)

PC 836(c)(1) states that the officer shall make an arrest even without a warrant, and whether or not the violation occurred in the officer's presence. (PC 836(c)(1).)

* Important: Per Penal Code section 13710(b), the terms and conditions of a Restraining or Protective Order remain enforceable, *notwithstanding the acts of the parties, and may be changed only by order of the court.* This means that, "protected persons" are not in violation of protective orders when they acquiesce or invite the restrained party's contact, and should not be arrested. (PC 13710(b).)

In situations where mutual protective orders have been issued, liability for arrest applies only to those persons who are reasonably believed to have been the dominant aggressor. (PC 836(c)(3).) In those situations, before making an arrest, Law Enforcement shall make reasonable efforts to identify, and may arrest the dominant aggressor involved in the incident. The dominant aggressor is the person determined to be the most significant, rather than the first aggressor. In identifying the dominant aggressor, Law Enforcement shall consider a) the intent of the law to protect victims or domestic violence from continuing abuse, b) the threats creating fear of physical injury c) the history of Domestic Violence between the persons involved and d) whether either person involved acted in self-defense. (PC 836(c)(3).)

III. WHAT IS A "DOMESTIC VIOLENCE RESTRAINING ORDER/ PROTECTIVE ORDER?"

Any order that enjoins one person from contacting another. (Orders issued pursuant to Family code section 2040, Family Code section 6218, Penal Code section 136.2, and those issued by a Criminal Court pending a criminal proceeding, *and Emergency Protective Orders.*)

IV. HOW TO DETERMINE WHETHER THE ORDER IS VALID:

A. Law Enforcement can check with dispatch to see if a served order is on file.

B. Law Enforcement can access full information about the terms of the order through SDLAW.

C. Law Enforcement can also check on *www.sdsheriff.net* which lists limited restraining order information for all protective orders that are entered into CLETS.

D. Law Enforcement can also call the Sheriff's Department 24-Hour Law Enforcement Line (law enforcement only) at (858) 974–2457 and ask the following questions:

1. Is there a restraining/protective order on file? (If so, it will be filed under the name of the restrained party)

IMPORTANT: If Sheriff personnel cannot verify the order, it may still be enforceable. If the responding officer believes in good faith that an order presented to him or her at the scene is valid and the suspect was on notice (see questions B through E below), a *private person's arrest* may be made even though the Sheriff's Department was not provided a copy to enter into DVROS.

2. What is the date of the order? When did/does the Order become effective?

3. What is the expiration date? Has the Order expired?

4. What are the terms of the order? For instance, whether peaceful contact is allowed is important information in determining whether a violation has occurred.

5. Was the restrained person served with the Order? Is there a Declaration of Service on file or has another officer given the needed notice to the person to be restrained?

E. NO RECORD OF SERVICE. If no record of service exists:

1. Advise the restrained person that there is an Order in effect,

2. Give a copy of the Order to the restrained person or, if no copy is available to give, have the terms of the Order read over the phone and then verbally inform him/her of those terms,

3. Advise him/her that s/he is now subject to the terms of the Order and can be arrested for any further violations,

4. Notify the Sheriff's Department and report that you have served a copy of the Order on the defendant (The Sheriff will record your name, ID number, date, time and location that the suspect received notice),

5. Prepare and sign a Proof of Service, and

6. File the Proof of Service as part of the report. Investigations personnel shall ensure the original Proof of Service is filed with the court issuing the Order and a copy retained with the police report.

V. VICTIMS SHALL BE ADVISED ABOUT AVAILABILITY OF EMERGENCY PROTECTIVE *ORDERS:*

An Emergency Protective Order (EPO) can be an important tool for law enforcement in the prevention of future violence. Law Enforcement shall inform victims of the availability of EPO when they have reasonable grounds to believe there is an immediate and present danger 1) of Domestic Violence based on the person's allegation of recent abuse or threat of abuse, or 2) the EPO is necessary to prevent the occurrence or recurrence of Domestic Violence. *If the person requests such an order, the officer shall request an EPO from the court.* (Family Code sections 6275, 6251, 6250, PC 646.91.)

A. EPOs are available 24-hours a day, 7-days a week.

B. This is not just an after-hours or weekend remedy.

C. The fact that no crime has yet been committed does not eliminate the duty to advise victims about EPOs.

D. Law Enforcement does not need permission from victims or the request from victims in order to request an EPO from the court. Law Enforcement can request EPOs on their own. (See Family Code 6250(a).)

E. Whether the respondent is in custody or the protected person left the home for safety reasons should have no bearing on the availability of an EPO, and should not be factored into the immediate and present danger determination.

F. If a Protective Order is *obtained,* a Crime/DV Incident Report shall be prepared on the incident.

VI. HOW TO OBTAIN AN EMERGENCY PROTECTIVE ORDER:

This procedure may be utilized 7 days a week, 24 hours a day.

A. If a protective order is being sought, the officer will complete Form EPO–001 (rev. 1–07) Application for Emergency Protective Order (CLETS).

B. After court hours, weekends and holidays, the officer will telephone the duty judge through the duty telephone at the Sheriff's Office at 858–974–2493 (this is a non-public number).

C. During court hours (8:00 a.m.–5:00 p.m.) the officer will contact a judge through the Family Court at 619–844–2942 (this is a non-public number).

D. Upon approval by the judge, the officer will complete Form EPO–001 (rev. 1–07), Emergency Protective Order (CLETS). This order may be granted for up to five (5) full court days and will expire at 5:00 p.m. on the last specified court day.

E. The officer will provide the pink copy of the application and the order to the issuing agency and the canary yellow copy to the protected party. The officer will submit the white copy of the application to the restrained party.

The goldenrod copy of the application will be attached to the crime report for the court.

F. The officer requesting the Order shall carry copies of the order while on duty. (Pen. Code, § 13710(c) requires the law enforcement officer to make a reasonable effort to serve the restrained party with the EPO.)

G. The officer will encourage the protected party to carry a copy of the Emergency Protective Order with him/her.

H. Make sure to fax the front and back pages of the approved Emergency Protective Order to the Sheriff's office at (858) 974–2492 whether or not the EPO was served to the restrained party.

I. Verbal admonishment by a law enforcement officer shall constitute valid service of the order under the following conditions:

a. Verbal admonishment must be conducted in person.

b. The terms and conditions must be read to the restrained person. Terms and conditions can be obtained by calling (858) 974–2457.

c. Advise restrained person to go to the local court to obtain a copy of the order containing the full terms and conditions of the order per Family Code section 6383(g).

Prepare a Crime Report for Every DV Restraining Order/Protective Order Violation

Law enforcement should always prepare and submit a crime report of the appropriate restraining order violation regardless of whether or not the suspect is still present at the scene.

A. Out of State Orders

Officers shall enforce out-of-state protective or restraining orders that are presented to them if conditions below are met. "Out-of-state" orders include those issued by U.S. Territories, Indian tribes, and military agencies.

1. The order appears valid on its face.
2. The order contains both parties' names.
3. The order has not yet expired. (Full Faith and Credit Provision of the Violence Against Women Act, Family Code 6400–6409.)

Officers should check CLETS to determine if the order has been registered in California. If the order is not registered, an attempt should be made to contact the foreign jurisdiction or its registry for confirmation of validity.

If validation cannot be substantiated, contact the Duty Judge for an EPRO, but the out-of-state protective or restraining order must still be enforced if it meets the above criteria. If not registered in California parties should be advised to immediately register the order through the Family Court.

B. When it appears the protected party invited the Restraining Order violation

Occasionally, officers may encounter a situation wherein a protected party has encouraged or invited a restrained party to violate the terms of an order by initiating contact. Officers should remember that the order remains in effect until canceled by the court, and that the *restrained party* is the only person in violation of the order in such a situation. (PC 13710(b).)

ADDENDUM G: CROSS-REPORTING REQUIREMENTS

Law Enforcement Cross-Reporting Requirements

LOCATION OF ABUSE	CROSS-REPORTING REQUIREMENT
Long term care facility	Long Term Care Ombudsman Program (1–800–510–2020) and the State Department of Public Health (916–558–1784) and to the licensing agency. (W&I 15640(e).)
State mental health hospital or a state developmental center	Refer to the office of Protective Services (916–651–7185) or Regional Center (858–576–2996)
Anywhere else	Adult Protective Services (APS) telephone report to (San Diego: 1–800–510–2020) and (outside San Diego: 1–800–339–4661) and send written report within two working days, or complete referral to the AIS Web Portal. *www.AisWebReferral.org*
TYPE OF ABUSE	CROSS-REPORTING REQUIREMENT
Any case of known or suspect abuse	Local Law Enforcement
Any case of known or suspected criminal activity	Attorney General's Bureau of Medical Fraud and Elder Abuse (1–800–722–0432)
WHO COMMITTED THE ABUSE	CROSS REPORTING REQUIREMENT
Licensed Health practitioner	Appropriate licensing agency
ADULT PROTECTIVE SERVICES CROSS-REPORTING REQUIREMENTS	
LOCATION OF ABUSE	CROSS-REPORTING REQUIREMENT
Long Term Care facility	Shall immediately inform reporting party that he or she is required to make the report to the Long Term Care Ombudsman program or to a local law enforcement agency. Shall not accept the report by phone but shall forward any written report received to the long term care ombudsman.

(Continued)

TYPE OF ABUSE	CROSS-REPORTING REQUIREMENT
Financial abuse	Prior to making any cross report of allegations of financial abuse to local law enforcement, APS shall first determine whether there is a reasonable suspicion of any criminal activity (W&I 15640(a)(1)).
Any case of known or suspected criminal abuse	Local law enforcement
Incidents of suspected abuse	Cross report to any other licensing or public agency charged with responsibility for investigation of incidents of suspected abuse (W&I 15640(b)).
WHO COMMITTED THE ABUSE	CROSS-REPORTING REQUIREMENT
Licensed Health Practitioner	Cross report to appropriate licensing agency

Letter Submitted by John M. Harper

U.S. Senate
Committee on Finance
Dirksen Senate Office Bldg.
Washington, DC

Re: SENATE HEARING ON ABUSE AND NEGLECT: “Not Forgotten: Protecting Americans from Abuse and Neglect in Nursing Homes” (Wednesday, March 6, 2019)

Submitted By: John Harper, Systems Advocate, Independent Living, Inc., 441 East Main St., Middletown, New York, 10940

Friends:

Thank you for this opportunity to provide written testimony regarding the above cited Senate Hearing. I offer the following points to consider.

Research has shown that when abuse and/or neglect occurs in the nursing home setting, one or more of the following played a part in causing harm to a resident or patient:

1. Negligent hiring.
2. Understaffing.
3. Inadequate training.
4. Breach of statutory or regulatory obligations, and
5. Medication errors.

Signs of such abuse and neglect include:

1. Poor personal hygiene.
2. Unsanitary living conditions.
3. Physical issues from lack of nutrition.
4. Loss or lack of mobility.
5. Unexplained injuries.
6. Psychological issues.

When a person reaches moment in his or her life when self-care requires assistance, the first priority is to ensure that every attempt possible is made for the individual to enjoy the most integrated setting and to the extent possible remain in one's regular night-time residence. If that is not possible, then, and only then, should a congregate setting be considered.

As with any congregate care service model, such as a nursing home, the quality of service is directly tied to the capacity and competency of the Direct Care Practitioners. This Practice must include eligibility criteria for potential practitioners, be valued within the service industry and include a competitive compensation in order to attract the level of professionalism which is required to consistently deliver the highest level of quality care.

A standardized curriculum of training, resulting in a credential, must be developed to address, comprehensively, all of the necessary best practice skills and competencies needed to ensure quality service. Candidates in such training must be tested and required to fulfill on-going continuing education in the field annually to maintain credentialing.

A universal Code of Ethics specific to this particular practice which reflects the desired culture to be developed and maintained in the nursing home setting must be formulated and adhered to. Any deviation from the Code must be addressed in a timely, uniform and consistent manner.

Respectfully Submitted

John M. Harper

The Hebrew Home at Riverdale, Statement for Daniel Reingold, MSW, JD, President and CEO

Chairman Grassley, Ranking Member Wyden and members of the Committee, on behalf of The Hebrew Home at Riverdale, New York and the SPRiNG Alliance (Shelter Partners: Regional, National and Global), I submit this statement for the record of the Senate Finance Committee hearing, "Not Forgotten: Protecting Americans from Abuse and Neglect in Nursing Homes." It is important that this hearing will shed light on this small part of a much larger national epidemic of elder abuse.

We share the Committee's commitment to the quality of care and quality of life of residents in nursing homes. We unequivocally condemn abuse and neglect, whether in a nursing home or in the community. We do not excuse abusive or neglectful treatment of older adults, who deserve respect and dignity as they age, and where they age.

Our nursing home, The Hebrew Home at Riverdale, is a non-profit organization serving poor older adults of all faiths for over a century. The Hebrew Home has been dedicated to community service since its founding in 1917, when a small synagogue in Harlem opened its doors as a shelter for poor, homeless, elderly people. Now recognized as one of the best nursing homes in the country, we push the boundaries of what's possible in skilled nursing care. Innovative programs like vision care, therapeutic activities, college courses, memory care, and exercise programs are underscored by individual attention and passion for our residents— which makes a real difference in their quality of life. Ideal for a range of older adults—from those needing assistance with the tasks of daily living to those requiring specialized treatments and ongoing care—we take pride in transforming the landscape of aging, every day. This past October, I was recognized by the senior healthcare field's highest award- the Award of Honor- at the LeadingAge Annual Conference in Philadelphia, Pennsylvania. The Award of Honor is the highest award LeadingAge bestows. It is presented to an individual who has been provided transformative leadership in aging services to advance the common good. I am grateful to have accepted the Award of Honor on behalf of the thousands of dedicated people who care for our nation's most vulnerable older adults every day.

The Hebrew Home serves more than 18,000 people in the greater New York City area. Our organization encompasses residential healthcare, rehabilitation, palliative care, low-income HUD housing, middle income housing communities, and a Medicaid managed long term plan. Our community services division offers a full spectrum of healthcare and supportive services to help maintain the independence of older persons who choose to remain in their own homes. This includes long term home health care and in-home personal care.

In 2005, we opened the Harry and Jeanette Weinberg Center for Elder Justice on the Hebrew Home campus. It was then the nation's first temporary shelter for victims of elder abuse residing in the community and is today a national leader and advocate in the fight against elder abuse.

The mission of the Harry and Jeanette Weinberg Center for Elder Justice at the Hebrew Home at Riverdale is to champion justice and dignity for older adults. We are pioneers of safe shelter for older adults experiencing abuse. Through the inception of the SPRiNG (Shelter Partners: Regional. National. Global) Alliance, we assist communities around the United States and the world in adopting our flexible model to create their own unique version of shelter. My testimony will address care within nursing homes but also raise the critical need to address abuse in the larger community and the role elder care providers can play to protect older adults.

Elder Abuse Is a Serious and Complex Problem

Elder abuse is a large yet poorly understood problem that often cannot be addressed in the same way that we address domestic violence.[84] Almost 90% of elder abuse occurs in the community, often perpetrated by family, friends, caregivers, and financial or other trusted "advisors." As with child abuse and domestic violence, elder abuse is under-reported. Elder abuse victims may be dependent on the perpetrator financially, physically or emotionally; they may be unable to access assistance because of physical and mental impairments (e.g., dementia). In addition, the older adult may not know who to ask for help, or where it is safe to make a report. As the Otto and Quinn report notes, there is a dearth of appropriate interventions for victims of elder abuse.

As Senator Cortez Masto noted in her questions to the second panel at the hearing, there is no one entity responsible for assuring protection for older adults in the community. The Elder Justice Coordinating Council, created with our support in 2010 by the Elder Justice Act, serves as a critical center for the federal government to assess, coordinate and improve federal and local response to elder abuse. The valuable work done by the EJCC underscores the need to have equally robust and significant investment by communities, a role that the elder abuse shelter movement effectively addresses. I have been proud to work with the EJCC in their important work.

Prevention of Abuse in Long-Term Care Settings

In many ways, it is easier to address prevention of elder abuse in nursing homes and other longterm care entities than it is in the community at large. These are contained by settings; the owner/provider hires, fires and trains staff; and the requirements for care are set by regulation and contract.

Providers must follow extensive regulations and corporate compliance, to ensure that regulatory requirements are met and care is delivered not just appropriately but at the highest level and with the greatest concern for the resident. But compliance alone does not guarantee quality.

Leadership and staffing are the two key elements that ensure high quality care and services. Leadership sets the tone—as a mission driven, faith-based organization, The Hebrew Home is committed to preventing all forms of elder abuse, neglect, and exploitation, and our entire body of staff understands and shares this commitment. Leadership includes creating a workplace culture of safety, transparency, clear reporting lines, upper level professionals who know how to respond to changes in resident conditions.

---

[84] See e.g., Otto and Quinn, Barriers to and Promising Practices for Collaboration Between Adult Protective Services and Domestic Violence Programs (National Center on Elder Abuse, May 2007).

Not only does the Weinberg Center for Elder Justice address the needs of elders in the community, it has also transformed the way our staff looks at our own residents. We have been providing person-centered, trauma-informed care, for over a decade. We screen for elder abuse at every entry point into the nursing home, and the Weinberg Center Team responds to any red flags of elder abuse, throughout the residential and rehabilitative care provided at the Hebrew Home. The impact of the shelter and of the type of care provided to abuse victims on the Hebrew Home cannot be over-stated.

In Shelter: The Missing Link in a Coordinated Community Response to Elder Abuse, published by the Center in January 2019 (available at weinbergcenter.org), we noted at pp.16-17:

> If we think of elder abuse at all, we tend to understand it as a discrete response to a known victim of abuse. But a system that shelters even a small number of older victims annually can have benefits that accrue to many, many elders throughout a community. This payoff is perhaps most visible within care facilities. Once facility staff understand the dynamics of elder abuse –and staff training is essential—they're more likely to become attuned to comments, behaviors and other signs by non-shelter residents that might indicate ongoing or past abuse. Opportunities to stop abuse, ideally early on, and to support healing are created where they probably would not have been.
>
> Care facilities often believe they're helping to solve a problem 'out there' in the community, as opposed to one under their own roof, but victims of elder abuse are everywhere. Recent data collected by the Hebrew Home backs up this common sense conclusion.
>
> In addition to providing skilled nursing and assisted living levels of care, the Hebrew Home operates a sub-acute residential and rehabilitation center on its main campus. Using an evidence-based screening tool developed by the Weinberg Center (cite omitted) that focuses on circumstances and events within the past year, as well as current and future risks, Hebrew Home staff screened 536 rehab patients over a yearlong period from May 2017 to May 2018. Nearly 12 percent, or 63 individuals, had positive indicators for abuse, roughly mirroring the rate of elder abuse in the community at large—typically cited as affecting 10 percent of adults.
>
> More generally and over time, trauma-informed care provided to shelter clients can influence a facility's culture, fostering environments where the experiences and desires of residents are more likely to be seen, heard and honored.

For nursing home and other care facilities, we find that the key elements to ensuring the best quality of care and quality of life for our residents is more than rules-based care—it is in the environment, the training, the recognition of the individual's needs and interest, the desire to serve. As a leader, I have the responsibility not only to ensure that the rules are followed but that the conditions are in place to enhance the work we do.

Sheltering Abused Elders: The Weinberg Center for Elder Abuse Prevention and SPRiNG Alliance

Elder abuse in the community is difficult to detect, and even when suspected, difficult to address. As noted above, it is estimated that 10 percent of older adults have been or are being abused, and that 90 percent of elder abuse victims do not live in nursing homes or other care settings. To put it differently, current estimates indicate that there are far more victims of elder abuse living in the community with no regulatory oversight than the total number of residents living in all U.S. nursing homes. And the amount of money stolen from older adults each year exceeds fifty percent of the national cost of Medicaid for nursing home care. I urge the Committee to expand its inquiry to this population of forgotten older adults. We know that it is difficult for victims of domestic violence to escape the cycle of poverty, to find the resources and emotional strength to leave the abusive relationship, as well as to find a safe haven. But it is even more difficult for older adults who can suffer from cognitive and physical disabilities. Traditional domestic violence shelters are not equipped to meet the needs of a person with dementia, or who is bed bound, as the Otto and Quinn paper note. This gap in service led to the collaboration between the Pace Women's Justice Center and The Hebrew Home to integrate a shelter for elder abuse victims into the infrastructure of the Home in 2005. The shelter is not just a setting. The Weinberg Center provides emergency short term housing, legal assistance and support services to victims of elder abuse. The Center continues a long-standing partnership between the Hebrew Home and the Bronx, New York and Westchester County District Attorneys to provide education and training to community, social services, law enforcement professionals and the judiciary. The Center has an outreach program designed to target older adults most at risk, visiting senior centers, retirement communities and shopping centers to disseminate information about available resources. In addition to prevention and intervention, The Hebrew Home has a research division that tracks and documents all Center cases with the ultimate goal of helping to identify the prevalence and incidence of elder abuse. Over the last 15 years since the first shelter opened, we have shepherded the creation of over 15 more shelters throughout the United States, and have expanded the vision from non-profit nursing homes to broad-based community programs. Though the SPRiNG Alliance (springalliance.org) was founded with the intention of spreading the shelter movement to every community with a long-term care facility, the call for each shelter model to adapt according to the needs and resources of each community has been clear.

Now each SPRiNG Alliance partner shares the vision of safety for older adults, and serves as the grounds for sharing research, education and community. The shelter movement is timely, relevant and pioneering.

First, we are mission-driven and mostly faith-based, non-profit long-term care providers with a moral obligation to assist elder abuse victims, and we have the knowledge and ability to do so. We provide not only a physical place for shelter, but also medical care, social work and legal assistance. Our goal is to safely return the older adult to the community.

Second, preventing and intervening in cases of elder abuse in the community, requires education and collaboration. We train judges, lawyers, pharmacists, doormen, Meals on Wheels delivery personnel and other professionals in the community to recognize and respond to elder abuse; we collaborate with police and prosecutors, hospitals and medical staff and we go directly to older adults. We involve everyone in the community who comes into contact with an older adult who needs assistance and protection. And we facilitate creation of multi-disciplinary terms to efficiently and effectively address the complexity of elder abuse cases.

Third, shelter is a way to raise awareness about elder abuse and to help influence state and federal policies. We support expanded funding for Adult Protective Services, training and education grants in elder abuse recognition and response, and other similar federal efforts.

Conclusion

Creating the elder abuse shelter has been an extraordinarily rewarding experience for our staff, our board, the community and the older adults we have helped. We would like to see an elder abuse shelter housed in every non-profit aging services provider in America.

I appreciate the opportunity to discuss these issues with you and congratulate you on your efforts to bring justice to our elders. We look forward to working with you to achieve that goal.

Letter Submitted by Patricia Johnson

Wednesday, March 6, 2019

I would like to thank the Senate Finance Committee for giving consumers an opportunity to voice their views on issues concerning nursing home practices which are often unfair, abusive, neglectful, and discriminatory in nature found throughout nursing homes across America.

My name is Patricia Johnson, daughter and Durable Power of Attorney, for Lillie M. Vaughan. She is a long term resident at Burcham Hills Center for Health and Rehab in East Lansing, MI after suffering a massive stroke, at the age of 89, in Detroit in April of 2016.

Let me share with you a little about this strong, dynamic black woman. Born and raised in Macon, GA, she moved to Detroit, MI in 1947. She got married, raised a family, secured employment at GM Fisher Body Plant in Livonia, MI from which she retired with full benefits. A great cook, gifted seamstress and tailor, dedicated church worker and went above and beyond providing care to family and neighbors with a smile.

My battles with inner city hospital physicians were nothing short of warfare. What gives them the right to determine care or lack thereof? She has aphasia and dysphagia, but is able to hear and understand conversations. Lacking the necessary resources to care for her myself, we only had 2–3 days to find a skilled nursing care rehab center upon discharge from hospital. On June 27, 2016, she was admitted into Burcham Hills for rehabilitation and long term care. It has been a roller coaster ride to this day! I will highlight some of the issues raised by presenter Dr. Grabowski of Harvard Medical School at the above mentioned hearing.

Primary Care Physicians 'Missing in Action'

There has been very little direct communication with the designated medical director/primary care physician at Burcham Hills. In December of 2016 Lillie was sent to the emergency room with a cold, swollen violet-colored, with weeping blisters on left leg, unresponsive and unarousable. Lab work done revealed many out of range numbers and blood sugar was also high and out of range as well as a UTI. The hospital physician informed me that this condition did not develop overnight. It appears an infection had been brewing over a two week period. Later, I requested copies of Lillie's medical records from Burcham Hills, her blood sugar levels had been elevated weeks prior and the nurse practitioner had been contacted by floor nurse but did not respond. After spending three weeks in hospital Lillie returned to Burcham Hills on hospice due to gangrene of left leg in January of 2017 with a dim prognosis. Through the care of the wound nurse and lots of prayer the leg started to heal on its own.

In May of 2018 this same leg started to self-amputate at the ankle and we went back to Sparrow Hospital emergency room and an orthopedic surgeon, provided counsel. He was willing to do the surgery on an out-patient basis but would not manage her overall care. Prior to this we had never been given been the option of consulting an orthopedic surgeon. Previously we were told mostly by Burcham Hills' staff that she probably wouldn't survive the surgery and there would probably be a sepsis infection. On July 17, 2018, arrangements for surgery were made, but there was a glitch. I received an email from the nurse practitioner which stated the surgeon wanted a PCP to admit to Sparrow Hospital. The medical director/primary care physician does not admit to Sparrow, therefore she was seeking a Medical Internal Service who admits for him. Who the hell has been managing my mother's care during the past two years?

The surgery was a success, with no sepsis infection present in Lillie's system. The surgeon discharge orders included some physical therapy, procedures for a prosthesis leg which would help with transfers to wheelchair, and a sense of overall dignity to a quality of life. Again, I have been met with opposition from the medical director/primary care physician—"she is too weak for a prosthetic leg"—and the nurse manager stating that there is no specific plan available according to Burcham Hills standards, which I have seen nothing in writing. However, I make sure Lillie is up and moving about in her wheelchair daily!

The post op checkups with CIMA group was a positive experience. Blood pressure medication was lowered to a manageable dose and Lillie was more awake and granted referrals for an eye exam and neurologist exam which had not been done at Burcham Hills in over two years.

Overmedicated

Upon review of listed medications, I discovered two different medications for acid indigestion and bowel health. Lillie has been given Reaglan, for nausea, quite a while before I was given a consent form to sign for use of psychoactive medication in July of 2018. I was unaware of the "black box warning" by FDA on elderly women who had been on this drug for a long time. Lillie had also been given Dilantin, antiseizure medication for stroke victims. At one time dosage was greatly increased due to a low therapeutic level reading from a blood test. During the initial exam with neurologist, questions as to why she was on a high dosage and who prescribed it. Her medical history and records from the stroke suffered in 2016 did not show evidence of any seizures. An order was written to discontinue this medication due to its side effects and recommended another drug, if seizures were noted and an EEG was scheduled months later. No seizure activity was indicated past or present. Why are they not held accountable? These actions effect one's quality of life regardless of being elderly.

Lack of Transparency

I have filed numerous complaints and grievances, some come back and changes are made, some don't, especially those requiring a detailed written response to critical questions regarding care. Both Medicare and Medicaid allow for residents to select their own primary care physician. However, Burcham Hills CHA require a certification process for outside physicians or staff to come on the premises to treat patients. I made a request in September of 2018 and after the forms were delivered I have not heard any feed back. I continue to advocate for Lillie. She is strong and deserving of much better care. She just celebrated her 92nd birthday a few weeks ago. All elderly Americans who have contributed in some way to the betterment of society deserve better. She has medicare (UAW Retiree Blue Cross Blue Shield) and Medicaid. I can still take her to medical specialists. The problem does not exist with the day to day care provided by CNAs, and RNs, but with the nurse managers, nurse practiconers, administrators, and medical director. Family members like myself, residents are not given a voice when it comes to ratings and our satisfaction. We are met with many obstacles.

Thank you for allowing a consumer's voice! Patricia Johnson

Senate Finance Committee, Not Forgotten: Protecting Americans from Abuse and Neglect in Nursing Homes March 6, 2019, Statement for the Record

Mr. Chairman and Mr. Ranking Member, LeadingAge appreciates the opportunity to submit this statement for the record of the Senate Finance Committee hearing, *Not Forgotten: Protecting Americans from Abuse and Neglect in Nursing Homes*.

The mission of LeadingAge is to be the trusted voice for aging. Our 6,000+ members and partners include nonprofit organizations representing the entire field of aging services, 38 state associations, hundreds of businesses, consumer groups, foundations and research centers.

LeadingAge is also a part of the Global Ageing Network, whose membership spans 50 countries. LeadingAge is a 501(c)(3) tax-exempt charitable organization focused on education, advocacy and applied research.

Since its founding in 1961, LeadingAge has stood for quality nursing home care. We participated in the development of the Nursing Home Reform Act, enacted as part of the Omnibus Budget Reconciliation Act of 1987 (OBRA '87). We have worked with the Centers for Medicare and Medicaid Services on the development of regulations to carry out OBRA. We have taken leadership roles in numerous initiatives like Quality First and Advancing Excellence in America's Nursing Homes, designed to give nursing homes tools and accountability measures to improve care. We and our 38 state associations provide extensive educational resources for our nursing home members not only on regulatory requirements and how to comply, but also on the deeper and more extensive issues of developing sound and forward-thinking leadership, recruiting and retaining well-qualified staff, and best practices for meeting the challenges of caring for extremely frail and vulnerable people. Our goal is for every nursing home in the country to be a place where any of us would be willing to live if we needed the level of care nursing homes provide.

Some recent examples of quality enhancement efforts our members and state associations have initiated:

Safe Care for Seniors, a program spearheaded by LeadingAge Minnesota, is designed to eliminate preventable harm in the course of caregiving. Through both words and actions – and with the senior at the center of all they do – providers renew their commitment to give safe, quality care to ensure a high quality of life for those they serve. Providers, team members, residents and families partner together to promote a culture of safety that allows residents to thrive in a community built on safety, trust, dignity, and respect. Providers and individuals take a two-fold pledge to increase the safety of the people they serve. They promise to always treat the people for whom they care with respect and dignity, to take steps to get to know them as individuals, and to speak up if they see something that may be unsafe or makes them feel uncomfortable.

Gayle Kvenvold, President and CEO of LeadingAge Minnesota put it this way: "…we began by asking this question: *what is in our power to do to bring about the best lives for our elders*? And that led us to renew our commitment to the heart and soul of our work – respect, safety and dignity for those we serve – and to commit as a statewide caregiving community and as LeadingAge Minnesota to some of the most meaningful work we will ever do. This is our calling, our commitment and our culture. Together we will prevent harm before it occurs and create a culture of safety. Together we will help those whose lives we touch, live their best lives." As the national partner of LeadingAge Minnesota, LeadingAge will seek to build on and promote the positive results of this initiative to our members in other states.

Another example involves two of our member nursing homes' collaboration with Altarum in its Program to Improve Eldercare. Altarum has received funding from civil monetary penalties collected by the state of Michigan for a three-year nursing home culture change initiative. LeadingAge members Martha T. Berry Medical Care Facility in Mount Clemens and Beacon Hill at Eastgate in Grand Rapids will be two of the six nursing homes participating in this initiative.

This "Accelerating Quality Improvement for Long-Stay Residents in Michigan Nursing Homes Using Culture Change" project will involve education and coaching from the Eden Alternative, a well-known proponent of fundamental nursing home organizational transformation toward truly person-centered services. Project participants will be trained in directing their organizations' operations to services oriented by resident choices and values. Altarum will monitor developments at the participating nursing homes, evaluate progress, and determine sustainability and economic impact. We and our members are excited by this opportunity to demonstrate the ways in which the principles of culture change can be put into practice and potentially replicated in other areas.

We also want to mention the work done by RiverSpring Health in Riverdale, New York. In addition to comprehensive services for its residents, RiverSpring maintains the Weinberg Center for Elder Justice, established in 2005 as this country's first shelter for victims of elder abuse. The Weinberg Center provides legal, social, and care management services to elders who have been victimized. At the Weinberg Center, elders who have experienced physical, emotional, or sexual abuse; neglect or abandonment; or financial exploitation can find shelter and help to regain control over their lives. Multi-disciplinary teams at the Weinberg Center provide trauma-informed care and services to help the older person recover, deal with legal issues, and often return to the community.

RiverSpring Health is part of the Shelter Partners Regional, National, & Global (SPRING) Alliance, a growing network of regional shelters supporting older people who have been victims of elder abuse. Several other LeadingAge members have joined the Alliance, including Eliza Bryant Village in Cleveland, Ohio; St. Elizabeth Community in Providence, Rhode Island; Lifespan in Rochester, New York; Jewish Senior Life in metropolitan Detroit, Michigan; and Jewish Senior Services in Bridgeport, Connecticut.

These organizations collaborate, sharing resources, technical assistance, and training to serve elders who have experienced abuse.

These are only some of the examples of the work LeadingAge members do every day to ensure the highest possible quality of care and quality of life for older people who need long-term services and supports. We make no apology for bad nursing home care. There is no excuse for abuse or neglect of older people whether they are living in nursing homes or in the larger community.

We understand and share the committee's concern about abuse and neglect in nursing homes. We also question the accuracy and adequacy of information now available to consumers through the Nursing Home 5-Star Quality Rating System on the Center for Medicare and Medicaid Services (CMS) website. As we have commented previously to Congress, the 5-Star system compares a nursing home's performance on quality measures, staffing, and health inspections only against the performance of other nursing homes in the same state. A 5-Star rating means only that a nursing home is performing much better than other nursing homes within its state.

LeadingAge believes that this system of rating nursing homes does not give consumers as much information as they need and should have to pick the best nursing home for themselves or their family members.

The 5-Star system also grades nursing homes on a bell curve, which requires some nursing homes to be graded at the one- and two-star level and relatively few nursing homes to be graded at the four- or five-star level. No matter how well its nursing homes may perform, no state may have a preponderance of four- and five-star nursing homes.

While the 5-Star system was conceived as a tool to help consumers choose a nursing home, few consumers understand the actual meaning of the 5-Star ratings. In addition, the ratings have been applied to contexts for which they were never intended, such as partnership in accountable care organizations, inclusion in managed care plans, and distribution of revenues under state Medicaid value-based purchasing initiatives.

On June 27, 2017 CMS announced an 18-month freeze on the health inspections portion of nursing homes' 5-Star ratings. The committee has noted that the 5-Star freeze has prevented consumers from detecting deterioration in a nursing home's quality that may have occurred since the nursing home's last survey in 2017. By the same token, we have heard from several of our member nursing homes that have committed time and resources to improving quality but are still stuck with their ratings from two years ago. We urged CMS to provide updated information on Nursing Home Compare about improvements nursing homes achieve during the freeze period.

We also have recommended that CMS should take a national approach to rating nursing homes under the 5-Star system. In its November 2016 report, *Nursing Homes: Consumers Could Benefit from Improvements to the Nursing Home Compare Website and Five-Star Quality Rating System,* the Government Accountability Office said:

> According to CMS Five-Star System documentation, the rating system is not designed to compare nursing homes nationally. Instead, ratings are only comparable for homes in the same state. CMS made the decision to base the health inspection component on the relative performance of homes within the same state primarily due to variation across the states in the execution of the standard surveys. Because the health inspection component most significantly contributes to the overall rating, this means that the overall rating also cannot be compared nationally. However, the addition of national ratings would be helpful for consumers and we have previously made recommendations to CMS that would help decrease survey variation across states.

And the 5-Star rating system should not include a bell curve. Every nursing home should have the potential to achieve a 5-Star rating by providing the highest-quality services. Every nursing home should be a place where we would not be reluctant to live or have a family member go to live when that level of care and services is needed.

An incident to be discussed at the committee's hearing, of the death of an Iowa nursing home resident due to reported neglect and inadequate care, is disturbing. It is the kind of incident for which no excuses can be made.

The case to some extent illustrates the challenges faced by rural long-term care providers and by people living in rural areas who need long-term care. According to news reports, Patricia Blank's mother, Mrs. Virginia Olthoff, lived at the Timely Mission Nursing Home in Buffalo Center, Iowa.

Buffalo Center is a town of 891 people, whose population is both aging and declining, according to census data. The town is 86 miles from the nearest moderate-sized city, Rochester, Minnesota. Timely Mission is the only nursing home in Buffalo Center, and the town has no home health care provider or hospital. Timely Mission has 46 beds certified for Medicare and Medicaid but currently has 38 residents, giving it an 82% occupancy rate.

During 2018, LeadingAge held town hall conversations in every state where we have members. Overwhelmingly we heard from our members, especially in rural areas, about the difficulties they have recruiting and retaining staff. This is true not only of certified nursing assistants, the backbone of the long-term care system, but also administrators, nurses, social workers, pharmacists, mental health professionals, and other essential care providers. We would note that, according to news reports, Timely Mission had no administrator at the time the incident in question occurred.

Concern reportedly has been expressed that as a result of care deficiencies that resulted in Mrs. Olthoff's death, CMS assessed a fine of $77,462. Questions have been raised as to whether the amount of that fine was appropriate, given the egregious circumstances in this case, and whether a much heavier fine should have been imposed, for example by using the per-day calculation CMS has used in the past.

Again, we make no excuses for bad care. However, we think the impact of steep fines on small, stand-alone nursing homes needs to be considered. The fine CMS assessed on

Timely Mission likely had a measurable impact on the nursing home's finances. A fine approaching $1 million, which might have been assessed under the per-day method of calculation, almost certainly would have caused the facility to close.

And what of that? Do we care whether an underperforming small nursing home in a rural area gets closed as a result of fines for care deficiencies? We think the committee should care. Because what happens to the 36 people now living at Timely Mission if it closes down? Where are they supposed to go? Alternative nursing home care is many miles away; home care services are even more distant. Maybe we should all be responsible for contributing to constructive solutions that improve care and preserve the ability of rural Americans to have access to nursing home services if they need them.

What happens to the people who work at Timely Mission if it closes? In many rural communities, the local nursing home is the primary source of employment. If another provider were to take Timely Mission's place, who would the new provider be able to recruit to provide the long-term services and supports residents of the area will need as they age?

LeadingAge represents many rural long-term services and supports providers who do an outstanding job in caring for their residents and clients. Residents of rural areas need and deserve the highest quality of long-term services and supports. But the challenges of financial and human resources that generally prevail in the long-term services and supports field are magnified in rural and frontier areas where the working-age population is declining, the aging population is growing, and health, long-term care, and human resources are few and far between. This is a concern not only for us as providers but also for those representing individuals and families who need long-term services and supports.

We need to consider whether the imposition of fines that might amount to several times a nursing home's annual revenues is the best or only way to ensure quality. We would note that the Nursing Home Reform Act of 1987 provides an array of remedies for care deficiencies in addition to civil monetary penalties; these remedies include directed plans of correction, inservice trainings, and appointment of temporary management. A recent *Health Affairs* article, *The Future of Nursing Home Regulation: Time for a Conversation?* by David Stevenson comments that:

> [I]t is important to note that there is relatively limited evidence about whether penalties effectively deter poor-quality care and what their optimal level or form might be.

We believe it is time to forge a new path forward: one of close collaboration between providers, policymakers, regulators and consumers that will better help providers meet the challenges faced to achieve the type of care older adults need as they age. Nursing homes play a critical role in our healthcare system and will continue to do so. This is not an us versus them situation. We – providers, policymakers, consumers and elected officials – are all in this together. We ask for an honest conversation on how all providers, and rural ones in particular, can attract and retain the staff they need; a clear assessment about the true costs of care, and how the nursing home oversight system can effectively promote systemic organizational change leading to measurable and sustained quality improvement within nursing homes. We owe it to older adults and those who care for them to figure this out.

Long Term Care Community Coalition et al.

The Long Term Care Community Coalition, Center for Medicare Advocacy, National Consumer Voice for Quality Long-Term Care, Justice in Aging, California Advocates for Nursing Home Reform, and National Academy of Elder Law Attorneys thank the Senate Finance Committee for holding the March 6, 2019, hearing "Not Forgotten: Protecting Americans From Abuse and Neglect in Nursing Homes." Our organizations are dedicated to improving the lives of long-term care residents across the country and are writing this Committee to highlight both recent and ongoing concerns that place nursing home residents at risk of experiencing abuse, neglect, and other forms of harm.

As this Committee knows, the Nursing Home Reform Law requires every nursing home to provide residents with the services they need to attain and maintain their "highest practicable physical, mental, and psychosocial well-being."[85] To ensure that residents receive the care that they need and deserve, the law and its implementing regulations detail specific resident rights and protections that all nursing homes must adhere to when they voluntarily participate in Medicare, Medicaid, or both. Unfortunately, the Centers for Medicare & Medicaid Services (CMS) has been rolling back these resident rights and protections, often at the request of the nursing home industry, for the purpose of reducing so-called provider "burdens."[86]

The following actions represent only a few of CMS's deregulatory efforts over the past two years:

1) CMS placed an 18-month moratorium on the full enforcement of eight standards of care.[87] These standards relate to important resident protections, such as baseline care planning, staff competency, antibiotic stewardship, and

---

[85] 42 U.S.C § 1395i–3(b)(2).

[86] *See, e.g., Don't Abandon Nursing Residents*, CANHR et al., available at https://nursinghome411.org/dont-abandon-nursing-home-residents-series/.

[87] *Temporary Enforcement Delays for Certain Phase 2 F-Tags and Changes to Nursing Home Compare*, Ref: S&C 18-04-NH, CMS, Nov. 24, 2017, available at https://www.cms.gov/Medicare/Provider-Enrollment-and-Certification/SurveyCertificationGenInfo/Downloads/Survey-and-Cert-Letter-18-04.pdf.

psychotropic medications. The moratorium means that nursing homes will not be financially penalized when these safeguards are violated.

2) CMS shifted the default civil money penalty (CMP) from per day (for the duration of a violation) to per instance.[88] *The New York Times* reported that "the change means that some nursing homes could be sheltered from fines above the maximum per-instance fine of $20,965 even for egregious mistakes."[89]
3) CMS issued a notice of proposed rulemaking (NPRM) to roll back emergency preparedness requirements. Most notably, the proposed rule would allow nursing homes to review their programs and train staff every two years instead of annually.[90]
4) In response to industry lobbying, CMS is carrying out plans to revise the federal nursing home Requirements of Participation to "reform" standards that have been identified as "excessively burdensome" for the nursing home industry.[91] The Requirements were recently revised in October 2016 (for the first time in 25 years) to better address longstanding problems, including persistent abuse and neglect.[92] These standards need to be implemented, not watered down.

Nursing home residents are some of the most vulnerable individuals in the nation. CMS's deregulatory agenda puts residents in danger of experiencing harm or being placed in immediate jeopardy of health, safety, or well-being. This potential for resident harm is in direct opposition to the HHS Secretary's duty under the law. The law makes clear that the Secretary is responsible for assuring the "requirements which govern the provision of care in skilled nursing facilities..., and the enforcement of such requirements, are adequate to protect the health, safety, welfare, and rights of residents and to promote the effective and efficient use of public moneys."[93] CMS's deregulatory actions indicate that the Secretary is ignoring this long-standing mandate.

CMS's efforts are even more dangerous because they exacerbate existing problems in nursing homes. Multiple reports from the HHS Office of the Inspector General (OIG) and the Government Accountability Office (GAO) document persistent and widespread

---

88 *Enforcement Weakens as Civil Money Penalties Shift from per Day to Per Instance*, Center & LTCCC, available at https://www.medicareadvocacy.org/enforcement-weakens-as- civil-money-penalties-shift-from-per-day-to-per-instance/.

89 Jordan Rau, *Trump Administration Eases Nursing Home Fines in Victory for Industry*, N.Y. Times (Dec. 24, 2017), available at https://www.nytimes.com/2017/12/24/business/trump-administration-nursing-home-penalties.html.

90 Medicare and Medicaid Programs; Regulatory Provisions To Promote Program Efficiency, Transparency, and Burden Reduction, 83 Fed. Reg. 47686 (Sept. 20, 2018), available at https://www.govinfo.gov/content/pkg/FR-2018-09-20/pdf/2018-19599.pdf.

91 *Requirements for Long-Term Care Facilities: Regulatory Provisions to Promote Program Efficiency, Transparency, and Burden Reduction (CMS-3347-P)(Section 610 Review)*, Office of Information and Regulatory Affairs (Fall 2018), available at https://www.reginfo.gov/public/do/eAgendaViewRule?pubId=201810&RIN=0938-AT36.

92 Medicare and Medicaid Programs; Reform of Requirements for Long-Term Care Facilities, 81 Fed. Reg. 68688 (Oct. 4, 2016), available at https://www.govinfo.gov/content/pkg/FR-2016-10-04/pdf/2016-23503.pdf.

93 42 U.S.C. § 1395i–3(f)(1).

problems facing nursing home residents. For instance, a 2014 OIG report found that one-third of Medicare beneficiaries experienced harm within, on average, 15.5 days of entering a nursing home; the OIG stated that 59 percent of these events were preventable.[94] Similarly, a 2008 GAO report highlighted that studies since 1998 indicate state surveyors "sometimes understate the extent of serious care problems in homes because they miss deficiencies . . .."[95] Such persistent problems over the years have created greater insecurity for residents, requiring additional legislation and regulations, not less.

The following problems indicate only some of the ongoing concerns:

1) More than 95 percent of all citations for violations of the federal minimum standards of care result in findings of no resident harm.[96] A "no harm" citation does not mean that the resident did not, in fact, experience pain, suffering, or humiliation. However, a finding of "no harm" all too often does mean that the nursing home is not penalized for poor care.[97]
2) Staffing is essential to resident care and quality of life. Too often, insufficient staffing is the underlying cause of other health violations.[98] By law, nursing homes must have a registered nurse on duty for eight consecutive hours and 24-hour licensed nurse services every single day.[99] These two requirements are recognized as the minimum necessary to ensure that residents receive the "skilled nursing" care and monitoring that they need and which facilities are paid to provide. However, CMS noted in a 2017 memorandum that about six percent of nursing homes that submitted nurse staffing data for the third quarter of 2017 had seven or more days with no reported RN hours and that 80 percent of these days were on weekends.[100] *The New York Times* further described the federal data as documenting that, for at least one day in the last quarter of 2017, 25 percent of nursing homes reported no registered nurses at work.[101]

---

94 Daniel R. Levinson, *Adverse Events in Skilled Nursing Facilities: National Incidence Among Medicare Beneficiaries*, HHS OIG (Feb. 2014), available at https://oig.hhs.gov/oei/reports/oei-06-11-00370.pdf.

95 *Federal Monitoring Surveys Demonstrate Continued Understatement of Serious Care Problems and CMS Oversight Weakness*, GAO (May 2008), available at https://www.gao.gov/assets/280/275154.pdf.

96 *Nursing Home Data Compendium 2015 Edition*, CMS, available at https://www.cms.gov/Medicare/Provider-Enrollment-and-Certification/CertificationandComplianc/Downloads/ nursinghomedatacompendium_508-2015.pdf.

97 *See generally, Elder Justice: What No Harm" Really Means for Residents*, LTCCC & Center, available at https://nursinghome411.org/news-reports/elder-justice/.

98 *The New York Times Shows Nursing Homes Are Not Meeting Staffing Requirements*, LTCCC & Center, available at https://nursinghome411.org/the-new-york-times-shows- nursing-homes-are-not-meeting-staffing-requirements/.

99 42 U.S.C. § 1395i–3(b)(4)(C).

100 *Transition to Payroll-Based Journal (PBJ) Staffing Measures on the Nursing Home Compare tool on Medicare.gov and the Five Star Quality Rating System*, Ref: QSO-18-17- NH, CMS (Apr. 6, 2018), available at https://www.cms.gov/Medicare/Provider-Enrollment-and-Certification/SurveyCertificationGenInfo/ Downloads/QSO18-17-NH.pdf.

101 Jordan Rau, *It's Almost Like a Ghost Town. Most Nursing Homes Overstate Staffing for Years*, N.Y. Times (Jul. 7, 2018), available at https://www.nytimes.com/2018/07/07/health/nursing-homes-staffing-medicare.html.

3) Antipsychotic Drugs. About 20 percent of nursing home residents are administered antipsychotic drugs every day.[102] However, less than two percent of the population will ever have a diagnosis for a clinical condition (e.g., Schizophrenia) identified by CMS when it risk-adjusts for potentially appropriate uses of these drugs. In a 2011 statement addressing widespread and inappropriate use of antipsychotic drugs in nursing homes, the HHS Inspector General stated that "[g]overnment, taxpayers, nursing home residents, as well as their families and caregivers should be outraged – and seek solutions."[103] Nevertheless, seven years later, in the absence of meaningful enforcement, the problem of overuse and misuse of antipsychotic drugs is still widespread.
4) Transfer and Discharge. CMS has stated that "facility-initiated discharges continue to be one of the most frequent complaints made to State Long Term Care Ombudsman Programs."[104] Although the Nursing Home Reform Law places specific restrictions on when and how a resident can be transferred or discharged, many residents fall victim to inappropriate and unsafe discharges. Residents have been discharged to unsafe and inappropriate settings, such as homeless shelters, storage units, and motels.
5) The buying and selling of nursing homes and the transfer of licenses to new managers raise questions about who these operators are and whether there are sufficient state and federal law, regulations, and practices in place, and meaningfully enforced, to protect residents.[105] For instance, Skyline Healthcare took over 100 nursing homes across the country starting in 2015 before ultimately collapsing in 2018.[106] Officials from various states indicated that Skyline facilities were at imminent risk of running out of necessary food and medication, and were unable to meet payroll. Many of Skyline's nursing homes were acquired from Golden Living, another chain that was sued by the Pennsylvania Attorney General in 2015 for providing poor care to residents. [107]

---

[102] *Despite Promised Crackdown, Citations for Inappropriate Drugging Remain Rare*, LTCCC (Nov. 8, 2018), available at https://nursinghome411.org/ltccc-news-alert-despite- promised-crackdown-citations-for-inappropriate-drugging-remain-rare/.

[103] Daniel R. Levinson, *Overmedication of Nursing Home Patients Troubling*, HHS OIG (May 9, 2011), available at https://oig.hhs.gov/newsroom/testimony-and- speeches/levinson_051011.asp.

[104] *An Initiative to Address Facility Initiated Discharges that Violate Federal Regulations*, Ref: S&C 18-08-NH, CMS (Dec. 22, 2017), available at https://www.cms.gov/ Medicare/Provider-Enrollment-and-Certification/SurveyCertificationGenInfo/Downloads/ Survey-and-Cert-Letter-18-08.pdf.

[105] *Joint Statement on Turmoil in the Nursing Home Industry*, LTCCC & Center, available at https://nursinghome411.org/wp-content/uploads/2019/01/LTCCC-CMA-Joint- Statement-on-Turmoil-in-the-Nursing-Home-Industry.pdf.

[106] Kimberly Marselas, *Skyline's implosion continues with Pennsylvania takeover*, McKnight's Long-Term Care News (May 3, 2018), available at https://www.mcknights.com/news/ skylines-implosion-continues-with-pennsylvania- takeover/.

[107] Wesley Robinson, *Harrisburg, Camp Hill nursing homes among 14 sued by state*, Penn Live (Jul. 1, 2015), available at https://www.pennlive.com/midstate/index.ssf/2015/07/14_nursing_homes_of_chain_nam e.html.

Nursing home residents are in need of urgent action to protect their quality of care and quality of life. Given the ongoing problems that already exist in nursing homes, CMS's deregulation places residents at an even greater risk of experiencing harm. We applaud the Senate Finance Committee's decision to hold a hearing on nursing home resident abuse and neglect, and hope that this Committee will continue to shine a spotlight on these issues until real change occurs and is sustained. Our organizations would like the opportunity to work with this Committee on future hearings and legislation to find solutions to these problems.

Contact Information:
Richard J. Mollot, Executive Director
Long Term Care Community Coalition

Toby S. Edelman, Senior Policy Attorney
Center for Medicare Advocacy

Dara Valanejad, Policy Attorney
Center for Medicare Advocacy
Long Term Care Community Coalition

Lori. O. Smetanka, Executive Director
The National Consumer Voice for Quality Long-Term Care
202-332-2275 | lsmetanka@theconsumervoice.org
Robyn Grant, Director of Public Policy and Advocacy
The National Consumer Voice for Quality Long-Term Care

Eric Carlson, Directing Attorney
Justice in Aging

Natalie Kean, Staff Attorney
Justice in Aging

Janet Wells, Public Policy Consultant
California Advocates for Nursing Home Reform

Tony Chicotel, Staff Attorney
California Advocates for Nursing Home Reform

Michael Connors, Long Term Care Advocate
California Advocates for Nursing Home Reform

David M. Goldfarb
National Academy of Elder Law Attorneys (NAELA)

Letter Submitted by Cherrie A. Miller

To Senator Grassley,

I am writing to you today regarding the death of Duane M. Dingman. I want to give you an accurate picture of the events that led up to my Dad's death. You are one of the very few who have taken the time to listen to what is actually happening in Iowa. As you have witnessed with the death of Mrs. Olthoff, Inspections and Appeals does absolutely nothing to monitor the nursing homes, care facilities, and hospice providers who are supposedly providing care to those who are most vulnerable. In the case of Mrs. Olthoff, Buffalo Center retained a 4 star rating. In the case of my Dad, the director of Windsor Manor and the nurse were fired and went across town and got the same jobs at another facility the next day. Inspections and Appeals gave Unity Point Hospice a citation and monitored for one year. That was it.

Kepro did an investigation into the death of my Dad and they said what Unity Point did was cruel and he suffered to die. In their report they stated that Unity Point did NOT "meet the minimum standard of care." Kepro is the investigative branch of Medicare. The staff at Kepro is comprised of doctors and nurses who have worked in hospice or directly with it.

Dad is a two time veteran. I went to the head of the Veteran's Administration for the state of Iowa. We met with the head physician. They were also appalled at the lack of care my Dad was given.

I have filed formal complaints to the Iowa Board of Nursing about the hospice nurse who withdrew Dad's heart medication without our knowledge and or consent. I specifically told them not to do that because he was in congestive heart failure. We found out by accident what they had done. They are going to keep an eye on her. Do you have to hurt a certain number of people before any action is taken? What is that number?

I have filed a formal complaint with the Iowa board of Medicine. Dr. Nikki Ehn was his physician for several years. She removed all his medications based on a call from a "case manager" that she had never met in her life. The family was never notified. They are going to keep an eye on her too. Please keep in mind the heart medicine that was helping to provide some comfort for him is about the size of a BB. What happened to care, comfort, and the "do no harm" oath? They were done with him.

I have notified the Iowa Attorney General's office and talked with the office of the Governor of Iowa, Kim Reynolds. Senator Ernst has a formal report and so does Congressman Kevin Yoder for the State of Kansas. It is the office of Kevin Yoder that finally got my Dad his well-deserved veteran benefits.

At the federal level I have also called the division of Medicare.

I absolutely want to testify before the committee on Elder Abuse and Neglect. We have done a lot of talking and filing reports, now it is time to do something for those who need and deserve care. You have the power to do that.'

Respectfully,

Cherrie A. Miller

We are filing this complaint against Unity Point Hospice, Fort Dodge, Iowa, on behalf of my deceased Father, Duane M. Dingman of Webster City, Iowa. This complaint specifically addresses their failure to meet a "standard of care." On September 22, 2015, Amanda Gascho, the case worker from Unity Point removed all of my Dad's medications without our permission. At my insistence, all medications were to be reinstated immediately. She did not comply with the families instructions. We were not told the medications had not been reinstated. On September 26, 2015, the week-end hospice worker named Erin informed us that Dad had not received any medications except Oxycodone for the last 4 days. Specifically no Lasix for the congestive heart failure. Erin left shortly after that. She did not stay to see if he was comfortable or that the medications were reinstated. We never saw Unity Point Hospice again. On the fifth day, the 27th, he was filled with fluid and he struggled for over 3 hours and finally died. It was a horrible nightmare. Our family is sickened and devastated over this. I watched him die a very difficult death and no one showed up to help.

The entire point of hospice care was to provide comfort to Dad in the final weeks of his life and for a peaceful transition when the time came. In their records they noted in the plan they made that this was the family's wishes. They did none of it.

Please meet my Dad. I have enclosed his memorial for you. If you look at the back you will see he is a two time veteran that proudly served in World War II and the Korean conflict. He was honorably discharged twice. He was married to my Mother for 57 years and the resided at their home for over 50 years. He worked at Electrolux for 43 years and retired with an impeccable record. At the age of 84, Congressman Kevin Yoder helped my Dad get the VA benefits he so richly deserved.

At the beginning of September 2015, as a family we decided to start hospice care for Dad. We were given Unity Point's name by Windsor Manor. We chose them because they were fairly close to Webster City and when it was critical they could be there. We were told by the Windsor nurse that they will come on week-ends to provide care. This was very important to us because we wanted to be sure that they would be available to keep him as comfortable as possible and especially during the transition time. Early on, the care was minimal. They did vital signs and actually spent very little time with Dad. The aids at Windsor Manor were carefully monitoring his oxygen levels, vital signs, helping with showers and daily care. On several occasions I suggested they came to help at meal time, taking him out in his wheelchair for fresh air, or going to the cafe for a cup of soft serve ice cream, or assisting with showers. They were not receptive to that. One Unity Point employee said they did not have time for that and they don't do that. During that month they gave him 2 showers, a massage and I insisted Mandy take him out for fresh air on September 22, 2015—very reluctantly she did.

Early on they wanted to stop his medications. We said none would be stopped other than three vitamins. On September 17, 2015, Dad was having difficulty and the Windsor Nurse called me to come to Windsor. I left Kansas City and spent the night sleeping next to Dad. He rebounded on the 19th. I spent the day with him. My brother, Mike came and was surprised to see me. Mike was there to see him every day about lunchtime before he went to work. I spent the day with Dad and went home later that day. Please note Mike was there every day and I called at least twice a day to check on him. Dad had a telephone in his room so we talked a lot.

On September 22, 2015, the Windsor Manor nurse, Laura Lavender, called to say that Dad was not swallowing well and they felt it was best to take all the medications and give him liquid morphine. We were very apprehensive about stopping all medications, and Mike and I wanted to talk it over. Amanda, the case manager stopped all medications. He had been getting oxycodone every 2 hours. During that time he did not get any morphine or oxycodone. I called the Windsor aid and she told me Dad had not had any pain medication for over 6 hours. I spoke with Amanda. I insisted she reinstate them all. She said all the meds were out of the building. I told her she was wrong and to walk down to the nurses station while I was on the phone with her. I insisted she get them, bring them down and restart them right now. ALL the meds were there. We did not know she only brought the oxycodone down. I stayed with her on the phone while she gave the medication to Dad. I have phone records to document this. According to Nikki Ehn, our family doctor, Amanda never asked to reinstate all the meds—only the oxycodone. A critical medicine for Dad was the lasix. This helped to eliminate the fluid from the heart, legs, arms, and mid region. It was important for his comfort.

On September 23rd, Dad had a good day. Mike checked on him and noted he was doing well today. When Mike arrived for his daily check, Dad was at the table eating. Obviously he was able to swallow. I made my normal phone calls and things were better. During the rest of this week Mike was dropping off the normal meds the VA sent to him at his home and then he would bring them to Windsor Manor. He dropped off meds 3 times that week. No one at Windsor Manor said that he was no longer getting those meds. As far as we knew everything was reinstated as requested. I let them know that I was coming on Saturday and planned to stay for an extended time. The nurse did call me and told me to bring bigger slacks because Dad was so swollen his slacks no longer fit him. I purchased 4 pairs to bring on Saturday.

On September 24th and September 25th, Dad was eating a pretty good breakfast, moderate lunch, and not much supper. Mike noted his arms and legs looked more swollen.

On September 26th, I called the after hours hospice line to get an update from them. It was the hospice number they gave me to call when we started with them. They did not know who Dad was. FOUR hours later they figured out who he was. They routed me to a woman at her home with a barking dog in Sioux City, and several other places. I got to Windsor Manor and both Mike and I noted Dad's legs and arms were very swollen. The week-end hospice worker, Erin, finally showed up. This is when we were told Dad was only getting oxycodone. Mike stayed in with Dad while he laid down. I went outside with my cell phone and started raising hell to get his meds back. Erin left. We never saw Unity Point Hospice again. At 8 PM on Saturday night Erin left me a voice mail saying she got a hold of Nikki Ehn and all the meds were reinstated except for the blood pressure one. The key was the lasix were reinstated. I called the Windsor nurse. She was at a dance. The director was at a birthday party. The only worker up front was an aid named Kay and she did not have a key to get in the nurses office to get the meds. The director, Jill Scott called Kay when I was standing there. Jill Scott was yelling in the phone that I was raising hell trying to get my Dad's medicine back. She told her she was not coming in. There was not a nurse in the building and no one could get a key to restart the meds. We were just stone walled—another day with no lasix. We are now on day 4 without them. Mike helped Dad dress for bed. At that time his legs were so heavy Mike lifted them into bed, he could no longer lift them himself. I slept in a chair next to him. He was up and down all night. He kept trying to spit up fluid. We later learned the Windsor nurse had all his medications removed and sent them to Thrifty White Pharmacy. The Pharmacy was closed and would not reopen until Monday. Dad did not make it to Monday.

September 27, 2015, Dad woke up at 5:15 AM. I helped him in the bathroom and then sat him in the recliner. His breathing was heavy and labored. We are now on day 5 with no lasics. His breathing is going from labored to wheezing. I am trying to comfort him and it is not working. I called the director and the nurse and neither one is coming until after lunch. Unity Point Hospice did not show up either. At that time I am begging for help. The nurse told me we had to be dismissed from hospice to call an ambulance. We later learned that is not true. We learned that from one of the prosecuting attorneys for the State of Iowa. While I stepped out to call for help, Dad panicked. I told him I would stay close and I held his hand. With one hand I held his hand, and the other I was calling and begging for help. The aid shift changes and Lisa Sandkamp arrives. She used to be a hospice aid for Gehtiva. By then it is 6:15. It is going very badly. After calling the Windsor nurse, Lisa brought in some liquid drops. By then Dad is convulsing and his body and face are in spasms and gasping for air. You could hear the sound of fluid. He kept trying to spit it up. He was really struggling. It was awful. I called Mike to come. Hospice did not show up and no one from Windsor showed up either. Finally at 7:55 they used a cell phone to pronounce him dead. The director from Windsor showed up and so did the nurse. Hospice wanted to show up for grief counseling. I told them to stay away. They did not show up when we needed them—we did not need them now. I am not sure why the director of Windsor and the nurse showed up. When I was begging for help, they did not show up either. They all came running as soon as he was dead.

These people cut Dad's life short and made the final hours of his life a nightmare. They are monsters. This is not what hospice should be. He is a great man and he deserved better than this. Their disrespect and disregard for his precious life is not acceptable. This family is devastated.

Amanda J. Gascho needs to be held accountable for her actions. She is a lot of things, hospice manager is not one of them. Nikki Ehn was his doctor. Her inappropriate behavior is disgusting. Windsor Manor was Dad's home for 5 years. Birthday cake and dancing are more important than end of life help. That says a lot about them. My Dad deserved more care, regard, and respect. I also want to make sure that this cannot happen to another family.

The death certificate shows he died of natural causes. There was nothing natural about it. They were not there—I was. They cannot even speculate what the final hours of his life were like—they never showed up when he was alive. Unity Point billed Medicare $10,000. They are all about the money. Care and Comfort are not included when you sign an agreement with them for hospice care

Thank you for your immediate attention to this matter. I will gladly forward any and all documents you request.

Sincerely,

Cherrie A. Miller

In Loving Memory of Duane M. Dingman, March 16, 1928–September 27, 2015

Duane Dingman, 87, of Webster City, died Sunday, September 27, 2015 at Windsor Manor. A Celebration of Life will be held at 2:00 p.m. on Thursday, October 1, 2015 at St. Paul's Lutheran Church with Pastor Mark Eichler officiating. Burial will follow the services at Graceland Cemetery with military rites by the American Legion Post #191. Visitation will be prior to the services from 12:00 p.m. until 2:00 p.m.

Duane M. Dingman, the son of James W. and Ethel Vandeventer Dingman was born March 16, 1928 in Webster City. He attended school in Webster City. He enlisted in the United States Army and proudly served two times. He enlisted on November 8, 1945 at Fort Des Moines, Iowa and served overseas with the Third Infantry. He was honorably discharged on March 16, 1948. He was recalled in the Korean Conflict on September 17,

1950 to Fort Hood, Texas. He was shipped overseas and served until June 30, 1951. He was honorably discharged on July 9, 1951, at Fort Lawton, Washington.

Duane married the love of his life, Nadine F. Lunning, on November 14, 1952 at the First Baptist Church of Webster City. Duane and Nadine were members of St. Paul's Lutheran Church and remained faithful members. They were married for 57 years. They resided at 1623 Sparboe Court for over 50 years. In later years Duane resided at Windsor Manor in Webster City.

Duane was employed at Webster City Products for 43 years. He retired at the age of 65. He is survived by two children, Cherrie A. Miller of Overland Park, Kansas and Michael and Catheryn Dingman of Webster City. He has two grandchildren, Jason D. and Christine Dingman of Webster City and Teresa and Andrew Miller of Grimes; many nieces and nephews.

Duane and Nadine enjoyed many historical society events and remained active in genealogy throughout their married life. They loved learning about their families and helped many others locate their family members too. Duane loved spending time with his grandchildren and was active in their lives. For many years he enjoyed his coffee group at McDonalds.

He is preceded in death by his wife, Nadine; his parents; his brothers, Isaac, Francis (as child), Vernon, William, Dale and Gerald; sisters, Wilma Graham, Lillian Logston, Viola Doolittle, Belva Neubauer, Lila Mix and Mavis Kleckner.

Duane will always be remembered as a loving husband, loving father and a loving grandfather. We will miss you Dad, Grandpa and friend.

Memorials may be given to St Paul's Lutheran Church, Kendall Young Library or the Alzheimer's Association in memory of Duane. Write a personal tribute for the family at *www.fosterfuneralandcremation.com.*

Statement Submitted by Jill K. Mount, R.N., BSN, MSN, Ph.D.

I would like to thank the Senate Finance Committee for holding the March 6, 2019, hearing "Not Forgotten: Protecting Americans From Abuse and Neglect in Nursing Homes." As a volunteer Washington State Long-Term Care Ombudsman, I have visited nursing homes where there have been instances of abuse and neglect.

I believe it is very important that the Centers for Medicare and Medicaid Services not roll back on resident rights and protections because nursing home residents need their rights to be protected. Please do not continue the 18-month moratorium on the full enforcement of eight standards of care. Also, please do not continue to shift the default civil money penalty from per day to per instance because that will shelter nursing homes from fines. I live in Washington State and we have many different types of natural disasters including landslides, floods, record snowfall and earthquakes. Please do not rescind the new emergency preparedness requirements because they protect nursing home residents when disasters like these occur. There is such great turnover in nursing home staff that requiring emergency preparedness program review and training staff every 2 years instead of annually will fail to protect residents. Also, please do not revise the federal nursing home Requirements of Participation that were revised in October 2016, please implement these standards, do not weaken them. As Senator Grassley noted, he has been involved in this issue for over 20 years and yet we continue to have neglect and abuse in nursing homes.

Letter Submitted by Christina A. Nappo

U.S. Senate
Committee on Finance
Dirksen Senate Office Bldg.
Washington DC

On March 9, 2019, you completed the hearing "Not Forgotten: Protecting Americans from Abuse and Neglect in Nursing Homes." On the same day CNN reported on this hearing. Senate hearing examines "devastating" nursing home abuse, summing up what was discussed at this hearing and it is this summery that I would like to respond to as part of my response to your hearing.

CNN reported that there was only a small section of this hearing for the victim of the increased reporting of the abuse that occurs in nursing homes. Matter of fact it was one line that talked about the innocent getting reported. I was that innocent who was reported on, this is my story and how your system has failed me and has continued to fail me for almost a year now. You want improvements on your system of abuse reporting I seen the system fail first hand and can tell you every part of the failure.

On May 12, 2018 I reported to work as I did for the last year with my clean uniform, my body and hair washed, my makeup minimum and my body spray light as not to offend any of my patients with my odor. I punched in at the time clock signed in at the unit floor and got my room assignments. It was Saturday night so it would be the same two showers one with my patient who I have had for the last year and one who I have had for a few Months, but have earned her trust and learned her bathing ritual that she likes. Nothing different I thought until my Floor Supervisor "Ricky" tried to assign a new girl Osanna Craig, Ozzy, to Richard for her on-sight training time, she was only hired three days ago as a permanent full time employee and just completed her on the job school training on April 8, 2018. Richard refused to take Ozzy so she was assigned to me; even though I was not cleared for training I took her as long as she could keep up with me.

We took vitals from my patients as usual, fed them dinner, cleaned up after dinner and I started my showering of my two patients. Ozzy was with me as I entered into the shower area with my female patient a 50s something lady who was in a wheelchair (HIPAA will not allow more information). I undressed her placed her on the toilet and began the first part of her showering process her shave. This patient liked to be shaved during her shower her face, side burns, arm pits, privates and legs. Which I did on the toilet it was less confining and the shower did not need to be running only the sink which allowed the humidity in the shower area to remain low until the washing process of the actual shower.

Ozzy remained quiet and did not ask questions she observed only as I worked with my patient, she never asked any questions and I did ask her if she had any questions and she told me that she did not.

I transferred my patient to the shower chair and rolled him into the shower, I washed her hair, rinsed and washed the rest of her. When I rinsed my patient with warm water and got to her private area she laughed and I said, "well that is the end of our shower" I continued briefly to rinse her legs and turned off the water. At the same shower event the RN who we were working under Marylou wanted to her required skin check on my patient. Since I had Ozzy in the shower with me I left to get Marylou for the skin check. Marylou completed her skin check on my patient and I dressed her and took her back to her room where she was placed into bed.

Her shower was done at 7:00–7:30 p.m. I lost track of Ozzy, she was going on a few smoke breaks and since I didn't go on breaks I just thought she was smoking or that she got pulled from me to do some training, which was not uncommon. You go where you are needed almost like a floater, so I did not question it. It was not until around 10 p.m. when I was told to report to the office that I knew that something happened, something so wrong, something that would change my life forever.

I entered into the office that the Floor Supervisor Rickey was in with Nicole a new LPN, who was recently upgraded from a CNA, when she graduated from college and earned her LPN certification. Both co-workers that I have worked with for a year, I asked, "what happened now, did I miss a blood pressure or something." They were not joking Rickey looked at me and asked for me to sit down. Nicole never made eye contact, I knew it was bad. "What's going on?" Rickey proceeded to tell me that, "Ozzy has reported you as sexually stimulating your patient in her shower." I was shocked. He let me read her statement, he told me that I will be able to write a statement of what happened. I told him what happened in the shower and that the patient does not moan she laughs she has never moaned with me she is not a moaner.

This 21 year old 3 day employee reported that my patient moaned in the shower when I rinsed her off with water and that I said that she would have a days of happiness after this shower because she likes her showers and that I asked my patient if it was okay to show her how to wash her because I need to make sure that she does it the right way when I am not here. This little sick girl used the word moaned not laughed, that turned the report sexual which made the report mandated reporting according to The Elder Law. It was Sexual and needed to be reported.

I told Ozzy she likes her showers and would have a few days of happiness, because she is stuck in her wheelchair 24/7 and when she is not in bed is always in her wheelchair. Ozzy never asked any questions during the shower so when I told her that she took it sexual since her mind was already there with the moaning that Ozzy said my patient did. Again, this patient never moans she only laughs. My patient is very private and I asked her permission to show Ozzy how I bathed her the right way before I bathed her, for viewing permission, this again in the statement that Ozzy wrote was written sexual. I asked my patient if I could show Ozzy how I wash you (not), Can I show Ozzy how I wash you (in sexy tone).

Under the Elder Act and our Work Policy (Consulate of Bayonet Point), we were to write our statements. Ozzy wrote her statement and was sent home I wrote my statement at 11pm handed my statement into the Floor Supervisor and was sent home. I wrote in my statement that I thought it was a misunderstanding and that if Ozzy would have asked questions during the shower I could have explained the showering details that she did not understand. We all were trained by a nurse how to give showers and I did my showers no different than anyone else so I did not understand what part of the shower Ozzy did not understand.

After I was sent home the Risk Manager/Executive Director of the Facility (MaryAnne Dimingo) came to the facility and Rickey told her what happened and that he sent us both home per policy. She told Rickey she didn't know what she was going to do and went down to her office for 15 minutes, reportedly, she called the police, an Elder Abuse requirement. The Risk Manager/Executive Director of the facility never called me, to this day she never called me. She came back to Rickey in his office and told him she called the police. She went down to my patients room and woke her with Nicole and a nurse and asked her about the shower I gave her at which time she said that I gave her a good shower and that I am her favorite aide.

The Sheriff came to the facility talked to the Executive Director, and Rickey. Never talking to my patient. Left the facility to talk to Ozzy at a gas station for about an hour, came back to the facility to see the shower head and came to my home and arrested me for Lewd and Lascivious. It was 2 a.m. on Mother's Day. The arrest report had all of Ozzy's words, none of mine, no misunderstanding, no new aide and lack of questions during a shower, nothing. Even though I was working in this type of field since I was 18 trained in home health, had all As in the class that I took to become a certified nurse's assistant, Personal Care Tech (PCT), EKG Tech, Medical Assistant, and Phlebotomist. I worked in a hospital a year before this facility and another nursing home a year before that with no problems and a stellar background check.

The officer was tasked with completing the investigation that the Executive Director should have done. This officer never met with my patient, he met with management for a half hour before meeting with Ozzy and talked with me for about five minutes. When he arrested me he told me that it was his opinion and the evidence for the reason of the arrest. I told him I know for a fact that there is no evidence because I did not do anything wrong, I would never hurt my patients.

His investigation the investigation that should have been done by the facility has been determined by the Attorney's that I have talked to. Was the way to go and way they would have told their clients to proceed with the investigation of the events. Have the police investigate it.

As the victim in this process I have a problem with this. I had the worst sheriff on staff, I talked to a Sgt. who told me that the arresting officer did not do his job correctly and he should have taken a statement from my patient even though she had trouble talking, there were other ways she could communicate. He also said our State Attorney does not do a no file, he never should have arrested you.

Allowing the local Sheriff to handle the investigation in this type of matter is the worst possible outcome for anyone. My officer complained all through my arrest that he would not be working overtime and that if his supervisor thinks he is she has another thing coming. My life was being shattered and he was worried about his overtime.

Abuse is a horrible thing and I do not want anyone to think that I condone any of it, but when it is reported it needs to be investigated the proper way no short cuts should ever be done, this is a persons' life. In my case several persons were involved and continue to be.

I was taken to jail, my jewelry taken off my wedding rings threatened to be cut off if I could not pull them over my fingers. My insulin pump which was useless because the controller was at home was taken off and put with my belongings. I was finger printed and a mug shot was taken, I sat with the nurse who asked me if I felt like killing myself. I was forced to undress in front of an officer holding my naked body parts away from view as she went to get my prison clothes I was going to be wearing for the next few hours. I was at the lowest part of my life ever, PTSD was created.

I cried until my eyes could not make tears any longer my sugars were in the 300 ranges, they had given me one shot of insulin when I was checked in and did not check my sugars again. My husband made my bail and I heard that when they were getting the group together to see the judge in the morning. I was given my clothes back, my jewelry, rings and an insulin pump that didn't work. I was released with no money and no way to call home, all alone. Mother's Day morning.

Sunday morning I heard from my sons for Mother's Day; I told them what happened. Shocked and disgusted friends and family all said sue and asked what we were going to do. My mind broken from the arrest and being charged with a Felony I didn't know what to do. The story hit the news my mug shot was shown with the story that Ozzy told the police officer, the story she wrote in her statement at work. Her confidential statement that was not confidential, the sheriff who was to do the investigation wrote the arrest report word for word as to what Ozzy reported to the Executive Director, she would verify this when being interviewed by the State Health Department Investigator Ms. V, months later.

The Executive Director of Consulate of Bayonet Point, Maryanne, Rickey the Floor nurse, and Linda Patton the Director of Nursing the next day met with Ozzy to go over what happened, she did not tell the same story and work began to suspect something was wrong with her story. She could not even keep the days straight as she kept recalling it as a Wednesday and it was a Saturday, and at one point she said in a report that she was bathing my patient and wasn't even touching her. They did not call the police on her, or do any paperwork. They had to keep Ozzy employed due to the fact that if she was fired that she could have sued them for reporting and them firing her, even though she lied.

My arrest story about went out all over the Internet, local news, and worldwide news. My face, my mug shot went all over. People wanted to kill me, reporters hacked my Facebook account and got family information, schooling and past job information. Unfortunately for me one of my past employers was Assisting Hands and as you can imagine the sick people in this world had a field day with that. I was now an Aide that taught my patients how to pleasure themselves, when you look up my name you will find this arrest as the first story under my name it has ruined me.

I cannot sue the Consulate of Bayonet Point for anything, they did what they were required to do according to the Elder Act. They had a report of abuse and followed the reporting guidelines, somewhat. Did they have 24 hours to investigate the case before calling the police? Yes, this was not an endangered patient. Did they investigate as they should have—no, are there guidelines in place that tell you how to investigate—no. Attorney's reported to me that they would have the police do the investigation, this is their job. My Sheriff was a training officer who did not want to work overtime.

Required data to AHCA was done, they removed me from the data base and I was unable to work. My job fired me May 15, 2018, and did not even tell me they just removed me from the schedule. Again, they never called me or talked to me to this day about what happened.

Nursing homes are so afraid to talk to the employees when they are suspended that a friend of mine was under an investigation when a senior woman accused a man on the shift of touching her, he was the only man on shift so he was suspended and the police were called. When the police came in to talk to her she said she made it up that he did not do anything, the police cleared him through their investigation. AHCA was contacted as required it took a few weeks to determine that he did nothing wrong through their investigation and his work determined that he did nothing wrong, that they lady made a false accusation. This is what the innocent has to go through, we are accused, arrested in my case, name ruined in my case. All the time the facility will not contact the employee with any information. My friend was called and put back on the schedule after two weeks of not knowing what was going on. The Facilities are afraid of doing something wrong management needs to be trained.

In the reports I have been able to obtain from my investigations, my job would have hired me back after everything was cleared. I did not know this, not that I would work for them, as they left me hanging even after they determined that Ozzy wasn't telling the truth. They never contacted the District Attorney's Office. My one eyed, can't walk, can hardly talk wheel chaired Patient did and told them nothing happened, when no my case was not getting cleared.

In Reporting Reasonable Suspicion of a Crime in a Long-term Care Facility (LTC) Section 1150B.

Section D. Time Period for Individual Reporting.

2. All others-within 24 hours if the events that cause the reasonable suspicion do not result in serious bodily injury to a resident, the covered individual shall report the suspicion no later than 24 hours after forming the suspicion.

In my case the Risk Manager/Executive Director had 24 hours to investigate, they knew within hours of the next day that Ozzy lied about what had happened. She changed her story five times by the time the investigations were over. Consulate called the police immediately and got me arrested on a Felony Charge.

3. Allegations of facility failure to comply with Section 1150B.

You have your laws written that the agencies are fearful that they will lose the funding that they so desperately need.

For example, an allegation that covered individuals did not report or were not informed of their duty to report under 1150B of the Act could lead to a determination that the facility did not comply with existing Federal requirements for reporting incidents, or provide training and have certain policies and procedures in place. Consulate has procedures in place a reporting system that states all parties involved in a case will be interviewed, I was not talked to by management and I was only asked to fill out a statement form to which I did and then per policy I was sent home, waiting further investigation. In my case, I was arrested by the local sheriff who did not interview my patient, and who talked long enough to my accuser to get her whole story written on the arrest report.42 CFR § 483.13 needs to be looked at closer; this reporting to the director immediately is a good requirement if the director does the required investigations which in this case is part of Consulate of Bayonet Points reporting guidelines. MaryAnne Dimingo did not do an investigation as required by law as part of the "Plan in place to investigate all suspicions of a crime." Turning the investigation over to local law enforcement to investigate needs to be addressed. When the Attorneys have told me that they would advise the facility directors to contact the police and not do an investigation it is a violation of the system that you have put into place.

Within three days of my arrest I got my criminal attorney for my felony charge, at a cost of $2,000.00 to start, which I borrowed from my sister. It could have been to start if we went to Court $5,000.00 more. Not to mention the 5 years in jail. My bail was $500.00 part was paid by my husband the other was paid by my Mother in Law. I waited and waited to find out what would happen with my case, my attorney had me call work and find out if I was on paid or unpaid leave and not to talk about anything else this was four days after the arrest. Which I did, unpaid, I received my last pay check. I applied for unemployment and Consulate of Bayonet Point denied me. I went to Court and found out at my unemployment hearing that Consulate of Bayonet Point found me innocent of charges and that AHCA found me innocent of charges. No one called me I found out through unemployment, the referee during the case said she thought something strange was going on with this case and told me she was not an attorney but recommended that I get a copy of the hearing. I did get a copy of the hearing. My last attorney I met with said I do have a case but it is too costly on his part to have his staff working on my case to clear my name and to get them for defamation. He would not make money on my case and I would not get the money I was entitled to. The Child and Family Services (DCF) investigator had already found me innocent. I called my Attorney once a week along with my bail bonds man to find out if they heard anything, three Months had passed. August 22, 2018, one day before the District Attorney found that they could not charge me with this crime and cleared me. I got a visit from the State or Florida Health Department Ms. V, she wanted me to surrender my CNA license the arrest came up in a finger print check. My License was never revoked, just the ability to run a background check through AHCA. Ms. V would end up doing all the interviewing I could not, she would be my best Ally for information. Ms. V did her reports and the Health Department did not file any charges on my CNA license. My handicapped patient ended up asking her Father to take her to the District Attorney's Office to meet with him. She met with them and cleared this case for me. I still cannot talk to her since I had an order of protection. Even if I could I cannot go back to the facility—I'm shell shocked. I have PTSD, Depression, and Anxiety. I have autoimmune disorders that are affected by stress and they are in full force from this, sores on my head from picking and I see a counselor two times a month to prevent myself from doing anything I would regret. I contacted several different Attorneys they all said the same thing Consulate of Bayonet Point followed reporting laws. They did what was required with a suspicion of a crime. I cry every day. I am your innocent victim, a victim of a girl in one report that just wanted some attention. I know the employees that are innocent are stuck in the middle of all the mess of drugs, sex, stealing and violence, but we are out there and we are victims too it took a long time for me to be able to call myself a victim every time you don't protect us too we are abused over and over again and no one is fighting for us.

Christina A. Nappo

National Association of State Long-Term Care Ombudsman Programs

March 14, 2019

U.S. Senate; Committee on Finance

Dirksen Senate Office Building

Washington, DC

RE: Senate Finance Committee Hearing: "Not Forgotten: Protecting Older Americans From Abuse and Neglect in Nursing Homes," Wednesday, March 6, 2019

Chairman Grassley and Ranking Member Wyden:

Introduction

The National Association of State Long-Term Care Ombudsman Programs (NASOP) extends its thanks to you for the hearing held on March 6 that continued raising awareness of the plight of many nursing home residents who suffer abuse and neglect while residing in a nursing home. As Chairman Grassley noted in his opening remarks, instances of abuse and neglect of nursing home residents are wide spread. Chairman Grassley noted that the Inspector General reported that one-third of nursing home residents experienced harm while receiving care in federally funded nursing homes.

NASOP agrees with Ranking Member Wyden that the update to nursing home regulations that were published in 2016 should be implemented as originally approved to require nursing homes to develop plans to prevent infections, policies to reduce abuse, neglect, mistreatment and theft, stop the practice of using psychotropic drugs unless they are prescribed for a specific, diagnosed condition, and prohibit the practice of requesting or requiring residents to sign pre-dispute arbitration agreements. While witnesses testified about transparency in serving residents, arbitration often requires confidentiality of the complaint and the outcome, obscuring the problems and the steps proposed to be taken to correct the problems. When this happens, residents, families, policy makers and the public are kept in the dark about the problems in nursing homes.

Long-Term Care Ombudsman Advocacy for Residents Abused in Facilities

Abuse and neglect of residents happens far too often in nursing homes. Residents will sometimes confide in Long-term Care Ombudsman Representative (ORs) because residents know that ORs are advocates for residents. Too often, residents will not give permission to the OR to report the abuse or take any other action because the resident fears retaliation, fears that the resident won't be believed, and because the resident feels shame at being so vulnerable and unable to care of him or herself as they were once able.

David Gifford testified that steps facilities can take to address abuse are all "after the fact." However, ORs regularly visit nursing homes to educate residents about their rights and often provide in-service training to staff about resident rights, including the right to be free from abuse and neglect, and to inform staff about abuse reporting requirements. These activities are before the fact, not after the fact. These "before the fact" interventions could and should be a part of the nursing home continuing training program, as well. In addition, having more staff in the building, noted below, would also help to prevent other harm, including reducing the occurrence and seriousness of pressure ulcers, reducing falls, attending to residents with cognitive declines who may communicate their needs and problems in ways that are aggressive because they have lost the ability to communicate in other ways.

Recommendations

Nursing Staffing

A running theme throughout witness testimony is the concern for not enough staff in facilities. ORs often hear this complaint from residents, families and even staff. When facilities are understaffed, residents do not get the care, supervision and monitoring that they should. When facilities use agency staff to provide care, residents do not know the caregivers and are even less inclined to report to the caregiver that they have experienced abuse. NASOP and other advocates have long urged staffing ratios in nursing homes. It just makes sense to set a minimum number of direct care workers and other healthcare providers for every day of the week and every shift, relative to the number of residents in the nursing home, because even the best staff can't do a good job when they have too many residents for whom they are responsible to provide care. Additional healthcare staff must also be required based on an assessment of the resident population needs.

Improving Conditions for Nursing Home Healthcare Staff

Direct care workers are involved in the most intimate care of residents including bathing, grooming and toileting. These workers are woefully under paid, and are often overworked when a nursing home does not have enough staff. If Congress increased Medicare and Medicaid reimbursement, that increase should require that a significant portion of that increase go toward direct care worker wages. It could also provide for other incentives to workers. Improving worker experience could reduce abuse and neglect in nursing homes. With more and better-paid direct care workers, the workers have more time to spend with each resident, more time to observe what is happening around them, more time to redirect a resident who may be aggressive and more time to notice when a resident has changed care needs that require additional interventions.

Supporting Survey Agencies in Sanctioning Nursing Homes

The agencies tasked with surveying nursing homes must be supported when they find deficiencies and determine that sanctions are appropriate. Urge the Centers for Medicare and Medicaid Services (CMS) to support the survey agencies' scope and severity findings. Urge CMS to continue per diem fines, rather than per instance fines. While compliance is the goal, without strong sanctions for violation of regulations, compliance is a dream, not a reality.

Conclusion

I believe that every member of NASOP could relate to the committee heartbreaking stories of resident abuse and neglect, like those of Patricia Olthoff-Blank and Maya Fischer. Despite the claim that abuse and neglect in nursing homes occurs only as isolated incidents, residents experience abuse and neglect across the country. When it is just statistics, it is easy to minimize the harm. But when it is your own loved one, one incident is one too many.

Please support changes to address abuse and neglect in nursing homes including:

1. At least a minimum of staff to the number of residents in a building on all shifts, every day of the week, and requiring additional staff to meet resident needs;
2. Increase the reimbursement for nursing home services requiring that a significant portion of the increase go to increase wages for direct care and other healthcare staff;
3. Requiring CMS to implement the 2016 regulations as originally approved; and
4. Continue holding more hearings and taking other actions to address the serious, ongoing problem of abuse and neglect for the approximately 1.5 million vulnerable residents in nursing homes across our country.

Sincerely,
Melanie S. McNeil

National Association of States United for Aging and Disabilities

March 18, 2019
U.S. Senate
Committee on Finance
Washington, DC

Dear Chairman Grassley and Ranking Member Wyden:

On behalf of the National Association of States United for Aging and Disabilities (NASUAD), I give this statement for the record in response to the recent Finance Committee hearing entitled "Not Forgotten: Protecting Americans From Abuse and Neglect in Nursing Homes" that was held on Wednesday, March 6, 2019. NASUAD represents the 56 officially designated state and territorial agencies on aging and disabilities. Each of our members oversees the implementation of the Older Americans Act (OAA); and many also serve as the operating agency in their state for Medicaid waivers and managed long-term services and supports programs that serve older adults and individuals with disabilities. Together with our members, we work to design, improve, and sustain state systems delivering home and community-based services (HCBS) and supports for people who are older or have a disability and for their caregivers.

NASUAD appreciates that your committee is looking into challenges that have occurred in facilities around the country and is seeking to improve protections for individuals who live in nursing homes. Our members share your interest in protecting the rights, safety, and health and wellness of all residents in long-term care facilities. We first want to recognize that the tragedies recounted by Ms. Patricia Olthoff-Blank and Maya Fischer are unacceptable and that our system of care must continue our work to prevent abuse, neglect, and exploitation as well as to respond appropriately and effectively when such tragedies occur.

In light of these tragedies, we think it is appropriate to consider improvements that could assist with both prevention of and response to abuse, neglect, and exploitation. We specifically noted the reference to the Long-term Care Ombudsman program in Chairman Grassley's questions of the witnesses. While we agree that the Ombudsman could be helpful in addressing and resolving the broader operational issues related to Nursing Homes, we note that the Ombudsman is not able to serve the role of fact-finder or provide Adult Protective Services (APS). In fact, the enacting regulations specifically note that co-locating the Ombudsman and APS could represent a conflict of interest for the program.[108] Given the basic functions of the Ombudsman coupled with the tragic deaths described by these family members, it makes sense that law-enforcement or a separate APS agency would be more likely to investigate the issues and communicate with the family.

With that background, we do note that the Ombudsman program has the responsibility to both "identify, investigate, and resolve complaints made by or on behalf of residents" and "advocate for changes to improve residents' quality of life and care."

However, the national Ombudsman program is largely underfunded and relies heavily on volunteers. Our state members report struggles with securing sufficient

[108] 45 CFR 1324.21.

volunteers as well as with recruiting and retaining sufficient staff for the Ombudsman programs which, in part, is due to the limited and stagnant funding for the Om- budsman program.

Similarly, there is no dedicated Federal funding for APS or for Elder Justice activities. Though we acknowledge that Congress has appropriated some funding for Elder Rights Support Activities over the past several years, this funding has been insufficient to provide APS and related services. The Administration for Community living has developed voluntary guidelines for APS systems[109] which have been reviewed by our members and are received favorably. Unfortunately, these voluntary guidelines are largely aspirational given the lack of Federal funding to accompany these supports. We strongly encourage the Finance Committee to work within your jurisdiction and collaborate with the Appropriations Committee to enact a national framework and dedicated funding stream for APS and to also improve the capacities of the Ombudsman program nationwide.

Sincerely,

Martha A. Roherty
Executive Director
NASUAD

Statement of Penny Cook, MSW, President and CEO

Pioneer Network
Rochester, NY
www.pioneernetwork.net
email: info@pioneernetwork.net

Chairman Grassley, Ranking Member Wyden, and distinguished members of the committee, thank you for the opportunity to submit this written statement for the hearing record. My name is Penny Cook and I'm the President and CEO of Pioneer Network, a national nonprofit organization dedicated to changing how our society views aging, treats elders and provides care and support to those elders and others. We are the umbrella organization for the culture change movement which, among other goals, is dedicated to transforming nursing homes from institutions to real homes for those who live there.

As Dr. David Grabowski stated in his testimony, "Traditional nursing homes fall short in several domains. Care is often directed by the staff rather than the resident. Ideally, residents should be offered choices about issues personally affecting them like

[109] *https://acl.gov/programs/elder-justice/final-voluntary-consensus-guidelines-state-aps-systems.*

what to wear and when to go to bed . . . Many nursing homes are quite institutional with long hallways with a nurse's station on one end, linoleum floors and two residents in a room . . . . These nursing homes feel more like a hospital than a home. The staff structure at these 'facilities' is often quite hierarchical with very little direct empowerment of direct caregivers. Nursing homes are not just suboptimal places to live, they are often difficult places to work. . . . a more participatory management structure that engages in CNAs in the decision-making process would help with staff turnover and performance."

Pioneer Network is working to change this reality. We provide resources and training to long-term care communities across the country to help them transform their culture and create real home in their communities, so people are living life the way they want to live it. We work with everyone who impacts the residents from CNAs to CEOs to nurses to dietary professionals and many more. And we believe that to sustain this change, we need to transform the negative perceptions we have about growing older. We convene people who work in aging and long-term care through our annual conference, state coalitions, monthly webinars and weekly newsletters to increase awareness, share resources and disseminate best practices. We are trying to create the kind of culture of care and support that we all want as we grow older.

In order to make culture change the norm in this country, we need to move beyond the fact that it is the "right thing to do" and present the business case as well as advocate for public policies that provide incentives for providers to change the culture of their organizations and the way care is delivered so that it is person-centered and residents have as much control over their daily lives as possible. As stated in "The Prevalence of Culture Change Practice in U.S. Nursing Homes: Findings from a 2016–2017 Nationwide Survey" by Susan C. Miller, Ph.D., and her colleagues at Brown University (Medical Care, 2018), "while more rigorous research is needed, panel studies have found nursing home culture change adoption is associated with reductions in Medicare/Medicaid survey deficiencies, decreases in the prevalence of feeding tubes, restraints and pressure ulcers, and higher resident satisfaction with the quality of care and quality of life." As is also stated, "Culture change-related practices align with the 2016 nursing home Medicare/Medicaid regulatory changes mandating person-centered care in nursing homes and with the person-centered care directive of the Patient Protection and Affordable Care Act (ACA)" and "State Medicaid Pay for Performance Programs (P4P) that include culture change and person-centered care quality criteria like the Kansas PEAK 2.0 program found high culture change adoption." Pioneer Network advocates for more states to have P4P programs that include these criteria as incentives for nursing homes to deliver person-centered care.

Culture change is not only about improving the quality of care and quality of life for nursing home residents but quality of work life for staff. As Dr. Grabowski stated in his testimony, "Nursing homes are not just suboptimal places to live, they are often difficult places to work. . . . A more participatory management structure that engages CNAs in the decision-making process would help staff turnover and performance." Pioneer Network educates providers about how to do this as well as other ways to support CNAs so that these important caregivers who have developed relationships with the people they take care of will want to stay rather than get a job somewhere else. Nursing homes that have the reputation of being a good place to work do not have as much of a problem recruiting staff, which is a huge issue, given the current workforce shortage. Pioneer Network is partnering with PHI (formerly Paraprofessional Health Care Institute) on a Workforce track at our 2019 Pioneering a New Culture of Aging Conference in Louisville, KY in August.

As Dr. Grabowski stated in his testimony, "Quality of life is an important part of a resident's nursing home experience which generally corresponds to those characteristics of nursing home care that affect the resident's sense of well-being, self-worth, self-esteem, and life satisfaction." He further stated that "measures such as resident and family satisfaction are important indicators of nursing home quality." Nursing Home Compare and the Five Star Quality Rating System currently use quality of care measures and information about quality of life and resident and family satisfaction are not included. Dr. Gifford pointed out in his testimony that "nursing homes are the only sector without a CMS public reporting requirement on resident and family satisfaction." Since long-term care residents of nursing homes live in the home, it is even more important that this be part of Nursing Home Compare and the Five Star Quality Rating System so we sent a letter to Dr. Kate Goodrich, Director of the Center for Clinical Standards and Quality and Chief Medical Officer urging CMS to seriously consider adding resident and family satisfaction to Nursing Home Compare and the Five Star Quality Rating System.

Pioneer Network stands ready to help the Senate Finance Committee and CMS in any way we can to improve the quality of care and quality of life for current and future residents of our nation's nursing homes.

Sincerely,

Penny M. Cook, MSW
President and CEO; Pioneer Network

Letter Submitted by Judith Purdy, R.N.

March 12, 2019
U.S. Senate
Committee on Finance
Dirksen Senate Office Bldg.
Washington, DC

Not Forgotten: Protecting Americans From Abuse and Neglect in Nursing Homes

Hearing Date: Wednesday, March 6, 2019

My 90-year-old father fell, fractured a hip and an elbow, had surgery and then went to a skilled nursing facility for therapy to regain mobility. He arrived on December 23rd—for 4 days no one re-positioned him in bed nor got him up. When he turned on his call light no one came. They failed to give him the oxygen he needed at night. There was no medical assessment completed by the doctor of his condition or needs within the required 48 hours.

I requested staff bathe my father, but 4–5 days later he still had not been bathed. On day 6 when my husband was helping my father to bed, he noticed my father's sock was wet, and when he pulled back the sock there was a large pressure ulcer on his heel. The sock had not been changed since his arrival on the 23rd.

I am a registered nurse, so I know more than most, but anyone would have recognized the basic lack of nursing care, cleanliness, medications, and oral hygiene that my father failed to receive. When my oft-repeated requests for attention to my father's fundamental needs were not responded to, I took action. I talked with the nurse in charge, I asked for a meeting with the facility administration, I called the facility's corporate office, and I called the hotline at the Kansas Department for Aging and Disability Services—KDADS (800–842–0078). I was prepared, giving the person who answered the hotline the list of inaction and wrong actions that occurred. I also put the same in writing and sent it to KDADS. The inspectors came within the week to investigate and cited deficient practices by the facility, not only for my father's care but for another individual as well.

You can't get something taken care of if you don't bring it forward. I am calling the poor care that we experienced and that was happening to others in the facility, to your attention as the higher oversight authority. We must challenge things not done right for older adults in nursing facilities. We must not be afraid to speak out. Otherwise who knows how many people will be harmed.

Judith Purdy, R.N.

Statement Submitted by June Schneider

My mom, Millicent Anderson, fell from a Hoyer lift in November 2017 due to negligence from the staff at Springtree Health and Rehab in Roanoke, VA. I filed a complaint with CMS (Kepro) as well as the Department of Health in Richmond. Kepro determined that Springtree did not provide the acceptable standard of care for her to prevent the fall, since there were three certified nursing assistants in the room attending to her and transferring her in the Hoyer lift. Because of the fall, my mom suffered a two-inch laceration to the side of her head and bled profusely and was taken to the hospital where she received staples to the wound. Thankfully she did not suffer any long-term adverse effects. Which is not usually the case. I consulted several attorneys who determined that they would not take her case because she did not die or suffer long-term injury.

The problem with nursing homes, such as Springtree, is that not enough staffing (especially certified nursing assistants) is mandated. There is usually not enough staff to care for the total amount of residents in a reasonable manner. There is also lack of communication and supervision between the nursing staff and certified nursing assistants. I have had multiple meetings and complaints about the standard of care my mom receives.

Not enough family members care, or report incidents of injuries caused by negligence. The residents are afraid to speak up for fear of retaliation, or do not have the "wherewithal" to seek help. They are not even aware that there is an ombudsman! The ombudsman is usually overworked with one ombudsman for a large amount of nursing homes. Adult Protective Services will visit and investigate incidents, but nothing usually improves, they are powerless. Nursing homes also know when inspectors are coming, even though the unannounced visits are supposed to be a surprise, they are not in reality. When an inspection visit is suspected, the nursing home gets everything in order to impress the inspectors, including hiring extra staff and falsifying information.

An attorney I consulted after my mom's fall, told me that another problem is that our representatives in the state of Virginia (and perhaps this is also true for other states) are shareholders in the big companies that own the nursing homes. Medical Facilities of America owns Springtree and most of the nursing homes in Virginia. They have government representatives on their boards as well as "big name" lawyers, and they are able to "fix things" to avoid fines. MFA recently joined in lobbying the government for the penalties to be reduced in nursing homes (less fines) with the excuse that they need less time to focus on defending fines and more time to focus on care, which is ridiculous because they really don't care, it's all about the money. That request was granted by the government. The elderly in nursing homes are the forgotten of society and the system is rigged against them. Please investigate the condition of nursing homes across America. What is on paper is not reality because I and the few family members who care have seen it firsthand. Thank you for reading.

Letter Submitted by Laura Smart, MSW, LGSW

March 6, 2019
U.S. Senate
Committee on Finance
Washington, DC

I attended the Senate Finance Committee hearing on March 6th, 2019 titled "Not Forgotten: Protecting Americans from Abuse and Neglect in Nursing Homes." I have been a social worker since December 1999; while getting my master's degree in 2015, I interned at a for-profit nursing home in Bethesda, Maryland. I was then made aware of the desperate and dangerous places nursing homes can be. Since 2015, I have worked in 4 nursing homes as either a social worker or social worker director. Three were for-profits and one was a non-profit. The for-profits were by far much worse than the non-profit; however, the non-profit also had many problems. I am going to keep this submission short due to being mindful of the committee's numerous other submissions. I have witnessed abuse and neglect in nursing homes—and I would describe the overall culture to be negligent and minimizing of the urgency of human suffering. It is as if the staff become desensitized (including myself to a degree) in order to remain working inside a nursing home. To formally address these serious concerns I emailed the Elder Justice Task Force on August 7, 2016—and told them what I had witnessed and that I would be available to them in any way (to testify, etc.)—they did respond back thanking me for the email; but that was the last I heard from them. After working for one of the largest for-profit providers in this country—CommuniCare—I sent them the following letter in December 2017:

This letter is meant to be read by the Owners of CommuniCare.

Hello, I am Laura Smart, MSW, LSW, a social worker who worked for your company in Kensington, Maryland (from September 2016—January 2017) and in Cincinnati at Clifton Healthcare Center (CHC) from March 2017 until October 27, 2017.

I have been a social worker since 1999 and am bound by a code of ethics and therefore am reporting to the owners of CommuniCare the realities of what I've encountered. Many times I shared with the administrators and upper management that the residents were not receiving adequate care. I am going to try to paint a picture so that you can understand what I am saying with the hope for change. At CHC on the 3rd floor is 58 beds—2 nurses shared that floor which I witnessed was very difficult (ideally that many beds needs to have at least 3 nurses)—medications were passed late, wounds not properly attended to, very little time spent with residents—29 residents for 1 nurse is not "best practice." The STNA's (nurse's aides) had far too many residents to take care of—best practice is no more than 8 residents on 1st shift—there is mountains of research to back that up—I have attached one study but there are hundreds of peer-reviewed studies proving that. When STNA's have 14 + residents to care for what that means is that someone is not getting changed, fed, bathed, etc. Often the STNA's have 14 + residents to care for which is routine on that floor; when there are only 3 STNA's on that floor they are caring for 19 + which is a recipe for disaster and you are approving neglect to occur. There is also not enough activities staff. So on top of not properly taking care of your residents physical/medical needs—their psycho-social needs are not being met as well. To have adequate activities—including field trips which remain very rare—would go a long way for your residents. To have a sufficient social services department you must have at least 3 social workers in a building of 130 + beds. Being the social services director at CHC I also had about 70 residents that were on my caseload— that is far too many residents to tend to properly. When all the tasks that is required (MOS assessments, progress notes, care conferences, meetings, etc.) is laid out there is not enough time in a day to sufficiently address those tasks so even though I am a diligent social worker and wanted to complete everything thoroughly, it was not possible. Ideally a social worker should not have more than 40–50 residents—considering ail the intakes, discharges, MOS assessments, care conferences, etc. To sum it up—you need more staff in every department in order to properly take care of your residents. I left your company for the sole reason of not wanting to be a part of an organization who fails at providing adequate care. Everything that I said above I said repeatedly to my administrators. I don't blame the administrators however, they often said they wished they could hire more but they had their constraints placed on them from corporate. I am attaching many resources to assist with improving care.

Laura Smart, MSW, LSW

I then worked for a non-profit in Cincinnati, OH. I can report that they usually had adequate staffing but the same type of culture existed; mainly lack of compassion. With so much CMS regulations to adhere to the majority of the day had to be spent on those regulations instead of trying to provide a more "person-centered environment" approach that includes "trauma-informed care" towards residents, etc. After working in four nursing homes and researching how to remedy the current state of nursing homes in this country, here is what I believe needs to happen:

- CMS needs to befriend nursing homes staff instead of having an adversarial stance.
- CMS needs to simplify their MEGA RULES that they have initiated and become friendly educators of their policies and procedures—instead of being the fearful overseers of their overwhelming massive policies.
- Social Workers or any staff in nursing homes should be able to call or email CMS and get friendly advice for help requested on proper policy enactment. Currently there is a culture of fear regarding reaching out to CMS.
- With regard to caseload size of residents to social workers in a nursing home—the law (which I believe to be in the Social Security Act) needs to change to 1 social worker to 50 residents instead of the current 1 social worker to 120 residents.
- A federal mandate regarding staffing for nurses and nurse's aides needs to be established. The current law uses the word "adequate" staffing which is giving the industry giants (and others) much leeway and therefore they are choosing to not properly staff their facilities which is why they (the for-profit owners) are

making tremendous profits. The current recommended staffing ratio is for Nurses on dayshift 1 nurse for 10–12 residents, and 1 nurse's aide for 5–7 residents.

Although I have seen and heard so much heartbreak and trauma in nursing homes, I continue to want to work in a nursing facility while also working on assisting with the much needed changes in policy. I recently moved back to the DC area and will likely get a job in a nursing home as a social worker. Although I overall enjoy working in a nursing home at the same time I fear my own safety and license because I know that these environments are dangerous places. I will make myself available for any questions or comments or however I am needed to assist with this social issue.

Thank you.

Laura Smart, MSW, LGSW

Letter Submitted by Ann E. Stanton

March 10, 2019
U.S. Senate
Committee on Finance
Dirksen Senate Office Bldg.
Washington, DC

NOT FORGOTTEN: PROTECTING AMERICANS FROM ABUSE AND NEGLECT IN NURSING HOMES

March 6, 2019

This submission concerns my sister, Kathleen (Kitty) Koehler, who died on July 24, 2012 after being the subject of abuse and neglect at Manorcare Nursing Home in Pittsburgh, PA. My views come from a very personal experience with nursing home neglect. I have had a continuation of letters and emails to various government agencies and elected officials at both the State and Federal levels for the past 6 years. I refuse to give up and say it was a natural death like the physician noted on her death certificate. He told me early on that he would never blame anyone for a person's death. He subsequently left his position at UPMC and began working for Heritage Valley Health Systems so the "falsified" death certificate will never be corrected. Several physicians told me that her anoxic brain injury was keeping Kitty in a vegetative state so that should have been noted as the immediate cause of death. The signer of the death certificate also completely omitted the respiratory arrest as a contributing factor in her death. He later stated that he never saw the nursing home medical record and was not interested in what happened there.

I also recently wrote to my new U.S. Representative, Conor Lamb, about the recent article in the newspaper relating to nursing home abuse and neglect. I explained to him the problems I have had during the past years trying to get answers from State and Federal officials and their ongoing cover-up of the events that took place on April 16, 2012.

My sister, Kitty, had quite suddenly developed kidney failure in July 2011 and the doctors were surprised that it came on so quickly but they didn't have many answers. She had been diabetic for years and was eventually placed on insulin as an adult. After three months, she suffered a severe sepsis and was admitted to the hospital. They found that she had a staph infection in her central venous catheter used for dialysis. She came close to death several times while in the hospital ICU for three weeks but with an extreme amount of excellent care, she eventually pulled through. After being transferred to a monitored unit for continuing care due to her debilitated state, a possible sexual assault had occurred by a sitter. The hospital ensured us that they would handle this situation and requested not to get the police involved so I listened to them because there were many other severe issues that needed my attention. That was my first BIG mistake because they never did anything about it which I found out much later after my sister's death. They, however, decided suddenly that Kitty needed to be discharged for rehab two days after the report was made.

For about the next six months, Kitty was admitted and discharged from numerous medical facilities where she was the victim of injuries or other medical problems. She finally was ready for rehab in late March 2012 and we tried finding a nursing home that we were familiar with but all the good ones had no beds and a waiting list. A sales rep from Manorcare had been at the UPMC hospital that day and the patient advocate stated that Kitty would be discharged there or she would pay for each additional day that she remained in the hospital. There had been three other facilities that the hospital had called but none of them (two were UPMC facilities) would accept her so we had no other choice.

Kitty had a couple of minor problems the first week there but she did like the rehab therapists and they worked very hard with her to try and get her standing and walking again. After a week, she had to return to the hospital so her dialysis catheter could be replaced because of kinks in the current one and her blood was not being cleaned. They sent her back to the nursing home the same day and she passed out and the outpatient dialysis center said they would not do dialysis for her in that condition so it was back to the UPMC hospital. She remained in the hospital for about five days and then it was back to Manorcare nursing home.

They started out with problems the first day back when they set her up in her room and forgot to provide the portable oxygen machine and she had trouble breathing. We had to get a nurse to get one for her. They also forgot to note her new medication that was added for Small Intestine Bacterial Overgrowth (SIBO) which was a very specific antibiotic to help with a chronic diarrhea condition that she had for five years. Two GI specialists at UPMC were the first ones to do a test to find this problem and put her on a medication. She seemed to be doing well for a few days and then on April 13, 2012, her rehab therapist told us it may be only a couple more weeks before she could be discharged because she was coming along so well. They found that she would need a special insert for one shoe because one leg was a bit shorter than the other due to previous heel fractures in 2008 that hadn't been treated properly. That was great news and that afternoon we had to take Kitty out to check into ACCESS transportation since Manorcare stated they could no longer transport Kitty to dialysis on Saturday. ACCESS transportation could not do this because they stated Manorcare should be providing that transportation. When we returned back to Manorcare, her items were thrown all over the room as if someone had been looking through her nightstand but we put everything back and were discussing if we should report it. We went out to get Kitty something for dinner since they were going to have a meal that night that caused problems for her. When we returned, she was not hungry and was having difficulty breathing. We got a nurse and Kitty's oxygen level was very low. The nurse then held her down and tried putting some sort of mist for her to breathe through a mask. Kitty was struggling and fighting to get it off and her oxygen level was going all over with highs and lows and she was getting worse. They called their contract ambulance and when the paramedic got there, he noticed her nasal cannula was not attached to the oxygen concentrator. He attached it and within minutes, Kitty's breathing was back to normal. Her appetite returned and the paramedic checked her vitals and noted that everything was in normal limits. He gave her the option of going back to the ER but she stated she was feeling good and we left it at that. The nurse became upset when he told her that she should always check to ensure that the nasal cannula is attached to the concentrator, especially before using other techniques.

We (my other sister and I) went in on Sunday (April 15, 2012) to visit and stayed several hours while she ate dinner which we brought in. She talked and laughed about how well she was beginning to feel and for the first time, she actually was full after eating her dinner. She was going to watch TV and then go to sleep and we were going to meet her the next day at her endocrinologist's office for her visit. She had been having some problems with hypoglycemia and he wanted to adjust her medications. Kitty's sugar had dropped early that morning and she was able to call the nurse and was given juice with sugar added. They continued that day to check it and she remained at a good level. That night the nurse promised us that she would ensure that someone would check on Kitty every two hours to check that her sugars weren't dropping. THAT NEVER HAPPENED. According to the record, Kitty was given insulin with no snack about 9:00 p.m. (they did not know if she was asleep or not) and long acting insulin at 10:00 p.m. The next record was about 4:00 am when they found her severely hypoglycemic.

On April 16, 2012, a nursing home aide found Kitty in an extremely lethargic condition with altered level of consciousness shortly after 4:00 a.m. She notified the RN on duty and the RN didn't know what to do so she called the on call doctor. I felt she should have called 911 in order to avoid wasting time since I later found out that Kitty's sugar was registering "low" . . . under 20. The doctor gave a phone order to the RN to give a Glucagen shot and this was noted in the medical record that it was given at 4:15 a.m. It was noted in the progress notes, SBAR, and the Medication Administration Records. According to the medical records, the RN noted after 20 minutes that the patient was unresponsive and her condition was worsening and called the doctor again and was told to call their contract ambulance. It took another 15 minutes for patient contact and they noted that oral glucose gel was given prior to their arrival. This was one of many false statements the RN made. The paramedics noted that Kitty went from a 5 on the Glasgow Coma Scale on their arrival to a 3 within 10 minutes. They noted she was having agonal breathing and placed a bag valve mask on her and rushed her to UPMC Shadyside Hospital ER. At the hospital, Kitty's blood pressure was 204/140.

The RN then called me at 4:49 a.m. I was not told the truth but was told that Kitty's sugar was running a little low and they were going to have an ambulance take her to Shadyside Hospital so they could give IV dextrose to get her sugar up. I needed to know if Kitty was still going to see her endocrinologist that morning but the RN said she could not call me back when Kitty returned. She told me to call back in about two hours because the ER is sometimes busy with emergencies and Kitty may be there a while. I didn't think there was any reason for her to lie to me but that's exactly what she did. ANOTHER FALSE STATEMENT. UPMC Shadyside Hospital had me listed as the healthcare POA and emergency contact but they also did not call when she arrived to notify me of her condition or why she was there. In the past, they called me regularly whenever they wanted to verify that a procedure could be performed or to update me but no contact for this very severe problem. I waited almost the two hours and was getting anxious when I called the nursing home three times and the line was constantly busy. I called the Administrator's number and left a message on her voice mail. I then called the ER at Shadyside Hospital and asked if they sent Kitty back yet to the nursing home. They told me that she was going to be admitted and that she was brought into the ER in respiratory arrest and that her sugar was not the reason for the emergency. She told me they had to put in a breathing tube and she had continued to be unresponsive and that her sugar was in a good range. I was told that numerous tests were being done and no one was quite sure what happened at the nursing home and the doctor wanted me to sign some papers when I came in later so they could get authorization to do some very specialized tests. I was confused and called the nursing home back again and they said they were told not to talk to me and hung up. I knew at this point it would be my job alone to find out what they were hiding.

That afternoon, I got a call from the Administrator to come and pick up Kitty's belongings. They would leave boxes and to pack them and leave without talking to anyone. While there, we noticed an empty tube of oral glucose gel in the trash can and rubber mats lying on the bed but no Glucagen kit. I called and told her of the lies and that I was not done with this and asked why they did not call 911. She said 911 does not respond to nursing homes and they had to wait for their contract ambulance. With this information, I sent an email to Pittsburgh EMS several days later stating what I was told. I got a call back on two occasions from them that they do respond to nursing home and they have responded to Manorcare in the past (without giving specifics). They stated that nursing homes don't want to call 911 for emergencies because a report is made of it. The EMS contact who called then said it was a shame because they could have been there with five minutes based on the location and could have put in an IV and gotten her to the hospital. He told me that as healthcare POA, I should be able to figure out if I'm entitled to the medical record which I found out I was.

The Administrator gave me a hard time about them but eventually released them to me. I continued to ask the Administrator why Glucagen was noted as being given and she continued to state it was. I told her I received a copy of the report from Transcare Ambulance as Healthcare POA and she was furious because their report showed the true nature of this emergency. She said that if they felt it was an emergency based on Kitty's condition given over the phone, then they should have called 911 themselves. As it was, Transcare changed the call for BLS to ALS which costs more but they felt it was necessary. I had called both Pharmaceutical companies that made glucagon injections to get more information about this drug and they took a volume of information from me for their reports. They were going to call the nursing home because they stated you cannot put in a medical record that this was given . . . if it was not. If it was not effective, then the nursing home would need to contact the company or the FDA for a possible recall. Based on the information that they said needs to be on the MAR, I began to believe that it definitely was not given.

I sent a letter to the PA Health Department and when they called, I told them about some problems but also told them to find out why they said they gave Glucagen but gave oral glucose gel. The Health Department questioned me as to how I got a copy of the medical record because when they recently spoke to the Administrator, they were told no one was entitled to the records. The Health Department sent me a letter stating that Glucagen was *not* given on April 16, 2012 as noted in the record but was given the previous night. Just another lie because my sister's sugar was a bit low early morning of April 15, 2012 and she called the nurse and was given juice with sugar in it. This was reported to me. I wondered why the PA Health Department was doing everything to protect the nursing home but not the victim. They eventually posted their online report on May 17, 2012 and it noted the only problem being that the nursing home did not properly report how much insulin was given during that week. They went on a sliding scale and it had been reported properly the first week of Kitty's stay so what changed? This was a "no actual harm" citation. What happened to the online report that they should have done relating to the RN's refusal to give a doctor-ordered Glucagen injection for severe hypoglycemia? Now I saw that the PA Health Department also was involved in a cover-up for the nursing home. The surveyors didn't care how much suffering Kitty endured that morning for 35 minutes while they forced oral glucose gel down her throat as she must have struggled to breathe. The RN just wanted to get Kitty's sugar up and she succeeded while causing a brain injury.

When I later received UPMC's medical records, I found out that Kitty went to the hospital ER in a respiratory arrest (primary reason for admission), hypoglycemic coma, and at the hospital they determined she had developed an anoxic brain injury and was being treated for aspiration pneumonia. This was in addition to C-Diff that she also got, making her sacral ulcer much worse. Kitty remained in an unresponsive condition for the next three months and the only feeling she realized was pain requiring continuous pain medication. On Manorcare's Interdisciplinary Team Discharge Summary signed on April 25, 2012, they noted that patient was "able to communicate needs, oriented to person, oriented to place" but they completely omitted that she was close to death at discharge. After three weeks in the hospital ICU, they had to replace the breathing tube with a trach tube and decided to do this at bedside in the ICU. She then developed numerous infections that required additional medications and care and developed sepsis again when she almost died. After five weeks in that ICU, she was discharged to a long-term acute care hospital where she remained on a vent, feeding tube and dialysis for two months. I removed her from this vegetative state to let her die which happened on July 24, 2012. Physical Medicine had even tried for two weeks using brain stimulants with no real success or change so I made that very hard decision to end her life.

This is when I began writing to every government agency and elected official to make them aware of the dangers in nursing homes. I found out early on that the PA Health Department was not about to change their online report and that is when I requested a copy of their investigation through the Right-to-Know office which was denied and then filed an Appeal which was also denied. I felt I had a right to find out what actually happened at the nursing home and why they felt justified to lie to me from the beginning. I filed an FOIA request through HHS and was told this chapter should be available to me but PA Health Department still denied it. I went through CMS and sent all the backup information needed to show my case but these managers all stated no actual harm and no falsification of records. I've attached a copy of one letter that was absolutely ridiculous indicating falsification of records does happen but the surveyors can't cite them for it. Falsification only happens when a facility is trying to hide a wrongdoing. I then checked with the Allegheny County Medical Examiner to see about having a review of the case since the doctor who signed the death certificate noted a natural death, but after waiting a month his office said they were not interested in reviewing the records. I requested that the PA Attorney General review the records in 2013 since the PA Health Department did not forward the information to them but that office refused. I then once again in 2017 requested that the new PA Attorney General (Shapiro) review this case since there is a Crime Code in PA that covers what occurred and they also refused. He ran on bringing back ethics and integrity to that office but this pertained only to his own agenda.

I have been fighting this for the past six years because my sister has never received justice relating to her death. Several advocates have told me to continue with my fight and others told me that the government is protecting the nursing home because Manorcare in PA is owned by the Carlyle Group (or was at that time) and no one will go up against such a powerful group. I have seen that this is true. In 2013, I did file a small claim suit against the nurse and Manorcare for my sister's funeral/burial costs. I eventually won that suit but the attorney from the law firm representing them told me I could continue fighting what happened to my sister and fight for better care at nursing homes but the settlement would state that neither I nor my sisters could go after Manorcare for any more money. I'm sure he knew that wrongful death in PA severely restricts who can file a lawsuit. Kitty did not have life insurance and my other sister and I used our personal money to pay for her funeral and burial so I felt it was their responsibility to cover her costs. To me, this was definite proof that her death was their fault because nursing homes don't pay out just because they feel bad. She is with God now but I'm still here so my fight continues.

One last item was that Manorcare sent a packet containing financial documents that needed to be signed but they had already been done earlier in the week. At the end was an "Arbitration Agreement" asking for someone to sign and return it. I did not respond but I only found out later how important this document was to them. They sent this to Kitty's address a day or two after she was rushed to the emergency room on April 16, 2012.

Thank you for allowing me to continue my fight. The pledge states "with liberty and justice for all" but I've found that justice is only another word that doesn't mean anything.

Ann E. Stanton

Department of Health and Human Services

Centers for Medicare and Medicaid Services (CMS)
Philadelphia, Pennsylvania
Northeast Division of Survey and Certification

The Honorable Patrick J. Toomey
U.S. Senate
June 19, 2013
Allentown, PA
Attn: Steve Meridith

Dear Senator Toomey:

This is in response to your letter of June 6, 2013, inquiring on behalf of your constituent, Ms. Ann Stanton.

The role of the health-care surveyor, state or federal, is to evaluate the care given in any particular health-care setting in terms of it meeting the minimal regulatory requirements. To the best of our knowledge, the word "falsification" appears in the long term care regulations only in regard to resident assessments (42 CFR 483.20(i)). The "falsification" of the mandatory resident assessment data that is required to be submitted through the MDS system carries a civil monetary penalty for the person falsifying data or causing it to be falsified. That, however, is not part of the survey process, and such penalties would be assessed by the Office of the Inspector General.

That is not to say the falsification of records does not happen, but it is not something in and of itself surveyors could cite as a deficient practice. "Falsification" is, as you point out in your letter, a legal distinction. The falsification of records for the purpose of fraudulently billing Medicare would be a criminal act. "False swearing" on several attestation forms used in the process of certifying other types of providers carries civil or criminal penalties. There is, however, no analogous "falsification" standard in the survey process.

As we have previously pointed out to Ms. Stanton, there is no dispute that the facility her mother[110] resided in had problems with record keeping, and the State had cited them for those issues. However, there is no evidence to suggest that ManorCare falsified[111] any records pertaining to her mother's care.

Sincerely,
Dale Van Wieren
Principal State Representative
Certification and Enforcement Branch

---

[110] After reviewing the letter, I realized they stated it was my mother; it was my sister. There is no reason to falsify a medical record unless a person has done the wrong thing.

[111] MDS records showed false statements all through them, but no one cared.

Statement Submitted by Stephanie Walker Weaver

I am writing to you in reference to the tragic death of my grandmother Bonnie Walker. Despite the assurances by the senior living facility where she lived that she would be safe and cared for, she suffered a horrific and entirely preventable death. I am seeking accountability from the facility responsible for her neglect to ensure that no one else suffers as she did. I have become aware of a tremendous impediment to that: forced arbitration. My grandmother, who suffered from dementia, walked away from Brookdale Senior Assisted Living in Charleston on July 27, 2016. It took over seven hours for anyone on staff to notice she was missing and even longer to notify my family. Frustrated with the fact that the staff still not found my grandmother and was not even actively looking for her. I took it upon myself to start searching the grounds. As I came around the back of the facility, I observed a police officer and a staff member going out the back door with a first aid kit. I followed behind. When we reached the pond to my absolute horror, I saw my grandmothers dismembered remains floating in the pond. We later learned that an alligator had killed her in the pond.

We initially had placed my grandmother at Savannah House in January of 2016. We removed her roughly June 2016 and placed her at Brookdale. We removed her from the Savannah House based on many things that started to alarm us with her care and the overall facility. The activity director quit and they were providing little to no activities for the residence. The residence were receiving poorly prepared meals by care staff members. My father witnessed a resident be shoved down by another resident. No staff would help her up. My father had to assist her up. They were also having frequent elopement issues with a resident the ultimately ended up eloping and dying. We felt we needed to move her to a new assisted living home and ultimately we chose Brookdale based on their commitment to her care.

When we received the autopsy report, it showed my grandmother had not received her medication for two days. She was back at Brookdale for 48 hours after visiting my parents that weekend at their home. It was common for her to stay at Brookdale from Sunday evening to Thursday evening and on weekends with my parents. My mother was told when she spoke with staff early that week not to stay with her that they would be monitoring her for the next few days to assess if she was needing to go in the memory care unit. So not only did no staff check on my grandmother early that evening until the next morning at 7:00 am. They did not give her medication for two days. They also were not monitoring her for the memory care unit despite the family being told to not stay with her. They also tested five residence that January 2017 after her death and four of the five were not receiving medications. Our family in the short six weeks my grandmother had multiple prescriptions come up missing. We had issues of prescriptions being destroyed by Brookdale staff and not given back to the family. We have documentation where charts have white out on them. The door did not alarm early that morning when my grandmother managed to slip out. There was only one staff member on in the evenings with over 30 residents. When the final report came out on Brookdale from DHEC. They only received right around $6,000 in fines. Most of the fines were not part of my grandmother case. My grandmother was last seen on video surveillance wandering the halls around midnight. We are still unclear of all the violations and negligence on Brookdale's part and what really occurred in the early hours of the morning on July 27, 2016. There are a few things I am certain of she was not being cared for properly, she was stolen from, and she deserved better care. My grandmother was taken from us in such a horrific way with so many wrongful dynamics that come into play with her story. No one deserves to die this way and suffer this way.

We are a country whose population is growing daily. We are also living longer. We are owed better care facilities, better training and better laws to protect our family members and future generations. I will continue to keep telling my grandmother's story and I will continue to fight for better care for our elders in her memory. Thank you for your time and your efforts going into looking at this epidemic of neglect in our care facilities that goes on nationwide.

https://www.nytimes.com/2018/12/13/business/assisted-living-violations-dementia-alzheimers

https://www.postandcourier.com/news/charleston-assisted-living-facility-where-woman-was-killed-by-nearby/article_537435a2-624c-11e7-9288-8b8d44af7005.html

https://www.postandcourier.com/news/granddaughter-suing-west-ashley-senior-facility-over-grandmother-killed-by/article_8207d9fa-5752-11e7-b322-6736aac8aff9.html

https://www.postandcourier.com/health/report-brookdale-charleston-nursing-home-director-suspects-employees-of-stealing/article_4f4ae148-e974-11e6-bf30-9f36642b0fc0.html

Statement Submitted by Carole H. Woolfork

Subject: "Not Forgotten: Protecting Americans From Abuse and Neglect in Nursing Homes"

Earlier today I sat at my computer from 10:15 a.m. to 1:00 p.m. to hear remarks from Senators and from the two panels that had been convened. The stories of the two daughters who told of the plight of their mothers at the time they were nursing home residents was tragic, seemingly avoidable and heartbreaking.

Based on past experience as a nurse manager and current experience as an advocate, I can attest to the fact that there are facilities that strive to provide and do provide quality of care and quality of life. However, it is also painfully obvious that many facilities fall short of meeting that standard. Therefore, more needs to be done to strengthen regulations and outcomes for failing to follow regulations and meet standards.

Nursing home residents are some of the most vulnerable individuals in the nation. CMS's deregulatory agenda puts residents in danger of experiencing harm or being placed in immediate jeopardy of health, safety, or well-being. This potential for resident harm is in direct opposition to the HHS Secretary's duty under the law. The law makes clear that the Secretary is responsible for assuring the "requirements which govern the provision of care in skilled nursing facilities . . . and the enforcement of such requirements, are adequate to protect the health, safety, welfare, and rights of residents and to promote the effective and efficient use of public moneys." CMS's deregulatory actions indicate that the Secretary is ignoring this longstanding mandate. Multiple reports from the HHS Office of the Inspector General (OIG) and the Government Accountability Office (GAO) document persistent and widespread problems facing nursing home residents. In my opinion, the following actions by CMS illustrate how existing problems in nursing homes have been exacerbated:

- Placing an 18-month moratorium on the full enforcement of eight standards of care that relate to important resident protections—baseline care planning, staff competency, use and monitoring of antibiotic, and psychotropic medications. The moratorium means that nursing homes will not be financially penalized when these safeguards are violated.
- Shifting the default civil money penalty (CMP) from per day (for the duration of a violation) to per instance. *The New York Times* reported that "the change means that some nursing homes could be sheltered from fines above the maximum per-instance fine of $20,965 even for egregious mistakes."
- Proposing rulemaking (NPRM) to roll back emergency preparedness requirements. Most notably, the proposed rule would allow nursing homes to review their programs and train staff every two years instead of annually.
- Responding to industry lobbying by carrying out plans to revise the federal nursing home Requirements of Participation to "reform" standards that have been identified as "excessively burdensome" for the nursing home industry. The Requirements were recently revised in October 2016 (for the first time in 25 years) to better address longstanding problems, including persistent abuse and neglect. These standards need to be implemented, not watered down.

There are numerous ongoing concerns. The following describes some of them:

- More than 95 percent of all citations for violations of the federal minimum standards of care result in findings of no resident harm. A "no harm" citation does not mean that the resident did not, in fact, experience pain, suffering, or humiliation. However, a finding of "no harm" all too often does mean that the nursing home is not penalized for poor care.

- Staffing is essential to resident care and quality of life. Insufficient staffing is often the underlying cause of other health violations. By law, nursing homes must have a registered nurse on duty for eight consecutive hours and 24-hour licensed nurse services every single day. These two requirements are recognized as the minimum necessary to ensure that residents receive the "skilled nursing" care and monitoring that they need and which facilities are paid to provide. However, CMS noted in a 2017 memorandum that about six percent of nursing homes that submitted nurse staffing data for the third quarter of 2017 had seven or more days with no reported RN hours and that 80 percent of these days were on weekends. *The New York Times* further described the federal data as documenting that, for at least one day in the last quarter of 2017, 25 percent of nursing homes reported no registered nurses at work.
- About 20 percent of nursing home residents are administered antipsychotic drugs every day. However, less than two percent of the population will ever have a diagnosis for a clinical condition identified by CMS when it risk adjusts for potentially appropriate uses of these drugs. In response to this concern, in 2011 the HHS Inspector General stated that "government, taxpayers, nursing home residents, as well as their families and caregivers should be outraged— and seek solutions." Nevertheless, currently in the absence of meaningful enforcement, the problem of overuse and misuse of antipsychotic drugs is still widespread.
- CMS has stated that "facility-initiated discharges continue to be one of the most frequent complaints made to State Long Term Care Ombudsman Programs." Although the Nursing Home Reform Law places specific restrictions on when and how a resident can be transferred or discharged, many residents fall victim to inappropriate and unsafe discharges. Residents have been discharged to unsafe and inappropriate settings such as homeless shelters, storage units, and motels.
- The buying and selling of nursing homes and the transfer of licenses to new managers raise questions about who these operators are and whether there are sufficient state and federal law, regulations, and practices in place, and meaningfully enforced, to protect residents. A health care entity that took over 100 nursing homes across the country starting in 2015 and collapsed in 2018. Various states officials indicated that the facilities were at imminent risk of running out of necessary food and medication, and were unable to meet payroll. This is just one of many illustrations that nursing home residents are in need of urgent action to protect their quality of care and quality of life.

CMS's deregulation places residents at an even greater risk of experiencing harm. Thank you to the Senate Finance Committee's decision to hold a hearing on nursing home resident abuse and neglect. It is the hope that this Committee will continue to highlight these issues until verifiable and demonstrable change occurs and is sustained.

Thank you in advance for being advocates for nursing home residents, and for exercising legislative power to facilitate changes to ensure quality of care and quality of life for all nursing home residents, with special scrutiny for the well-being of the frail, the voiceless, and the vulnerable.

In: Elder Justice
Editor: Vince D. Anderson

ISBN: 978-1-53619-447-0

Chapter 2

THE ELDER JUSTICE ACT: BACKGROUND AND ISSUES FOR CONGRESS*

Kirsten J. Colello

SUMMARY

Elder abuse is a complex issue. As such, it often leads to calls for a multifaceted policy response that combines public health interventions, social services programs, and law enforcement. To address this complexity, the Elder Justice Act was enacted on March 23, 2010, as part of the Patient Protection and Affordable Care Act (ACA, P.L. 111-148, as amended). The Elder Justice Act is intended to provide a coordinated federal response to elder abuse by emphasizing various public health and social service approaches to prevent, detect, and treat abuse. The Elder Justice Act is Congress's first attempt at comprehensive legislation to address abuse, neglect, and exploitation of the elderly at the federal level.

Elder Justice Provisions

Enactment of the Elder Justice Act under the ACA contained certain public health and social services approaches to the prevention, detection, and treatment of elder abuse, primarily under the Department of Health and Human Services (HHS) authorities and administration. The elder justice provisions enacted under the ACA did not fully incorporate the comprehensive multidisciplinary policy approach (public health, social services, and criminal justice) envisioned in earlier versions of introduced legislation. Unlike earlier versions of the Elder Justice Act, which included a multidisciplinary approach that incorporated criminal justice provisions, the Elder Justice Act enacted

* This is an edited, reformatted and augmented version of Congressional Research Service Publication No. R43707, dated June 15, 2020.

under ACA did not include a criminal justice response for addressing the prevention, detection, and prosecution of elder abuse crimes under the Department of Justice (DOJ). With enactment of the Elder Justice Act under the ACA, criminal justice provisions were introduced as separate stand-alone legislation in subsequent Congresses. On October 18, 2017, the Elder Abuse Prevention and Prosecution Act of 2017 (EAPPA; P.L. 115-70) was signed into law establishing certain DOJ requirements with respect to investigating and prosecuting elder abuse crimes and enforcing elder abuse laws. In addition, Section 501 of P.L. 115-70 amended the Elder Justice Act to authorize certain court-appointed guardianship oversight activities under Adult Protective Services (APS) demonstration grants.

Federal Funding for Elder Justice Activities

The authorizations of appropriations for most Elder Justice Act activities expired on September 30, 2014. However, Congress continues to appropriate some funding for authorized activities. To date, most programs and activities authorized under the Elder Justice Act have either not received funding since enactment or have not received funding at their previously authorized levels. For FY2020, the Further Consolidated Appropriations Act, 2020 (P.L. 116-94), provided $14.0 million in discretionary appropriations under the Elder Rights Support Activities line item appropriation within the Administration for Community Living's (ACL's) Aging and Disability Services Programs budget authority, of which $12.0 million is for the Elder Justice and Adult Protective Services program. ACL funding under the Elder Justice and Adult Protective Services program is also used for activities authorized under Older Americans Act (OAA) Sections 411 and 751. FY2020 funding of $12.0 million for the Elder Justice and Adult Protective Services program was the same as the FY2019 funding level.

Topics Covered in This Chapter

This chapter provides a brief legislative history of the Elder Justice Act, summarizes elder justice provisions enacted as part of ACA, and describes administrative efforts related to implementation and funding, along with several issues for Congress regarding the act's reauthorization.

Elder abuse is gaining attention as a public policy issue in the United States. Although the extent of such abuse is largely unknown, some studies indicate that it is prevalent and that many incidents of abuse are never reported.[1] A 2010 study of the extent of elder abuse in the United States found that 11% of individuals aged 60 and older residing in the community reported some type of abuse in the past year.[2] A 2008 study found that 9% of community-residing older adults aged 57 to 85 reported verbal

[1] National Center on Elder Abuse, *Statistics and Data*, https://ncea.acl.gov/What-We-Do/Research/Statistics-and-Data.aspx#prevalence.

[2] Acierno, Ron, M. A. Hernandez, A. B. Amstadter, et al., "Prevalence and Correlates of Emotional, Physical, Sexual, and Financial Abuse and Potential Neglect in the United States: The National Elder Mistreatment Study," *American Journal of Public Health*, vol. 100 (2010).

mistreatment, 3.5% reported financial mistreatment, and 0.2% reported physical mistreatment by a family member in the past year.[3]

Studies such as these likely underestimate the full extent of elder abuse because they do not include all categories of abuse, exclude individuals who reside in institutional settings such as nursing facilities, and generally exclude individuals with significant cognitive impairment (see text box "What is Elder Abuse?"). In addition, incidents of elder abuse may go unreported, as older individuals may be reluctant to report abuse by an individual they rely upon for their personal care and well-being.[4] The physical and emotional effects of elder abuse can have lasting effects and may lead to disability or even premature death.[5] Moreover, research indicates that there is an association between victims who have physical and cognitive impairments, as well as inadequate social supports, and an increased risk of elder abuse.[6]

What Is Elder Abuse?

Behaviors that constitute elder abuse and neglect, also referred to as *elder mistreatment*, are considered to be "intentional actions that cause harm or create a serious risk of harm (whether or not harm is intended) to a vulnerable elder by a caregiver or other person who stands in a trust relationship to the elder or failure by a caregiver to satisfy the elder's basic needs or to protect the elder from harm."[7]

Elder abuse and neglect may occur in domestic or institutional settings, as described below.

- *Domestic* elder abuse generally refers to any of the following types of mistreatment that are committed by someone with whom the elder has a special relationship (e.g., a spouse, sibling, child, friend, or caregiver).
- *Institutional* elder abuse generally refers to any of the following types of mistreatment occurring in residential facilities (e.g., a nursing facility, assisted living facility, group home, board and care facility, or foster home) and is usually perpetrated by someone with a legal or contractual obligation to provide some element of care or protection.

---

[3] Laumann, Edward O., S. A. Leitsch, and L. J. Waite, "Elder Mistreatment in the United States: Prevalence Estimates From a Nationally Representative Study," *The Journals of Gerontology Series B: Psychological and Social Sciences*, vol. 63 (2008).

[4] Centers for Disease Control and Prevention, *Understanding Elder Abuse: Fact Sheet*, Division of Violence and Prevention, National Center for Injury Prevention and Control, 2016, http://www.cdc.gov/violenceprevention/pdf/em- factsheet-a.pdf.

[5] Lachs M.S., C.S. Williams, S. O'Brien, et al., "The Mortality of Elder Mistreatment," *Journal of the American Medical Association*, vol. 280 (1998).

[6] U.S. Government Accountability Office, *Stronger Federal Leadership Could Enhance National Response to Elder Abuse*, GAO-11-208, Mar 2, 2011, http://www.gao.gov/assets/320/ 316224.pdf. Reissued on March 22, 2011.

[7] Richard J. Bonnie and Robert B. Wallace, eds., *Elder Mistreatment: Abuse, Neglect and Exploitation in an Aging America*, National Research Council (Washington, DC: National Academy Press, 2003).

The following are generally considered the major categories of elder abuse and neglect:[8]

- *Physical abuse* is the use of force that may result in bodily injury, physical pain, injury, or impairment.
- *Emotional or psychological abuse* is the infliction of mental anguish, pain, or distress through verbal or nonverbal acts.
- *Sexual abuse* is nonconsensual sexual contact of any kind with an older adult.
- *Financial or material exploitation* is the illegal or improper exploitation or use of funds, property, or assets of an older adult.
- *Neglect* is the refusal or failure to fulfill any part of a person's obligations or duties to care for an older adult.
- *Abandonment* is the desertion of an older person by an individual who has assumed responsibility for providing care or by a person with physical custody.
- *Self-neglect* is behavior that threatens a person's own health or safety, including refusal or failure to provide himself/herself with adequate food, water, clothing, shelter, personal hygiene, or medication.[9] Self-neglect is often considered distinct from elder abuse—the distinction being that self-neglect is a form of violence a person inflicts upon himself or herself (self-directed violence), whereas elder abuse is violence inflicted by another individual (interpersonal violence). Self-neglect may co-occur alongside or be triggered by elder abuse. However, research indicates that self-neglect prevention strategies differ from elder abuse prevention strategies.

Because elder abuse is a complex issue, it often leads to calls for a multifaceted policy response combining public health initiatives, social services programs, and criminal law enforcement to address abusive behavior. In response to this complexity, the Elder Justice Act was enacted on March 23, 2010, as part of the Patient Protection and Affordable Care Act (ACA, P.L. 111-148, as amended).[10] The Elder Justice Act was enacted to provide a coordinated federal response to elder abuse by emphasizing various public health and social service approaches to prevent, detect, and treat such abuse. The act represents Congress's first attempt at comprehensive legislation to address abuse, neglect, and exploitation of the elderly at the federal level. Enactment of the Elder Justice Act places the issue of elder abuse on par with similar legislation Congress has enacted with respect to child abuse and neglect, under the Child Abuse Prevention and Treatment Act,[11] and domestic violence, under the Violence Against Women Act.[12]

---

[8] National Center on Elder Abuse (NCEA), *Frequently Asked Questions*, Administration on Aging, https://ncea.acl.gov/ FAQ.aspx; Krug, Etienne G., et al., eds. World Report on Violence and Health: Chapter 5, Abuse of the Elderly, 2002.

[9] Centers for Disease Control and Prevention, *Elder Abuse Surveillance: Uniform Definitions and Recommended Core Data Elements*, Version 1.0, National Center for Injury Prevention and Control Division of Violence Prevention, Atlanta, Georgia, 2016.

[10] §6703(a) through (c) of ACA (P.L. 111-148).

[11] For more information on the Child Abuse Prevention and Treatment Act, see CRS Report R43458, *Child Welfare: An Overview of Federal Programs and Their Current Funding*.

As with other grant programs authorized under the ACA, the implementation of new grants and activities under the Elder Justice Act has been hampered by the lack of federal discretionary spending for authorized activities, which are subject to the annual appropriations process. Agencies have implemented some elder justice programs and activities with limited funding. However, a coordinated federal response to the issue as envisioned by the Elder Justice Act has been challenging, in part due to actions Congress has taken since FY2010 to curb federal discretionary spending.[13]

The extent of elder abuse has the potential to grow in scope as the older population continues to increase in size, and as individuals live longer post-retirement. In 2018, an estimated 16.0% of the total U.S. population was aged 65 and older (about one in every six Americans).[14] The U.S. Census Bureau projects that by 2040 one in every five Americans, or 21.6% of the U.S. population, will be age 65 or older.[15] Thus, Congress will likely have a continued interest in shaping the federal role and response to elder abuse going forward. This chapter provides a brief legislative history of the Elder Justice Act, summarizes elder justice provisions enacted as part of the ACA and any administrative efforts related to implementation and funding, and describes several issues for Congress with respect to the act's potential reauthorization.

Elder Justice Defined

Elder justice is defined in statute, from a societal perspective, as efforts to (1) prevent, detect, treat, intervene in, and prosecute elder abuse, neglect, and exploitation; and (2) protect elders with diminished capacity while maximizing their autonomy.

From an individual perspective, *elder justice* is defined as the recognition of an elder's rights, including the right to be free of abuse, neglect, and exploitation.

Source: SSA §2011 as amended by Section 6703(a) of ACA [42 U.S.C. §1397j].

---

12 For more information on the Violence Against Women Act, see CRS Report R45410, The Violence Against Women Act (VAWA): Historical Overview, Funding, and Reauthorization.

13 The Budget Control Act of 2011 (BCA; P.L. 112-25) included provisions authorizing increases in the debt limit, as well as provisions designed to reduce the federal deficit. One way the BCA seeks to reduce deficits is by establishing discretionary spending caps, which limit the amount of money that can be provided through the annual appropriations process for each of the next 10 fiscal years. For a more detailed explanation of the BCA, see CRS Report R44874, The Budget Control Act: Frequently Asked Questions.

14 CRS estimate based on U.S Census Bureau, Older Americans Month, "Population and Housing Estimates," https://www.census.gov/newsroom/stories/2020/older-americans.html.

15 U.S. Census Bureau, 2017 National Population Projections Tables: Main Series, "Table 2. Projected age and sex composition of the population," https://www.census.gov/data/tables/ 2017/demo/popproj/2017-summary-tables.html.

LEGISLATIVE HISTORY OF THE ELDER JUSTICE ACT

Congressional interest in the issue of elder abuse spans more than a quarter of a century, with numerous hearings and reports concerning the need for a federal response to abuse, neglect, and exploitation of the elderly. Prior to enactment of the Elder Justice Act as part of the ACA, Congress took a number of steps toward addressing elder abuse, including authorizing federal assistance to state Adult Protective Services (APS) programs through the Social Services Block Grant (SSBG) program. In addition, Congress amended the Older Americans Act (OAA) to provide separate funding for elder abuse prevention and vulnerable elder rights protection activities, including establishment of the Long-Term Care Ombudsman Program (LTCOP) under Title VII, Vulnerable Elder Rights Protection Activities. Provisions regarding elder justice were also incorporated under Title VII in the OAA reauthorization of 2006 (P.L. 109-365).[16]

In 2002, the 107th Congress first introduced comprehensive legislation to address elder abuse incorporating public health, social services, and criminal justice provisions under the Elder Justice Act (S. 2933). After that, Elder Justice Act legislation was reintroduced in subsequent Congresses with Senate Finance Committee action on the public health and social services provisions of the bill in the 108th, 109th, and 110th Congresses.[17] The Elder Justice Act of 2009 (S.795) was introduced in the 111th Congress and only included the public health and social services approaches to the issue. S. 795 was incorporated into the Senate Finance Committee's health reform bill (S. 1796) and subsequently adopted in the Senate health reform bill (H.R. 3590), which became the ACA (P.L. 111-148).

The elder justice provisions enacted under the ACA did not fully incorporate the comprehensive multidisciplinary approach (public health, social services, and criminal justice) envisioned in earlier versions of introduced legislation. Enactment of the Elder Justice Act under the ACA contained certain public health and social services approaches to the prevention, detection, and treatment of elder abuse, primarily under the Department of Health and Human Services' (HHS) authorities and administration. Unlike earlier versions of the Elder Justice Act, which included a multidisciplinary approach, the act did not include a criminal justice response for addressing the prevention, detection, and prosecution of elder abuse crimes under the Department of Justice (DOJ). With the enactment of the Elder Justice Act under the ACA, criminal justice provisions were subsequently introduced as separate stand-alone legislation in subsequent Congresses

---

[16] Congress included several provisions related to elder justice activities in the OAA Amendments of 2006 (P.L. 109- 365). For example, the law added various elder justice activities to be carried out by the Assistant Secretary for Aging. These provisions include responsibility for the Administration on Aging (AoA) to develop and implement systems for elder justice and to conduct an elder abuse national incidence study. It also added a requirement that the Assistant Secretary award funds for competitive grants to states for developing and implementing elder justice activities under Title VII of OAA.

[17] The Elder Justice Act has been introduced in the 108th Congress (S. 333; H.R. 2490), 109th Congress (S. 2010; H.R. 4993), and 110th Congress (S. 1070; H.R. 1783).

with legislative activity in the 115th Congress.[18] On October 18, 2017, the Elder Abuse Prevention and Prosecution Act of 2017 (EAPPA; P.L. 115-70), was signed into law establishing certain DOJ requirements with respect to investigating and prosecuting elder abuse crimes and enforcing elder abuse laws.[19] In addition, Section 501 of P.L. 115-70 amended the Elder Justice Act (Section 2042(c) of the SSA) to authorize certain court-appointed guardianship oversight activities under APS demonstration grants. Thus far, in the 116th Congress, no bills have been introduced in to reauthorize the Elder Justice Act.[20]

ELDER JUSTICE ACT PROVISIONS

The Elder Justice Act provisions enacted under the ACA and amended under EAPPA authorize entities and programs that address the federal coordination of elder abuse and the administration of new grant activities, as well as certain protections for residents of long-term care facilities, and other specified studies.[21] The following sections describe these provisions in greater detail.

Elder Justice Act Provisions Under the Social Security Act

Several of the Elder Justice Act provisions amended the Social Security Act (SSA), which incorporated elder justice into a renamed Title XX, entitled Block Grants to States for Social Services and Elder Justice. The ACA subsequently reorganized the structure of SSA Title XX, by placing previously existing sections under a new Subtitle A, Block Grants to States for Social Services, and adding a new Subtitle B, Elder Justice.

National Coordination of Elder Justice Activities and Research

Several SSA elder justice provisions address federal coordination and research activities. Specifically, SSA Title XX, Subtitle B, establishes an Elder Justice Coordinating Council and an Advisory Board on Elder Abuse, Neglect, and Exploitation. It also addresses research protections and awards grants to establish and operate

---

[18] In the 114th Congress, these bills included S. 3270, the Elder Abuse Prevention and Prosecution Act; S. 2747/H.R. 5018, the Elder Protection and Abuse Prevention Act; S. 1663, the Robert Matava Elder Abuse Victims Act of 2015; and H.R. 4963, the Elder Abuse Victims Act of 2016.

[19] For more information on the Elder Abuse Prevention and Prosecution Act of 2017 (EAPPA; P.L. 115-70), see https://www.justice.gov/elderjustice/eappa. Further discussion of the provision under the Elder Abuse Prevention and Prosecution Act, P.L. 115-70, is beyond the scope of this report.

[20] Elder Justice Act reauthorization bills were introduced by Rep. Peter King in the 114th Congress (H.R. 988) and 115th Congress (H.R. 2639).

[21] §6703(a) through (c) of the ACA.

stationary and mobile forensic centers. These provisions and any administrative or other actions to implement authorized programs or activities are described below.[22]

Elder Justice Coordinating Council

The Elder Justice Act established the Elder Justice Coordinating Council at HHS (SSA §2021). The council includes the HHS Secretary as chair and the U.S. Attorney General as a permanent member, as well as the head of each federal department or agency, identified by the chair, as having administrative responsibility for administering programs related to elder abuse, neglect, and exploitation.[23] The council is required to submit a report to the appropriate committees of Congress within two years of enactment and every two years thereafter that describes its activities and challenges. The council is also required to make recommendations for legislation, model laws, and other actions deemed appropriate.[24] Such sums as necessary are authorized to be appropriated to carry out the council's functions.[25] (See the "Authorizations of Appropriations" section of this chapter for further information.)

On October 11, 2012, the HHS Secretary convened the inaugural meeting of the Elder Justice Coordinating Council. The council is a permanent group, expected to meet twice a year. The HHS Secretary assigned responsibility for implementing the council to the Administration for Community Living (ACL). The work of the council is supported by a staff-level Elder Justice Interagency Working Group also led by ACL, which was established prior to ACA. Since the inaugural meeting, the council has convened several times. During these meetings, Elder Justice Interagency Working Group members presented proposals for federal action and a summary of steps for federal involvement in the prevention, detection, and prosecution of elder abuse. The working group also coordinated a report of federal activities in elder justice since 2010.[26] At the May 2014 meeting, the council agreed to a set of eight recommendations for increased federal involvement in addressing elder abuse (see text box "Elder Justice Coordinating Council: Recommendations for Increased Federal Involvement in Elder Abuse"). More recent meetings have focused on the opioid crisis and elder abuse and elder justice concerns faced by rural and tribal communities.

---

[22] Prior to Part I, new Subtitle B begins with Sections 2011 (Definitions) and 2012 (General Provisions), which are not discussed here.

[23] The Elder Justice Coordinating Council members include heads of the following departments and agencies: U.S. Department of Health and Human Services (Chair), Consumer Financial Protection Bureau, Corporation for National and Community Service, U.S. Department of Housing and Urban Development, U.S. Department of Justice, U.S. Department of Labor, U.S. Department of the Treasury, U.S. Department of Veterans Affairs, U.S. Postal Inspection Service, U.S. Securities and Exchange Commission, Federal Trade Commission, and the Social Security Administration.

[24] On June 22, 2015, HHS submitted the *Elder Justice Coordinating Council 2012-2014 Report to Congress*, as required, https://acl.gov/sites/default/files/programs/2016-09/EJCC-2012-2014-report-to-congress.pdf.

[25] Authorizations of appropriations language are indefinite; that is, they do not specify a year and therefore do not expire.

[26] For a copy of the report, a list of EJCC members, and information on EJCC meetings and proposals, see https://acl.gov/programs/elder-justice/elder-justice-coordinating-council-ejcc.

Elder Justice Coordinating Council: Recommendations for Increased Federal Involvement in Elder Abuse[27]

- Support the Investigation and Prosecution of Elder Abuse Cases—Support the investigation and prosecution of elder abuse, neglect, and financial exploitation cases by providing training and resources to federal, state, and local investigators and prosecutors.
- Enhance Services to Elder Abuse Victims—Support and protect elder abuse victims by improving identification of elder abuse and enhancing response and outreach to victims.
- Develop a National Adult Protective Services (APS) System—Develop a national APS system based on standardized data collection and a core set of service provision standards and best practices.
- Develop a Federal Elder Justice Research Agenda—Establish a coordinated research agenda across federal agencies to identify best practices for the prevention of and intervention in elder abuse and elder financial exploitation.
- Develop a Broad-Based Public Awareness Campaign—Develop a comprehensive, strategic, and broad- based national public awareness campaign, with clear and consistent messaging to raise awareness and understanding of elder abuse, neglect, and exploitation.
- Cross-Disciplinary Training on Elder Abuse—Develop training to educate stakeholders across multiple sectors and disciplines on preventing, detecting, intervening in, and responding to elder abuse, neglect, and exploitation.
- Combat Elder Financial Exploitation, Including Abuse by Fiduciaries—Prevent, detect, and respond to elder financial exploitation through federal enforcement activities, policy initiatives, coordination, oversight and education, and by collaborating with industry to enhance fraud detection and provide resources for victims.
- Improve Screening for Dementia and Cognitive Capacity, Financial Capacity, and Financial Exploitation—Improve the ability of APS and first responders to screen for diminished capacity, diminished financial capacity, and vulnerability to or victimization by financial exploitation.

Advisory Board on Elder Abuse, Neglect, and Exploitation

The Advisory Board on Elder Abuse, Neglect, and Exploitation (SSA §2022) is established to create a short- and long-term multidisciplinary plan for development of the field of elder justice and to make recommendations to the Elder Justice Coordinating Council. The Advisory Board must be composed of 27 members from the general public appointed by the Secretary and must have experience and expertise in prevention of elder abuse, neglect, and exploitation. The Advisory Board is required to submit a report to the Elder Justice Coordinating Council and the appropriate committees of Congress within 18 months of enactment and annually thereafter that contains information on the status of federal, state, and local elder justice activities, and that makes specified

[27] Administration for Community Living, *Eight Recommendations from the Elder Justice Coordinating Council for Increased Federal Involvement in Addressing Elder Abuse*, May 2014, https://acl.gov/sites/default/files/programs/2016- 09/Eight_Recommendations_ for_ Increased_Federal_Involvement.pdf.

recommendations. Such sums as necessary are authorized to be appropriated to carry out the functions of the Advisory Board.[28] On July 14, 2010, HHS published a notice establishing the Advisory Board;[29] however, no subsequent public announcement by HHS has been made about board appointments or activities. (See the "Authorizations of Appropriations" section of this chapter for further information.)

Research Protections

The HHS Secretary is required to promulgate guidelines to assist researchers working in the areas of elder abuse, neglect, and exploitation with issues relating to human research subject protections (SSA §2023). For the purposes of the application of certain specified federal regulations to research conducted under this subpart, it defines "legally authorized representative" to mean, unless otherwise provided by law, the individual, or judicial or other body authorized under the applicable law to consent to medical treatment on behalf of another person. No public information on the status of guidance promulgated by HHS Secretary was found. (See the "Authorizations of Appropriations" section of this chapter for further information.)

Authorizations of Appropriations

To carry out the above functions of the Elder Justice Coordinating Council (SSA §2021), the Advisory Board on Elder Abuse, Neglect, and Exploitation (SSA §2022), and research protection guidelines for human subjects (SSA §2023), a new SSA Section 2024, Authorization of Appropriations, authorized to be appropriated $6.5 million for FY2011, and $7.0 million for each of FY2012 through FY2014. To date, Congress has not provided discretionary funding for these activities through the annual appropriations process. However, as previously mentioned, the Elder Justice Coordinating Council has convened several times since 2012.

Elder Abuse, Neglect, Exploitation Forensic Centers

SSA elder justice provisions also added a provision regarding the establishment and support of elder abuse, neglect, and exploitation forensic centers (SSA §2031). This provision requires the HHS Secretary, in consultation with the U.S. Attorney General, to award grants to eligible entities to establish and operate both stationary and mobile forensic centers and to develop forensic expertise pertaining to elder abuse, neglect, and exploitation. It authorized to be appropriated $4 million for FY2011, $6 million for FY2012, and $8 million for each of FY2013 and FY2014 to carry out these activities. To

[28] Authorizations of appropriations language are indefinite; that is, they do not specify a year and therefore do not expire.

[29] U.S. Department of Health and Human Services, "Establishment of the Advisory Board on Elder Abuse, Neglect, and Exploitation," *75 Federal Register 40838*, July 14, 2010.

date, Congress has not provided discretionary funding for these activities through the annual appropriations process.

Programs to Promote Elder Justice

SSA elder justice provisions establish several grant programs and other activities to promote elder justice through various enhancements to the workforce and electronic health record technology, grants to adult protective services programs, and training for long-term care ombudsmen, among other activities. These provisions are described below.

Enhancement of Long-Term Care

Under SSA Section 2041, the Elder Justice Act required the HHS Secretary, in coordination with the Secretary of Labor, to carry out activities that provide incentives for individuals to train for, seek, and maintain employment providing direct care in long-term care (LTC) facilities. In doing so, the HHS Secretary is required to award grants to eligible entities to conduct programs that offer direct care employees continuing training and varying levels of certification.

The act further authorized the HHS Secretary to make grants to LTC facilities for specified activities that would help such entities offset costs related to purchasing, leasing, developing, and implementing certified electronic health records (EHR) technology designed to improve patient safety and reduce adverse events and health care complications resulting from medication errors. This section also requires the Secretary to adopt electronic standards for the exchange of clinical data by LTC facilities and, within 10 years of enactment, to have in place procedures to accept the optional electronic submission of clinical data by LTC facilities pursuant to such standards. The standards adopted must be compatible with standards established under current law, as specified, and with general health information technology standards.

The section authorized to be appropriated $20.0 million for FY2011, $17.5 million forFY2012, and $15.0 million for each of FY2013 and FY2014 to carry out the activities under this section. To date, Congress has not provided discretionary funding for these activities through the annual appropriations process.

Adult Protective Service Functions and Grant Program

Adult Protective Services (APS) programs are social services programs established through legislation enacted in all 50 states, the District of Columbia, Guam, Puerto Rico, and the U.S. Virgin Islands. APS programs serve seniors and adults with disabilities by offering a system for reporting and investigating abuse, as well as providing social services to victims. State APS laws vary in the age of eligibility for APS assistance, definition of abuse, types of abuse covered, classification of the abuse as criminal or civil, mandatory reporting requirements, investigative procedures, and remedies for abuse. Prior to enactment of the Elder Justice Act, no dedicated federal funding authority was available for state APS programs. However, some states have used federal funding provided under the OAA and the Social Services Block Grant program to supplement state and local funding for APS programs.

Several SSA elder justice provisions addressed federal funding and additional resources for state APS programs. Specifically, SSA Section 2042(a) requires the HHS Secretary to ensure that the department (1) provides authorized funding to state and local APS offices that investigate reports of elder abuse, neglect, and exploitation; (2) collects and disseminates data in coordination with DOJ; (3) develops and disseminates information on best practices regarding, and provides training on, carrying out APS; (4) conducts research related to the provision of APS; and (5) provides technical assistance to states and other entities that provide or fund APS. To carry out these functions, the section authorized to be appropriated $3.0 million for FY2011 and $4 million for each of FY2012 through FY2014.

The HHS Secretary is also required to establish two grant programs. The first are grants to enhance APS services provided by states and local governments under SSA Section 2042(b). Annual grants awarded to states to enhance APS are to be distributed to states based on a formula. For each of FY2011 through FY2014, it authorized to be appropriated $100.0 million for annual grants to enhance APS programs. To date, Congress has not provided discretionary funding for these activities through the annual appropriations process.

The second grant program are grants to states (and high courts of states, as amended by P.L. 115-for APS demonstration programs under SSA Section 2042(c). Grant funds may be used for a variety of activities, such as methods to detect or prevent elder abuse (e.g., training modules and training in abuse forensics to enhance detection), methods that focus on financial exploitation, and activities to address guardianship and conservatorship proceedings (see text box entitled "Guardianship and Conservatorship"). For each of FY2011 through FY2014, it authorized to be appropriated $25.0 million for APS demonstration grants.

Although Congress has not explicitly provided discretionary funding for these activities through the annual appropriations process, beginning in FY2015, Congress provided discretionary funding more generally for Elder Justice and Adult Protective Services through the annual appropriations process.[30] ACL has used this funding for data collection activities, technical assistance to state APS programs, and to award discretionary grants to states to enhance APS services (see the "Funding for Elder Justice Activities" section of this chapter)

---

[30] The Further Consolidated Appropriations Act, 2020 (P.L. 116-94), provided $14.0 million in discretionary appropriations for FY2020 under the Elder Rights Support Activities line item appropriation within ACL's Aging and Disability Services Programs budget authority, of which $12.0 million is for the Elder Justice and Adult Protective Services program. ACL Funding under the Elder Justice and Adult Protective Services may also be used for activities authorized under OAA Sections 411 and 751.

Guardianship and Conservatorship[31]

Subject to state law, a court may appoint a guardian who is responsible for making all decisions—including legal, financial, and health decisions—for an individual, or a conservator who makes financial decisions regarding an individual's property. In general, guardians are appointed by a state court based on a determination by a judge or other official that an individual lacks the capacity to make decisions regarding their personal health, welfare, or property. According to a 2016 Government Accountability Office (GAO) report, states and local courts have primary responsibility over the guardianship and conservatorship process. While the federal government does not regulate or directly support such programs, federal programs and activities may provide indirect support to state programs.

The Elder Abuse Prevention and Prosecution Act of 2017 (EAPPA; P.L. 115-70) amended the APS demonstration grant authority under SSA §2042(c) to allow authorized funds to be used for activities related to guardianship and conservatorship proceedings. Specifically, it authorized the awarding of state demonstration grants to the highest courts of states to assess adult guardianship and conservatorship proceedings and to implement changes deemed necessary from such assessments. Such changes may include background checks for all potential guardians and conservators, as well as implementing electronic systems to simplify the guardianship and conservatorship process and to better enable courts to identify and detect fraud and exploitation. In awarding grants to state courts for demonstration programs, the HHS Secretary is required to consider the recommendations of the U.S. Attorney General and the State Justice Institute. Grantees are required to collaborate with the state-level agency on aging and the APS agency in conducting the demonstration program. To date, HHS not provided grant funding to state courts for these activities.

Long-Term Care Ombudsman Program Grants and Training

The Long-Term Care (LTC) Ombudsman Program is a consumer advocacy program that aims to improve the quality of care, as well as the quality of life, for residents in long-term care settings by investigating and resolving complaints made by, or on behalf of, such residents. Established under Title VII of the Older Americans Act (OAA), the Administration on Aging (AoA) within the Administration for Community Living (ACL) under HHS administers the nationwide program. As of 2018, there were 53 state LTC Ombudsman Programs operating in all 50 states, the District of Columbia, Guam, and Puerto Rico, and 523 local programs.[32] States and territories receive an annual allotment

---

[31] GAO, *Elder Abuse: The Extent of Abuse by Guardians Is Unknown, but Some Measures Exist to Help Protect Older Adults*, GAO-17-33, November 2016, https://www.gao.gov/assets /690/681088.pdf.

[32] ACL, Long-Term Care Ombudsman Program, https://ltcombudsman.org/about/about-ombudsman; ACL, AGing Independence and Disability Program Portal, Data-at-A-Glance, National Ombudsman Reporting System (NORS), 2018 data, https://agid. acl.gov/DataGlance/NORS/.

for ombudsman activities based on a statutory funding formula.[33] For FY2020, the total appropriated funding for the LTC Ombudsman Program was $17.9 million.[34]

SSA Section 2043 requires the HHS Secretary to award grants to eligible entities with relevant expertise and experience in abuse and neglect in LTC facilities or state LTC ombudsman programs to (1) improve the capacity of state LTC ombudsman programs to respond to and resolve abuse and neglect complaints; (2) conduct pilot programs with state or local LTC ombudsman offices; and (3) provide support for such state LTC ombudsman programs and such pilot programs. It authorized to be appropriated $5 million for FY2011, $7.5 million for FY2012, and $10 million for each of FY2013 and FY2014. The section also requires the Secretary to establish programs to provide and improve ombudsman training with respect to elder abuse, neglect, and exploitation for national organizations and state LTC ombudsman programs. It authorized to be appropriated $10 million for each of FY2011 through FY2014. To date, Congress has not provided discretionary funding for these activities through the annual appropriations process.

Protecting Residents of Long-Term Care Facilities

Provisions enacted under the Elder Justice Act establish (1) a National Training Institute for Surveyors and grants to state survey agencies and (2) requirements for reporting crimes in federally funded LTC facilities.[35]

National Training Institute for Surveyors

As specified under SSA Titles XVIII (Medicare) and XIX (Medicaid), each state has a licensing and certification agency that inspects long-term care facilities that participate in Medicare and/or Medicaid. These state agencies conduct standard and extended surveys and, under certain circumstances, impose remedies for noncompliance. The surveys they conduct examine both a facility's processes for delivering care and the outcomes of residents' care to ensure that minimum standards are met. CMS's Survey & Certification Group provides some instruction and training to state and federal surveyors through classroom and web-based training applications.[36]

The Elder Justice Act requires the HHS Secretary to establish and operate the National Training Institute for federal and state surveyors to carry out specified activities

---

[33] For more information on OAA funding formulas, see CRS Report RS22549, *Older Americans Act: Funding Formulas*.

[34] Personal communication from Steve Hagy, Director, Office of Budget and Finance, Administration for Community Living, U.S. Department of Health and Human Services, January 10, 2020.

[35] ACA Section 6703(b).

[36] CMS, *Survey & Certification – Surveyor Training*, http://cms.hhs.gov/Medicare/Provider-Enrollment-and-Certification/SurveyorTraining/index.html.

that provide and improve the training of surveyors who investigate allegations of abuse, neglect, and misappropriation of property in programs and LTC facilities that receive payments under Medicare or Medicaid. It authorized to be appropriated $12 million for the period of FY2011 through FY2014 to carry out these activities. The HHS Secretary is also required to award grants to state survey agencies that perform surveys of Medicare- or Medicaid-participating facilities to design and implement complaint investigation systems. It authorized $5 million for each of FY2011 through FY2014 to carry out these activities. To date, Congress has not provided discretionary funding for these activities through the annual appropriations process.

Reporting to Law Enforcement of Crimes Occurring in Federally Funded Long-Term Care Facilities

The Elder Justice Act amended SSA Title XI, Part A, by adding a new SSA Section 1150B, requiring the reporting of crimes occurring in LTC facilities that receive at least $10,000 in federal funds during the preceding year. The section requires owners, operators, employees, managers, agents, and contractors of nursing facilities (covered individuals) to report any reasonable suspicion of a crime (as defined by the law of the applicable political subdivision) against a resident or individual receiving care from the facility to the appropriate entities. Failure to report suspicion of a crime would result in a civil monetary penalty, and the Secretary may make a determination to exclude the covered individual from participation in any federal health care program. If an individual is classified as an "excluded individual," a LTC facility that employs that person is not eligible to receive federal funds under the SSA.

SSA Section 1150B also requires applicable nursing facilities to annually notify covered individuals that they are required to report any reasonable suspicion of a crime to the appropriate entities. It prohibits an LTC facility from retaliating against an employee for making a report. If retaliation occurs, the LTC facility may be subject to a civil monetary penalty, or the HHS Secretary may exclude the facility from participation in any federal health care program for a period of two years, or both. In addition, each LTC facility is required to post conspicuously, in an appropriate location, a sign specifying the rights of employees under this section.

In June 2011, CMS issued guidance to state survey agency directors describing the regulations related to the reporting of reasonable suspicion of a crime in applicable nursing facilities and provided responses to frequently asked questions.[37] A 2014 report by the HHS Office of Inspector General found that 61% of nursing facilities (9,487 facilities) had documentation to support meeting both reporting requirements (1) to

[37] 42 C.F.R. 483.12, Freedom from abuse, neglect, and exploitation (references SSA Section 1150B); CMS, *Reporting Reasonable Suspicion of a Crime in a Long-Term Care Facility (LTC): Section 1150B of the Social Security Act*, S&C: 11-30-NH, June 17, 2011 (revised January 20, 2012), see http://www.cms.gov/Medicare/Provider-Enrollment-and-Certification/SurveyCertificationGenInfo/Downloads/SCLetter11_30.pdf.

annually notify covered individuals of their obligation to report reasonable suspicion of crime, and (2) to clearly post a sign specifying the rights of employees to make such reports.[38]

National Nurse Aide Registry

Nurse aides generally work in nursing facilities under the direction of a nurse and provide the majority of direct care to residents, helping with activities of daily living (ADLs) (i.e., eating, bathing, dressing, toileting, transferring, and mobility). Nurse aides may also provide health- related and other housekeeping tasks, such as administering medications, checking vital signs, assisting with medical equipment, making a resident's bed, or cleaning a resident's room. However, the scope of work performed by nurse aides can vary according to state licensing requirements and the provider.

Federal regulations require each state and DC to establish and maintain a nurse aide registry of individuals who have completed training and are registered to work as nurse aides in that state.[39] State-based nurse aide registries also must include individuals who have been prohibited from employment as nurse aides in LTC facilities due to substantiated findings of abuse, neglect, or misappropriation of property. LTC providers use nurse aide registries to conduct background checks on potential employees, as LTC facilities are required to check their state nurse aide registry and other state-based registries that might contain information on a potential employee. Such databases can be an effective resource in identifying individuals with a history of abuse.

The HHS Secretary is required, in consultation with appropriate government agencies and private sector organizations, to conduct a study on establishing a national nurse aide registry.[40] No later than 18 months after the date of enactment, the Secretary is required to submit a report to the Elder Justice Coordinating Council and appropriate congressional committees containing the findings and recommendations of the study. The Elder Justice Act authorizes to be appropriated such sums as necessary to carry out these activities, with funding for the study not to exceed $500,000. To date, Congress has not provided discretionary funding for this activity through the annual appropriations process and no study has been completed or report submitted to these entities.

[38] HHS, Office of Inspector General, Nursing Facilities' Compliance with Federal Regulations for Reporting Allegations of Abuse of Neglect, OEI-07-00010, August 2014.

[39] 42 C.F.R. §483.156.

[40] ACA §6703(c).

FUNDING FOR ELDER JUSTICE ACTIVITIES

Although the authorizations of appropriations for most Elder Justice Act activities expired on September 30, 2014, Congress continues to appropriate some funding for authorized activities. However, to date, most programs and activities authorized under the Elder Justice Act either have not received funding since enactment or have not received funding at their previously authorized levels.[41] For FY2020, the Further Consolidated Appropriations Act, 2020 (P.L. 116-94), provided $14.0 million in discretionary appropriations under the Elder Rights Support Activities line item appropriation within ACL's Aging and Disability Services programs budget authority, of which $12.0 million is for the Elder Justice and Adult Protective Services program. ACL funding under the Elder Justice and Adult Protective Services program is also used for activities authorized under OAA Sections 411 and 751. Funding of $12.0 million for FY2020 was provided at the same FY2019 funding level (see *Table 1*).

Table 1. Funding for elder justice activities for FY2012-FY2020 ($ in millions)

	FY 2012[a]	FY 2013[b]	FY 2014	FY 2015	FY 2016	FY 2017	FY 2018	FY 2019	FY 2020
Elder Justice/ Adult Protective Services	$6.0	$2.0	—	$4.0	$8.0	$10.0	$12.0	$12.0	$12.0

Source: FY2012 to FY2020 Labor-Health and Human Services (HHS)-Education Appropriations Acts and accompanying report and explanatory statement language available at the CRS appropriations status table; various HHS, Administration on Aging (AOA) and Administration for Community Living (ACL) budget documents, including budget justifications (FY2013 and FY2021), and operating plans for FY2012 through FY2013.

[a] FY2012 appropriated amounts to the Public Health and Prevention Fund (PPHF) transferred to ACL; amounts are the final year funding amounts after rescissions, sequestration, and transfers.

[b] FY2013 appropriated amounts to the PPHF transferred to ACL; amounts are the final year funding amounts after rescissions, sequestration, and transfers.

Prior to Congress funding elder justice activities through the annual discretionary appropriations process, some activities received funds transferred from mandatory appropriations within the Prevention and Public Health Fund (PPHF). Under the ACA, Congress provided the PPHF with a permanent annual appropriation.[42] PPHF funds are to be transferred by the HHS Secretary for prevention, wellness, and public health activities and are available on October 1, the beginning of each new fiscal year.[43]

---

[41] The ACA reauthorized funding for numerous existing discretionary programs administered by HHS. The ACA also created many new discretionary programs, including those authorized under the Elder Justice Act, and provided for each an authorization of appropriations. While most of those existing discretionary programs continue to receive an annual discretionary appropriation, albeit at levels below the amounts authorized by the law, few of the new grant programs authorized under the ACA have received any discretionary funding. For more information, see CRS Report R41390, *Discretionary Spending Under the Affordable Care Act (ACA)*.

[42] ACA §4002; 42 U.S.C. §300u-11.

[43] CRS Report R44796, The ACA Prevention and Public Health Fund: In Brief.

For FY2012, the HHS Secretary transferred $6.0 million to ACL from the PPHF for new grants to states and tribes to test elder abuse prevention strategies (authorized under SSA Section 2042 and OAA Section 751). For FY2013, $2.0 million was transferred to ACL from the PPHF for elder justice activities, which funded development of the National Adult Maltreatment Report System (see the "National Adult Maltreatment Reporting System" section of this chapter). No PPHF funds were transferred to ACL for elder justice activities for FY2014 or subsequent fiscal years.

In FY2015, for the first time, Congress appropriated $4 million for Elder Justice/Adult Protective Services activities through the annual discretionary appropriations process. Another $8 million was appropriated for these activities in FY2016 and $10.0 million in FY2017. For each of fiscal years 2018 through 2020, Congress appropriated $12 million for elder justice activities. The following section describe selected elder justice programs, projects, and activities that have been funded.

Elder Abuse Prevention Intervention Demonstrations

In FY2013, ACL awarded five grants to states and tribal organizations for an evaluation of the state grantees under the Elder Abuse Prevention Interventions Program.[44] Projects included using forensic accountants to prevent elder financial exploitation, increasing medication adherence to prevent elder self-neglect, and developing screening tools to identify elder abuse. In addition to grants to states, three tribal organizations received grant funding for the development of a multidisciplinary team to address elder abuse in Indian Country, development and testing of culturally appropriate evidence-based screening tools, and culturally appropriate train-the-trainer modules to improve skills on addressing and intervening with elder abuse issues.[45]

Elder Justice Innovation Grants

In FY2016, ACL established the Elder Justice Innovation Grants program, which funded eight competitive grants to various entities (e.g., higher education institutions, nonprofit organizations, local government entities) to increase knowledge about effective

---

[44] Hafford, C., and K. Nguyen, *An Evaluation of AOA's Program to Prevent Elder Abuse: Final Report*, NORC at the University of Chicago, Prepared for Office of Disability, Aging and Long-Term Care Policy Office of the Assistant Secretary for Planning and Evaluation U.S. Department of Health and Human Services, August 1, 2016, https://aspe.hhs.gov/pdf-report/evaluation-aoas-program-prevent-elder-abuse-final-report.

[45] Administration for Community Living, *Protecting American's Seniors: The Elder Abuse Prevention Interventions Program*, at http://acl.gov/NewsRoom/Publications/docs/ Protecting_Americas_Seniors-%20The_%20Elder_%20Abuse_%20Prevention_%20 Interventions_%20Program.pdf.

ways to address the prevention or intervention of abuse, neglect, and exploitation of older adults.

Multi-Disciplinary Teams[46]

A number of collaborative community models exist to address elder abuse, including Multi-Disciplinary Teams (MDTs). One example of an MDT is the elder abuse forensic center model, which brings together a team of professionals in health care, social services, and criminal justice (e.g., law enforcement, attorneys, and victim advocates). In this context, forensic science involves elder abuse experts from different disciplines investigating and resolving cases of abuse or neglect. Developed out of a need to integrate services that have been historically fragmented and difficult to navigate, the MDT model can bridge different disciplines by employing a full-time staff, conducting regular face-to-face meetings to review cases of abuse and neglect, engaging in problem-solving, and facilitating recommended actions. Team members, who may work for either the organizing entity or a participating organization, may conduct joint visits and trainings, and engage in frequent and ongoing collaboration and consultation. Other MDT approaches address specific kinds of abuse (e.g., financial abuse) or serve as medical response teams that perform certain tasks (e.g., psychological or medical assessments).

Grants were awarded for forensic center innovation, to address abuse in Indian Country, to address abuse in guardianship, and to understand self-neglect.[47] In FY2017, ACL awarded another five grants to higher-education institutions and nonprofit organizations to help state APS programs assess the cognitive decision-making capacity of their clients and to develop curriculum and training on integrating elements of trauma-informed care. Other grant awards provided legal assistance and access to community-based services to older adults who have experienced maltreatment.

National Adult Maltreatment Reporting System (NAMRS)

The National Adult Maltreatment Reporting System (NAMRS) is the first data system of its kind to collect national data on abuse and exploitation of older adults and

---

[46] Cafaro Schneider, Diana, Laura Mosqueda, Erika Falk, et al., "Elder Abuse Forensic Centers," *Journal of Elder Abuse & Neglect*, vol. 22 (2010); Navarro, Adria E., K. H. Wilber, J. Yonashiro, et al., "Do We Really Need Another Meeting? Lessons From the Los Angeles County Elder Abuse Forensic Center," *The Gerontologist*, vol. 50 (2010); Twomey, Mary S., Glenda Jackson, Heidi Li, et al., "The Successes and Challenges of Seven Multidisciplinary Teams," *Journal of Elder Abuse & Neglect*, vol. 22 (2010); Consumer Financial Protection Bureau, *Report and Recommendations: Fighting Elder Financial Exploitation through Community Networks*, Office of Older Americans, August 2016; Consumer Financial Protection Bureau, *A Resource Guide for Elder Financial Exploitation Prevention and Response Networks*, Office of Older Americans, August 2016.

[47] For more information, see Administration for Community Living, https://acl.gov/programs /elder-justice/elder-justice-innovation-grants-0.

adults with disabilities, as reported to state APS agencies.[48] Although the system is still early in its development, the data collected is used to report national statistics on the policies and practices of state APS agencies. NAMRS gathers case-level data on client and perpetrator characteristics; types of maltreatment allegations and related findings; risk and protective factors associated with clients; services received or identified; and client outcomes, based upon the knowledge available to APS agencies. State participation in NAMRS is voluntary, and data are collected annually. The first year of NAMRS reporting was FY2016; as of FY2018, all states, the District of Columbia, and U.S. territories voluntarily participate.[49]

Development of the National Adult Maltreatment Report System[50]

In FY2013, $2.0 million was transferred to ACL from the PPHF for elder justice activities. Through an interagency agreement between ACL and HHS's Office of the Assistant Secretary for Planning and Evaluation (ASPE), funds were used to design, develop, and pilot the National Adult Maltreatment Reporting System (NAMRS). Nine states—Colorado, Georgia, Illinois, Maine, Massachusetts, Missouri, Montana, Pennsylvania, and Texas— participated in a pilot of the data system. The project team also had a multiagency steering committee with representatives from ACL, ASPE, DOJ, and the Centers for Disease Control and Prevention (CDC). In addition, the National Center on Elder Abuse and the National Adult Protective Services Association provided consulting expertise. States and stakeholders also provided input into project planning. Based on the pilot, further refinement to the reporting system was made after consideration of project team suggestions and team recommendations with respect to full implementation and participation of all states and U.S. territories in NAMRS.

Other Adult Protective Services Activities

In addition, starting in FY2015 funding has been awarded to state grantees to address innovations and improvements in the practice, services, data collection, and reporting

---

[48] For further information and annual NAMRS reports for FY2016 through FY2018, see Administration for Community Living, *National Adult Maltreatment Reporting System (NAMRS)*, http://www.aoa.acl.gov/AoA_Programs/Elder_Rights/NAMRS/index.aspx.

[49] G. Aurelien, G., M. Beatrice, J. Cannizzo, et al., *Adult Maltreatment Data Report 2018*. Administration for Community Living, U.S. Department of Health and Human Services, 2019.

[50] For further information and links to the two-part final report, see *Administration for Community Living, National Adult Maltreatment Reporting System (NAMRS) Background*, https://acl.gov/programs/elder-justice/national-adult- maltreatment-reporting-system-namrs-background.

under the State Grants to Enhance Adult Protective Services demonstration grant program.[51]

To further assist state APS programs, ACL has established the National Adult Protective Services Technical Assistance Resource Center (APS TARC), as well as Voluntary Consensus Guidelines for State APS Systems. These initiatives provide some assistance to states in developing efficient and effective state APS programs. In addition, training and assistance on NAMRS is provided to states through APS TARC.[52]

Issues for Congress

The ACA created several new discretionary programs, including those authorized under the Elder Justice Act, and provided for each an authorization of appropriations.[53] Most elder justice programs and activities have yet to receive funding through the annual congressional appropriations process, thereby limiting the Administration's response to implementation. In addition, the authorizations of appropriations for most Elder Justice Act provisions expired on September 30, 2014 (see *Table A-1* for information on specific Elder Justice Act authorizations of appropriations).

In considering the reauthorization of the Elder Justice Act, Congress faces a decision whether or not to extend the authorizations of appropriations associated with existing programs and activities. Some policymakers may consider new language to modify or repeal existing authorities, as well as to authorize new programs or activities. While Elder Justice Act legislation enacted as part of ACA primarily sought to address incidents of abuse in domestic settings, two reports published in 2019 by the HHS Office of Inspector General and GAO have focused attention on abuse in institutional settings such as nursing homes.[54] Congress may choose to focus greater attention on prevention and detection of abuse in such settings.

Congress may also consider the relationship between Elder Justice Act authorities and other similar or related authorities in other statutes. For example, the OAA establishes the LTC Ombudsman Program, administered by AoA within ACL. The Elder Justice Act authorizes grants under the Social Security Act to improve capacity and provide assistance to state LTC Ombudsman Programs, as well as provide training to

---

[51] For more information, see Administration for Community Living, *State Grants to Enhance Adult Protective Services*, https://acl.gov/programs/elder-justice/state-grants-enhance-adult-protective-services; for FY2019 grant funding, see award announcement at https://acl. gov/news-and-events/announcements/acl-elder-justice-grants-strengthen-legal-assistance-programs-aps.

[52] For more information, see Administration for Community Living, *Elder Justice & Adult Protective Services*, https://aoa.acl.gov/AoA_Programs/Elder_Rights/index.aspx.

[53] For further information, see CRS Report R41390, Discretionary Spending Under the Affordable Care Act (ACA).

[54] HHS, OIG, Incidents of Potential Abuse and Neglect at Skilled Nursing Facilities Were Not Always Reported and Investigated, June 2019, https://oig.hhs.gov /oas/reports/ region1/11600509.pdf; GAO, Nursing Homes: Improved Oversight Needed to Better Protect Residents from Abuse, June 2019, https://www.gao.gov/assets/700/699721.pdf.

ombudsmen. As authorized, these programs have different committees of jurisdiction responsible for program authorization and oversight.

In the context of these actions, policymakers may look to existing federal administrative or oversight activities for areas of continued legislative emphasis.

Federal Funding and Leadership

Congress first appropriated dedicated funding for elder justice activities in FY2015. This investment has been critical to the development of a national APS data collection system and the development of evidence-based research and programs. In addition, ACL has provided leadership in establishing federal resources for state APS systems, including the National APS Resource Center and voluntary consensus guidelines for state APS systems. However, the lack of full federal funding as authorized in the act has hampered the ability of the federal government to further its role in addressing the prevention, detection, and treatment of elder abuse. The OAA first called attention to the importance of federal leadership in the area of elder justice. Under the OAA, the AOA has primary responsibility for federal leadership in carrying out elder justice activities.[55] However, similar to EJA, funding under the OAA for such activities has been limited.

According to GAO, the Elder Justice Act "reaffirmed the importance of federal leadership of elder justice activities and provides a vehicle for establishing and implementing national priorities in this area."[56] Although the Elder Justice Coordinating Committee has appointed members and convened several times, an Advisory Board on Elder Abuse, Neglect, and Exploitation tasked to put forth a plan to develop the field of elder abuse has yet to be established. Further federal efforts to develop objectives, priorities, policy, and long-term planning on these issues may be limited by available funding.

Elder Abuse Data Collection

Federal efforts to collect data on elder abuse at the national level are complicated by variation in state statutory definitions of elder abuse, which makes it difficult to identify actions that constitute elder abuse, and by the absence of a uniform reporting system

---

55 42 U.S.C. 3011.

56 U.S. Government Accountability Office, *Stronger Federal Leadership Could Enhance National Response to Elder Abuse*, GAO-11-208, March 2, 2011, http://www.gao.gov /assets/320/ 316224.pdf. Reissued on March 22, 2011.

across states. A 2011 GAO report recommended that the HHS Secretary conduct a pilot study to collect, compile, and disseminate APS administrative data.[57]

To this end, ACL has used Elder Justice Act funding to design, develop, and implement the National Adult Maltreatment Reporting System (NAMRS). Title II of the Elder Abuse Prevention and Prosecution Act (EAPPA, P.L. 115-70) requires the U.S. Attorney General, in consultation with local, state, and federal entities, to establish best practices for elder abuse data collection and, in consultation with the HHS Secretary, to annually engage in certain interagency federal data collection efforts.[58] Policymakers may have a continued interest in these initiatives and in further funding efforts to continue these data collection activities.

Elder Abuse Prevention

According to ACL, "most communities do not have comprehensive elder abuse prevention efforts that engage a broad set of individuals and institutions that can play a role in combating abuse, such as health professionals, law enforcement and legal services agencies, social workers, clergy, and community organizations."[59] To implement the Elder Justice Act, the ACL funded several grants to states and tribal organizations that test interventions designed to prevent elder abuse, neglect, and exploitation. These multidisciplinary models draw on prevention strategies from other family violence prevention programs and can assist in developing the evidence base for more widespread dissemination. ACL has invested in an evaluation of such grants. Based on findings from research, such initiatives could be disseminated more broadly to other states and entities through federally funded websites such as the National Center for Elder Abuse, federal technical assistance, and further funding opportunities.

Concluding Observations

The Elder Justice Act represents one set of policies in the broader context of domestic social policy to address the complex issue of elder abuse. As a federal legislative response, the Elder Justice Act may best serve as a catalyst for further federal

---

[57] Ibid.

[58] DOJ, EAPPA Data Overview and Data Collection Recommendations for State and Local Law Enforcement, https://www.justice.gov/elderjustice/eappa.

[59] Administration for Community Living, *Protecting American's Seniors: The Elder Abuse Prevention Interventions Program*, at http://acl.gov/NewsRoom /Publications/docs/ Protecting_Americas_Seniors-%20The_%20Elder_%20Abuse_%20Prevention_%20Inter ventions_%20Program.pdf.

coordination and action that can focus greater public awareness and attention on the needs of a growing, and potentially vulnerable, aging population.

According to GAO, the Elder Justice Act "provides a vehicle for setting national priorities and establishing a comprehensive, multidisciplinary elder justice system in this country."[60] Such a response touches on a range of domestic policy programs and issues that are not specific to one congressional committee's jurisdiction or area of expertise. Furthermore, congressional oversight into federal administration, implementation, and related activities must rely on different committees of jurisdiction, as well as the experience of select committees such as the Senate Special Committee on Aging. According to subject matter experts, elder abuse is not an easy problem to address, as it is

> a complex cluster of distinct but related phenomena involving health, legal, social service, financial, public safety, aging, disability, protective services, and victim services, aging services, policy, research, education, and human rights issues. It therefore requires a coordinated multidisciplinary, multi-agency, and multi-system response.[61]

Achieving such a response will likely require congressional interest in overseeing the range of elder justice programs and activities that currently exist across federal agencies. In addition, further research may help policymakers address areas where service delivery is either fragmented, lacks sufficient resources, or both. According to stakeholders, there are numerous challenges in responding to elder abuse, including lack of coordination, data, and resources.[62] Addressing these challenges could help develop an informed strategic and coordinated federal response.

APPENDIX A. ELDER JUSTICE ACT: AUTHORIZATIONS OF APPROPRIATIONS

Table A-1 provides a section-by-section list of Elder Justice Act provisions with an authorization of appropriations.

---

[60] U.S. Government Accountability Office, *Stronger Federal Leadership Could Enhance National Response to Elder Abuse*, GAO-11-208, March 2, 2011, http://www.gao.gov/assets/320/ 316224.pdf; U.S. Government Accountability Office, *Survey of Adult Protective Services Program Administrators* (GAO-11-129SP, March 2011), an E-supplement to GAO-11-208, GAO-11-129SP, Mar 2, 2011, http://www.gao.gov/products/GAO-11-129SP.

[61] Connolly, Marie-Therese, B. Brandl, R. Breckman, The Elder Justice Roadmap: A Stakeholders Initiative to Respond to an Emerging Health, Justice, Financial and Social Crisis, 2014.

[62] Ibid.

Table A-1. Elder Justice Act: authorizations of appropriations

ACA Section	Statutory Authority	Provision	Authorization of Appropriations
6703(a)	SSA §2021	Elder Justice Coordinating Council	Such sums as necessary (no years specified), see also new SSA Section 2024 below
6703(a)	SSA §2022	Advisory Board on Elder Abuse, Neglect, and Exploitation	Such sums as necessary (no years specified), see also new SSA Section 2024 below
6703(a)	SSA §2024	Authorization of appropriations	$6.5 million for FY2011, and $7.0 million for each of FY2012 through FY2014
6703(a)	SSA §2031	Forensic centers and expertise	$4 million for FY2011, $6 million for FY2012, and $8 million for each of FY2013 and FY2014
6703(a)	SSA §2041(a)	Incentives for LTC staffing	For new SSA Section 2041: $20 million for FY2011, $17.5 million for FY2012, and $15 million for each of FY2013 and FY2014
6703(a)	SSA §2041(b)	Certified EHR technology grant program	See above authorization of appropriations for SSA Section 2041
6703(a)	SSA §2041(c)	Standards for transactions involving clinical data by LTC facilities	See above authorization of appropriations for SSA Section 2041
6703(a)	SSA §2042(a)	Adult protective service functions	$3 million for FY2011, and $4 million for each of FY2012 through FY2014
6703(a)	SSA §2042(b)	Grants to enhance provision of adult protective services	$100 million for each of FY2011 through FY2014
6703(a)	SSA §2042(c)	Adult protective services demonstration grants	$25 million for each of FY2011 through FY2014
6703(a)	SSA §2043(a)	Long-term care ombudsman program grants	$5 million for FY2011, $7.5 million for FY2012, and $10 million for each of FY2013 and FY2014
6703(a)	SSA §2043(b)	Ombudsman training programs	$10 million for each of FY2011 through FY2014
6703(b)	New authority	National Training Institute for Surveyors	$12 million for the period of FY2011 through FY2014
6703(b)	New authority	Grants to state survey agencies	$5 million for each of FY2011 through FY2014
6703(c)	New authority	National nurse aide registry study and report	Such sums as necessary (no years specified) to carry out these activities, with funding not to exceed $500,000

Source: Table prepared by the Congressional Research Service based on the text of the Patient Protection and Affordable Care Act (ACA; P.L. 111-148, as amended).

Notes: EHR = Electronic Health Records; LTC = Long-Term Care; SSA = Social Security Act.

APPENDIX B. ELDER JUSTICE RESOURCES

The resources below provide further information on elder justice issues.

- *National Center on Elder Abuse* (U.S. Administration on Aging) https://ncea.acl.gov/
  The National Center on Elder Abuse (NCEA) compiles and publishes resources for policymakers, consumers, researchers, and social service, justice, and health care workers on elder abuse and neglect. The website includes frequently asked questions and resources on topics such as financial exploitation, emotional abuse, the mistreatment of LGBT elders, and the abuse of people with dementia. Some of the resources are available in multiple languages.
- *State Resources* (National Center on Elder Abuse)
  https:// ncea.acl.gov/Resources/State.aspx
  A directory of state hotlines and agencies for reporting suspected elder abuse, neglect, or exploitation. If the situation is serious, threatening, or dangerous, constituents should call 911 or the local police for immediate help. This directory also lists state laws, agencies, and statistics related to elder abuse and neglect.
- *Elder Abuse* (Centers for Disease Control and Prevention)
  http://www.cdc.gov/violenceprevention/elderabuse/
  A collection of statistics, prevention strategies for practitioners, and the consumer "Fast Facts" sheet on "Preventing Elder Abuse."
- *Elder Abuse* (National Library of Medicine)
  https://medlineplus.gov/elderabuse.html
  A compilation of consumer resources and journal articles on elder abuse.
- *Elder Justice Initiative* (U.S. Department of Justice) http://www.justice.gov/elderjustice/
  A collection of elder justice resources for victims and families (including a "Find Help Near You" state and local directory for reporting elder abuse), prosecutors (including sample federal and state pleadings and elder justice statutes), and researchers (including curated selections of research articles and an Elder Abuse Prevention and Prosecution Act [EAPPA] data overview).
- Consumer Financial Protection Bureau (CFPB)
  http://www.consumerfinance.gov/
  A compilation of consumer tools, education resources, data, and other research to protect consumers in the financial marketplace, and includes information for older Americans and prevention of financial exploitation.
- *Key Issues: Elder Abuse* (U.S. Government Accountability Office) http://www.gao.gov/key_issues/elder_abuse/issue_summary
  A summary of types of elder abuse and diagrams of federal agency missions and responsibilities to combat elder financial exploitation. Click the "Key Reports" tab for GAO reports on elder justice issues.

- *Statute Compilations* (U.S. House of Representatives, Office of the Legislative Counsel)
  https://www.govinfo.gov/app /collection/comps/p
  The statutory text of the Elder Justice Act appears at Title VI, Subtitle H, Sections 6701 through 6703, of the Patient Protection and Affordable Care Act, which is listed under "P" on this web page.

In: Elder Justice
Editor: Vince D. Anderson

ISBN: 978-1-53619-447-0

Chapter 3

ELDER JUSTICE: HHS COULD DO MORE TO ENCOURAGE STATE REPORTING ON THE COSTS OF FINANCIAL EXPLOITATION*

United States Government Accountability Office

ABBREVIATIONS

ACL	Administration for Community Living
APS	Adult Protective Services
CFPB	Consumer Financial Protection Bureau
COVID-19	Coronavirus Disease 2019
DOJ	Department of Justice
FBI	Federal Bureau of Investigation FinCENFinancial Crimes Enforcement Network
FTC	Federal Trade Commission
HHS	Department of Health and Human Services
NAMRS	National Adult Maltreatment Reporting System
NIBRS	National Incident-Based Reporting System
SAR	Suspicious Activity Report
Sentinel	Consumer Sentinel Network
Treasury	Department of the Treasury

* This is an edited, reformatted and augmented version of the United States Government Accountability Office Report to the Special Committee on Aging, United States Senate, Publication No. GAO-21-90, dated December 2020.

Why GAO Did This Study

Elder financial exploitation—the fraudulent or illegal use of an older adult's funds or property—has far- reaching effects on victims and society. Understanding the scope of the problem has thus far been hindered by a lack of nationwide data. In 2013, HHS worked with states to create NAMRS, a voluntary system for collecting APS data on elder abuse, including financial exploitation. GAO was asked to study the extent to which NAMRS provides information on elder financial exploitation.

This chapter examines (1) the status of HHS's efforts to compile nationwide data through NAMRS on the extent of financial exploitation and the challenges involved, and (2) what is known about the costs of financial exploitation to victims and others. GAO analyzed NAMRS data from fiscal year 2016 through 2019 (the most recent available); reviewed relevant federal laws; and interviewed officials from HHS, other federal agencies, elder abuse prevention organizations, and researchers. GAO also reviewed APS documents and spoke with officials in eight states, selected based on their efforts to study, collect, and report cost data; and reviewed studies on financial exploitation.

What GAO Recommends

GAO recommends that HHS (1) work with state APS agencies to collect and submit cost data to NAMRS, and (2) develop a timeframe to share states' tools to help collect cost data. HHS did not agree with the first recommendation, but GAO maintains that it is warranted, as discussed in the report. HHS agreed with the second recommendation.

What GAO Found

Most state Adult Protective Services (APS) agencies have been providing data on reports of abuse to the Department of Health and Human Services (HHS), including data on financial exploitation, although some faced challenges collecting and submitting these data. Since states began providing data to HHS's National Adult Maltreatment Reporting System (NAMRS) in 2017, they have been voluntarily submitting more detailed data on financial exploitation and perpetrators each year (see figure). However, some APS officials GAO interviewed in selected states said collecting data is difficult, in part, because victims are reluctant to implicate others, especially family members or other caregivers. APS officials also said submitting data to NAMRS was challenging initially because their data systems often did not align with NAMRS, and caseworkers may not have entered data in the system correctly. HHS has provided technical assistance and grant funding to help states address some of these challenges and help provide a better picture of the prevalence of the various types of financial exploitation and its perpetrators nationwide.

Number of States That Provide Data on Financial Exploitation and Perpetrators to NAMRS

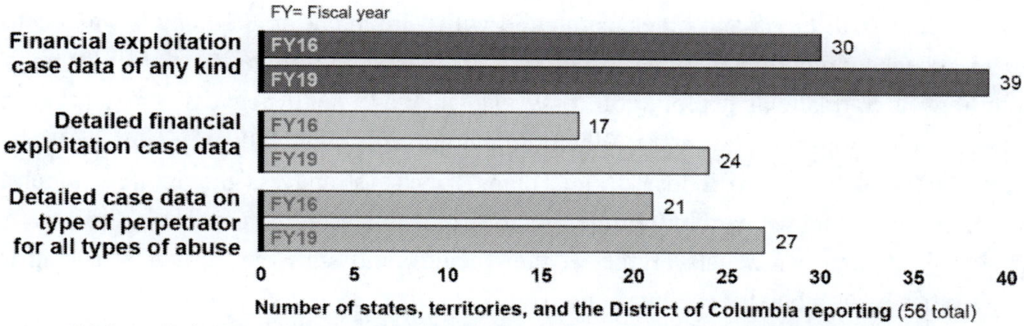

Source: GAO analysis of National Adult Maltreatment Reporting System (NAMRS) | GAO-21-90.

Studies estimate some of the costs of financial exploitation to be in the billions, but comprehensive data on total costs do not exist and NAMRS does not currently collect cost data from APS agencies. The Consumer Financial Protection Bureau found actual losses and attempts at elder financial exploitation reported by financial institutions nationwide were $1.7 billion in 2017. Also, studies published from 2016 to 2020 from three states—New York, Pennsylvania, and Virginia—estimated the costs of financial exploitation could be more than $1 billion in each state alone. HHS does not currently ask states to submit cost data from APS casefiles to NAMRS, though officials said they have begun to reevaluate NAMRS with state APS agencies and other interested parties, including researchers, and may consider asking states to submit cost data moving forward. Adding cost data to NAMRS could make a valuable contribution to the national picture of the cost of financial exploitation.

Recognizing the importance of these data, some APS officials GAO interviewed said their states have developed new data fields or other tools to help caseworkers collect and track cost data more systematically. HHS officials said they plan to share this information with other states to make them aware of practices that could help them collect cost data, but they have not established a timeframe for doing so.

December 18, 2020

The Honorable Susan M. Collins
Chairman
Special Committee on Aging, United States Senate

The Honorable Robert P. Casey, Jr.
Ranking Member
Special Committee on Aging, United States Senate

Elder financial exploitation—the fraudulent or illegal use of the resources of an elder for monetary or personal benefit—is a growing problem, especially as the U.S. population ages.[1] The U.S. Census Bureau projects that by 2030, more than 20 percent of U.S. residents will be 65 and older, compared with 13 percent in 2010 and 9.8 percent in 1970.[2] As the population of older Americans increases, the prevalence of elder abuse, including elder financial exploitation, may also increase, with negative impacts on the victims, their families, and society. When older adults are financially exploited by trusted others (such as family, friends, or guardians) or by strangers, the money is rarely recovered. Those losses can undermine the ability of older adults to support and care for themselves, which can negatively affect their health, and shift the burden of caring for them to family members or society in general.

With a goal of building the information base necessary to improve prevention, interventions, and services for exploited, abused, and neglected older adults, the Department of Health and Human Services (HHS) began to develop the National Adult Maltreatment Reporting System (NAMRS) in 2013 to collect data—including data on financial exploitation—from states' Adult Protective Services (APS) agencies. You asked us to study the extent to which NAMRS provides information on elder financial exploitation. This chapter examines (1) the status of HHS's efforts to compile nationwide data through NAMRS on the extent of elder financial exploitation and the challenges state APS agencies face providing this information, and (2) what is known about the costs of elder financial exploitation to victims and others.

To determine the status of HHS's efforts to compile nationwide data through NAMRS on the extent of elder financial exploitation and the perpetrators of this abuse, we analyzed NAMRS data from fiscal years 2016 through 2019, which included all the data collected and available at the time of our review.[3] We reviewed documents from HHS's Administration for Community Living (ACL) and ACL's APS Technical Assistance Resource Center to understand trends in and the quality of the NAMRS data,

---

[1] The Elder Justice Act of 2009 (Elder Justice Act) defines exploitation as "the fraudulent or otherwise illegal, unauthorized, or improper act or process of an individual, including a caregiver or fiduciary, that uses the resources of an elder for monetary or personal benefit, profit, or gain, or that results in depriving an elder of rightful access to, or use of, benefits, resources, belongings, or assets." See Pub. L. No. 111-488, tit. VI, subtit. H., sec. 6703, § 2011(8), 124 Stat. 119, 782-83 (2010) (codified at 42 U.S.C. § 1397j(8)). For purposes of this report, we use this definition of "elder financial exploitation," unless otherwise noted. Federal and state laws vary in their definitions of financial exploitation. The examples described in this report may not meet the Elder Justice Act's definition.

[2] See U.S. Department of Commerce, Economics and Statistics Administration, U.S. Census Bureau, *An Aging Nation: The Older Population in the United States, Current Population Reports* (Washington, D.C.: May 2014) and U.S. Census Bureau 2017 National Population Projections Tables.

[3] HHS's Administration for Community Living (ACL) has publicly released NAMRS summary data reports for fiscal years 2016 through 2019.

and ACL's plans for the database moving forward. In addition, we interviewed officials from the APS Technical Assistance Resource Center, which is responsible for maintaining the NAMRS database and providing NAMRS-related technical assistance to state APS agencies. Based on our review of documents and information provided by officials during these interviews, we determined that the NAMRS data on financial exploitation and perpetrator characteristics were sufficiently reliable for the purposes of describing the status and quality of the data at the time of our review. Additionally, we reviewed studies on financial exploitation and the perpetrators of this type of abuse.

To examine what is known about the costs associated with elder financial exploitation, we analyzed the methodology and findings of 15 studies that contained cost estimates. We identified these studies through discussions with representatives from elder abuse prevention organizations and federal agency officials, and through a literature search. We limited our literature search to studies published in the United States in the past 10 years (from January 2010 through January 2020) in academic peer- reviewed journals, trade or industry publications, and government reports.[4] Once we identified these 15 studies, two GAO economists reviewed the studies in detail, including their data sources, methods, limitations, and key findings. We found the cost estimates in nine of the 15 studies to be sufficiently reliable for our purposes of describing what is known about the costs of elder financial exploitation to victims and others. The remaining six studies were not included in our review.[5]

To address both of these research objectives, we interviewed ACL, Consumer Financial Protection Bureau (CFPB) and Department of Justice (DOJ) officials, as well as researchers and representatives with national elder abuse prevention organizations about any challenges in collecting information on and estimating the costs of elder financial exploitation.[6] We reviewed relevant federal laws, regulations, agency guidance, and also gathered documents from and interviewed APS agency officials in eight selected states: California, Florida, Maine, Nevada, New York, Oregon, Pennsylvania, and Virginia. We

---

[4] Our literature search identified about 300 publications using search terms that would capture information on costs of elder financial exploitation to victims and others, such as family members and taxpayers. Two analysts reviewed the summary information of these publications to identify studies that contained original cost estimates. While we limited our literature search to publications from January 2010 through January 2020, we included in our analysis several studies identified through discussions with organizations and agency officials that were published more recently.

[5] Two of the six studies that did not meet our inclusion criteria, but are commonly cited studies of the costs of elder financial exploitation, include a 2011 study from MetLife and a 2015 study from True Link. The MetLife study relied on newspaper articles as its main data source. (See MetLife Mature Market Institute, The MetLife Study of Elder Financial Abuse: Crimes of Occasion, Desperation, and Predation Against America's Elders (June 2011).) The True Link study's authors extrapolated total losses based on an assumption that all older adults had the same annual financial loss as those of their survey respondents. (See True Link Financial, The True Link Report on Elder Financial Abuse 2015 (January 2015).)

[6] We interviewed the following national elder abuse prevention organizations and national organizations with specific elder abuse prevention efforts: AARP Public Policy Institute, American Bar Association Commission on Law and Aging, National Adult Protective Services Association, National Association of Attorneys General, and National Center on Elder Abuse. We also interviewed researchers from the following institutions: New York State Office of Children & Family Services, Stanford Center on Longevity, University of Minnesota, University of Southern Maine, and Virginia Polytechnic Institute and State University.

selected these states based on various factors, including states that had conducted a study of the costs of financial exploitation in their state; reported varying levels of financial exploitation data to NAMRS in fiscal year 2018; have elder abuse multidisciplinary teams; and were recommended by national elder abuse prevention organizations and researchers because they collect cost data on financial exploitation. We also compared ACL efforts to collect data on elder financial exploitation, including cost data, to its information sharing mission and to HHS's goals for NAMRS.

In each of the eight selected states, we requested information to determine what data APS agencies collected on financial exploitation, the perpetrators of that abuse, and the tools or training they provided to caseworkers related to financial exploitation. We also interviewed state APS administrators and data managers about their agency's role in collecting data on the costs of financial exploitation and what challenges, if any, they face reporting these data to NAMRS.[7] In several of these states, we also spoke with representatives of elder abuse multidisciplinary teams (e.g., collaborative groups that bring together stakeholders from different sectors, including APS, law enforcement, legal services, guardians and conservators, financial services, etc., to build relationships and share knowledge to improve their community's response to elder abuse) and APS caseworkers who specialize in financial exploitation cases. Our interviews with officials in these states are not generalizable to all state APS agencies, but they provide illustrative examples about selected state APS agencies' experiences collecting financial exploitation data, the challenges state agencies may face reporting these data to NAMRS, and actions state APS agencies may be taking to collect and report data on financial exploitation. (See app. I for more information about the role of APS agencies in each of these selected states.)

We conducted this performance audit from October 2019 to December 2020 in accordance with generally accepted government auditing standards. Those standards require that we plan and perform the audit to obtain sufficient, appropriate evidence to provide a reasonable basis for our findings and conclusions based on our audit objectives. We believe that the evidence obtained provides a reasonable basis for our findings and conclusions based on our audit objectives.

BACKGROUND

Older adults are particularly vulnerable to financial exploitation for several reasons. For example, older adults are often targeted because they have acquired more wealth over

[7] We were unable to conduct interviews with officials from New York's APS agency because of impacts on government operations related to the Coronavirus Disease 2019 (COVID-19). Instead, New York APS officials provided written responses to our interview questions. All interviews with the seven remaining states were conducted via telephone.

a longer period of time compared to younger people. Also, research has shown that the likelihood of making poor financial decisions increases with age, including diminished capacity to manage money and financial assets in ways that meet one's needs.[8] Research has also found that the incidence of Alzheimer's disease and other dementias in older adults can undermine their judgment, and may result in financial exploitation going unnoticed by family or other caregivers until it is too late to recover financial losses.[9]

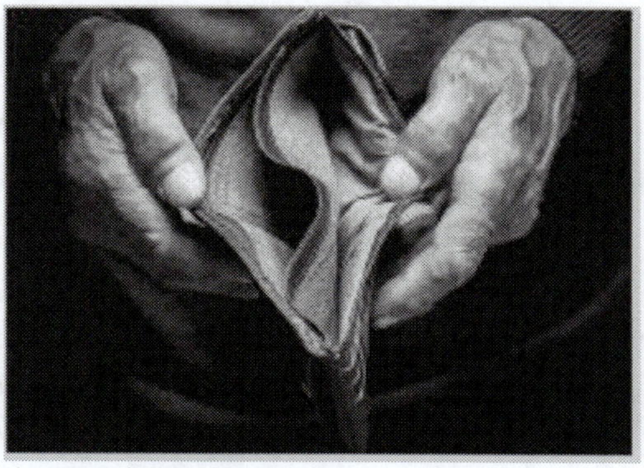

Source: perfectlab/stock.adobe.com. | GAO-21-90.

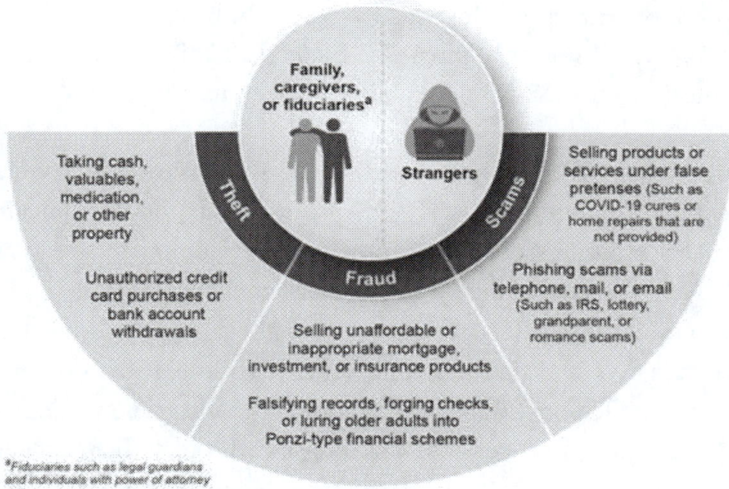

Source:GAO review of documents from federal agencies and elder abuse prevention organizations. | GAO-21-90.

Note: Federal and state law may differ in how they define what constitutes financial exploitation. There can be overlap between these categories, depending on the definition.

Figure 1. Examples of Perpetrators and Types of Elder Financial Exploitation.

---

[8] Sumit Agarwal et al., "The Age of Reason: Financial Decisions over the Life-Cycle with Implications for Regulation," *Brookings Papers on Economic Activity*, vol. 2 (2009), 51- 117.

[9] Liesi E. Hebert et al., "Alzheimer Disease in the US Population," *Archives of Neurology*, vol. 60 (August 2003), 1119-1122.

In addition, elder financial exploitation may take a variety of forms, ranging from a caregiver or family member stealing money or medications off a victim's dresser or charging items for their personal use to a victim's credit card, to a legal guardian withdrawing funds from the victim's bank account, to a scam that entices a victim to share bank information or wire money (see Figure 1). Each of these types of elder financial exploitation may require a different strategy to try to reduce the prevalence, as well as different skills and expertise to investigate and respond to a report of possible financial exploitation.

Role of Federal and State Agencies

Various federal, state, and local agencies are involved with identifying, investigating, and prosecuting incidents of elder abuse. Within HHS, the Administration for Community Living (ACL) works to protect older adults and those with disabilities from abuse by providing grants to state APS agencies to help them carry out their responsibilities and to various resource centers.[10] ACL also plays a role in generating and sharing knowledge relevant to protecting older adults, including by planning for the coordination and development of elder justice research, programs, studies, training, and other efforts nationwide.[11] For example, ACL funds the National Center on Elder Abuse, which disseminates information on elder abuse, neglect, and exploitation to professionals and the public.

ACL also funds the APS Technical Assistance Resource Center, which provides a variety of educational opportunities for APS professionals, and technical assistance to state and local APS programs on policy, practice, and administrative issues, including supporting state APS agencies as they prepare their annual NAMRS data submissions.

The Department of Justice (DOJ) helps to monitor and address elder abuse through its Elder Justice Initiative and through collaboration with HHS and other federal, state, and local partners.[12] In October 2020, DOJ announced that it had awarded $9.4 million in grant funding for direct victim services and research projects that enhance the field's

---

[10] HHS established ACL in 2012, merging the Administration on Aging, the Administration on Intellectual and Developmental Disabilities, and the Office on Disability. The Administration on Aging, a component of ACL, principally administers the Older Americans Act of 1965, as amended, which provides grants to states that they can allocate to state APS agencies.

[11] See Pub. L. No. 111-488, tit. VI, subtit. H., sec. 6703, 124 Stat. 119, 782-804 (2010) (codified at 42 U.S.C. §§ 1320b-25, 1395i-3a, and 1397j to 1397m-5). Specifically, the Elder Justice Act of 2009 provides for formula grants to enhance the provision of adult protective services and demonstration grants to conduct programs to detect and prevent elder abuse. See sec. 6703, § 2042(b)-(c) (codified at 42 U.S.C. § 1397m-1(b)-(c)).

[12] In 2019, we reported on the status of the Department of Justice's (DOJ) elder justice activities. See GAO, *Elder Justice: Goals and Outcome Measures Would Provide DOJ With Clear Direction and a Means to Assess Its Efforts*, GAO-19-365 (Washington, D.C.: June 7, 2019).

response to elder abuse and financial exploitation.[13] In addition, DOJ investigates and prosecutes financial crimes against older adults that violate federal laws, such as health care fraud and large-scale mail fraud. For the past 3 years, DOJ has conducted an "Elder Fraud Sweep" to bring enforcement actions in criminal and civil cases throughout the country. In March 2020, DOJ announced that its annual sweep had resulted in charges involving more than 400 defendants in elder fraud schemes with alleged losses totaling over $1 billion.[14]

In addition, ACL collects and disseminates data regarding elder abuse, neglect, and exploitation, in coordination with DOJ.[15] Under provisions of the Elder Justice Act of 2009, HHS, as the designated chair of the Elder Justice Coordinating Council, has delegated leadership to ACL for coordinating activities related to elder abuse, neglect, and exploitation across the federal government.[16] As of December 2020, 15 other federal agencies were members of the Council including DOJ (as a permanent member), CFPB, the Department of the Treasury (Treasury), and the Federal Trade Commission (FTC).[17] Through their participation in the Elder Justice Coordinating Council, these federal agencies are committed to identifying and proposing solutions to the problems surrounding elder abuse, neglect, and financial exploitation. In addition, agencies in the social services, criminal justice, and consumer protection systems in each state lead the state and local efforts to prevent, detect, and respond to elder financial exploitation.

Source: Du Visu/stock adobe.com. | GAO-21-90.

[13] U.S. Department of Justice, *Justice Department Awards over $9 Million to Combat Elder Fraud and Abuse* (Oct. 1, 2020).

[14] U.S. Department of Justice, Attorney General William P. Barr Announces the Results of the Department of Justice's 2020 Elder Fraud Sweep and New Nursing Home Initiative (Mar. 3, 2020).

[15] See sec. 6703, § 2042(a)(1)(B)-(C) (codified at 42 U.S.C. § 1397m-1(a)(1)(B)-(C)).

[16] See sec. 6703, § 2021 (codified at 42 U.S.C. § 1397k).

[17] The other Elder Justice Coordinating Council member agencies include the Corporation for National and Community Service, the Departments of Agriculture, the Federal Communications Commission, Homeland Security, Housing and Urban Development, Interior, Labor, Veterans Affairs, the Postal Inspection Service, the Securities and Exchange Commission, and the Social Security Administration.

State APS agencies provide social services that are administered at the state and local level, and APS caseworkers investigate and substantiate reports of suspected abuse, including reports of financial exploitation.

ACL prepared a report about the characteristics of state APS programs and policies in 2018.[18] According to ACL's report, some state APS agencies are administered by the state's aging agency, but in most states, APS is under the state's department of human services and, similar to the federal level, serves a broader population, including adults with disabilities who are age 18 or older.[19] APS investigates reports of abuse that occur in non-institutional community settings, such as in an individual's home, and in many states, APS also investigates reports of abuse in residential facilities, such as nursing homes or long-term care facilities, where many older adults live.[20] Following a report of abuse, APS can arrange for services to secure the person's safety and meet their basic needs. If a report of financial exploitation is substantiated, and the caseworker determines there is evidence of criminal activity, APS generally refers the case to law enforcement for further investigation.

Whether a financial exploitation case comes to the attention of law enforcement authorities through referral from APS or some other means, law enforcement agencies and district attorneys have broad discretion in deciding whether to pursue a case.

Federal Data Sources on Financial Exploitation

HHS and other federal agencies maintain different data sources that collect and report various financial exploitation data (see Table 1). For example, DOJ, in consultation with HHS, is required to collect statistical data related to elder abuse cases from federal law enforcement and other federal agencies as appropriate, and to publish the data on its website.[21] DOJ and the FTC are also each required to submit an annual report to Congress detailing the enforcement actions it has taken for cases involving financial schemes or scams that targeted or largely affected elders.[22]

---

[18] See WRMA, Inc., *Adult Protective Services Policy Final Report*, a report prepared at the request of the Department of Health and Human Services, Administration for Community Living (September 21, 2018).

[19] According to ACL's report, this is the case in 49 states. Depending on the state's social service structure, APS programs are either operated at the state level or by counties. See WRMA, Inc., *Review of Adult Protective Services Policy Final Report* (2018).

[20] According to ACL's report, in 14 states, APS does not investigate reports of abuse in residential facilities. In these states, there may also be a regulatory agency such as a Medicaid Fraud Control Unit or Long-Term Care Ombudsmen that is responsible for responding to reports of abuse or neglect in these settings. See WRMA, Inc., *Adult Protective Services Policy Final Report* (2018).

[21] his is required by the Elder Abuse Prevention and Prosecution Act. See Pub. L. No. 115-70, § 202(a), 131 Stat. 1208, 1211 (2017).

[22] See U.S. Department of Justice, *Attorney General's Annual Report to Congress on Department of Justice Activities to Combat Elder Fraud and Abuse* (Washington, D.C.: Oct. 18, 2020); and Federal Trade Commission, *Protecting Older Consumers 2019-2020 A Report of the Federal Trade Commission* (Washington, D.C.: Oct. 18, 2020) for the most recent annual reports to Congress from these agencies.

Table 1. Key sources of financial exploitation data maintained by federal agencies

Administering federal agency	Name of data source	Description of information collected
Department of Health and Human Services (HHS)	National Adult Maltreatment Reporting System (NAMRS)	Data on adult maltreatment from state Adult Protective Services (APS) programs.
Department of the Treasury (Treasury)	Financial Crimes Enforcement Network's (FinCEN) Bank Secrecy Act E-Filing System	Data on suspected elder financial exploitation submitted by financial institutions (referred to as Suspicious Activity Reports).
Federal Bureau of Investigation (FBI)	National Incident-Based Reporting System (NIBRS)	Data on crimes collected from state, local, and federal law enforcement agencies that participate in the system.
Federal Trade Commission (FTC)	Consumer Sentinel Network (Sentinel)	Information on consumer complaints from multiple sources such as state and local law enforcement.

Source: GAO analysis of HHS, FBI, FTC, and Treasury information. I GAO-21-90.

The Older Americans Act of 1965, as amended, does not require HHS to report data on elder abuse or exploitation, but does require HHS to establish federal guidelines and disseminate best practices for uniform data collection and reporting by states.[23] In our 2011 report on elder justice, we found that HHS had taken limited steps to implement this requirement.[24] Agency officials at the time expressed concern about the practicability of collecting the data given that there is no common state- level definition of elder abuse, and that the amount of funding being provided would not justify the burden on states if they were asked to report uniform data.

Nevertheless, partially in response to a recommendation we made in that 2011 report,[25] as well as calls from program officials, policymakers, and subject matter experts for more nationally aggregated data from state APS agencies, HHS began to work with state APS agencies in 2013 to develop a voluntary nationwide system to collect data on adult maltreatment from all 50 states, the District of Columbia, and five territories. This system became the National Adult Maltreatment Reporting System (NAMRS). According to HHS, an important goal of NAMRS is to collect consistent and accurate national data on investigations and services by APS programs in response to reports of abuse (referred to by NAMRS as adult maltreatment), including physical, sexual, and psychological abuse, financial exploitation, and neglect.

---

[23] See 42 U.S.C. § 3011(e)(2)(A)(iii) and (iv).

[24] GAO, *Elder Justice: Stronger Federal Leadership Could Enhance National Response to Elder Abuse*, GAO-11-208 (Washington, D.C.: Mar. 2, 2011).

[25] The conference report accompanying the legislation cited findings and recommendations from our 2012 and 2011 reports. See S. Rep. No. 115-9 (2017) (Conf. Rep.). See also GAO, *Elder Justice: National Strategy Needed to Effectively Combat Elder Financial Exploitation*, GAO-13-110 (Washington, D.C.: Nov. 15, 2012); and GAO-11-208.

States Have Increased Their Financial Exploitation Reporting to NAMRS Each Year and HHS Is Helping States Address Challenges

HHS released its first report of NAMRS data in 2018, which summarized state APS agency data from fiscal year 2016.[26] Since then, HHS has released three more NAMRS reports summarizing state APS agency data from fiscal years 2017 through 2019.[27] Each year, more states have been providing NAMRS with more data on financial exploitation and on the perpetrators of abuse based on APS casefiles. While APS data are an important source of information on the extent of financial exploitation nationwide and perpetrators of this abuse, gaps remain in states' reporting of these data. HHS, through its Administration for Community Living (ACL), has provided technical assistance and grant funding to help states address challenges submitting data to NAMRS. Other studies have produced nationwide estimates of certain types of fraud or theft based on data from financial institutions and surveys of older adults.

State APS Programs Are Providing More Data Each Year to NAMRS, but Gaps Remain

ACL asks APS agencies in all 50 states, the District of Columbia, and five territories to voluntarily provide information to NAMRS about their policies, practices, and data on reports of abuse.[28] APS agencies may submit one of two levels of data on reports of abuse: either summary data (referred to by NAMRS as "key indicator component" data) or, if possible, more detailed case-level data (referred to by NAMRS as "case component" data), which includes data on client characteristics, services provided, and perpetrator characteristics for specific reports of abuse (see Table 2).[29] Beyond the

---

[26] See Administration for Community Living, *NAMRS FFY 2016 Background Report* (Washington, D.C.: May 5, 2018) and related materials which summarize fiscal year 2016 NAMRS data received from state APS agencies on the ACL website accessed on July 28, 2020 at https://namrs.acl.gov/Learning-Resources/Adult-Maltreatment-Reports.aspx.

[27] See Administration for Community Living, *Adult Maltreatment Report 2019* (Washington, D.C.: 2020) and *Adult Maltreatment Report 2018* (Washington, D.C.: 2019) summarizes fiscal year 2019 and 2018 NAMRS data, respectively. Fiscal year 2017 NAMRS data can be found in several reports on the ACL website at https://namrs.acl.gov/Learning- Resources/Adult-Maltreatment-Reports.aspx.

[28] According to ACL's report, in 49 states, APS agencies are responsible for serving adults with disabilities between the ages of 18-59 or 18-64, in addition to older adults. See WRMA, Inc., *Adult Protective Services Policy Final Report* (2018). Therefore, NAMRS data include reports of abuse affecting individuals eligible for APS services—both older adults and younger adults with disabilities. As a result, throughout this report, when discussing NAMRS data and other services provided by APS, we generally refer to financial exploitation rather than elder financial exploitation. Also, hereinafter in this report, we refer to the 56 APS reporting entities, including states, the District of Columbia, and the U.S. territories as "states."

[29] State APS agencies may choose one or the other reporting level each year, but do not submit both. The annual reporting period for NAMRS data is the federal fiscal year (October 1 through September 30).

summary reports issued to date, according to HHS officials, NAMRS is expected to begin releasing more detailed case-level data publicly in fall 2021.

Some states only submit data when reports of abuse have been confirmed or "substantiated"; other states also submit at least some data on unsubstantiated cases. In the first year's submission of data to NAMRS, for fiscal year 2016, NAMRS reports show that 46 states provided either summary or detailed case-level data on their reports of abuse.[30] For fiscal year 2019, the most recent year of data available at the time of our review, NAMRS reports show that 51 states provided either summary or detailed case-level data on reports of abuse.

Table 2. Information ACL requests for NAMRS on the prevalence of financial exploitation and perpetrators of abuse at the summary and detailed case-level

Summary ("Key Indicator Component") data: Aggregated data on key statistics of investigations and victims, provided by agencies that are unable to provide detailed case-level data. These summary data include statistics on 20 data elements describing all reports of abuse received and investigated in a fiscal year, in aggregate.
Prevalence: ACL asks states to provide NAMRS with summary data on their investigations of reports of abuse by type of abuse, including financial exploitation.
Perpetrators: ACL asks states to provide NAMRS with summary data on perpetrator characteristics when their investigations of reports of abuse are substantiated. For example, ACL asks for summary data such as whether perpetrators had a kinship relationship or caregiving association with the victim. (Note: These summary data cannot be analyzed by type of abuse.)
Detailed case-level ("Case Component") data: Data on client characteristics, services, and perpetrator characteristics, provided by state agencies that are able to track and report these data for specific reports of abuse. These detailed case-level data include information on 54 data elements describing all reports of abuse received and investigated in a fiscal year, for each case individually.
Prevalence: ACL asks states to provide NAMRS with detailed case-level data on their investigations of reports of abuse by type of abuse, including financial exploitation, and whether the report was substantiated.
Perpetrators: ACL asks states to provide NAMRS with detailed case-level data on the victim-perpetrator relationship when reports of abuse are substantiated, including reports of financial exploitation. For example, ACL asks for information such as whether there is cohabitation, what the kinship relationship is, what the caregiving relationship is, and whether there is a substitute decision-maker relationship, such as with a health care or financial proxy, a guardian or conservator, or representative payee. (Note: These case-level data can be analyzed by type of abuse.)

Source: GAO analysis of information that the Administration for Community Living (ACL) requests for the National Adult Maltreatment Reporting System (NAMRS). | GAO-21-90.

In their fiscal year 2019 submissions, most states were providing financial exploitation data to NAMRS at least at the summary level, and the number of states submitting data on perpetrator types at the case-level had also increased. As more states contribute data to NAMRS, ACL officials said there will be enough detailed case-level

[30] In addition, all 56 states provided information on their policies and practices (referred to by NAMRS as "agency component" data) since their first submission of fiscal year 2016 data.

data from states to be able to sort and regroup the data in various ways. For example, researchers would be able to tabulate the types of abuse by the types of perpetrators, and provide estimates of the percent of financial exploitation cases that involve adults over age 65 and that are perpetrated by family members, legal guardians, or strangers.

States have been providing more data to NAMRS, but in their fiscal year 2019 submissions, over one-half of the states were still not providing detailed case-level data elements on financial exploitation, or detailed case-level data on the relationship between victims and the perpetrators (see Figure 2). According to an ACL gap analysis of NAMRS data, among the states that submitted detailed case-level data on financial exploitation cases in fiscal year 2018, most provided less than one-half of the 29 requested data elements examined by the gap analysis, and eight of 31 states provided no financial exploitation data.[31] With respect to perpetrator data, ACL officials acknowledged that, even at the summary data level, these data are the least complete type of data and a known gap.

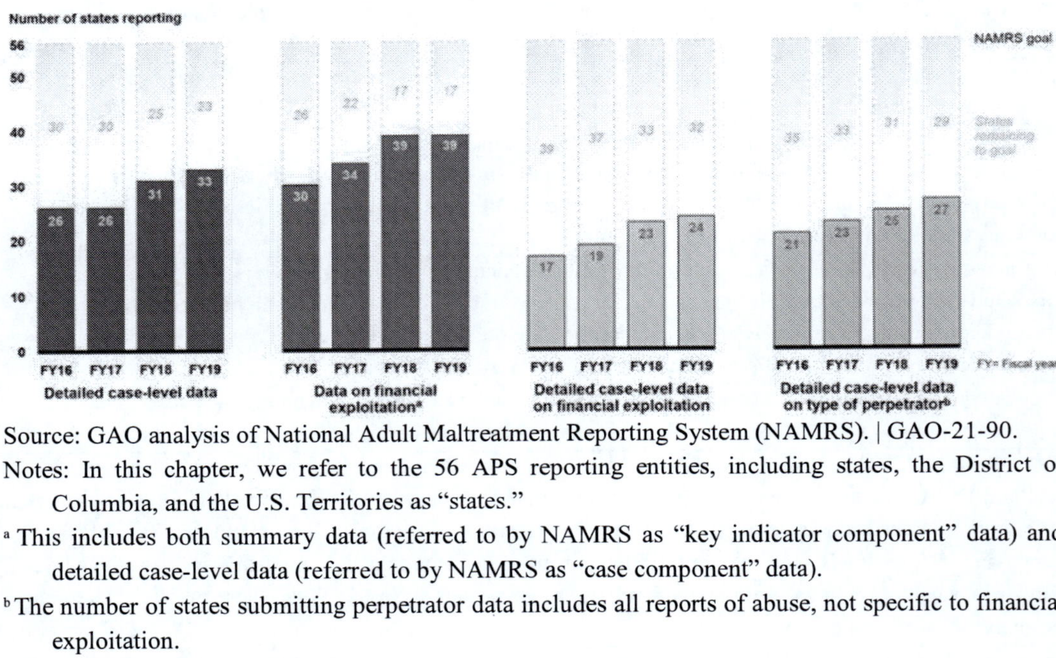

Source: GAO analysis of National Adult Maltreatment Reporting System (NAMRS). | GAO-21-90.

Notes: In this chapter, we refer to the 56 APS reporting entities, including states, the District of Columbia, and the U.S. Territories as "states."

[a] This includes both summary data (referred to by NAMRS as "key indicator component" data) and detailed case-level data (referred to by NAMRS as "case component" data).

[b] The number of states submitting perpetrator data includes all reports of abuse, not specific to financial exploitation.

Figure 2. Number of States That Provide Data on Reports of Abuse to the National Adult Maltreatment Reporting System (NAMRS).

[31] ACL officials said that the APS Technical Assistance Resource Center conducted this overall NAMRS gap analysis to understand what additional data elements are needed from states to improve data reliability, and to assess the overall status of states' reporting to inform what further technical assistance will be needed. According to that gap analysis, for fiscal year 2018, most of the 29 requested data elements were provided by less than one-half of the 56 states. The challenges states face in collecting and reporting these data are discussed later in the report.

ACL officials also said that many states were initially unsure if they would be able to provide certain data on perpetrators because the data may not be captured in the state-level data systems, and some states may have policy or legal concerns about recording perpetrator information before affording the perpetrator due process. Also, state APS programs place their primary focus on the victims, not the perpetrators. Nevertheless, ACL officials said that the agency has provided technical assistance to states that have requested it to increase the amount of perpetrator data they provide, and they believe that perpetrator data will likely become more complete over time, to the extent that more states continue to provide more data to NAMRS each year. (See text box for more information on common types of perpetrators and various intervention strategies.)

Types of Financial Exploitation Perpetrators and Intervention Strategies

Trusted others. Perpetrators can include an array of people known to or trusted by the older adult, such as family members and paid home care workers, as well as those with fiduciary responsibilities, such as financial advisors.[a] When the perpetrator is a family member, researchers have suggested that the intervention approach needs to include the family member, not just the victim, so that the family can stay intact, if possible.[b]

Strangers. Perpetrators can also include strangers who use various methods, such as mail, telephone calls, or email to deceive a victim by misrepresenting facts about promised goods, services, or other benefits. This type of activity is usually referred to as a scam or fraud.[c] In these cases, it has been suggested by researchers that one of the best interventions is to keep older adults from becoming socially isolated. For example, they noted that older adults who are lonely and desire companionship can be more susceptible to strangers perpetrating various scams and frauds.[d]

Legal guardians and other proxies. Perpetrators can also include substitute decision-makers, such as legal guardians, conservators, and representative payees, as well as health and financial proxies. According to a report from the American Bar Association (ABA), states bear responsibility for judicial appointment, administrative cost, and guardianship monitoring, yet lack the resources to do so adequately. The ABA adopted a resolution in August 2020 recommending that Congress create an adult Guardianship Court Improvement Program to help support efforts to improve state guardianship systems for adults.[e]

Source: GAO review of studies and information from the National Adult Protective Services Association, and the American Bar Association. I GAO-21-90.

[a] National Adult Protective Services Association, Exploitation Resources, accessed November 3, 2020, https://www.napsa-now.org/get-informed/exploitation-resources/.

[b] Shelly L. Jackson and Thomas L. Hafemeister, Financial Abuse of Elderly People vs. Other Forms of Elder Abuse: Assessing Their Dynamics, Risk Factors, and Society's Response, (August 2010). This unpublished paper is available on the Department of Justice website, accessed on Sept. 1, 2020, at https://www.ncjrs.gov/pdffiles1/nij/grants/233613.pdf.

[c] Exploitation is commonly used to refer to theft that occurs over a longer period of time, often by someone known to the victim. See Michaela Beals, Marguerite DeLiema, and Martha Deevy, Framework for a Taxonomy of Fraud, (July 2015).

[d] Jackson and Hafemeister, Financial Abuse of Elderly People vs. Other Forms of Elder Abuse (August 2010) and Marguerite DeLiema, "Elder Fraud and Financial Exploitation: Application of Routine Activity Theory," Gerontologist, vol. 58, no. 4, (2018), 706-718.

[e] American Bar Association, Report to the House of Delegates: Resolution. Approved August 2020. Accessed on Sept. 1, 2020, at https://www.americanbar.org/news/ reporter_resources/annual-meeting-2020/house-of-delegates-resolutions/ 105/.

ACL officials told us that one of their goals is to have all states report detailed case-level data to NAMRS, and that the APS Technical Assistance Resource Center continues to work with states towards this goal. According to ACL's 2019 NAMRS annual report, having more data is important for avoiding inaccurate conclusions that could be drawn from less complete data, and will result in more consistent and useful NAMRS data for observing trends over time.[32] But officials said that even without all of the states providing detailed case-level data, NAMRS will still be a useful source of national data to inform and prevent elder abuse by enabling analysis of abuse investigations nationwide. Therefore, ACL officials said that they plan to publicly release NAMRS data after collecting 5 years of data—currently scheduled for fall 2021.

Some State APS Agencies Faced Initial Challenges Submitting Data to NAMRS

APS agency officials we spoke with in some selected states noted that they initially faced several challenges adjusting their data collection and reporting processes to make this submission of data to NAMRS possible (see Figure 3). ACL provided technical assistance and funding through grants to help address the various difficulties states faced.

Source: GAO analysis of National Adult Maltreatment Reporting System (NAMRS) documentation and interviews with Adult Protective Service (APS) agency officials. | GAO-21-90.

Figure 3. Typical Process for State APS Agencies Submitting Financial Exploitation Data to NAMRS.

Difficulties Aligning State Data Elements

While acknowledging the benefits of participating in NAMRS, officials in four of the selected states said that the initial process of aligning the existing APS data elements to the NAMRS data elements (referred to as "mapping") was time consuming. Further, officials in Nevada and Pennsylvania said that it was expensive to modify their state data systems to add additional data elements requested by NAMRS. Pennsylvania officials

[32] See Administration for Community Living, *Adult Maltreatment Report 2019* (2020).

said that adding additional data elements means additional work for caseworkers, who may already have heavy caseloads. However, officials we interviewed in these and other states that had completed this mapping process said that after the initial mapping effort, there were fewer challenges in subsequent years. Maine APS officials added that there would likely only be new challenges if NAMRS changed a data element to be collected. ACL officials also noted that mapping was a one-time event supported by thousands of hours of ACL technical assistance, and that the mapping will remain valid unless they adopt changes to the data elements.

The absence of a single statewide data system in some states can also make it more difficult for APS agencies to align data elements statewide to provide detailed case-level data to NAMRS. For example, state APS officials in California said that having 58 counties, each with a separate data system, created challenges in providing statewide data, especially with respect to providing detailed case-level data. In contrast, Oregon officials said that they had recently moved to a new statewide data system and that this had enabled them to provide detailed case-level data. In Virginia, officials said they also had recently moved to a new statewide data system and expected that this will facilitate collecting and reporting detailed case-level data to NAMRS.

Difficulties Converting State Data into a Specific Format

Even after the state data elements are aligned with NAMRS, the detailed case-level data must be converted into the XML file format before it can be submitted to NAMRS. According to ACL officials, the agency requests NAMRS data in this format because it is a data format that allows a significant amount of information about the data to be included, allows for data validation, and was the most cost-efficient at the time NAMRS was developed. State officials in some states said that reformatting the data to XML required technical expertise or added expenses to buy special software or hire a contractor. Officials in Oregon said they were able to complete the coding of this data conversion themselves but that it was difficult and time consuming to do so. Nevada officials said they had to contract with a vendor to convert their state data into the XML format. In Florida, APS officials said that they had not yet converted their data to this format because they do not have access to the funding that would be required to go through a vendor or purchase conversion software. As a result, they said that while they collect the requested data elements, they are unable to provide these data to NAMRS.

Difficulties with Caseworkers' Data Entry

APS agency officials we spoke with in several states said they also face data entry challenges that may affect the collection of financial exploitation-related case data. State APS officials in several states said that data gaps are caused by errors when APS caseworkers initially enter data into the system. These initial errors can include entering data into narrative fields instead of data fields, or not entering data at all. Officials in three states noted that this may be due, in part, to caseworkers often being required to perform multiple jobs and work quickly. To help address these issues, state APS officials said that they provide training to caseworkers about good data collection practices.

ACL Efforts to Help Address These Challenges

ACL officials and the APS Technical Assistance Resource Center staff are working with states to improve their NAMRS data submissions by providing technical assistance and funding through APS enhancement grants.

Technical assistance. ACL contracts with the APS Technical Assistance Resource Center to provide a variety of technical assistance that may include helping states align their data elements with the NAMRS system data elements, providing training for state staff on reporting data to NAMRS, and answering questions. APS agency officials we interviewed in most of the selected states said this technical assistance helped them report data to NAMRS.

APS enhancement grants. ACL provided enhancement grant funding to state APS agencies during fiscal years 2015, 2016, 2018, and 2019 that could be used by states to improve their data systems and align their data with NAMRS, among other things.[33] State APS agency officials we spoke with told us that they have used funding from these grants in various ways. For example:

- Virginia officials said they used a grant to move to a single statewide data system, and they plan to use another grant to transition to reporting detailed case-level data to NAMRS rather than summary data.
- Nevada officials used a grant to modify their existing data system so that they could incorporate NAMRS data elements and provide detailed case-level data. These officials said the funding also supported training caseworkers for who will be using the new system.
- Pennsylvania officials said they used a grant to help purchase XML conversion software that enabled them to convert their state data to the NAMRS required data format.

APS Data Provide Important Information on Financial Exploitation but Are Not Comprehensive

APS casefiles are an important source of data on financial exploitation, but do not provide a comprehensive picture of all the financial exploitation that may be occurring.

[33] ACL's grant announcement in fiscal year 2019 specifically invited applicants seeking to achieve improvements in the state's ability to document and report APS case, client, and perpetrator characteristics and services in a manner that is consistent with NAMRS.

APS casefiles contain specific information about the nature of the abuse and the perpetrator, information that may not exist anywhere else, according to national elder abuse prevention organization officials. At the same time, not all incidents of financial exploitation are reported to APS, for reasons described below.

Some incidents of financial exploitation are reported directly to law enforcement or other entities. For example, in some states, allegations of exploitation that occur in residential facilities are reported to other state- level entities, such as Medicaid Fraud Control Units, or Long-Term Care Ombudsmen,[34] and some state APS programs do not respond or investigate reports of abuse in these settings.[35] Similarly, elder financial exploitation identified by financial institutions is often reported to Treasury's Financial Crimes Enforcement Network (FinCEN) through Suspicious Activity Reports (SAR) filed by financial institutions.[36] According to a recent Consumer Financial Protection Bureau (CFPB) study, suspicious activity is rarely reported to APS, law enforcement, or other authorities.[37] Also, given that state definitions of financial exploitation vary, incidents reported to APS in some states may not be reported in others.[38] For example, some states—such as Nevada—have a definition of exploitation that includes acts taken by trusted others, guardians, or those holding a power of attorney, while other states—such as New York and Virginia—have definitions that would also include acts taken by strangers.[39] Also, as noted earlier, some states limit APS investigations to cases involving adults age 60 or 65 and older, while other states serve adults with disabilities who are 18

---

[34] Medicaid Fraud Control Units can investigate and prosecute Medicaid provider fraud, as well as patient abuse or neglect in health care and nursing home facilities. As of September 2020, there were 53 of these units, the majority of which were located in the state attorney general's office. HHS certifies these units annually. Similarly, Long-Term Care Ombudsmen programs can address complaints about abuse of nursing home residents. These programs operate in every state and are typically located in a state's unit on aging.

[35] Most state APS programs investigate allegations of abuse in these settings under some circumstances, but in 14 states, APS does not investigate any allegations of abuse, neglect, or exploitation in facilities. See WRMA, Inc., *Adult Protective Services Policy Final Report* (2018).

[36] Financial institutions include a wide range of filers that include banks, credit unions, casinos, money transmitters, and insurance companies, among others.

[37] See Consumer Financial Protection Bureau, Office of Financial Protection for Older Americans, *Suspicious Activity Reports on Elder Financial Exploitation: Issues and Trends* (Washington, D.C.: February 2019).

[38] The way states define financial exploitation could also affect the way they report data to NAMRS. For example, one Nevada APS official we interviewed said their state includes financial exploitation under their definition of exploitation, which is treated as a separate data category in NAMRS. See Nev. Rev. Stat. § 200.5092(3) (2020). This official said that their state APS agency provides its financial exploitation data to NAMRS under the more general "exploitation" category. Other states, such as Maine, have a definition for both exploitation and financial exploitation. See Me. Stat. tit. 22, § 3472(9) & (9-A) (2019). For additional information about variation in state APS programs and reporting requirements, see WRMA, Inc., *Adult Protective Services Policy Final Report* (2018) and National Center on Elder Abuse and National Adult Protective Services Association, *Mandated Reporting of Abuse of Older Adults and Adults with Disabilities*, a report prepared at the request of the Department of Health and Human Services, Administration for Community Living, October 2020.

[39] Compare Nev. Rev. Stat. § 200.5092(3) (2020) (defining exploitation to refer to "any act taken by a person who has the trust and confidence of an older person or a vulnerable person or any use of the power of attorney or guardianship of an older person or a vulnerable person . . . "), with N.Y. Soc. Serv. Law § 473(6)(g) (McKinney 2020) (defining financial exploitation to mean the "improper use of an adult's funds, property, or resource by another individual . . . ") and Va. Stat. § 63.2-1606(C) (West 2020) (defining financial exploitation to mean, among other things, the illegal or fraudulent use of the assets of an older adult "for another's profit, benefit, or advantage, including a caregiver or person serving in a fiduciary capacity . . . ").

or older in addition to older adults. According to ACL officials, these and other variations among state APS policy and programs can have implications for the consistency of data submitted to NAMRS.

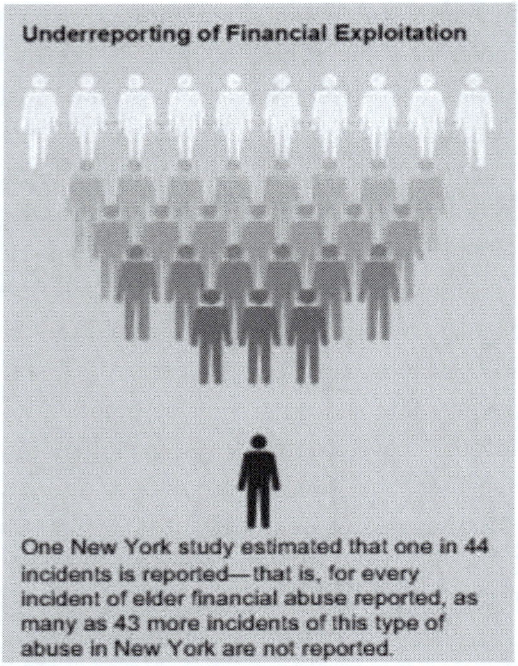

Source: GAO analysis of Lifespan of Greater Rochester, Inc.,Weil Cornell Medical Center of Cornell University, and New York City Department for the Aging, *Under the Reader: New York State Elder Abuse Prevalence Study* (2011). | GAO-21-90.

Also, research has shown that incidents of financial exploitation that could or should be reported to APS agencies are not always reported. In 2010, researchers estimated that elder abuse could directly affect at least 10 percent (roughly 5 million) of older Americans each year.[40] But APS officials in some of the eight states we contacted said that many older Americans, in particular, are reluctant to report abuse or exploitation for various reasons, such as feelings of embarrassment, or an unwillingness to implicate a family member or a trusted caretaker. One study estimated that for elder financial exploitation in New York specifically, just one in 44 incidents of this type of abuse is reported to APS.[41]

---

[40] Elder Justice Coordinating Council, U.S. Dept. of Health and Human Services, Report of the Secretary Detailing the Activities of the Elder Justice Coordinating Council for 2012– 2014, (June 2015).

[41] See Lifespan of Greater Rochester, Inc., Weill Cornell Medical Center of Cornell University, and New York City Department for the Aging, Under the Radar: New York State Elder Abuse Prevalence Study (2011). This study found that in New York only one in 44 incidents of elder financial abuse was reported, and only one in 24 incidents of elder abuse in general was reported. Some of the financial exploitation cost estimate studies we reviewed used underreporting factors for elder abuse more generally (such as one in 10 or one in 25), rather than a factor specific to financial exploitation.

Coronavirus Disease 2019 (COVID-19) Related Scams Targeting the Elderly

Examples identified by APS officials in selected states:

- Offering to buy groceries for seniors and then vanishing with the money.
- Asking potential recipients of CARES Act stimulus payments to provide personal information in order to receive their checks.
- Obtaining credit card information for personal protective equipment and not delivering it and/or stealing the credit card information.
- Charging for COVID-19 tests, protective equipment, or purported cures that were not delivered.

Source: GAO interviews with state Adult Protective Service (APS) officials in selected states. | GAO-21-90.

In addition, even when incidents of financial exploitation are reported to APS, the claims can be difficult to investigate and confirm, which can result in fewer of these incidents being substantiated and reported to NAMRS. State APS agency officials we interviewed said that lack of expertise or access to financial records can pose difficulties for caseworkers trying to investigate these cases,[42] and that victims of suspected elder financial exploitation often are not cooperative with these investigations, for various reasons (see text box).[43] Another challenge for some states, which can also affect the data that they collect and provide to NAMRS, is their states' standards of evidence for confirming abuse cases, according to officials with the National Association of Adult Protective Services Agencies. According to association officials, a survey they conducted in 2017 found that 34 states require a "preponderance of the evidence," but some states had higher standards, such as "clear and convincing" evidence. As a result, according to association officials, some states may report higher numbers of incidents to APS. Also, new types of scams are emerging constantly. For example, several new COVID-19-related scams were identified by APS workers during the first few months of the pandemic.

To help address challenges related to investigating and confirming reports of financial exploitation, some states have established Multidisciplinary Teams made up of various stakeholders, such as APS staff, law enforcement, and representatives of financial institutions, or court liaisons. These teams come together to discuss complex cases, including those involving financial exploitation, to improve investigations and outcomes. According to representatives of the Multidisciplinary Teams that we interviewed, successful collaboration can increase the number of incidents that APS is able to

---

[42] In our 2012 report, we also found that state agencies involved in combating elder financial exploitation experienced challenges collaborating and had difficulty accessing data and information, which hindered the response to elder financial exploitation. See GAO-13-110.

[43] The eight states we selected for our review are: California, Florida, Maine, Nevada, New York, Oregon, Pennsylvania, and Virginia.

substantiate and report to NAMRS, ultimately improving the completeness of the NAMRS data.

Examples of Challenges Cited by Caseworkers Investigating Financial Exploitation Cases

APS officials and caseworkers we interviewed across the eight selected states described the following challenges when trying to investigate financial exploitation cases:

Lack of expertise. Caseworkers often face challenges obtaining and interpreting financial documents, and may not have access to forensic accountants, who might be able to determine how money has been lost and how it can be recovered. Some financial exploitation cases can be extremely complicated because of multiple accounts, asset transfers, complex annuities, and more. Officials said that forensic accountants can be particularly useful in complex cases for clients with a large number of investments and assets, but these experts are often not available.

Lack of access. Caseworkers said they often have difficulty acquiring financial records from banks that could help verify the costs of financial exploitation. For example, officials in Nevada said that it can be particularly challenging for caseworkers to get financial records from out-of-state banks, as well as from the Social Security Administration, and that it can be difficult for victims to make record requests themselves if they have cognitive impairments.

Lack of cooperation. Following a report of suspected elder financial exploitation, older adults often are reluctant to work with APS caseworkers during the investigation for various reasons. For example, they may not know they are being exploited, they may be embarrassed about an incident, or they may not want to implicate a family member or caregiver who may be the perpetrator. The older adult's lack of mental capacity also can make it difficult to determine what kinds of financial transactions have occurred and whether permission was granted for those transactions, and for caseworkers to gain access to needed financial records.

Source: GAO interviews with Adult Protective Services (APS) officials and caseworkers in selected states. I GAO-21-90.

For example:

- Representatives from two teams that specialize in financial abuse told us that cases involving financial exploitation are especially complex, hard to investigate, and often require additional resources and consultation, but that involving a multidisciplinary team can help address these challenges.
- Representatives from one team reported an instance of elder financial exploitation where a family member opened a joint credit account and stole a substantial amount of the victim's money. The team had to involve the Federal Bureau of Investigation (FBI) since the perpetrator lived in a different state which limited the actions local law enforcement could take.
- Another multidisciplinary team we interviewed said that they are collaborating to develop a smartphone application designed to collect information that will improve referrals from APS to law enforcement, and strengthen the support for

increased criminal prosecutions in cases involving the abuse, neglect and exploitation of vulnerable adults.[44]

Other Research Provides Information on the Prevalence of Certain Types of Financial Exploitation

Research we identified that examined financial exploitation based on data sources other than APS casefiles can shed light on the prevalence of certain types of financial exploitation nationwide. For example, one research study analyzed the FBI's National Incident-Based Reporting System (NIBRS) data on police reports and described the types of incidents being reported to police involving financial exploitation, but did not seek to provide estimates of prevalence or type of perpetrator.[45] Other research, described in more detail below, has provided some nationwide estimates for certain types of financial exploitation based on certain data sources.

Source: alexyndr/stock.adobe.com. | GAO-21-90.

---

[44] The smartphone app is under development through a grant from the Department of Justice, Office for Victims of Crime.

[45] This study, published in 2011, analyzed 2007 National Incident-Based Reporting System (NIBRS) data on criminal incidents reported to the police about financial offenses. The study reported that only a small percentage of all individual crime victims experienced financial exploitation, which took the form of false pretenses, credit card/ATM fraud, impersonation, or counterfeiting/forgery. However, the study did not provide a nationwide estimate because the sample was not representative. See J. Stamatel, J. Mastrocinque, "Using National Incident-Based Reporting System (NIBRS) Data to Understand Financial Exploitation of the Elderly: A Research Note", *Victims and Offenders*, vol. 6, no. 2, (2011), 117-136. More recently, the Department of Justice analyzed 2018 NIBRS data and found that there were more than 137,000 incidents of financial exploitation reported to NIBRS for victims 51 and older during the time period they reviewed. See Department of Justice, Office of the Attorney General, *Attorney General's Annual Report to Congress on Department of Justice Activities to Combat Elder Fraud and Abuse* (Washington, D.C.: Oct. 18, 2020). This report did not include a nationwide estimate of the prevalence of this type of abuse. According to DOJ officials, the Bureau of Justice Statistics and the Federal Bureau of Investigation recently partnered to expand NIBRS coverage, and upon completion, NIBRS will capture crime data, including information on fraud and violent victimization of the elderly, from law enforcement agencies that serve an estimated two- thirds of American citizens.

Analysis of Data from Financial Institutions

In 2019, the CFPB reported that in 2017, financial institutions filed 63,500 elder financial exploitation Suspicious Activity Reports (SAR).[46] SARs include data on suspected elder financial exploitation submitted by financial institutions to Treasury's Financial Crimes Enforcement Network (FinCEN). Further, CFPB observed that the number of older adults involved in these suspicious activities likely represented less than 2 percent of an estimated 3.5 million victims in 2017. The report also indicated that strangers were the most common suspected perpetrators of elder financial exploitation reported in the SARs, but that the amount lost was greater when the older adult knew the suspect personally.[47] This study examined suspected exploitation of older adults occurring at certain types of financial institutions. For example, financial institution personnel may observe perpetrators financially exploiting an older adult by monitoring suspicious transfers within their accounts such as unusual amounts of activity and large transfers.

Nationally Representative Survey of Older Adults about Scams and Fraud

In 2018, the Teachers, Insurance, and Annuity Association reported nationally representative data on the prevalence of financial exploitation from a one-time module added to the 2016 Health and Retirement Study, administered to adults over age 50.[48] The study found that 8 percent of respondents reported at least one form of fraud. One- third of respondents indicated that others had used or attempted to use one of their accounts without permission. This study specifically focused on one type of financial exploitation—scams—and asked incident-based questions about subtypes of scams, such as investment fraud, account misuse, and advance fee scams.

---

[46] See Consumer Financial Protection Bureau, Office of Financial Protection for Older Americans, *Suspicious Activity Reports on Elder Financial Exploitation: Issues and Trends* (Washington, D.C.: February 2019). This report analyzed the number of unique incidents reported. Each SAR corresponds to a single incident of suspected elder financial exploitation, and therefore this does not necessarily reflect 63,500 potential victims of elder financial exploitation, as multiple SARs may be filed associated with a single individual.

[47] Further, there were differences reported based on the type of reporting financial institution. Money service businesses reported that common types of scams were committed by strangers and included romance, relative in need, and lottery/sweepstake scams. Depository institutions reported that common types of financial exploitation were committed by those known to the older adult and included theft, abuse of power of attorney, and other fraudulent activity.

[48] See DeLiema, M., Deevy, M., Lusardi, A., Mitchell, O., *Exploring the Prevalence, Risk Factors, and Financial Consequences of Fraud: Evidence from the Health and Retirement Study* (2018) *TIAA Institute Research Dialog*, Issue No. 143. Data was acquired for this study through use of a one-time survey module added to the University of Michigan's Health and Retirement Study in 2016. In 2017, DOJ's Bureau of Justice Statistics included this module as a permanent supplement to the National Crime Victimization Survey.
According to DOJ officials, data from the first 2017 fraud module added to the National Crime Victimization Survey are scheduled to be publicly released in March 2021. These data will provide new, nationally representative data on the prevalence of various types of personal financial fraud victimization that can be sorted by age of the victim (the survey is administered to persons age 18 or older). DOJ officials said the Bureau of Justice Statistics is evaluating factors to determine how often this fraud module will be conducted and when the next survey will take place.

Nationally Representative Survey of Older Adults Living in Residential Communities

A 2008 study surveyed 3,005 participants who were 57 to 85 years of age and were living in residential communities to ask whether they had experienced mistreatment in the past year.[49] With respect to financial exploitation, the study found that financial abuse by a family member had a prevalence rate of 3.5 percent. This was based on a single financial exploitation question about whether a family member had taken or withheld their money or belongings in the last year.

Nationally Representative Survey of Older Adults

A 2008 study surveyed adults 60 or older in a randomly selected national sample to determine the prevalence rates and risk factors for different types of abuse.[50] To identify whether financial exploitation had occurred, the survey asked participants a series of questions about people who may have made financial decisions for them and about various kinds of theft. The study reported that financial exploitation by family members in some form was present in 5.2 percent of respondents in the previous year, and that lifetime financial exploitation by strangers was present in 6.5 percent of respondents, usually in the form of fraud.

STUDIES ESTIMATE CERTAIN LOSSES TO BE IN THE BILLIONS AND SOME STATES ARE TAKING STEPS TO IMPROVE COST DATA

Although comprehensive cost data do not exist across all types of elder financial exploitation for all those affected, we identified several studies that each provided a cost estimate of more than $1 billion for a certain type of loss. In addition, although ACL's NAMRS does not currently ask state APS agencies to submit available information from casefiles on costs to victims and others, some states have taken steps to develop tools to collect cost data to help address this critical knowledge gap for those working to inform policy and prevent elder abuse.

Studies Have Estimated Certain Costs to Be in the Billions

Several studies identified in our review used various data sources to provide cost estimates of elder financial exploitation.[51] Two studies were based on federal data sources

---

[49] See E.O. Laumann, S.A. Leitsch, L.J. Waite, "Elder Mistreatment in the United States: Prevalence Estimates From a Nationally Representative Study," *Journals of Gerontology Series B*, vol. 63, no. 4 (2008), 1-7.

[50] See R. Acierno, M. Hernandez-Tejada, W. Muzzy, K. Steve, *The National Elder Mistreatment Study*, Criminal Justice Reference Service (2008).

[51] To identify information on costs, we interviewed ACL, CFPB, and DOJ officials and representatives of national elder abuse prevention organizations and conducted a literature search. We identified 15 studies that met our

and provided nationwide estimates, and seven studies were based on APS casefile data and provided state level estimates.

Nationwide Studies Using Federal Data

Three federal datasets currently collect information on certain costs resulting from elder financial exploitation (see Figure 4). Two recent studies published using federal data collected by Treasury's FinCEN and by FTC have provided reliable nationwide estimates of the cost of certain types of elder financial exploitation. FinCEN collects data from banks on financial losses and the FTC collects data from consumer complaints about fraud. Estimates contained in these two studies reflect data on certain parts of the costs resulting from elder financial exploitation. Given they are only capturing some aspects of cost, they may be viewed as a lower bound to the total nationwide cost of elder financial exploitation in a given year.

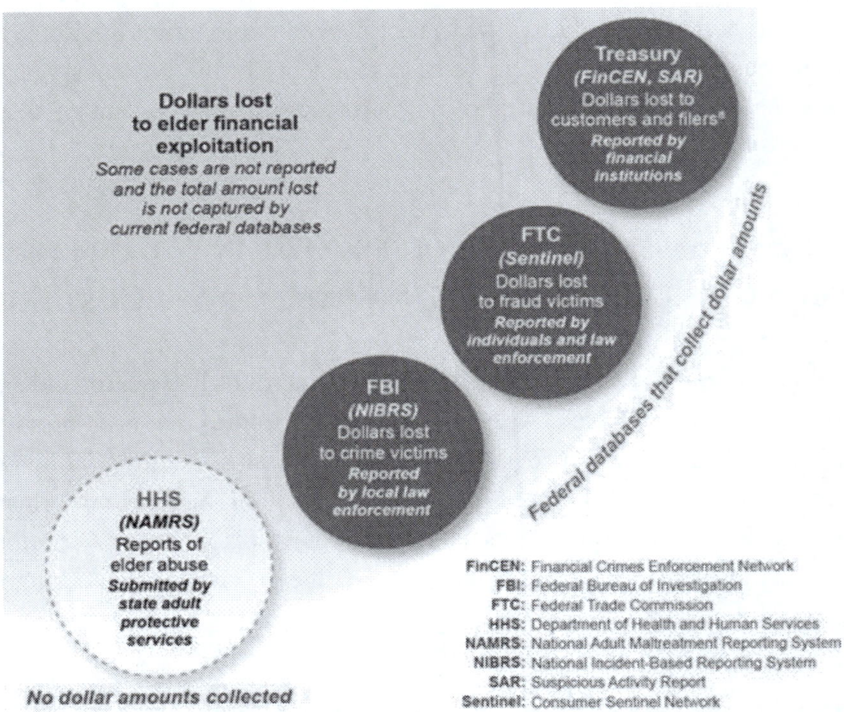

Source: GAO analysis of documents from federal agencies and information from federal agency websites. | GAO-21-90.

[a] Reported losses can include actual and attempted theft to victims and financial institutions that file suspicious activity reports.

Figure 4. Types of Information Collected by Federal Data Sources on Costs of Financial Exploitation.

criteria of including original cost estimates related to elder financial exploitation. Those 15 studies were reviewed for reliability by two economists, who determined that nine studies (two national studies and seven state studies) provided reliable estimates of certain types of costs.

CFPB Study

As previously noted, in 2019, the CFPB published a study based on analysis of data from Suspicious Activity Reports (SAR) filed with Treasury's FinCEN.[52] In this study, CFPB analyzed 2017 SARs data and found actual losses and attempts at elder financial exploitation that had been observed and reported by financial institutions were a combined $1.7 billion.[53] SARs are filed by financial institutions, such as banks and money services businesses, and submitted to FinCEN. These reports capture the actual losses to older adults or to financial institutions, as well as attempts to steal older adults' funds, or both.

FTC Study

In 2020, the FTC issued a report based on an analysis of Consumer Sentinel Network data on losses to victims of fraud.[54] Consumer Sentinel Network data are obtained through consumer complaints reported to the FTC by consumers or law enforcement.[55] Complaints were included in the study if they provided a dollar amount and their age. This analysis found that during 2019, more than 300,000 fraud reports associated with consumers who were age 60 or older were filed by consumers or law enforcement, totaling more than $440 million in losses. The total loss may be higher given that about one-half of the consumer complaints lacked age information and were therefore not included in the portion of the analysis that was based on the complainants' age. Also, the complaint data are self-reported and, therefore, respondents may not have accurately recalled the actual dollar amount lost.

In addition to data from FinCEN and FTC, the Federal Bureau of Investigation's National Incident-Based Reporting System (NIBRS) collects data on dollars lost to crime victims reported by local law enforcement. Our literature search did not identify any studies that estimate elder financial exploitation costs using the NIBRS data. Also, DOJ's forthcoming 2017 National Crime Victimization Survey fraud supplement survey will provide another federal data source containing nationally representative (self-reported) information about some of the costs of fraud to victims.[56]

---

[52] See CFPB, Suspicious Activity Reports on Elder Financial Exploitation: Issues and Trends (2019).

[53] CFPB's analysis excludes the top 1 percent of SARs by dollar amount involved per year to address outliers and data quality issues. Given that the national and state cost studies use different timeframes, including partial years, or different calendar and fiscal years, we did not adjust the estimates in the various studies for inflation. Importantly, estimates across these studies, both at the national and state levels, should not be compared or added together.

[54] See Federal Trade Commission, *Protecting Older Consumers, 2019-2020* (2020).

[55] Consumer Sentinel Network data include consumer complaint information from only those who elect to report it to the FTC, and therefore are not representative of the all consumers who experience fraud.

[56] According to DOJ officials, these data will be publicly released in March 2021 and will make an important contribution to knowledge in this area. In addition, in August 2020, CFPB awarded a contract to researchers for a study of financial loss and recovery for older victims of elder financial exploitation. As part of their work, researchers plan to interview victims, their family members, and professionals about the amount of money and property lost and recovered, as well as the methods of theft, among other topics. According to CFPB officials, this study is expected to be complete in August 2021.

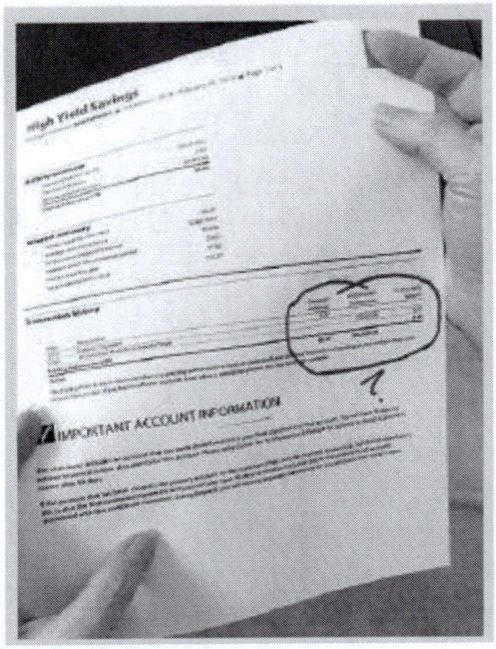

Source: GAO file photo. | GAO-21-90.

State Studies Using APS Data

APS casefiles offer another valuable source of data on the costs of elder financial exploitation. We found that some states had analyzed data from APS casefiles as well as other data sources to estimate the costs of financial exploitation in their states. Specifically, we identified seven state studies published in the last 10 years that include original and reliable cost estimates of financial exploitation reported to APS in their respective states.[57] Three of the state studies—in New York, Pennsylvania, and Virginia—projected that costs could be over $1 billion in each of these states alone. Six of the seven state studies compiled costs to victims, and three state studies calculated costs to taxpayers. For example, the 2020 Maine study estimated health care costs to taxpayers by matching APS data to Medicare and Medicaid cost data.

Six of the seven state studies also used a similar methodology to determine costs to victims by manually reviewing casefile notes from a sample of APS casefiles to record cost data.[58]

---

[57] We reviewed the methodology of these seven state cost studies and found their estimates to be reliable based on data reported to APS during the study period. We also identified one study from Wyoming, published in 2014, that included some information about costs based on a review of APS casefiles in that state. This study examined 10 cases from 2011, 16 cases from 2012, and six cases from 2013. Upon review, we determined that because the sample sizes in this study were small and the range of reported losses varied widely from year to year, the estimates were not generalizable. Therefore, we determined that estimates from Wyoming's study were not reliable enough to include in our report.

[58] The 2020 Maine study linked these APS data to Medicare and Medicaid claims data.

Table 3. Key Findings and Limitations from Seven State Studies of Financial Exploitation

Study year and state	Number of cases included	Observed costs (to victims and/or taxpayers)	Underreporting factors applied[a]	Projected costs (to victims and/or taxpayers) in dollars	Selected limitations identified by study authors and our review
2011 Utah	52 cases from 2011	5 million (victims)	10, 25, and 44	48 to 210 million (victims)	In some cases, there was not enough information in the casefile notes to make a valuation of costs or valuation of property, so these values were derived based on supplemental data.
2014 Oregon	969 cases from 2013	3 million (victims), 407,000 (taxpayers)	44	439 million (victims), 1.9 million (taxpayers)	The total loss to the taxpayers attributed in the sample cannot fully be calculated due to limitations in documentary evidence.
2016 New York	928 cases from fiscal year 2013	27 million (victims and taxpayers)	10 and 44	352 million to $1.5 billion (victims and taxpayers)	The study did not have full coverage of the state of New York and had to estimate costs for the larger population.
2016 Virginia	76 cases from state fiscal year 2015	2.1 million (victims)	44	1.2 billion (victims)	The findings do not include Fairfax County due to data compatibility issues, and Fairfax is the most populous county in Virginia.
2017 Maine	106 cases from state fiscal year 2016[b]	4.7 million (victims)	10 and 44	$47 to $205 million (victims)	The study used casefiles from both APS and Legal Services for the Elderly to sum losses, but the extent to which these organizations serve different populations is unclear, so there may be some double counting.
2020 Maine[c]	131 APS cases from 2007-2012 and 281 non-APS cases	0.3 million (annual costs for taxpayers)	24 and 44	7.2 to 13.2 million (annual costs for taxpayers)	The study included a specific group of older adults who are dual-eligible for Medicare and Medicaid for the entire period.
2020 Pennsyl-vania	315 cases between July 2017-June 2018	12 million (victims)	44	2.5 billion (victims)	The study did not have full coverage of the state of Pennsylvania and had to estimate costs for the larger population.

Source: GAO analysis of state cost estimate studies. | GAO-21-90.

Notes: For all seven studies, observed costs are cost estimates based on data found in Adult Protective Service (APS) casefile notes and projected costs are cost estimates for the state in the given time period that take into account missing cost data due to underreporting or a lack of data in APS casefiles. Given that the state studies use different timeframes, including partial years, or different calendar and fiscal years, we did not adjust the cost estimates in the various studies for inflation. Importantly, cost estimates across these studies should not be compared or added up.

[a] State study authors used various factors to account for underreporting, based on elder abuse studies estimating that just one in 10, one in 24, one in 25, or one in 44 incidents are reported to APS.

[b] The 2017 Maine study included 71 APS casefiles and 35 Legal Services for the Elderly casefiles from state fiscal year 2016. This study included data and analysis from 2010 through 2016.

[c] The 2020 Maine study linked APS data to Medicare and Medicaid claims data to estimate observed costs.

Some study authors and APS officials told us it was time- and resource-intensive to extract the available data from the casefile notes, in part, because the casefile notes are typically not standardized and further, they do not always include cost information. Once study authors retrieved the available cost data from the casefile notes, they typically used these data to attempt to calculate a statewide estimate. In some studies, they simply added the observed costs together. In other studies, they estimated an average cost per case based on those cases with cost data and then applied this average to a larger number of cases. Then, because research indicates that incidents of elder financial exploitation are under-reported, study authors typically generated a larger number based on one of the underreporting factors mentioned above to project costs statewide (see Table 3).[59]

These studies demonstrate that APS casefile data offer another potential source of nationwide data on the costs of elder financial exploitation; however, ACL does not currently ask state APS agencies to submit information on such costs in NAMRS. ACL officials said that when NAMRS was being developed, they considered including a cost data element, but decided against it because while data on costs can often be found in casefile notes, at the time, very few states' APS agencies collected this type of information in their data systems and ACL was focused on keeping the system simple enough to encourage state participation. At the same time, one of the goals for the development of NAMRS was to expand data that states routinely collect, in part to address critical gaps in knowledge at the national level.[60]

Officials said that while they do not currently have any concrete plans to ask states to submit cost data, they envision NAMRS changing over time to help ensure NAMRS data are relevant and can be used to inform policy and prevent elder abuse. To this end, ACL officials said that they will begin a consensus-based stakeholder engagement process in fiscal year 2021 to inform updates to NAMRS that could be implemented in February 2023 when they said the current approval for NAMRS data collection expires.[61] Officials said they will consider whether to add new data elements to NAMRS during this process, and that cost is one of the data elements that could be considered. Including cost data in future iterations of NAMRS could begin to help address this critical gap in knowledge. While ACL officials expressed concern about the reporting burden on state agencies if NAMRS were to add cost data elements, NAMRS remains a voluntary system and state agencies may choose whether to submit these data.[62] Several researchers and APS officials we spoke with said that adding cost data to NAMRS could make a valuable

[59] See appendix II for more details on each of these studies methodologies, findings, and limitations.

[60] See U.S. Department of Health and Human Services, Development of a National Adult Protective Services Data System: NAMRS Pilot Final Report (2015).

[61] According to ACL officials, this new approval will be accomplished through the Office of Management and Budget's publication of an Information Collection Request document in the Federal Register, with the opportunity for public comment. ACL officials said that state APS agencies are one of the key stakeholders they will consult with during this process.

[62] Should ACL decide to add new data elements to NAMRS in 2023 as a result of this stakeholder engagement process, states who choose to participate would have to align their systems with the addition of any new data elements, whether or not cost data elements are added.

contribution to the national picture of the costs of financial exploitation, and that having a clearer picture of these costs would be helpful to prevention programs and policymakers.

Some States Have Developed Tools to Collect Cost Data

Researchers we interviewed said that using information manually pulled from APS casefile notes is a time consuming and difficult way to retrieve data. To make this process easier, APS officials we interviewed from several states said that their states have created or were creating tools to help their caseworkers collect better cost data about financial exploitation moving forward.

One strategy described by officials in some states involved collecting dollar amounts or other related cost data in new separate fields in their data systems.[63] For example:

- An APS official from Sacramento County, California, stated that the county's data system includes a specialized financial exploitation page that collects both the value lost to victims and what was taken, including money, real estate, jewelry, and vehicles. According to this official, the county began collecting cost information in 2014.
- A Virginia APS official said that they published their 2016 state financial exploitation cost study at the request of the state legislature, and afterwards, added fields to the data system to collect the known or estimated amount of monetary loss and the method through which exploitation occurred. Methods include theft, fraud, forgery, or unauthorized credit card use.
- An Oregon APS official told us that the agency established a statewide data system in December 2018, which includes a new financial exploitation data entry page to collect dollar amounts of losses, along with information on the types and methods of exploitation.

Another strategy described by some APS programs involved developing tools to help caseworkers collect and document costs more consistently. The mission of APS is to investigate reports of elder abuse—including financial exploitation—and to develop a plan to ensure the victim's safety, health, and independence.[64] Some APS officials said that within this context, gathering cost data is relevant only to the extent it is needed to

[63] The eight states we interviewed were selected, in part, because representatives of national elder abuse prevention organizations or ACL officials told us that these state APS agencies systematically collected some cost information related to financial exploitation. (See app. III for more detailed examples of new data elements some states have added to their data systems.

[64] While APS programs vary at the state and local level with respect to populations served, services provided, and scope of the program, according to the National Adult Protective Services Association, the underlying mission is the same across programs. See National Adult Protective Services Association, *How APS Helps,* accessed September 21, 2020, https://www.napsa-now.org/get-help/how-aps-helps/.

substantiate that financial exploitation took place. If a report of financial exploitation is substantiated, and the caseworker determines there is evidence of possible criminal activity, APS refers the case to law enforcement for further investigation.

Source: Kate Derr/stock.adobe.com. | GAO-21-90.

ACL officials noted that once evidence of financial exploitation is substantiated and a case is referred to law enforcement, the APS caseworker's attention turns to ensuring that the victim is safe and that their basic needs are met. At that point, it is up to law enforcement to investigate the total amount of any losses. According to APS officials, the APS investigation may be complete and the case closed before all of the victim's financial losses are discovered. For example, Florida APS officials told us that its state APS agency completes investigations within 60 days, which officials said can make it difficult for them to determine a full loss amount in cases involving financial exploitation, because of the time required to investigate these often complex financial exploitation cases.

In addition to time constraints, according to APS officials, the same challenges that can make it difficult for caseworkers to confirm cases of financial exploitation can also make it difficult for APS caseworkers to collect cost data: lack of expertise and access to records, as well as lack of cooperation from victims. To help address these challenges, some state agencies have developed tools to assist their caseworkers in conducting financial exploitation investigations. APS officials we interviewed in several states said that they have developed or are developing tools that can help caseworkers collect more cost data during their investigations of financial exploitation cases.[65] For example:

---

[65] See appendix III for examples of tools some states have created to collect cost data.

- Maine developed a checklist of evidence for caseworkers to collect during their investigations. The checklist includes bank and credit card records from victims and suspects, Medicaid application information, and correspondence between a nursing home and family member or caregiver suspected of failing to pay for care.
- New York developed a suite of tools (called the Financial Exploitation Investigation Suite of Tools) to help APS caseworkers investigate reports of financial exploitation. These tools include questions to ask during the initial client meeting, a list of documents to request, income and expenses Tables, and a "red flag" checklist.[66]

ACL officials said they are aware of some states' recent efforts to add new data fields and develop tools to collect more cost data, and they acknowledged that sharing these tools with other states would help encourage states to collect cost data by providing states with ideas and models of how to do so. Under the Elder Justice Act of 2009, one of HHS's responsibilities (delegated to ACL) is to share information and provide technical assistance to state APS agencies, and ACL has established resource centers specifically to provide technical assistance to and share information with state APS agencies related to elder abuse. ACL officials said that they plan to share information on states' recent efforts to develop tools to collect more cost data, but they do not yet have a timeframe for doing so. Until ACL develops a timeframe for disseminating this information to states, state APS agencies may not be aware of tools and practices that could help them collect cost data more effectively.

Victims and Others Often Face Costs That Are Difficult to Collect and Quantify

Beyond the financial costs of exploitation that are more easily captured in dollars, victims often also experience other costs related to effects on their health or quality of life, but these costs are difficult to collect and quantify. Elder financial exploitation often results in costs to others as well, including family members, health care facilities, taxpayers, and community-based organizations.[67] While some of these costs can be quantified, these data are generally not collected or estimated more broadly.

---

[66] New York's Financial Exploitation Investigation Suite of Tools was created with funding from an ACL grant (specifically, a State Grant to Enhance Adult Protective Services).

[67] Marie-Therese Connolly, et. al., *The Elder Justice Roadmap: A Stakeholder Initiative to Respond to an Emerging Health, Justice, Financial and Social Crisis,* a report prepared for the Department of Justice with support from the Department of Health and Services (2014).

Costs to Victims' Well-Being

Elder Financial Exploitation Costs Related to Decline in Victims' Well-being

Examples described by APS officials in selected states:

- An older woman was financially exploited by a neighbor who stole thousands of dollars from her, and afterwards, she broke out in persistent hives that would not subside despite medical treatment.
- A perpetrator stole prescription medication from an older adult living in a health care facility, and the victim died without adequate pain relief.

Source: Information from Adult Protective Service (APS) officials in selected states. I GAO-21-90.

Financial exploitation can affect the physical, emotional, and mental well- being of older adults although these effects can be difficult to quantify. For example, living independently and maintaining relationships with family members can be critical to an older adult's physical, emotional, and mental well-being, and studies show that when victims lose their ability to live independently, or lose their relationship with a family member or trusted other who has betrayed them, the effects can be life-altering. None of the studies we identified attempted to quantify these costs related to declines in victims' well-being.

Elder Financial Exploitation Costs Related to Decline in Well-being

Examples described by APS officials in selected states:

- An older woman who was a diabetic lived with her son who controlled all of her money. He only purchased pizza for the two of them to eat, which caused the woman serious health consequences. APS officials said that while this was a form of exploitation and neglect, it would be impossible to capture this health decline in dollars.
- An elderly man had been living with a provider who had been exploiting him for the past 1-2 years. The provider is supposed to do laundry, get medications, and be physically present but doesn't do those things and sometimes may be absent. The APS official said it would be hard to quantify the effects of this exploitation, especially the emotional suffering or the health problems from not taking medication.

Source: GAO interview with Adult Protective Services (APS) officials in selected states. I GAO 21 90.

Studies of the effects of elder abuse, including financial exploitation, generally discuss intangible costs more broadly, without assigning a specific cost estimate. For example, in a 1995 study from the National Institute of Justice, researchers found that 14 percent of victims surveyed reported that they had suffered health or emotional problems directly related to having been the victim of a financial crime, but the authors did not estimate specific costs.[68] Three years later, a study published in The Journal of the American Medical Association showed that for participants in the study, elder mistreatment was associated with increased mortality in older adults.[69]

More recently, studies in various peer-reviewed journals that examined the effects of elder financial exploitation found similar effects, such as declines in physical health, depression, and generalized anxiety, or emotional costs—including loss of self-esteem and feelings of guilt or shame.[70] For example, a 2016 study published in The Journal of Elder Abuse & Neglect found that compared with other types of elder abuse, for its sample of victims, financial exploitation had one of the lowest survival rates.[71] A 2013 study found that financial exploitation, like other types of elder abuse, can be associated with increased rates of hospitalization.[72] In prior reports from 2010, 2011, and 2016, we have also reported on the significant negative effect of financial exploitation and other types of elder abuse on victims', citing health declines and a shorter lifespan.[73] Yet, capturing these costs is not easy. The authors of the New York state cost study said that not only are costs associated with declines in physical and emotional health difficult to quantify, but it is also difficult to determine causal relationships between the financial exploitation and the negative effects.

While none of the studies we identified attempted to quantify these potentially life-altering costs, these costs can take a toll. In our discussions with representatives from elder abuse prevention organizations and with researchers, as well as with APS officials in selected states, several said these types of negative effects on victims can be devastating. For example, one researcher said she believes it is the fallout from financial exploitation that can be life-changing and traumatic, severing relationships with family members or having to move the older adult into a facility. Several researchers and

---

[68] U.S. Department of Justice, National Institute of Justice, *Victimization of Persons by Fraud* (Washington, D.C.: 1995).

[69] The author of this study defined elder mistreatment as one or more of the following: abuse, neglect, or exploitation of an older adult. See Mark S. Lachs, et.al, "The Mortality of Elder Mistreatment," *JAMA (The Journal of the American Medical Association),* vol. 280, no. 5 (1998). Although this study does not address the issue of increased mortality as a result of financial exploitation separately from other types of abuse, it illustrates how there can be costs to victims' health as a result of abuse.

[70] See Gali H. Weissberger, et al., "Physical and mental health correlates of perceived financial exploitation in older adults: Preliminary findings from the Finance, Cognition, and Health in Elders Study (FINCHES)," *Aging & Mental Health,* vol. 24, no. 5 (2020), Michael J. Tueth, "Exposing Financial Exploitation of Impaired Elderly Persons," *American Journal of Geriatric Psychiatry,* vol. 8, no. 2 (2000); and Stacey Wood and Peter A. Lichtenberg, "Financial Capacity and Financial Exploitation of Older Adults: Research Findings, Policy Recommendations and Clinical Implications," *Clinical Gerontologist*, vol. 40, no. 1 (2017).

[71] Jason Burnett, et al., "Five-year all-cause mortality rates across five categories of substantiated else abuse occurring in the community," *Journal of Elder Abuse & Neglect,* vol. 28, no. 2 (2016).

[72] XinQi Dong and Melissa A. Simon, "Elder Abuse as a Risk Factor for Hospitalization in Older Persons," *JAMA (The Journal of the American Medical Association) Internal Medicine*, vol. 173, no. 10 (2013).

[73] See GAO-11-208, which focused on elder abuse more broadly. The following two reports focused specifically on financial exploitation: GAO-17-33, Elder Abuse: The Extent of Abuse by Guardians Is Unknown, but Some Measures Exist to Help Protect Older Adults (Washington, D.C.: Nov. 16, 2016) and GAO-10-1046, Guardianships: Cases of Financial Exploitation, Neglect, and Abuse of Seniors (Washington, D.C.: Sep. 30, 2010).

representatives of two elder abuse prevention organizations noted that attempting to quantify some of these negative effects warrants further study.[74]

Costs to Other Groups

Elder Financial Exploitation Cost to a Family Member

Examples described by researchers we interviewed:

- A family member of a victim of financial exploitation had to take out a second mortgage to pay attorney costs to pursue legal action against the perpetrator who had stolen all of her grandfather's money.
- Some of the major costs that affect family members include costs associated with the family member's loss of work to provide care (which affects employers, too), as well as the victim's health care and housing costs. These losses do not stop at the immediate victim, they trickle down through families and generations, multiplying the negative effects.

Source: GAO interviews with researchers. I GAO-21-90.

In addition to victims, other groups—such as family members, health care facilities, taxpayers, and community-based organizations—may face costs or experience losses resulting from elder financial exploitation.

Some of these costs can be quantified; however, data on such costs are generally not collected and, therefore, are difficult to estimate more broadly.

Family Members

When an older adult is a victim of financial exploitation, family members often must use their own financial resources or incur other costs.[75] For example, according to one state cost study we reviewed, family members may find it necessary to pay for care and housing for older relatives who were once financially independent, and may also pay legal costs if they try to sue perpetrators to recover lost funds.[76] According to researchers we interviewed, family members may also experience the loss of future inheritance. For example, if a parent has to move to a nursing facility after being financially exploited by a caregiver, the unexpected costs of this care could deplete funds that would have otherwise been passed down to their children. Finally, according to one researcher we

[74] One federal program that attempts to place a dollar value on the extent of a decline in physical or emotional health following trauma is the Veteran Affairs system of disability compensation, which includes compensation for post-traumatic stress disorder (PTSD). For example, based on 2020 compensation rates, a person with a 50 percent disability due to PTSD symptoms could be eligible to receive a benefit of $893.43 per month.

[75] While some family members may know how much they have spent to support a victim, these costs are not typically captured in APS casefiles.

[76] See New York State Office of Children and Family Services, The New York State Cost of Financial Exploitation Study (2016).

spoke with, family members may lose wages if they have to reduce their hours or stop working to take care of a victim. We previously found that employed parental and spousal caregivers experience a number of job impacts due to caregiving responsibilities that can negatively affect their retirement security.[77] Specifically, we estimated that 56 percent of parental and spousal caregivers went to work late, left early, or took time off during the day to provide care. Overall, we found caregiving was negatively associated with the number of hours caregivers worked, and spousal caregivers who were near retirement had lower retirement assets than non-caregivers.

Health Care Facilities

A CFPB manual for assisted living and nursing facilities highlights that financial victimization of older adults in these care settings can place them at risk of involuntary discharge or loss of housing for nonpayment. In such situations, the facility may have to bear the cost if the victim becomes destitute and the bills remain unpaid.[78] Some APS officials also told us that hospitals and long-term care facilities may lose money if a family member or other individual responsible for paying for the victim's care fails to do so. While some of these costs may be quantified by a facility, they generally are not collected or recorded in a victim's APS casefile, and capturing the costs across many victims or facilities would be difficult. For example, in states such as Virginia, where APS programs investigate reports of abuse that occur in residential facilities, a state official said that APS often gets financial abuse referrals from nursing homes stemming from non-payment. APS officials in this state said that a record of the amount of fees unpaid to the facility may be available from the facility, but generally these amounts would not be recorded in an individual's APS casefile.

Elder Financial Exploitation Costs to Health Care Facilities

Examples described by APS officials in selected states:

- The son of an older adult who was bed- bound in a health care facility refused to pay the facility because he said his father's assets were his birthright.
- The daughter of an older adult in a health care facility spent about $100,000 from her mother's savings account, but would not pay the facility; officials said the facility probably would never receive payment.

Source: Information from Adult Protective Services (APS) officials in selected states. I GAO-21-90.

[77] GAO, *Retirement Security: Some Parental and Spousal Caregivers Face Financial Risks,* GAO-19-382 (Washington, D.C.: May 1, 2019).

[78] Consumer Financial Protection Bureau. Protecting residents from financial exploitation: A manual for assisted living and nursing facilities (Washington, D.C.: 2014).

Taxpayers

Victims who experience a significant loss of money or assets may have to enroll in government programs for low-income individuals.

Although generally outside of the types of costs tracked by APS caseworkers, three state cost studies we reviewed estimated the costs to their states of providing public benefits to victims who had been financially exploited (see Table 3 above).

For example, to estimate Medicaid, Medicare, and other public assistance costs related to financial exploitation in New York, state APS workers coordinated with other state agencies to identify new or additional public benefits and social services provided to clients following an APS investigation of financial exploitation. In Maine, researchers compared the likelihood of incurring costs and expenditure levels of dual-eligible Medicare and Medicaid financial exploitation victims relative to control groups. While increased Medicaid spending at the national level could result in significant costs to taxpayers, researchers said that it would be challenging to match necessary APS data to Medicaid data nationally and such as Medicaid and the Supplemental Nutrition Assistance Program.[79] to determine if any increase in Medicaid spending was a direct result of the exploitation. Officials in four states also said that their APS programs had used emergency funds for food or rent to support financial exploitation victims who were unable to cover those costs, but in three of these states, APS officials said it would be difficult to tie these expenditures specifically to financial abuse because, for example, other types of abuse are often involved as well.

Taxpayers also face costs associated with the response to elder financial exploitation by APS workers, law enforcement, and other program resources, such as legal services. For example, APS may incur costs when caseworkers testify in court, enroll victims in Medicaid, and administer tests of victims' mental capacity to help prove lack of consent. Law enforcement costs can include the costs of investigating financial exploitation cases. One state study was able to quantify some of these types of costs by coordinating with law enforcement agencies.[80] Courts also incur costs for trying these cases, but APS officials said these costs would be difficult to estimate.

---

[79] Medicaid pays for low-income individuals' health care needs, including nursing facility fees, if necessary. According to the Centers for Medicare & Medicaid Services, state Medicaid reimbursement rates vary for those who are institutionalized, such as in a nursing facility. For example, according to our analysis of 2019 Medicaid reimbursement rate data from two states, the average reimbursement rate per Medicaid recipient for nursing facilities in the state of New York was $295 per day (or $107,791 if in care for a full year), while in the state of Nevada, the average rate was $129 per day (or $47,049 if in care for a full year).

[80] New York State Office of Children and Family Services, *The New York State Cost of Financial Exploitation Study* (2016).

Elder Financial Exploitation Cost to Taxpayers

Examples described by APS officials in selected states:

- A woman in her 80s was left impoverished when her daughter depleted over $200,000 of her funds. Because of this exploitation, the woman was unable to afford private at-home care, and was moved to a nursing facility and placed on Medicaid.
- The state's APS program sometimes provides funds for hotel or motel rooms to help keep a person safe from abuse, which could be due, in part, to financial exploitation.

Source: Information from Adult Protective Services (APS) officials in selected states. I GAO-21-90.

Community-Based Organizations

Community-based organizations, such as non-profit organizations that are not government-funded, can also incur costs that are difficult to quantify in their efforts to combat elder financial exploitation, according to several researchers and APS officials in Oregon. For example, APS officials told us about organizations that provide pro bono legal services to victims, including a legal services organization for the elderly in Maine and a law school in Sacramento, California. Non-profit organizations may provide other supports to victims, such as help obtaining food or health insurance. APS officials in Oregon said their agency does not have access to emergency funding for victims' necessities, so they rely on food banks for those who can no longer afford food.

Elder Financial Exploitation Costs to Community-based Organizations

Examples described by APS officials and researchers in selected states:

- Local senior resource advocates provided pro bono assistance to an older adult in obtaining health insurance after her granddaughter stole $75,000 of her money to buy a vehicle, pay personal bills, and support her own lifestyle.
- A 2016 state study found that 33 percent of referrals of financial exploitation led to involvement with other governmental agencies and community-based service programs.

Source: Information from Adult Protective Services (APS) officials and researchers in selected states. I GAO-21-90.

CONCLUSION

While comprehensive cost data do not exist across all types of elder financial exploitation, various estimates of certain types of financial losses have been in the billions. In many cases, these costs can be life-altering for the victims, who rarely recover their financial losses. Further, elder financial exploitation can have costs for others, including family members, taxpayers, and community-based organizations. ACL has successfully partnered with state APS agencies to begin collecting data on elder abuse from APS casefiles, including data on financial exploitation. With NAMRS, ACL is making progress toward capturing these important data on financial exploitation that may not exist anywhere else. Each year, more states are submitting more data to NAMRS, and in the coming years, NAMRS is expected to be able to help provide a better picture of the prevalence of the various types of financial exploitation and its perpetrators nationwide.

Researchers and agency officials we spoke with noted the value and importance of knowing more about the costs of financial exploitation. However, ACL currently does not request state APS agencies to submit information on the costs of financial exploitation to NAMRS. ACL has initiated an effort to work with state APS agencies and other stakeholders to reevaluate NAMRS data collection, which could provide an opportunity for ACL to add cost data as part of its future data collection. By requesting cost data, ACL could move states towards collecting this information more routinely and in more standardized ways—helping to address the critical gap in knowledge about the cost of financial exploitation nationwide, and informing efforts to better protect older adults from potentially life-altering financial losses.

Some states have developed tools to collect information on costs and record this information in their case management systems. As the agency responsible for developing and sharing information regarding research and training about the provision of APS services and strategies, ACL is well-positioned to help states learn from one another how to collect cost data, but it has not taken steps to disseminate this information across states. ACL officials said they plan to share this information to assist states, but until they do so, state APS agencies may not be aware of tools and practices that could help their states collect cost data.

RECOMMENDATIONS FOR EXECUTIVE ACTION

We are making the following two recommendations to the Administration for Community Living (ACL):

The Administrator of ACL should work with state APS agencies to develop data fields on the costs of financial exploitation to add to NAMRS to encourage more states to collect these data. This could be achieved, for example, during the stakeholder engagement process ACL is undertaking to discuss potential updates for the NAMRS system. (Recommendation 1)

The Administrator of ACL should develop a timeframe to share information and tools that state APS agencies have developed to collect cost information with other states, to provide states with strategies they can use to improve data collection on financial exploitation costs. This could be achieved, for example, by leveraging ACL's existing resource centers such as the APS Technical Assistance Resource Center or the National Center on Elder Abuse to disseminate this information to states. (Recommendation 2)

AGENCY COMMENTS AND OUR EVALUATION

We provided a draft of this chapter to the Department of Health and Human Services, the Consumer Financial Protection Bureau, and the Department of Justice for review and comment. All three agencies provided technical comments, which we incorporated into the report as appropriate. HHS also provided written comments which are reproduced in appendix IV and summarized below.

In its written comments, HHS agreed with the recommendation that the agency develop a timeframe to share information and data collection tools with other states that state APS agencies have developed. HHS stated that it would consider ways to conduct these information sharing activities in fiscal year 2022, when it enters into new contracts with its existing resource centers.

HHS did not agree with the recommendation that the agency work with state APS agencies to develop data fields for NAMRS on the costs of financial exploitation to encourage more states to collect these data. In its comments, HHS stated it could not guarantee that data elements capturing the cost of financial exploitation would be recommended for inclusion in NAMRS during the next renewal process. HHS noted that NAMRS is a voluntary data system and that HHS must consider the reporting burden on the state agencies of adding data fields to the system.

We understand that HHS must consider the reporting burden on state agencies and cannot guarantee the inclusion of cost data elements in NAMRS. However, as we note in the report, some state agencies are already collecting these cost data, and by requesting this information in NAMRS, HHS could move states towards collecting this information more routinely and in more standardized ways. As stated in the report, the agency plans to begin a stakeholder engagement process for NAMRS renewal in fiscal year 2021. HHS stated in its written response that it expects this process could result in updating or adding data elements to NAMRS based on input from stakeholders, balancing what would be valuable for understanding adult maltreatment with what is feasible for APS to collect and report with reasonable burden. This stakeholder engagement process is a valuable opportunity to engage with state APS agencies as well as other important stakeholders to consider whether to add new data elements to NAMRS about the cost of financial exploitation in the coming years. We continue to believe that working with states to add data elements to NAMRS to capture the cost of financial exploitation would help to determine the scope and magnitude of financial exploitation nationwide—currently a critical gap in knowledge about the costs of financial exploitation.

As agreed with your offices, unless you publicly announce the contents of this chapter earlier, we plan no further distribution until 30 days from the report date. At that time, we will send copies of this chapter to the appropriate congressional committees, the Secretary of Health and Human Services, the Attorney General, the Director of the Consumer Financial Protection Bureau, and other interested parties.

Kathryn A. Larin
Director, Education, Workforce, and Income Security

APPENDIX I: PROFILES OF SELECTED STATES

This appendix provides information on the eight states selected for our review, including demographic information, an overview of the Adult Protective Services (APS) program in each state, and the strategies that officials reported using to address financial exploitation. This information, summarized in state profiles on the following pages, is based on data from the U.S. Census Bureau, the National Adult Protective Services Technical Assistance Resource Center, and our interviews with APS officials in the selected states.[81]

We selected these eight states based on various factors, including whether they had made efforts to collect data on financial exploitation or had established an elder abuse multidisciplinary team. Figure 5 provides a U.S. map with the selected states highlighted.

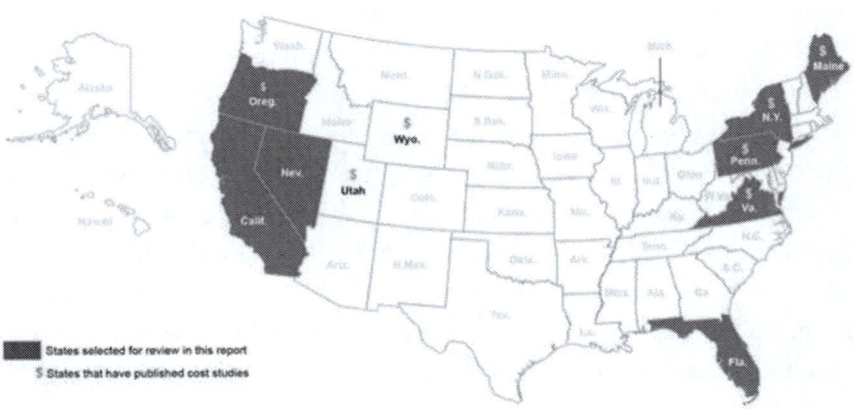

Source: GAO; National Atlas (map). | GAO-21-90.

Figure 5. Map of States Selected by GAO for Review of Elder Financial Exploitation.

---

[81] We did not conduct an independent review of state laws or regulations.

PROFILE 1. CALIFORNIA

State Demographics

California

Total population	39,512,223
Population age 65 and over (Percentage)	5,834,998[a] (15%)
Characteristics of population age 65 and over	Percentage
Female	55%
Male	45%
Age 85 and over	2%
With a disability	34%
With owner-occupied housing	73%
Income sources:	
Earned income	80%
Social Security income	85%
Other retirement income	54%
Cash public assistance	2%
Supplemental Nutrition Assistance Program (SNAP) benefits	6%
No telephone service	1%
No internet subscription (via computer)	7%

Sources: GAO analysis of U.S. Census Bureau's 2019 American Community Survey data, 1-year estimates; U.S. Geological Survey (map). | GAO-21-90.

Note: All estimates have a margin of error of +/- 0.4 percentage points or less at the 90% confidence level.

[a] The margin of error is +/-3410 at the 90% confidence level for the population age 65 and over.

State Adult Protective Services (APS)

APS at a Glance

Organizational structure	Administered by a component of each county's Health and Human Services agency.
Population served	Older adults with disabilities and younger adults with disabilities (including younger adult in a 24-hour health facility as an inpatient), and older adults by age alone.
Facility jurisdiction	APS investigates unlicensed facilities suspected of elder and dependent adult abuse.
Maltreatment types investigated	Abandonment, emotional abuse, financial exploitation, neglect, physical abuse, sexual abuse, self-neglect, and other.
APS response requirement for investigations	Case initiation occurs within 10 days.
Mandatory reporters	Medical, dental, pharmacy, guardian, conservator, nursing staff, residential care staff, foster parent, law enforcement, public safety, firefighter, and an employee of human services.

Source: GAO analysis of the National Adult Protective Services Technical Assistance Resource Center's review of state APS policy. We did not conduct an independent review of state laws or regulations. | GAO-21-90.

Strategies for Addressing Elder Financial Exploitation

California APS officials told us they:

- Improved coordination with law enforcement and financial institutions through education and outreach.
- Responded to elder financial exploitation using the Financial Abuse Specialist Team. This team is a multidisciplinary team of public and private representatives focused on the prevention, identification, and treatment of older and dependent adult financial abuse. APS officials said one way this group addressed elder financial exploitation is by educating its members on current issues and trends.
- Provided APS caseworker training through a partnership with the following universities: San Diego State University, California State University Fresno, and California State University Sacramento. They said each university has training academies that develop events or training content for outside speakers, internal trainers, and in-person and online trainings.

Source: GAO interviews with state APS officials. | GAO-21-90.

PROFILE 2. FLORIDA

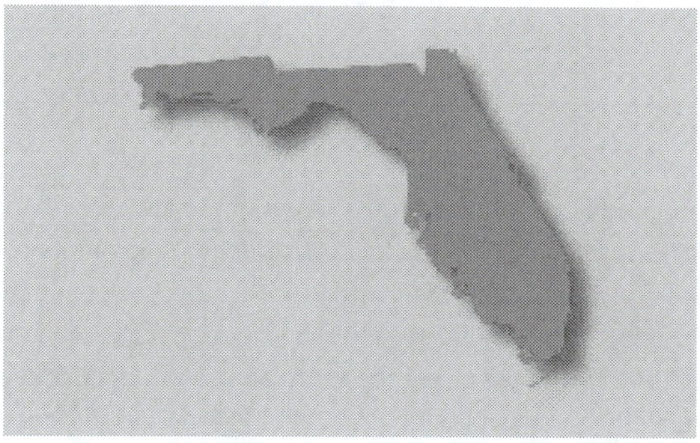

State Demographics

Florida

Total population	21,477,737
Population age 65 and over (Percentage)	4,498,198[a] (21%)
Characteristics of population age 65 and over	Percentage
Female	55%
Male	45%
Age 85 and over	3%
With a disability	32%
With owner-occupied housing	82%
Income sources:	
Earned income	72%
Social Security income	90%
Other retirement income	56%
Cash public assistance	2%
Supplemental NutritionAssistance Program (SNAP) benefits	10%
No telephone service	2%
No internet subscription (via computer)	9%

Sources: GAO analysis of U.S. Census Bureau's 2019 American Community Survey data, 1-year estimates; U.S. Geological Survey (map). | GAO-21-90.

Note: All estimates have a margin of error of +/- 0.6 percentage points or less at the 90% confidence level.

[a] The margin of error is +/-4208 at the 90% confidence level for the population age 65 and over.

State Adult Protective Services (APS)

APS at a Glance

Organizational structure	Administered by a component of the state's Health and Human Services agency.
Population served	Older adults with disabilities and younger adults with disabilities
Facility jurisdiction	APS investigates reports in community and institutional settings including mental hospitals, long-term residential care facilities, nursing homes, adult living facilities, facilities licensed by the Agency for Persons with Disabilities and facilities designed to restore individuals with intellectual disability deemed mentally incapacitated to proceed. Institutional settings do not include jails, correctional and detention facilities, federal veteran's hospitals/nursing homes.
Maltreatment types investigated	Emotional abuse, financial exploitation, neglect, physical abuse, sexual abuse, suspicious death, and self-neglect.
APS response requirement for investigations	Following a report of abuse, case initiation occurs within 1 day.
Mandatory reporters	Any person, including, but not limited to: medical, dental, pharmacy, mental health, social worker, case manager, nursing staff, residential care staff, foster parent, caregiver, law enforcement, public safety officer, firefighter, financial, legal, day care, senior services center, vocational rehab, coroner, medical examiner, embalmer, and long-term care ombudsman.

Source: GAO analysis of the National Adult Protective Services Technical Assistance Resource Center's review of state APS policy and information from state APS agency officials. We did not conduct an independent review of state laws or regulations. | GAO-21-90.

Strategies for Addressing Elder Financial Exploitation

Florida APS officials told us they:

- Developed a training module for newly-hired APS caseworkers on financial exploitation in partnership with the National Adult Protective Services Association.
- Attended a 2015 conference where many of the financial institutions agreed to share records concerning elder financial exploitation, which resulted in more collaboration regarding these cases including a request form for caseworkers to obtain client's account information from financial institutions.
- Established working agreements with law enforcement.
- Created a multidisciplinary team called the Adult Protection Team that meets monthly to discuss elder financial exploitation cases. The group also invites law enforcement, mental health, and health care administrators to the meetings to leverage their expertise concerning these cases.

Source: GAO interviews with state APS officials. | GAO-21-90.

PROFILE 3. MAINE

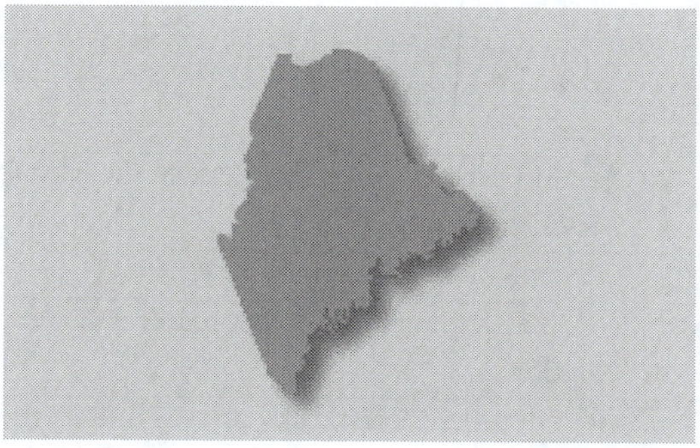

State Demographics

Maine

Total population	1,344,212
Population age 65 and over (Percentage)	285,978[a] (21%)
Characteristics of population age 65 and over	Percentage
Female	55%[b]
Male	46%
Age 85 and over	3%
With a disability	33%
With owner-occupied housing	78%
Income sources:	
Earned income	73%
Social Security income	91%
Other retirement income	59%
Cash public assistance	2%
Supplemental NutritionAssistance Program (SNAP) benefits	10%
No telephone service	1%
No internet subscription (via computer)	8%

Sources: GAO analysis of U.S. Census Bureau's 2019 American Community Survey data, 1-year estimates; U.S. Geological Survey (map). | GAO-21-90.

Note: All estimates have a margin of error of +/- 1.8 percentage points or less at the 90% confidence level.

[a] The margin of error is +/-1199 at the 90% confidence level for the population age 65 and over.

[b] The percentages for female and male do not add to 100% due to rounding.

State Adult Protective Services (APS)

APS at a Glance

Organizational structure	Administered by a component of the state's Health and Human Services agency
Population served	Dependent and incapacitated adults.
Facility jurisdiction	APS has authority to investigate reports of maltreatment across all locations.
Maltreatment types investigated	Abandonment, emotional abuse, financial exploitation, other or non- specific exploitation, neglect, physical abuse, sexual abuse, suspicious death, self-neglect, and other.
APS response requirement for investigations	Case initiation occurs within 5 days.
Mandatory reporters	Medical, dental, pharmacy, mental health, social worker, case manager, guardian, conservator, clergy, law enforcement, public safety, firefighter, coroner, medical examiner, and embalmer.

Source: GAO analysis of the National Adult Protective Services Technical Assistance Resource Center's review of state APS policy and information from state APS agency officials. We did not conduct an independent review of state laws or regulations. | GAO-21-90.

Strategies for Addressing Elder Financial Exploitation

Maine APS officials told us they:

- Provided training to financial institutions on how to address elder financial exploitation and the process for reporting it to APS officials
- Gave general investigation training to APS caseworkers that provides guidance on elder financial exploitation investigations. This training also provides information on how to collect related data.
- Submitted cases where the elder financial exploitation is a high dollar amount to investigators on the Financial Abuse Specialist Team. This team works with a separate Financial Abuse Specialist Committee to collaborate on financial exploitation cases. The committee includes prosecutors, detectives, and other community partners.
- Used a checklist that lists the type of evidence needed for elder financial exploitation investigations.

Source: GAO interviews with state APS officials. | GAO-21-90.

PROFILE 4. NEVADA

State Demographics

Nevada

Total population	3,080,156
Population age 65 and over (Percentage)	498,219[a] (14%)
Characteristics of population age 65 and over	Percentage
Female	53%
Male	47%
Age 85 and over	1%
With a disability	34%
With owner-occupied housing	72%
Income sources:	
Earned income	77%
Social Security income	89%
Other retirement income	57%
Cash public assistance	2%
Supplemental NutritionAssistance Program (SNAP) benefits	9%
No telephone service	2%
No internet subscription (via computer)	8%

Sources: GAO analysis of U.S. Census Bureau's 2019 American Community Survey data, 1-year estimates; U.S. Geological Survey (map). | GAO-21-90.

Note: All estimates have a margin of error of +/- 1.3 percentage points or less at the 90% confidence level.

[a]The margin of error is +/-1593 at the 90% confidence level for the population age 65 and over.

State Adult Protective Services (APS)

APS at a Glance

Organizational structure	Administered by a component of the state's Department of Health and Human Services.
Population served	Adults age 60 and older, and vulnerable adults age 18-59.
Facility jurisdiction	Nevada Adult Protective Services investigates reports of maltreatment for those living in the community in a private home, group residential facilities, and individuals within a skilled nursing facility.
Maltreatment types investigated	Abandonment, emotional abuse, financial exploitation, other or non-specific exploitation, neglect, physical abuse, sexual abuse, and self-neglect.
APS response requirement for investigations	Case initiation occurs within 3 business days.
Mandatory reporters	Medical, dental, mental health, social worker, home health aides, nursing home employees, financial advisors, law enforcement, public safety, coroner, and medical examiner, among others.

Source: GAO analysis of the National Adult Protective Services Technical Assistance Resource Center's review of state APS policy and information from state APS agency officials. We did not conduct an independent review of state laws or regulations. | GAO-21-90.

Strategies for Addressing Elder Financial Exploitation

Nevada APS officials told us they:

- Leveraged forensic accountants for its investigations of financial exploitation, when deemed necessary.
- Provided training to newly-hired investigators on how to conduct financial exploitation investigations.
- Established a training academy for all investigators in 2019. This academy was created in partnership with a subject matter expert. It is a 4-day training with a session on financial exploitation.
- Attend the annual National Adult Protective Services Association conferences. During each conference, staff attend a session on finanical exploitation.

Source: GAO interviews with state APS officials. | GAO-21-90.

PROFILE 5. NEW YORK

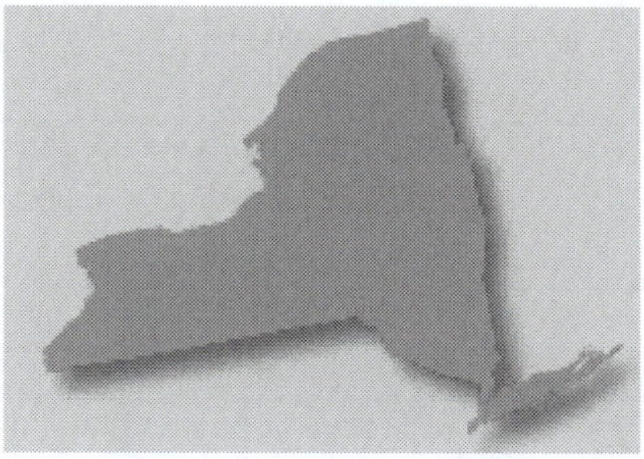

State Demographics

New York

Total population	19,453,561
Population age 65 and over (Percentage)	3,295,968[a] (17%)
Characteristics of population age 65 and over	Percentage
Female	57%
Male	43%
Age 85 and over	2%
With a disability	32%
With owner-occupied housing	65%
Income sources:	
Earned income	77%
Social Security income	87%
Other retirement income	58%
Cash public assistance	3%
Supplemental NutritionAssistance Program (SNAP) benefits	16%
No telephone service	2%
No internet subscription (via computer)	8%

Sources: GAO analysis of U.S. Census Bureau's 2019 American Community Survey data, 1-year estimates; U.S. Geological Survey (map). | GAO-21-90.

Note: All estimates have a margin of error of +/- 0.6 percentage points or less at the 90% confidence level.

[a] The margin of error is +/-3163 at the 90% confidence level for the population age 65 and over.

State Adult Protective Services (APS)

APS at a Glance

Organizational structure	Administered by a component of each county's Health and Human Services agency and supervised at the state level.
Population served	Older adults and adults age 18 and older with a physical or mental impairment.
Facility jurisdiction	APS does not investigate in a facility.
Maltreatment types investigated	Abandonment, emotional abuse, financial exploitation, other or non- specific exploitation, neglect, physical abuse, sexual abuse, and self-neglect.
APS response requirement for investigations	Case initiation occurs within 3 days. If the situation is life threatening, a response is required within 24 hours.
Mandatory reporters	There are no mandatory reporters.

Source: GAO analysis of the National Adult Protective Services Technical Assistance Resource Center's review of state APS policy and information from state APS agency officials. We did not conduct an independent review of state laws or regulations. | GAO-21-90.

Strategies for Addressing Elder Financial Exploitation

New York APS officials told us they:

- Provided training on financial exploitation investigations in their required core training for all APS caseworkers and supervisors. They also offer a course entitled, "Broken Trust: Financial Exploitation and Power of Attorney Abuse - A Guide for APS Professionals in NYS."
- Developed the Financial Exploitation Investigation Suite of Tools, which is a set of tools designed to guide the way elder financial exploitation is investigated. For example, they created a red flag checklist that made it easier for caseworkers to identify signs of potential financial exploitation.
- Used forensic accountants for elder financial exploitation cases in some local district APS operations.
- Through state and community partnerships established Enhanced Multi-Disciplinary Teams to address financial exploitation and complex cases of abuse for clients over 60 years of age.
- Established strong relationships with local agencies and the private sector that support coordination with elder financial exploitation investigations.

Source: GAO interviews with state APS officials. | GAO-21-90.

PROFILE 6. OREGON

State Demographics

Oregon

Total population	4,217,737
Population age 65 and over (Percentage)	767,496[a] (18%)
Characteristics of population age 65 and over	Percentage
Female	54%
Male	46%
Age 85 and over	2%
With a disability	35%
With owner-occupied housing	78%
Income sources:	
Earned income	76%
Social Security income	91%
Other retirement income	61%
Cash public assistance	2%
Supplemental NutritionAssistance Program (SNAP) benefits	12%
No telephone service	1%
No internet subscription (via computer)	7%

Sources: GAO analysis of U.S. Census Bureau's 2019 American Community Survey data, 1-year estimates; U.S. Geological Survey (map). | GAO-21-90.

Note: All estimates have a margin of error of +/- 1.1 percentage points or less at the 90% confidence level.

[a] The margin of error is +/-2795 at the 90% confidence level for the population age 65 and over.

State Adult Protective Services (APS)

APS at a Glance

Organizational structure	Administered by a component of the state's Health and Human Services agency.
Population served	Older adults with disabilities, younger adults with disabilities, and older adults by age alone.
Facility jurisdiction	APS is available to any adult residing in a licensed care facility, nursing facility (if alleged perpetrator is not employed by the facility), adult foster home, or in private residences.
Maltreatment types investigated	Abandonment, emotional abuse, financial exploitation, other or non-specific exploitation, neglect, physical abuse, sexual abuse, self-neglect, and other.
APS response requirement for investigations	APS uses a triage process of determining the nature and severity of risk to individuals and the immediacy of response required for case initiation.
Mandatory reporters	Medical, dental, pharmacy, mental health, social worker, case manager, guardian, conservator, clergy, nursing staff, residential care staff, foster parent, caregiver, law enforcement, public safety, firefighter, legal, and an employee of human services.

Source: GAO analysis of the National Adult Protective Services Technical Assistance Resource Center's review of state APS policy and information from state APS agency officials. We did not conduct an independent review of state laws or regulations. | GAO-21-90.

Strategies for Addressing Elder Financial Exploitation

Oregon APS officials told us they:

- Collaborated with subject matter experts in their unit such as policy analysts and quality assurance specialists for technical assistance concerning finanical exploitation cases.
- Required newly hired APS investigators to complete a Fundamental Training Course that includes a session focused on financial exploitation investigations.
- Hosted meetings every other month, where APS investigators receive specialized training by subject matter experts throughout the year.
- Specifically, the state's Central Office APS Unit that held this training had one session on abuse by a power of attorney and other trusted individuals. This session was presented by an elder law attorney.

Source: GAO interviews with state APS officials. | GAO-21-90.

PROFILE 7. PENNSYLVANIA

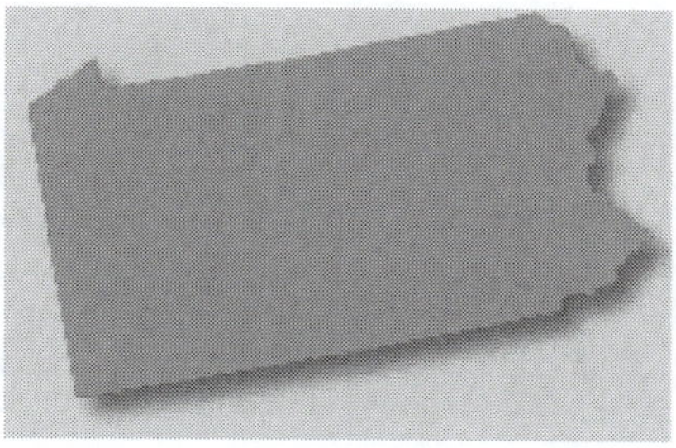

State Demographics

Pennsylvania

Total population	12,801,989
Population age 65 and over (Percentage)	2,388,218[a] (19%)
Characteristics of population age 65 and over	Percentage
Female	56%
Male	44%
Age 85 and over	3%
With a disability	32%
With owner-occupied housing	78%
Income sources:	
Earned income	75%
Social Security income	91%
Other retirement income	64%
Cash public assistance	2%
Supplemental NutritionAssistance Program (SNAP) benefits	11%
No telephone service	1%
No internet subscription (via computer)	7%

Sources: GAO analysis of U.S. Census Bureau's 2019 American Community Survey data, 1-year estimates; U.S. Geological Survey (map). | GAO-21-90 Note: All estimates have a margin of error of +/- 0.5 percentage points or less at the 90% confidence level.

[a] The margin of error is +/-2997 at the 90% confidence level for the population age 65 and over.

State Adult Protective Services (APS)

APS at a Glance

Organizational structure	The state's Older Adults Protective Services (OAPS) program is administered by the state Department of Aging, and implemented locally by each county's Area Agency on Aging.
Population served	Adults age 60 and over.
Facility jurisdiction	OAPS investigates in facility and community settings.
Maltreatment types investigated	Abandonment, emotional abuse, financial exploitation, other or non-specific exploitation, neglect, physical abuse, sexual abuse, suspicious death, self-neglect, caretaker neglect, and other.
APS response requirement for investigations	Case initiation occurs within 72 hours.
Mandatory reporters	Employers and administrators of facilities (as defined in state law).

Source: GAO analysis of the National Adult Protective Services Technical Assistance Resource Center's review of state APS policy and information from state APS agency officials. We did not conduct an independent review of state laws or regulations. | GAO-21-90.

Strategies for Addressing Elder Financial Exploitation

Pennsylvania Older Adults Protective Services (OAPS) officials told us they:

- Provided initial basic training to all new investigative staff. This training includes an overview of relevant laws and related regulations.
- It is 3-and-a-half days in duration and includes an introduction to financial exploitation, such as how to collaborate with banks and guidance on analyzing bank statements.
- Offered training from the Department of Aging's Institute on Protective Services at Temple University-Harrisburg. The curriculum includes in person or virtual basic training with a financial exploitation case review. According to OAPS officials, the virtual course was developed in response to the Coronavirus Disease 2019 (COVID-19) pandemic.
- Temple also provided them the Financial Exploitation Investigative Guide, which is a tool that caseworkers can use when conducting financial exploitation investigations.
- Offered online training modules with links to videos. One of the topics covered in the financial exploitation course includes investigations concerning fraudulent credit card use.

Source: GAO interviews with state APS officials. | GAO-21-90.

PROFILE 8. VIRGINIA

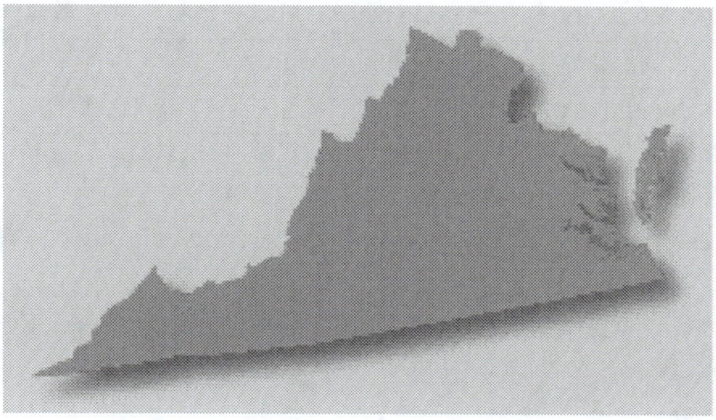

State Demographics

Virginia

Total population	8,535,519
Population age 65 and over (Percentage)	1,358,336[a] (16%)
Characteristics of population age 65 and over	Percentage
Female	56%
Male	44%
Age 85 and over	2%
With a disability	33%
With owner-occupied housing	81%
Income sources:	
Earned income	79%
Social Security income	88%
Other retirement income	65%
Cash public assistance	2%

(Continued)

Supplemental NutritionAssistance Program (SNAP) benefits	6%
No telephone service	1%
No internet subscription (via computer)	7%

Sources: GAO analysis of U.S. Census Bureau's 2019 American Community Survey data, 1-year estimates; U.S. Geological Survey (map). | GAO-21-90.

Note: All estimates have a margin of error of +/- 0.8 percentage points or less at the 90% confidence level.

[a] The margin of error is +/-4164 at the 90% confidence level for the population age 65 and over.

State Adult Protective Services (APS)

APS at a Glance

Organizational structure	Located in the state's Aging and Disability Agency, administered by local Departments of Social Services.
Population served	Adults age 60 or older and incapacitated adults age 18-59.
Facility jurisdiction	APS investigates reports of suspected abuse, neglect or exploitation in all settings (community, residential, and institutional) with the exception of state correctional facilities.
Maltreatment types investigated	Emotional abuse, financial exploitation, other exploitation, neglect, physical abuse, sexual abuse, and self-neglect.
APS response requirement for investigations	Case initiation within 24 hours unless there is need for an immediate response.
Mandatory reporters	Medical, dental, pharmacy, mental health, social worker, case manager, law enforcement officer, any person employed by or contracted with a public or private agency or facility and working with adults in an administrative, supportive or direct care capacity.

Source: GAO analysis of the National Adult Protective Services Technical Assistance Resource Center's review of state APS policy and information from state APS agency officials. We did not conduct an independent review of state laws or regulations. | GAO-21-90.

Strategies for Addressing Elder Financial Exploitation

Virginia APS officials told us they:
• Provided law enforcement and APS educational information concerning elder financial exploitation through regional multidisciplinary teams and elder justice coalitions. This opportunity to collaborate through this group helped them understand each others respective role as it relates to investigations. • Created online training modules for APS caseworkers with funds from a 2018 ACL grant. This training provided them helpful information that they leveraged when reporting the National Adult Maltreatment Reporting System's (NAMRS) case component data in fiscal year 2020. • Received an ACL grant in 2015 that supported the development of their unified APS data system that is statewide.

Source: GAO interviews with state APS officials. | GAO-21-90.

APPENDIX II: OVERVIEW OF STUDIES OF ESTIMATED COSTS OF FINANCIAL EXPLOITATION IN SIX STATES

This appendix provides additional details on the data source, methodology, key findings, and limitations described in the seven studies that estimate costs of elder financial exploitation in six individual states.[82] Two studies estimate the costs in Maine and the remaining five studies estimate costs in one of the following states: New York, Oregon, Pennsylvania, Utah, or Virginia. Six of the studies estimated costs to victims, and three state studies also calculated costs to taxpayers. Six of the seven state studies used a similar methodology to determine costs to victims, by manually reviewing casefile notes from a sample of Adult Protective Service (APS) casefiles to record cost data. Study authors typically used these data to calculate a statewide estimate. In some studies, they simply added the costs together. Then, study authors generated a larger number based on one of several underreporting factors to develop a statewide estimate.[83] See table 4 for detailed information on these studies.

---

[82] We identified one additional state study from Wyoming, published in 2014, that included some information about costs based on a review of APS casefiles. This study examined 10 cases from 2011, 16 cases from 2012, and six cases from 2013. Upon review, we determined this study's methodology was not described in enough detail for us to determine if the estimates generated from these data were reliable.

[83] State study authors used various factors to account for this underreporting, based on elder abuse studies estimating that just one in 10, one in 24, one in 25, or one in 44 incidents are reported to APS.

Table 4. Findings, methodology, and limitations of state financial exploitation cost studies

Study year and state	Title and author	Data sources and study population	Analysis methods	Results	Selected limitations identified by study authors and our review
2011 Utah	"The 2011 Utah Economic Cost of Elder Financial Exploitation," by Jilene Gunther	Utah APS cases for adults age 60 and over who had supported cases. Case file data were supplemented with Kelley Blue Book, Utah sold real estate and real estate estimate tools, and other valuation tools when value of losses were unavailable.	Fifty-two cases were reviewed in- depth to determine financial loss. Cases were reviewed regarding dollar amount taken and property stolen. In cases involving property, gathered information as available from case notes was used to determine the value of lost property. Projected costs by multiplying by underreporting factors of 10, 25, and 44.[a]	Observed cost: $5 million (victims) Projected cost: $48 to $210 million (victims)	In some cases, there was not enough information in the case file to make a valuation of costs or valuation of property, so these values were derived based on supplemental data.
2014 Oregon	"Financial Exploitation Data Book: A Retrospective Look At Community Based Financial Exploitation in Oregon in 2013," by Rebecca Fetters	Oregon APS cases, which include those physically disabled (age 18-64) or over the age of 65, which had substantiated cases.	Of 969 cases that had substantiated cases of financial exploitation, 623 were read and reviewed by hand. Added costs in case file notes for which it was possible to assign a specific dollar amount, and extrapolated costs for the broader number of cases for which there was no dollar amount in the case file. Determined the average loss per case, multiplied by the total number of substantiated cases, then multiplied by an underreporting factor of 44	Observed cost: $3 million (victims), $407,000 (taxpayer) Projected cost: $439 million (victims), $1.9 million (taxpayers)	The total loss to taxpayer-funded programs attributed the sample cannot fully be calculated due to limitations in documentary evidence.
2016 New York	"The New York State Cost of Financial Exploitation Study," by Yufan Huang, and Alan Lawitz	New York State APS cases within a 12- month period across 31 local social services districts. These data are not exclusive to the older population. All cases were coded using a 24- item case review document created specifically for the present study. Most districts submitted case reviews for all cases during the study window; others reviewed a randomly selected subset.	928 case reviews of APS cases involving allegations of financial exploitation; 479 cases were used to calculate alleged victim losses. The personnel hours associated with providing these services were defined as service agency costs. Public benefit costs were tracked by asking APS workers to identify new or additional public benefits provided to clients following an APS investigation. Evidence supporting the alleged exploitation was found in 52 percent of coded referrals. For these cases, workers provided additional information on the identity of the alleged perpetrator, the alleged methods used to exploit the victim, and the nature and value of the assets allegedly taken (victim losses).	Observed cost: $27 million (victims and taxpayers) Projected cost: $352 million to $1.5 billion (victims and taxpayers)	The study did not have full coverage of the state of New York and had to estimate costs for the larger population.

Study year and state	Title and author	Data sources and study population	Analysis methods	Results	Selected limitations identified by study authors and our review
			Adjusted to include estimates for districts lacking data, then multiplied by a high-end (44) and low-end (10) underreporting factor.		
2016 Virginia	"Adult Financial Exploitation in Virginia: Collaborative Approaches to Address the Issue," by Virginia Department for Aging and Rehabilitative Services	Virginia APS cases in State fiscal year 2015 for older adults (age 60 and over) and incapacitated adults (age 18-59) who had substantiated cases	76 cases with enough information to determine the extent of loss were reviewed, which identified a loss of $2.1 million, with an average of about $27,782 per case. The 76 cases were selected for review from 1,016 substantiated financial exploitation cases. Therefore the case average was multiplied by 1,061 to determine that these victims may have lost up to $28,226,512. The study projected costs by adjusting the number of substantiated cases by an underreporting factor of 44 and multiplied by the average cost per victim in sampled cases.	Observed cost: $2.1 million (victims) Projected cost: $1.2 billion (victims)	The findings do not include Fairfax County due to data compatibility issues, and Fairfax is the most populous county in Virginia.
2017 Maineb	"Financial Exploitation of Maine's Older Adults: An Analysis of Maine Adult Protective Services and Legal Services for the Elderly Case Records, State Fiscal Years 2010-2016," by Eileen Griffin, Catherine McGuire, and Kimberly I. Snow	Maine APS cases from State Fiscal Years 2010-2016 for adults 60 and over with at least one substantiated allegation of financial exploitation. Maine Legal Services for the Elderly (LSE) legal files from State Fiscal Years 2010 - 2016 for LSE clients involving allegations determined to have merit for further investigation	This study analyzes cases handled by Maine's APS and LSE to try and address underreporting of elder financial exploitation by multiplying underreporting factors of 10 and 44.	Observed cost (to victims): 2010: $4.6 million 2011: $2.9 million 2012: $3.2 million 2013: $3.3 million 2014: $4.9 million 2015: $4.5 million 2016: $4.7 million Projected cost (to victims): 2010: $46 to $205 million 2011: $29 to $127 million 2012: $32 to $139 million 2013: $33 to $146 million 2014: $49 to $215 million 2015: $45 to $199 million 2016:$47 to $205 million	The extent to which the populations are different in the two data sets is not estimated in the report. There were a relatively small number of cases.

Table 4. (Continued)

Study year and state	Title and author	Data sources and study population	Analysis methods	Results	Selected limitations identified by study authors and our review
2020 Maine	"Pent-up demand for care among dual- eligible victims of elder financial exploitation in Maine" by Yvonne Jonk, et al.	Maine APS database from 2006- 2014 for adults age 60 and over who were dual-eligible for Medicaid and Medicare with substantiated allegation of financial exploitation. APS cases were linked to Medicare and Medicaid claims data.	Health service utilization and costs were analyzed 1-year prior, during, and 2 years after the initial APS investigation. Used propensity scores to match each APS adult with a substantiated allegation of financial exploitation to two non-APS controls. Regression models were used to compare the likelihood of incurring costs and expenditure levels of financial exploitation victims relative to comparable non-APS controls, respectively. Used a range of under reporting rates: one in 24 and one in 44 to estimate range of the total Medicare and Medicaid costs associated with financial exploitation in Maine.	Observed cost: $0.3 million (annual costs for taxpayers) Projected cost: $7.2 to $13.2 million (annual costs for taxpayers)	The study is limited to a specific group of older adults who were dual-eligible for Medicare and Medicaid for the entire period. There were a relatively small number of cases. Given potential underreporting issue, some financial exploitation cases may have been included in the non-APS controls.
2020 Pennsylvania	"Financial Exploitation of Older Adults Study Report" by Pennsylvania Department of Aging	Pennsylvania cases from Social Assistance Management System database between July 2017- June 2018 for elders randomly selected from 10 Area Agencies on Aging.	The Department of Aging randomly selected a total of 455 cases from 10 Area Agencies on Aging (AAAs) encompassing the 14 counties with highest substantiated financial exploitation cases. 315 cases with dollar amount were used to calculate average financial exploitation. The authors projected the total cost by multiplying the average financial exploitation cost calculated earlier by the state wide number of total financial exploitation cases substantiated by the AAAs during this timeframe and an underreporting factor of 44.	Observed cost: $12 million (victims) Projected cost: $2.5 billion (victims)	This study did not have full coverage of the state of Pennsylvania and had to estimate costs for the larger population.

Source: GAO analysis of state cost estimate studies. | GAO-21-90.

Notes: Given that the national and state studies use different timeframes, including partial years, or different calendar and fiscal years, we did not adjust the cost estimates in the various studies for inflation. Importantly, cost estimates across these studies should not be compared or added up.

[a] State study authors used various factors to account for this underreporting, based on elder abuse studies estimating that just one in 10, one in 24, one in 25, or one in 44 incidents are reported to APS.

[b] The 2017 Maine study included data and analysis from 2010 through 2016. We reported cost estimates by year because the study did not adjust their dollar amounts for inflation.

APPENDIX III: SELECTED STATE APS AGENCY TOOLS FOR COLLECTING FINANCIAL EXPLOITATION COST DATA

This appendix provides examples of data elements or tools developed by Adult Protective Services (APS) in five of the selected states. Some states have added—or are planning to add—new data elements to their states' data systems to record dollar amounts, what was stolen, or the method used by the perpetrator. Other states have developed tools to assist caseworkers that are collecting cost data during financial exploitation investigations. The tools states have developed for caseworkers include checklists, lists of questions, and worksheets that can be used by caseworkers during their investigations. The following examples illustrate some states' efforts to improve the collection of cost data when investigating financial exploitation cases.

Examples of New Data Elements Capturing Costs in State Data Systems

New York

New York's APS agency developed a list of additional reportable data elements about the costs of financial exploitation which could be incorporated into their existing state data system for recording and reporting.[257] This template includes data elements such as the costs of items stolen from the client, the cost of additional public benefits needed due to financial exploitation, as well as costs incurred by APS and other public agencies during the investigation or assessment of the financial exploitation case. If these data elements are incorporated, the APS data system will prompt the caseworker to provide information such as the method of theft and the dollar amount for items stolen, including personal property, stocks or bonds, real estate, automobiles, and/or public benefits (see Figure 6).

Oregon

In Oregon, the state's data system collects the data elements shown below (see Figure 7), which include a description of the exploitation and the dollar amount lost.

Virginia

In 2019, Virginia's APS agency added a screen to its case management system to collect the known or estimated amount of monetary loss, amount recovered, and method

---

[257] This list of data elements was developed by New York APS with funds from an Administration for Community Living grant (specifically, a State Grant to Enhance Adult Protective Services) in fiscal year 2015.

of financial exploitation: theft, fraud, forgery, or unauthorized credit card use (see Figure 8).

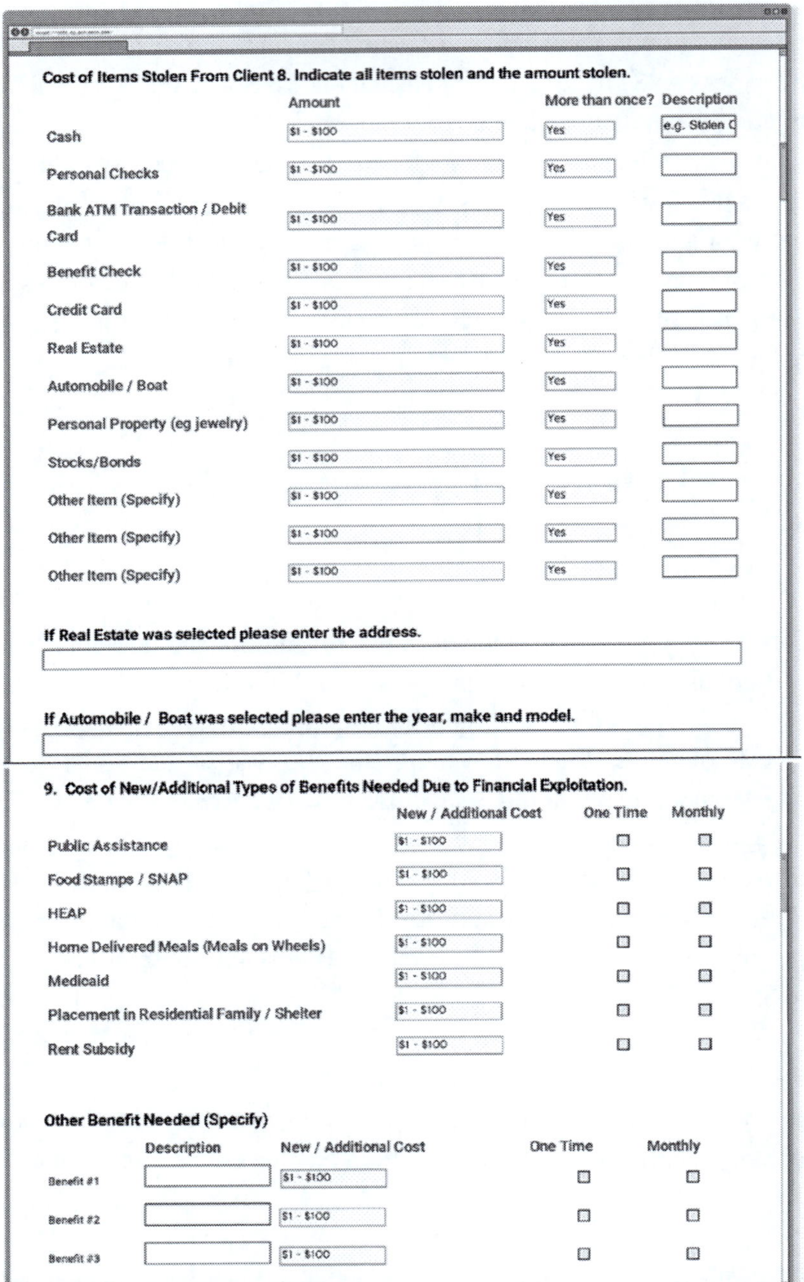

Cost of Items Stolen From Client 8. Indicate all items stolen and the amount stolen.

	Amount	More than once?	Description
Cash	$1 - $100	Yes	e.g. Stolen C
Personal Checks	$1 - $100	Yes	
Bank ATM Transaction / Debit Card	$1 - $100	Yes	
Benefit Check	$1 - $100	Yes	
Credit Card	$1 - $100	Yes	
Real Estate	$1 - $100	Yes	
Automobile / Boat	$1 - $100	Yes	
Personal Property (eg jewelry)	$1 - $100	Yes	
Stocks/Bonds	$1 - $100	Yes	
Other Item (Specify)	$1 - $100	Yes	
Other Item (Specify)	$1 - $100	Yes	
Other Item (Specify)	$1 - $100	Yes	

If Real Estate was selected please enter the address.

If Automobile / Boat was selected please enter the year, make and model.

9. Cost of New/Additional Types of Benefits Needed Due to Financial Exploitation.

	New / Additional Cost	One Time	Monthly
Public Assistance	$1 - $100	☐	☐
Food Stamps / SNAP	$1 - $100	☐	☐
HEAP	$1 - $100	☐	☐
Home Delivered Meals (Meals on Wheels)	$1 - $100	☐	☐
Medicaid	$1 - $100	☐	☐
Placement in Residential Family / Shelter	$1 - $100	☐	☐
Rent Subsidy	$1 - $100	☐	☐

Other Benefit Needed (Specify)

	Description	New / Additional Cost	One Time	Monthly
Benefit #1		$1 - $100	☐	☐
Benefit #2		$1 - $100	☐	☐
Benefit #3		$1 - $100	☐	☐

Source: New York Adult Protective Services (ASP). | GAO-21-90.

Figure 6. Example List of Reportable Data Elements on Costs of Financial Exploitation and Outcomes from the APS Agency in New York.

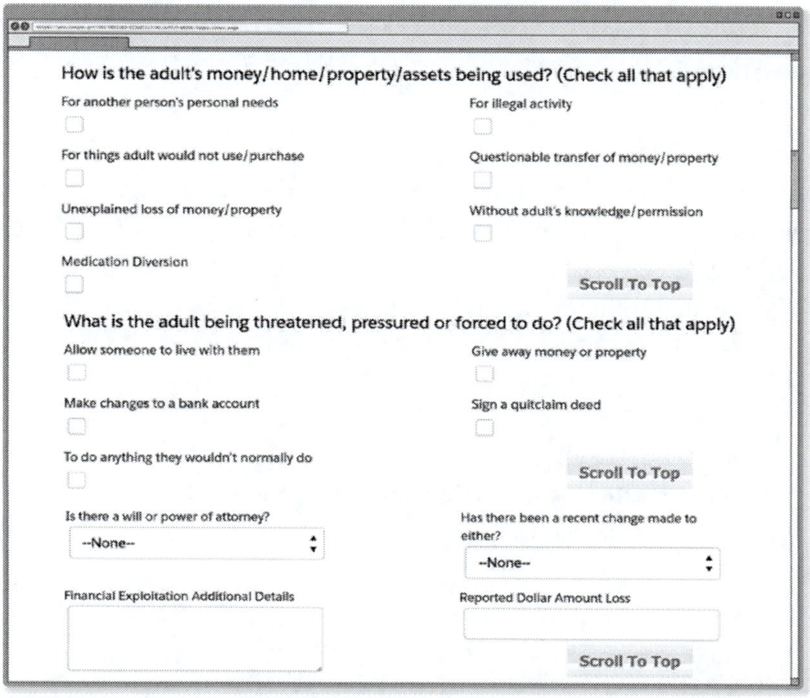

Source: Oregon Adult Protective Services (ASP). | GAO-21-90.

Figure 7. Example Data Collection Page on Financial Exploitation from the APS Case Management System in Oregon.

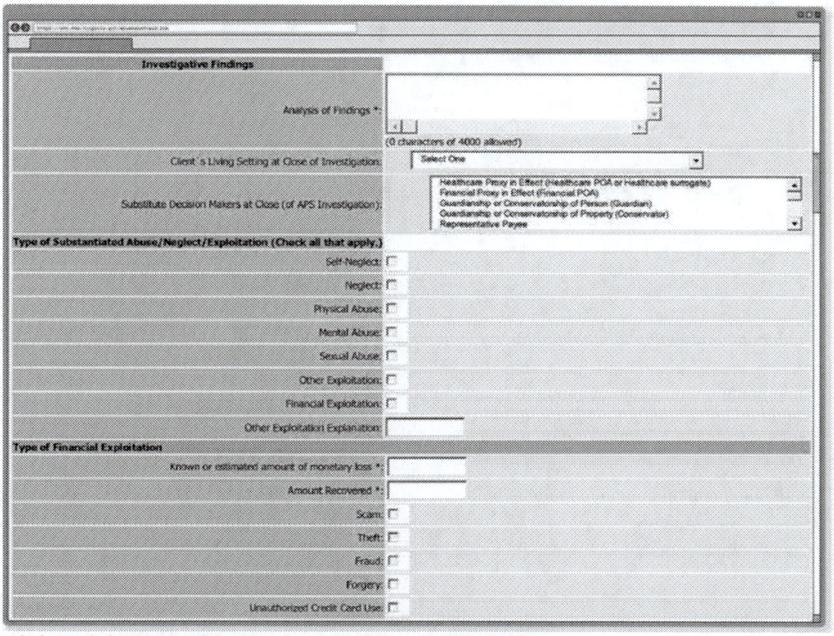

Source: Virginia Adult Protective Services (ASP). | GAO-21-90.

Figure 8. Example Data Collection Page on Financial Exploitation from the APS Case Management System in Virginia.

Examples of Tools to Assist Caseworkers That Are Collecting Financial Exploitation Data

California

APS officials in Sacramento County told us they developed a questionnaire in 2014 for caseworkers to use during financial exploitation investigations (see Figure 9). This questionnaire directs caseworkers to collect data such as asset taken, value of asset taken, method of financial exploitation, and value of the asset protected due to APS intervention.

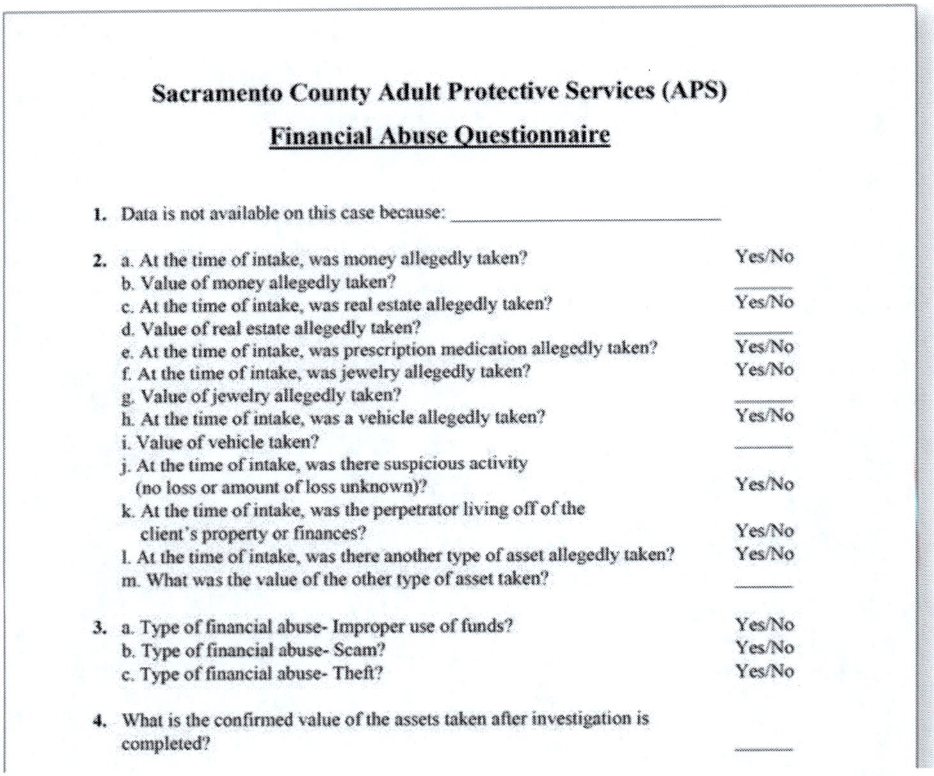

Sacramento County Adult Protective Services (APS)

Financial Abuse Questionnaire

1. Data is not available on this case because: ____________

2. a. At the time of intake, was money allegedly taken? Yes/No
   b. Value of money allegedly taken? ______
   c. At the time of intake, was real estate allegedly taken? Yes/No
   d. Value of real estate allegedly taken? ______
   e. At the time of intake, was prescription medication allegedly taken? Yes/No
   f. At the time of intake, was jewelry allegedly taken? Yes/No
   g. Value of jewelry allegedly taken? ______
   h. At the time of intake, was a vehicle allegedly taken? Yes/No
   i. Value of vehicle taken? ______
   j. At the time of intake, was there suspicious activity (no loss or amount of loss unknown)? Yes/No
   k. At the time of intake, was the perpetrator living off of the client's property or finances? Yes/No
   l. At the time of intake, was there another type of asset allegedly taken? Yes/No
   m. What was the value of the other type of asset taken? ______

3. a. Type of financial abuse- Improper use of funds? Yes/No
   b. Type of financial abuse- Scam? Yes/No
   c. Type of financial abuse- Theft? Yes/No

4. What is the confirmed value of the assets taken after investigation is completed? ______

Figure 9. (Continued)

5. a. Due to the APS intervention, what is the value of the income or pension protected each month?	______
b. Due to APS intervention, what is the value of savings, (money market accounts, IRAs, annuities, stocks, etc) protected?	______
c. Due to APS intervention, what is the value of the real estate protected?	______
d. Due to APS intervention, was prescription medication protected from theft?	Yes/No
e. Due to APS intervention, what is the value of the jewelry protected?	______
f. Due to APS intervention, what is the value of the vehicle(s) protected?	______
g. Due to APS intervention, what is the value of other assets protected?	______
h. Not applicable.	Yes/No
6. a. Social worker requested neurological exam or capacity declaration to address cognitive capacity?	Yes/No
b. Social worker assisted client/family in obtaining payee?	Yes/No
c. Social worker collaborated with family and friends to protect client's assets?	Yes/No
d. Social worker assisted client in obtaining a restraining order?	Yes/No
e. Social worker made crime report to law enforcement? (Do not check yes if only the 343 was completed)	Yes/No
f. Social worker facilitated or assisted in the recovery of client's assets?	Yes/No
g. Social Worker assisted client/family in closing bank accounts and/or opening new accounts?	Yes/No
h. Social worker made referrals to the criminal justice system (FTC, FBI IC3, Postmaster, DOJ, DA's Office, etc)?	Yes/No
i. Social worker educated the client and/or suspect about the law requiring the client's assets to be used for the client's benefit?	Yes/No
j. Social worker ensured appropriate level of placement for client?	Yes/No
k. Social worker educated client and/or family regarding financial scams?	Yes/No
l. Social worker referred the client for conservatorship?	Yes/No
m. Other interventions	Yes/No
n. None (either N/A or interventions completed by friend, family, or professionals prior to APS involvement)	Yes/No
o. Client has capacity and refused social worker interventions/services?	Yes/No

Source: Sacramento County Adult Protective Services (ASP). | GAO-21-90.

Figure 9. Example Questionnaire for APS Caseworkers to Use in Financial Abuse Investigations from Sacramento County, California.

Maine

In Maine, APS officials have created a checklist to assist its caseworkers collecting information when investigating financial exploitation cases. The checklist includes examples of evidence to obtain and interviews to pursue (see Figure 10).

CHECKLIST OF EVIDENCE TO OBTAIN IN FINANCIAL EXPLOITATION CASE

- ☐ Bank documents of victim, including
  - o Bank statements for saving, checking
  - o Copies of all checks written on victim's account (front and back)
  - o Copies of all deposits into victim's account
  - o Copies of loan paperwork, application, payment history
- ☐ Bank documents of the suspect (same as above)
- ☐ MaineCare Application file if person is on MaineCare
  - o Shows other assets
  - o Shows who applied – suspect?
  - o Correspondence or notes between financial worker and applicant
- ☐ Nursing home records
  - o Account history
  - o Trust account history – is the suspect giving victim and spending money
  - o Correspondence with suspect regarding non-payment
  - o Admission agreement (is suspect listed as financially responsible party?)
- ☐ Documentation of other assets/investments of the victim
  - o Annuities, mutual funds, bonds, stocks
  - o People on MaineCare typically will not have stocks, bonds, mutual funds – can only have assets of $3,000
- ☐ Documentation of any income that does no automatically go into victim's bank account (to see who is endorsing the checks and where they are being deposited/cashed)
  - o Social security
  - o Tax refunds
  - o Pensions
- ☐ Interviews
  - o Current POA/Conservator/Guardian (non-suspect)
    - ▪ Find out about usual expenditures of victim
    - ▪ Obtain financial information that might have already gathered
  - o Nursing home or group home staff
    - ▪ Obtain payment history and correspondence with suspect
    - ▪ If a trust account exists, inquire into procedure related to how the trust accounts are handled (i.e. how money is received and spent)
  - o Victim, if competent
    - ▪ Makes sure to verify victim was not giving gifts to the suspect and that she was not aware of the checks being written in her account.
    - ▪ Ask if victim is aware that her nursing home (etc) bill is in arrears.
    - ▪ Ask about any agreements for payment for services provided.
  - o Suspect (tape/video record)
    - ▪ Show him/her suspicious checks and ask what they are for.
  - o Relatives of victim
    - ▪ May have information on the suspect or financial info on the victim
    - ▪ May have witnessed interactions between suspect and victim which could show undue influence, harassment, duress
  - o Complainant (if none of the above)
  - o MaineCare worker
    - ▪ Inquire about any statements made to suspect about how to appropriately spend down the recipient's money
    - ▪ Ask about difficulties obtaining financial documentation from suspect to complete the application
    - ▪ Ask whether worker had any suspicions when reviewing the financial documentation during the MaineCare approval process
- ☐ Medical records of victim if competency is an issue
- ☐ Employee file (if suspect is a group home/nursing home/personal care attendant (PCA) employee
- ☐ Criminal history check
- ☐ Documentation of suspicious expenditures out of victim's account (if there are checks for unusual expenses, get the documents – loan paperwork, credit card – find out if victim has a credit card, etc.; if there are checks to other banks, find out if the victim or suspect have an account at the bank through subpoenas; if large ticket purchases are made see if you can find out form the company who made these purchases. If there are purchases for insurance, such as health insurance, not belonging to the victim, match the acct # to the suspect.)
- ☐ Credit card records of victim or suspect
- ☐ Invoices, receipts, etc (fiduciary should keep these, but they frequently don't)
- ☐ Conservatorship file documents (if suspect was the victim's conservator, they have to file annual accountings)
- ☐ Consider consulting a fiduciary expert (such as a professional conservator). Can sometime be used as an expert witness to explain fiduciary duty.

Source: Maine Adult Protective Services (ASP). | GAO-21-90.

Figure 10. Example Checklist of Evidence to Obtain When Investigating Financial Exploitation Cases from the APS Program in Maine.

New York

In New York, APS officials have developed a set of tools to assist caseworkers' investigations of financial exploitation. The Financial Exploitation Investigation Suite of Tools (FEIST) including a list of questions, red flags checklists, and worksheets in 5 steps.[258] For example, step 2 includes a red flag checklist for APS's initial inquiry (see Figure 11).

Financial Exploitation Investigation Suite of Tools (FEIST)
Phase I: Initial Inquiry & Observation
Step 2: Red Flags Checklist – Initial Inquiry & Observation

County ____________ Caseworker ____________________
Case No. ____________ Email Address ____________________

✓	**Red Flag**	**Reference to Indicators**
	Multiple referral sources indicate financial exploitation	
	Responses suggest lack of capacity, dementia, or severe disorientation	
	Client relies on others for ADLs/IADLs	
	Others speak for the client, or client defers to others for response	
	Client is evasive, hostile, or dismissive about finances	
	Client is isolated from resources/other contact	
	Client reports feeling threatened or ashamed	
	Client is unable to pay bills	
	Client is uncomfortable with the way finances are handled	
	Individual handling finances or care charges excessive fees	
	Client is uncomfortable with decisions made by POA or HCP	
	Others live in the home and do not contribute to household	
	Others use client's car/other asset	
	Client believes income does not cover regular expenses	
	Income should but does not cover regular expenses	
	Client has unexplained debt	
	Client has unexplained balances on credit cards	
	Client believes they have been financially exploited, scammed, or had their identity stolen	

After you have reviewed this Step 2: Red Flags Checklist, ask yourself the following additional questions based on what you know so far:

- Is there a reason to believe the client may be a victim of financial exploitation by the hands of another person? Is this something you cannot rule out?
- Is there a reason to believe someone may be taking the client's funds or property without the client's permission or knowledge?
- Is there a reason to believe that someone is using the client's funds or property in their own interest rather than the interest of the client?
- Does the client indicate he/she is being exploited, and this cannot be ruled out?

Figure 11. (Continued)

---

[258] Step 1 includes a list of questions to help the caseworker identify if financial exploitation is occurring and, if so, to understand the full scope of the abuse. Step 2 includes a red flag checklist (see Figrue 11). Step 3 includes a worksheet to collect data on client income and expenses. Based on what is known about the client's income and expenses, the caseworker can determine whether the client's income does not cover their bills, which can be an indicator of financial exploitation. Step 4 is a bank statement summary, which is used to help the caseworker identify unusual withdrawal and spending patterns. Step 5 pulls the above information together to submit the case to a third party for review, assessment, and possible intervention. The New York Financial Exploitation Investigation Suite of Tools can be accessed at https://www.justice clearinghouse.com/resource/investigating-financial-exploitation-new- yorks-feist-y-new-approach/.

If the answer to any of these questions is yes, **proceed with FEIST Phase II and take other needed action to gather additional information.**

- This includes making a prompt request for customer financial records from the financial institutions where the client is believed to have accounts. Use the standard request form approved by your local district.
- Where the client is believed to have given a power of attorney to an agent, send a 15-Day Letter to the agent, directing the agent to provide the power of attorney document and all written transactions made by the agent on behalf of the client. If the agent fails to timely respond, contact your counsel and ask for initiation of a special proceeding for a court to compel the agent's disclosure of such records.
- Consider requesting a credit report for the client (if capable of giving consent).

Developed by Webber CPA, PLLC in conjunction with a federal grant to Enhance Adult Protective Services awarded by the Administration for Community Living to the New York State Office of Children & Family Services.

If, on the other hand, it appears that the client is knowingly giving their funds or property away to another person, with the client's consent AND without coercion or intimidation, then it is unlikely to be financial exploitation. **If you can rule out financial exploitation, stop use of the FEIST.**

Source: New York Adult Protective Services (ASP). | GAO-21-90.

Figure 11. Example of a Tool for Investigating Financial Exploitation Cases from the APS Program in New York.

Appendix IV: Comments from the Department of Health and Human Services

DEPARTMENT OF HEALTH & HUMAN SERVICES

OFFICE OF THE SECRETARY

Assistant Secretary for Legislation
Washington, DC 20201

December 3, 2020

Kathy A. Larin
Director, Education, Workforce
and Income Security Issues
U.S. Government Accountability Office
441 G Street NW
Washington, DC 20548

Dear Ms. Larin:

Attached are comments on the U.S. Government Accountability Office's (GAO) report entitled, *"Elder Justice: HHS Could Do More to Encourage State Reporting on the Costs of Financial Exploitation"* (Job code 103828/GAO-21-90).

The Department appreciates the opportunity to review this report prior to publication.

Sincerely,

Sarah C. Arbes
Assistant Secretary for Legislation

GENERAL COMMENTS FROM THE DEPARTMENT OF HEALTH & HUMAN SERVICES ON THE GOVERNMENT ACCOUNTABILITY OFFICE'S DRAFT REPORT ENTITLED — "ELDER JUSTICE: HHS COULDDO MORE TO ENCOURAGE STATE REPORTING ON THE COSTS OF FINANCIAL EXPLOITATION" (GAO-21-90)

The U.S. Department of Health & Human Services (HHS) appreciates the opportunity from the Government Accountability Office (GAO) to review and comment on this draft report.

Recommendation 1

GAO recommends ACL work with state APS agencies to develop data fields for NAMRS on the costs of financial exploitation, and to encourage more states to collect and submit cost data to NAMRS. **(Recommendation 1)**

HHS Response

HHS does not concur with GAO's recommendation to include NAMRS data fields on costs of financial exploitation. As a voluntary reporting system, ACL employs a stakeholder engagement process to understand the needs and value to researchers and states for adding and updating NAMRS data fields. ACL must also consider the burden on states for consistently collecting data for any of the data fields and reporting to NAMRS. While useful in determining the scope or magnitude of the phenomena of financial exploitation, the actual cost of financial losses is not necessary information for APS caseworkers during investigations. This information is not necessary for determining eligibility nor service planning, and APS is not the entity that would seek restitution from, or prosecution of, perpetrators. Because of these facts, ACL cannot guarantee that data elements capturing the cost of financial exploitation would be recommended for inclusion in NAMRS during the next renewal process.

However, ACL has plans to begin the stakeholder engagement process for NAMRS renewal in the second quarter of FFY 2021. The stakeholder process is expected to complete by the end of FFY 2021. In February 2022, ACL will begin the formal process under the Paperwork Reduction Act for updating NAMRS by the existing expiration of February 2023. NAMRS data fields will be updated and/or added based on input from stakeholders on what data elements would be valuable for understanding adult maltreatment, balanced with what is feasible for APS to collect and report with reasonable burden.

Recommendation 2

GAO recommends ACL develop a timeline to share with other states information and tools that state APS agencies have developed to collect cost information, and to provide states with strategies to improve data collection on financial exploitation data. **(Recommendation 2)**

HHS Response

HHS concurs with GAO's recommendation. While currently outside the FFY 2021 scope for the APS Technical Assistance Resource Center and the National Center on Elder Abuse, ACL will consider ways to incorporate these activities beginning in FFY 2022.

INDEX

C

D

E

H

I

J

L

M

N

O

P

Q

R

S

T

U

V

W